IMAGES OF LABOUR

Instant propaganda for socialists in 1912 was available in the form of 'Red-Spots', strongly gummed paper stickers printed by J. Barlow of St James Street, Devonport. Advertised in the *Clarion* they were available from C.E. Holt of 77 Evelina Road, Nunhead, at 2s. for 1,000 or a guinea for 20,000.

SELECTED MEMORABILIA FROM THE
NATIONAL MUSEUM OF LABOUR HISTORY, LONDON

IMAGES OF LABOUR

JOHN GORMAN

SCORPION PUBLISHING LTD

IMAGES OF LABOUR

First published by Scorpion Publishing Ltd, 1985

ISBN 0 905906 46 2 Paper
ISBN 0 905906 47 0 Cased

Designed and Produced by Scorpion Pica
Editor Leonard Harrow
House Editor John Orley
Design and Art Direction Colin Larkin
Art Editors John Gorman and Colin Larkin
Design and Production team
Roger Kemlo, Dale Dawson, John Orley, Pat Ball and Christine Crossman
Typesetting Melior Roman and Bold
Paper Royal Sword matt art 135 gsm
Printing and Binding Hazell Watson and Viney Ltd, England

GLC
funded

Dedicated to my mother,
Lilian Buzzard, born South Shields, 1906,
daughter of John Thomas Buzzard, miner,
and Dora Elizabeth Cooper.

As we come marching, we battle, too, for men —
For they are women's children and we mother them again.
Our lives shall not be sweated from birth until life closes —
Hearts starve as well as bodies: Give us Bread,
but give us Roses.

JAMES OPPENHEIM

Labour's classic 1945 election poster, 'And *Now* Win the Peace', was designed by John Armstrong as a result of Labour Party consultations with Donald Zec, the brilliant wartime cartoonist of the *Daily Mirror*. Armstrong, who also designed the cover of Labour's election-winning manifesto, 'Let Us Face the Future', worked day and night for a week to produce eight poster designs for Labour, declining to accept any fee for his work.

The poster was one of a pack of nine double-crown pictorial posters sold to election agents at 4s. a set, or £10 for 100 sets. Together with single colour letterpress slogan posters, the Labour Party produced an astonishing total of 400,000 posters for their campaign. At a time of acute shortages of men and materials, the Labour Party invoked the help of George Isaacs, Secretary of NATSOPA (to become Minister of Labour and National Service in the Attlee cabinet), and E.W. Spackman of the National Union of Printing, Bookbinding and Paper Workers to produce the work in time, using the services of fourteen printing companies.

The Labour Party, in a well organised national propaganda campaign, made full use of the professional talents of socialist supporters, many of whom like O.G. Willey and C.T. Simmons had served with the Ministry of Information during the war. 284 tons of paper were used in printing a flood of pamphlets, leaflets, speakers' cards, speakers' handbooks, posters, manifestos and pictorial election booklets to present the socialist case for social change.

In 1975 the Armstrong victory poster was reprinted to mark the seventy-fifth anniversary of the founding of the Labour Party on 27 February 1900.

CONTENTS

WALTER CRANE'S GREAT CARTOON FOR "THE SUN."

Her message to Labour sweet May-Day doth bring,
From the city of Toil as the multitude streams
To rejoice in the Sun, as they read in his beams
The Hope of the world with the promise of spring.

The Sun was printed on salmon-pink newsprint, a colour that unwittingly reflected its political hue, when launched on Tuesday 27 June 1893. Edited by the Irish Nationalist MP, T.P. O'Connor, it supported the Gladstone Liberal Government, the cause of labour representation in Parliament and the Progressive Party in the London County Council. Horatio Bottomley, the charlatan financier, politician and newspaper owner, bought the Sun in 1902 and as a stunt 'gave the paper to Labour for a day' on May Day 1903. The paper was filled with labour news, and edited by Ben Tillett, but it is the cartoon by Walter Crane that Bottomley's publicity has bequeathed to posterity.

ACKNOWLEDGEMENTS

In compiling this book I have turned to many individuals and organisations for expert advice and professional assistance. I am grateful to Terry McCarthy, director of the National Museum of Labour History, for his ready agreement to the project and for allowing me full access to the museum collection. I record my special thanks to his staff, Jane Roberts, Ricky Davis, Bernadette Gillow, Deanna Cox and Bill Benfield, for their courteous and always helpful response to my requests for assistance that so often disrupted their normal work.

I was helped throughout in my research by Gareth Thomas, who pursued the vaguest of clues with Holmesian application, working with diligence and flair in an area that was new to him. Friends in the labour movement were always ready to help and I am particularly appreciative of the comradely co-operation given by Sid Brown, Ted Brake and Harold Smith. I acknowledge the specialist information given by Alan Clinton, Bill Fishman, Jean Gaffin, Bob Leeson, John May, J.P.M. Millar, Stan Newens, Frank Setchfield, Jim Simmons and John Smethurst. I am also obliged to all those, unnamed, who answered my many letters of enquiry.

I am grateful to those who granted me interviews relating to their direct connections with specific exhibits, especially Bill Alexander, Felicity Ashbee, George Mackley Browne, Frank Haxell, Lou Kenton, Cliff Rowe and Walter Southgate, all veterans of the labour movement.

My thanks are due to Ernie Greenwood, Bill Glasspool, Winston Mattis and John Warren for photography, to Eve Denney for the patient and immaculate typing of my near illegible manuscript and to Lisa Collins for typing my considerable correspondence. As ever, I was sustained throughout by my wife Pamela, as I retreated into my garden studio to research and write, deserting her for countless weekends during the best summer for years, a lifestyle she endured with loving tolerance.

I am indebted to the librarians, curators and staffs of the following libraries, museums and organisations who received Gareth Thomas and myself with courtesy and gave friendly and professional guidance:
Amalgamated Union of Engineering Workers Library; Association of Scientific, Managerial and Technical Staffs; British Broadcasting Corporation; British Library, Newspaper Library, Colindale; British-Soviet Friendship Society; Communist Party Library; Co-operative Union Library; Co-operative Party; Co-operative Wholesale Society Library; Dorset County Museum; Guildhall Library; Lancashire District Central Library; *Labour Leader*; Labour Party Archives; Labour Party Library; London Co-operative Society; London School of Economics; Marx Memorial Library; Medical Aid for Vietnam; Modern Records Centre, University of Warwick Library; *Morning Star*; Musicians' Union; National Coal Board Library; National Portrait Gallery Library; Norfolk Rural Life Museum; Public Records Office; Queen Mary College, University of London; North West Lancashire, Durham and Cumbria Textile Workers' Union; Registrar of Friendly Societies; Royal Academy of Arts; Royal Arsenal Co-operative Society; Royal Doulton Tableware Ltd.; Salvation Army; Science Museum; South Shields Central Library; Tower Hamlets Central Library; Transport and General Workers' Union; TUC Library; Union of Communication Workers Library; United States Embassy Library; Victoria and Albert Museum; Westminster Arts Library.

Finally, my thanks to the Arts Committee of the Greater London Council for their grant towards the colour printing of this book.

John Gorman,
December 1984.

The bronze, *Henry Fry, Socialist*, was sculpted by William Lawrence for the National Museum of Labour History in 1982. Lawrence was born in Barking in 1951, the son of a London docker, and his education began at the Keir Hardie Junior School, Canning Town, East London. After leaving secondary school in Plaistow, wanting to work with his hands he went to engineering school for two years as an apprentice at Plessey's. Whilst the training fulfilled a craft need, it did not provide the creative outlet he felt within himself and he left to travel around the world studying sculpture. Returning to England, he obtained a place at the Chelsea and Hammersmith School of Art and now works full time as a sculptor from his home in Covent Garden. Lawrence never met Henry Fry but, working from snapshots and tape recordings of his voice, succeeded in capturing the dimensional character of the man who was a dedicated socialist, a compulsive collector of the memorabilia of labour history and founder of the Trade Union, Labour, Co-operative, Democratic History Society.

HENRY FRY
SOCIALIST
1906 – 1982

PREFACE

During the past decade or so there has been an upsurge of interest in the history of the labour movement, not only for the preservation and scholarly study of archival material, but for the rich heritage of visual history that survives from the many organisations that together have contributed to the wider cause of Labour. The impetus has come not so much from academics who necessarily occupy the high ground as historians, but from a grass roots movement of worker historians, collectors, community workers, photographers, writers and artists who have brought a new dimension to the study of working class culture.

In many parts of Britain, working people from many trades — electricians, engineers, printers, miners and others — are separately and collectively engaged in the rescue, preservation and study of a tangible form of British history. It is a source that in the past has been neglected and even ignored by universities, museums and galleries. Yet here exists a powerful vein of historical material of primary source value for study by present and future historians. The visual evidence of labour history takes many forms: badges, banners, emblems, tokens, coins, commemorative ware, certificates, regalia, membership cards, paintings, prints and the day-to-day paraphernalia that emerges from the organisation of any group of people. As I write, there are mementoes around me that form part of my own family history: the jack plane used by my grandfather who was a cabinetmaker, the fifty years' trade union membership badge that belonged to my father (a carpenter), a miner's lamp from an uncle who was a Durham miner, a print of the 'Battle of Cable Street' by the East London artist John Allin, a cast-iron sign that reads 'Funerals to suit all classes', begged from a local undertaker. All belong to the history of working people and say something of the past lives and circumstances of the people who made and used them.

Two pioneers who recognised the intrinsic value of the memorabilia of labour were Henry Fry and Walter Southgate, two working men, socialists and trade unionists, without the benefit of formal history training, each consumed with a squirrel-like passion for the acquisition of anything connected with the history of labour. Two men of vision who rejected what Henry Fry so aptly termed 'Drum and bugle history' and saw the true history of Britain in the lives of common working people. They were also two men who shared a dream of a permanent home for their joint collections, a museum of Labour history. This book does not attempt to record the vicissitudes of their determined efforts to make that dream a reality: that is a book in itself. Neither is it my intention to cover the whole field of the iconography of the labour movement, for that would fill volumes. Rather, it is intended as an introduction to the scope of study offered by the visual history of Labour and as a tribute to Henry Fry, Walter Southgate and the little band of followers that realised the establishment of the National Museum of Labour History. For those reasons I have rejected the temptation to include many important relics that exist in private and public collections and include only such items as may be seen at the museum. The selection is personal and, of course, limited by the parameters of the collection. Nevertheless, there is a wide enough range of material to quicken the imagination and encourage others to help in the preservation of an alternative history, a history made not by kings, queens and generals, but by British working men and women.

Henry Fry was born in Corsham, Wiltshire, on 6 May 1906 and had his introduction to the real world of labour when he started working during his school holidays in a brush factory at the age of ten years. His involvement in trade unionism and Labour politics came early; as a postal worker he was Secretary of the Chippenham Trades Council at the age of nineteen and the Labour Agent for Reigate, Surrey, when he was twenty-four. A trade union scholarship took him to Ruskin College, Oxford, and there followed a life of political activity working with George Lansbury on *Lansbury's Labour Weekly*, with Wal Hannington in the National Unemployed Workers' Movement and with Sylvia Pankhurst for a short time on her *New Times and Ethiopia News*. Fry married in 1942 and it was about that time he began seriously to build his collection of labour memorabilia, when good books on obscure subjects like trade union history might be bought for coppers and second-hand shops were a repository of treasures amongst the junk and did not conceive of calling themselves antique shops. Sadly, the stories behind many of his major finds died with him and he left no catalogue of the sources of his acquisitions and deposits. The excitement of the chase in pursuit of specific items remains unrecorded, his successes and failures a matter for speculation. Henry Fry was tenacious in his searches not only for relics but for buildings and places connected with well-known personalities of radical history. He succeeded in tracing the burial spot of Henry (Orator) Hunt, of Peterloo fame, to Parham Church, but despite years of enquiry never did discover the final resting place of the English revolutionist, Thomas Paine, whose bones were brought back to England from America by William Cobbett in 1809.

In 1958 Fry brought together a group of people in Reigate, the town in which he lived, to form a group known as the Socialist History Society under the chairmanship of Councillor Tony Donavan. The aim of the society was to 'campaign for the collection and preservation of visual history material connected with the Labour Movement'.

Walter Southgate was born on 8 May 1890 in Bethnal Green, East London, in a solid working class street of artisans. Sixty years later he was still able to recall the occupations of his neighbours in that close community: 'eight cabinetmakers, two builders and decorators, four bookbinders, one painter, four builders' labourers, three carmen, two engineers, one coalman, five shopkeepers, one postman, one quill-pen cutter, three glassblowers, two clerks, three laundry workers, one bookmarbler, one seaman, one timekeeper and two pensioners'. In common with so many poor children at the turn of the century, Southgate was compelled by economic circumstance to work 'part time' whilst still at school. At the age of twelve, he worked forty hours a week, before and after school, delivering milk in metal cans for 3s. 6d. a week.

At fourteen he began work as a clerk in a solicitor's office and a year later he joined the Social Democratic Federation, the party of Marxist socialism. Later that year he founded, together with six colleagues, the Hackney branch of the National Union of Clerks and in 1910 he formed the North East London Clarion Cycling Club, carrying the message of socialism to the villages of Essex. A street-corner agitator, he was a conscientious objector in the First World War, refusing 'To be used as cannon fodder because a Parliament of old men had said so'. Before the end of the war, after working on the land, he started work with the National Union of Sheet Metal Workers as a clerk in head office where he worked until 1943. In the post-war years he worked as a gardener and handyman whilst continuing with his political activity. He retired in 1965 but never ceased working for socialism and in 1978 he was presented at the Labour Party Conference with a Certificate of Merit for 'outstanding voluntary service to the Labour Party' by Prime Minister James Callaghan. One job from which he has never retired is the old craft of quill-pen cutting, a skill learned from his father, the last professional quill-pen maker. The work is still called for by Lloyds of London who have a two hundred and fifty year tradition of making entries in their wrecks books with such pens.

From his time of joining the SDF in 1905, Southgate had been collecting handbills, posters, pamphlets and personalia connected with the labour movement. Like Henry Fry, he had little money to spend and picked up bargains, a first edition of Thomas Paine's *Rights of Man* for 6d. and an inscribed watch which once belonged to Tom Jones, first organising secretary of the London Trades Council, for £6.

In 1963 the town council of Reigate held a series of commemorative events to mark the centenary of Borough status granted by Queen Victoria. Two Labour councillors, Charles Pearce and Ron White, proposed that the Trades Council should sponsor an Exhibition of Trade Union History and Henry Fry was asked to organise the event. The exhibition was opened on 1 May by George Woodcock and for the first time items from Fry's collection were on public view. The publicity generated by the exhibition gave a new sense of direction to the Socialist History Society; it also reached the attention of Walter Southgate, who read of it in *Reynolds' News* and immediately wrote to Fry and his colleagues telling them of his own remarkable collection. The outcome was a broadening of the objects of the society and a change of name to the Trade Union, Labour, Co-operative, Democratic History Society, a title of nineteenth century trade union complexity, mercifully to be referred to as 'TULC'. Negotiations were also started to establish a trust for the Walter Southgate collection, the basis for a future museum.

At this stage, TULC was very much a cottage industry, the collection being stored in a bedroom of Henry Fry's small and crowded home in Reigate and in the garage of Richard West, the chairman of TULC. Fry's house had no telephone, outgoing calls being made from a public call box at the end of the road and incoming calls being made to Richard West, who lived several turnings away. Henry Fry's wife Betty, apart from sharing the home with her husband, two teenage daughters and stacks of memorabilia, provided refreshment and hospitality for curious and inquiring visitors. With scanty funds, the mounting of a series of exhibitions posed enormous problems. The TULC exhibition panels were homemade and to the dismay of professional archivists and museum curators, exhibits were affixed to the panels with drawing pins and Sellotape. Nevertheless, the society flourished and in 1968 purchased a small surburban house in Cornfield Road, Reigate. The house cost £4,500, of which Florence Willard, the TULC treasurer, gave £3,000, Richard West £500 and the balance was raised from donations. The house was later named the Florence Willard

History Centre and though conditions were cramped, the collection had a home that claimed to be the 'first visual history centre of Labour'.

The venture gave impetus to the development of the collection, two important deposits being made by Ivy Tribe, a former President of the National Council of British Socialist Sunday Schools and J.P.M. Millar, former Secretary of the National Council of Labour Colleges. Official support came from a number of trade unions, prominent Labour leaders and a few distinguished historians, but it was left to the rank and file workers of TULC to win a more suitable home for the collection and found the National Museum of Labour History, formally opened by Sir Harold Wilson on 19 May 1975. Now, splendidly housed in the old Limehouse Town Hall in East London, provided by the Tower Hamlets Council and recently renovated at a cost of £200,000, the museum flourishes. Re-opened by Labour leader Neil Kinnock on 2 July 1984, the museum attracts visitors from all parts of the world. Every item recorded by computer, the dream of the Reigate pioneers has become a reality. With so many voluntary and selfless workers involved in the formative years of TULC and the establishment of the National Museum of Labour History, it is invidious to name some without naming all, so it is better in this brief background to leave the main credit where it is due, to Henry Fry and Walter Southgate.

Unfortunately, no early records were kept of donations or exhibits to the collection and so, rather than name the few donors that are known, I have considered it fair to give no credits for the items documented or illustrated in this book unless necessary to prove provenance. Despite considerable research, the lack of documentation must inevitably mean that much of the personal history behind the exhibits remains untraced. I am aware, too, of areas crucial in the development of the labour movement that are not covered by the collection. The gaps are there for the movement to fill. Whatever the shortcomings, the National Museum of Labour History is an established and growing collection, the only museum solely devoted to the history of Labour. The collection stands as a witness to the efforts of our forebears, working men and women, the people who have built the wealth of Britain, to win a more equitable and just society in which all will yet share.

John Gorman
December 1984

Walter Southgate, last of the quill-pen cutters, aged ninety-four.

13

IMAGES OF LABOUR

'My heart is very good to it, and I am horrible busy with making standards, banners and bagies,' wrote Catherine of Aragon to Thomas Wolsey on 13 August 1513. She was writing of preparations for war and the standards, banners and badges were needed as symbols of identity, giving immediate visual recognition to determine friend from foe. Armorial bearings were painted on shields, tabards, standards and banners, symbols to which men swore allegiance, followed in battle and rallied to when the call came. The earliest images were religious in character, the national banner of England for centuries bore the ruddy cross of St George and, whatever banners were carried, this was foremost in the field. Henry V at Agincourt gave prominence to the banners of St George and St Edward, persuading his followers of divine and saintly aid. When the Earl of Surrey led an expedition against Scotland in the reign of Henry VIII he took with him the banner of St Cuthbert of Durham, described as being 'Suspended from a horizontal bar below a spear head, a yard or so in breadth and a little more than this in depth, the bottom edge had five deep indentations. The banner was of red velvet sumptuously enriched with gold embroidery and in the centre was a piece of white velvet half a yard square having a cross of red velvet upon it.' Throughout centuries of evolution of heraldic devices, the influence of religious imagery has survived to become woven into the iconography of craft guilds, masonic lodges, friendly societies and trade unions. In a French work on medieval guilds, the flag of the lawyers of Loudoun is said to have had 'a large eye on it', not an eye to business but the 'all-seeing eye of the Almighty', an image to recur on banners into the twentieth century.

In France the banners of the medieval craft guilds were carried into battle as insignia of the companies of men provided at the expense of those corporations. There is an account of 'a banner bearing a chevron between hammer, trowels and builder's square', in another 'a chevron between an axe and a pair of compasses'. The candlemakers of Bayeux marched beneath a black banner embroidered with three white candles, the metal workers carried a black flag with a silver hammer and files depicted, and there are descriptions of banners bearing 'extraordinary devices, boots, shoes, drinking vessels, anvils and the like' owing to the presence of the various guilds that had sent men to the fight. In England the craft guilds developed armorial bearings emblematic of the trades, carpenters, tailors, tin-plate workers, plasterers, painters and the rest weaving the materials, tools and mottos of their crafts into complex symbolism giving each an individual identity.

With the development of industrial capitalism in Britain in the eighteenth and nineteenth centuries, the new working class sought images to define and identify their own organisations, formed to protect their interests against the employers who owned the machinery of production. They turned first to the familiar arms of the guilds, a natural instinct, for the journeymen saw themselves as the true heirs to the tradition of the crafts of which they were so proud. As the first combination of working people came together, woolcombers, apronmakers, brushmakers, framework knitters, calico printers, coachmakers and a myriad of small and lesser known trades, they had no compunction in appropriating the devices and mottos of the guilds, whose imagery was already so familiar to the journeymen. In borrowing from the old established symbolism of the guilds they also invested their infant organisations with the stamp of respectability, creating an illusion of a past history offering a valid reason for existence, the protection of the trade. This, in part, was forced upon the early unions by the Act of 12 July 1799, to 'prevent unlawful Combinations of Workmen', the preamble to which read, 'Whereas great Numbers of Journeymen, Manufacturers and Workmen in various parts of this Kingdom have, by unlawful meetings and Combinations, endeavoured to obtain Advance of their wages, and to effectuate other illegal purposes; and the laws at present in Force against such unlawful Conduct have been found to be inadequate to the Suppression thereof, whereby it is become necessary that more effectual Provision should be made against such unlawful Combinations; and for preventing such unlawful practices in future, and for bringing such Offenders to more speedy and exemplary Justice.' The Act was an open invitation to employers to rule their workers by force of law, a government aspiration that has not yet been entirely abandoned. It is true that the penalties provided for in the Act were not as severe as those that might be imposed under common law: three months' hard labour or two months' hard labour and a fine of £20 (about three months' wages for a skilled worker). It did, however, mean that any group of workers who banded together to seek to raise wages, reduce hours of work, oppose a wage cut or call a strike could be hauled before a magistrate who in all probability was a factory owner, farmer or squire. The Act also provided for payment to informers and a worker might be condemned on the unsubstantiated word of any traitorous individual seeking reward.

The early unions sought to overcome the provisions of the Act by forming themselves as friendly societies, operating with insignia based upon guild arms and using the ritual and oaths of masonic lodges adapted to their own needs to protect themselves with secrecy. In 1835 the Friendly Boiler Makers had a lengthy initiation ceremony which included the secret signs of recognition: 'You will now receive the grip, words, signs and countersigns of the Order of Friendly Boilermakers.' The Operative Stonemasons' Society in 1834 swore an oath of loyalty and secrecy, 'Nor will I work with any illegal man or men but will do my best for the support of wages . . . nor will I write or cause to be wrote, print, mark,

either in stone, marble, brass, paper or sand, anything connected with this order, so help me God.' The initiation ceremony for an aspiring member included the baring of his left breast, blindfolding, kneeling and confrontation with a white shrouded figure, a painted skeleton and the union president regaled with apron, sash and sword, 'O Death, O Death, thy terror strikes us with dismay.' Having sworn to 'guard well the secrets of the lodge' the new member pledged to act on behalf of his brothers and uphold the union rules. The Coventry Weavers laid down the punishment for breach of their rules, 'The offender should be placed on an ass, with his face towards the tail of the animal and drawn about the town exposed to the ridicule and violence of the mob.' Ritual demanded regalia and in 1833 the Society of Preston Joiners bought 'A square and compasses'. When the Society joined the Builders' Union the same year they paid £1. 4s. 6d. for a 'new top coat for Tyler', and a further 11s. 6d. for a 'coct hat' and 'mufstaches'. The Warrington Lodge records show an entry of 'To painting and gilding the axe, 2s. 6d.' Two delegates of the Shoemakers' Union arrested at Exeter were found to be carrying 'two wooden axes, two large cutlasses, two masks and two white garments or robes, a large figure of death with dart and hourglass, a Bible and Testament'. The ritual of outside and inside doorkeepers, tilers, marshals, conductors, terrible oaths and secret signs was an inevitable response to laws that encouraged police spies and informers in an attempt to stop working people joining together to protect their wages and

Florence Willard with Vic Feather, General Secretary of the TUC, at the opening of 'Banner Bright', John Gorman's exhibition of trade union banners at the Whitechapel Art Gallery, May 1973.

conditions – laws that forced the Society of Ironfounders to meet on dark nights on peaks and moors of the Midland counties and bury the books of the Society in the ground. The Tolpuddle Martyrs, who formed the Friendly Society of Agricultural Labourers in 1834, were betrayed by an informer, Edward Legg ('black-legg'), sentenced by a judge who was a wealthy landowner, and charged not with forming a combination but administering an illegal oath. The charge enabled the judge to pursue his task of breaking the union by sentencing the six labourers to seven years' transportation.

The unions, anxious to persuade authority that they did not represent a seditious threat, saw the familiar guild images, not only as a form of early visual recognition by their members, but also as a kind of protection by association, an unspoken implication that they had been around for years. The Society of Tailors in the reform demonstration of 1832 carried a banner on which was a coat of arms with Adam and Eve as supporters, a design based upon the arms of the Worshipful Company of Tin-Plate Workers, alias Wireworkers. The United Kingdom Society of Coachmakers lifted the guild arms of the Worshipful Company of Coachmakers and Harnessmakers and gave added authority by adding the royal standard! Not content with the free use of the guild arms, the unions unhesitatingly purloined the dates of incorporation of the medieval guilds. The banner of the Dublin Operative Tailors carried the date 1418, that of the Dublin Brick and Stonelayers, 1670, the Dublin Silk Weavers, 1728. The Webbs wrote in their *History of Trade Unionism*, 'The trade unions not only in many cases bear the same arms as guilds, but often also the date of their incorporation. Thus, the old Society of Regular Carpenters claims to date from 1490, the Regular Operative Housepainters' Trade Union connects itself with the guild of St. Luke and the local union of Brick Layers and Plasterers assume the date of incorporation of the Bricklayers Company by Charles II.' The Greenwich lodge banner of the Amalgamated Society of Watermen and Lightermen carries the date 1514, the year of the first Act of Parliament to regulate fares upon the Thames, and even pre-dates the establishment of the Worshipful Company of Watermen in 1555. To dispel any further doubt as to their honourable and good intentions, the unions in conformity with heraldic practice added mottos, mostly of a conciliatory nature. 'Unite in Love' proclaimed the United Tin Plate Workers' Society in 1821, a direct translation of the Latin motto of the Worshipful Company of Tin-Plate Workers, alias Wireworkers. '*Humani nihil alienum*, to humanity nothing hostile' read the motto of the Friendly Boiler Makers' Society in 1834 beneath the first emblematic design for the union. 'Combined to protect, not to injure', Society of Farriers, 1833; 'Through love and unity we support each other', Friendly Sawyers of Whitehaven, 1838, while 'Defence not defiance' became the popular proclamation of hundreds of unions.

With the emergence to legality after the Reform Acts of 1824 and 1825, the imagery of trade unionism was slowly shaped by industrial development and the lessons of struggle. The illustrations upon their banners reflected craft pride, showing the tools of the trade and the products of their labours. Aproned carpenters with jack planes and saws, printers examining proofs, cotton operatives at the spinning mules, railway workers with oil cans and shunting poles, sailors coiling rope, miners hewing coal, every skill represented and a range of manufactured products displayed that could have filled the Great Exhibition. The beautifully painted banner of the Boyne Fishermen, painted by William Reynolds in 1873, shows three fishermen at work with a seine net in Drogheda Bay, adding for good measure portraits of St Brigid and St Patrick. The Drogheda Labourers' Society shows a labourer and his family harvesting. The huge banner of the Hull Seamens' and Marine Firemens' Union, 1888, depicts a sailing ship with inset cameos of the perils of life at sea. The Northampton branch banner of the National Union of Boot and Shoe Operatives, *c.*1920, shows the modern machinery of shoe-making and includes a large portrait of St Crispin, first painted on a shoemakers' union banner in 1834 when the Nantwich shoemakers 'engaged Mr Thomas Jones to paint for us a banner emblematical of our trade with the motto "May the manufactures of the sons of St Crispin be trod upon by the whole world."' With the growth of heavy industry, drop hammers, furnaces, iron ships, steel bridges, boilers and retorts, all became proud subjects of illustration on trade union banners. It was not until

Poster designed by J.T. Kent to commemorate the Chicago Martyrs of 1886.

the new unionism of the 1890s that the social and political aspirations of trade unionism were to be given visual form as part of the iconography of labour. Parallel with the increasing numbers, changing style and popularity of banners was the design and production of printed emblems, large certificates, usually of double crown size (762 x 508mm), lithographed or engraved in black and white, or more often in the latter half of the nineteenth century, printed in full colour, giant pictorial evidence of membership. Most of the early emblems follow the banners in depicting the authentic sign of the trade, the guild arms or an adapted version of the arms. The emblem of the United Society of Brushmakers, 1839, designed by J. Shury of Charterhouse Lane, London, has the guild arms, its supporters being a Russian boar, surmounted by a masonic-style handshake. It embodies the arms of six major towns, symbolic of the amalgamation of local societies into a united order. Beneath a patriotic illustration of Britannia is a scene of St Katherine's dock, an import point for the cargoes of foreign bristles. The emblem of another early union, the Friendly Boiler Makers' Society, carried the sign of the order, a hammer in an uplifted hand, the device of the Worshipful Company of Blacksmiths. The design includes a primitive steamship and the classic trade union symbol of unity, 'the clasped handshake of brotherhood the world o're'. With improved skills in printing and engraving, the late nineteenth century emblems became intricate and draughtsmanlike works of art, created by the finest artists and engravers. Typical of the period is the emblem of the Amalgamated Society of Carpenters and Joiners, designed in 1868 by A.J. Waudby. The artist had exhibited at the Royal Academy in 1844 and again in 1848 when two of his paintings, *An Interior of a Cottage* and *Devotion*, were hung. The monumental design carries an accurate illustration of the centring of an arch adapted from a plate in Nicholson's *Practical Carpentry*, flanked with the figures of a carpenter and joiner. Both figures are based on a portrait of James Blayne, chairman of the executive committee of the union in 1862. The outstanding feature of the emblem is that it is surmounted by a likeness of Joseph of Nazareth, claimed by the union as 'the most distinguished member of the craft on record, being the reputed father of our Saviour'! The Carpenters and Joiners were not alone in tracing their craft, if not membership of the union, to biblical times. The Shipwrights laid claim to Noah and his Ark, the Masons to the building of Solomon's Temple, the Bricklayers to the Tower of Babel, and the Tailors to having made the first suit of clothes – for Adam and Eve. Newer trades could not rival the ancient crafts in their claim to direct continuity from the time of creation, but did their best, the Letterpress Printers enrolling Caxton and the Amalgamated Society of Lithographic Printers, Alois Senefelder, the inventor of lithography. Waudby also designed the emblem of the Operative Bricklayers' Society, 1869, producing a large oil painting (page 126)

based upon the central theme of the design to hang in the union's head office. His design for the Bricklayers' emblem was overlooked by the 'all-seeing eye' of the 'omnipotent King of Kings, looking down and diffusing the rays of glory on all beneath, that never fails to light the path of the earnest worker and fearless spirit who believes in His almighty power.' The eye, to be found on the regalia and emblems of friendly societies, masonic lodges and innumerable trade union images, is of ancient origin, known as the 'blind point' in a circle, though it was thought by some to represent the eagle eye of the general secretary keeping a close watch on union affairs.

The emblems were sold to members, who regarded them with great pride. In mid-Victorian times a colour emblem would have cost about 3s., plus the cost of framing. Thousands were sold and, according to R.A. Leeson, 'the Ironfounders' Secretary is reported to have threatened to resign if he did not get a commission on emblem sales.' The Amalgamated Society of Carpenters and Joiners sold plate paper copies of their emblem in 1868 at half a crown each and in the same year the Stonemasons sold their Waudby designed emblem at 2s. 9d. plus frames at 5s. or 7s., the first 3,000 emblems selling rapidly. An expenditure of around 8s. to 10s. was a great deal to pay by a worker who might have been earning less than 30s. a week, yet thousands paid for the privilege of hanging the union emblem above the mantlepiece. The emblems expressed craft pride, with scenes of tools and work, traced ancient lineage with portrayals of historic figures, had an aura of mystery with allegorical symbols, the spindle of labour, the beehive of industry, the classical female figures of hope, truth, justice, art and commerce. Like the designs of union banners they reflected the development of modern industry, the emblem of the Amalgamated Association of Card and Blowing Room Operatives, c.1890 (page 79) for example, illustrating the heavy machinery of carding engines. The Amalgamated Society of Enginemen, Cranemen, Boilermen and Firemen (page 81) showed a steel mill on their 1890 emblem while the United Society of Boiler Makers and Iron and Steel Shipbuilders illustrated an iron shipbuilding yard and a factory scene of boiler making. Many of the emblems showed scenes of funeral benefit, superannuation, sick payment, unemployment relief and accident benefit (page 81), giving solid assurance to the family of the trade unionist in the days before state social security.

Some trade unions took to having the grand and intricate emblems of their craft emblazoned on their banners. Great silken sails of brilliant colour, with red, gold, silver and green predominating, they were hoisted aloft by teams of six, paraded with pride, each union vying with the other to present the most elaborate and stunning banner in the procession. The Bricklayers were one such union, with their Tower of Babel climbing to heaven, 'Every house is built by some man, but He that builds all things is God.' Crammed with verse, scenes, symbols, mottos, figurative virtues and every symbolic representation one can think of, Gwyn Williams has likened it to a stained-glass window, 'An heraldic assertion of presence in community . . . of those banners union men raised cathedrals to labour'. The Watford Bricklayers built theirs in 1888, 'the very next year the full round orb of the dockers' tanner rose over the horizon. Their cathedrals were about to be invaded by the multitude.'

The Great Dock Strike of 1889 changed the face and direction of trade unionism. To the ranks of the bowler-hatted watch and chain craftsmen of the great model unions, the skilled aristocrats of labour, came 200,000 cloth-capped unskilled labourers. The strike also changed the imagery of labour, for the new unions sought no imagined past but looked to the hope of the future. As day by day another union or branch of some section of the unskilled and previously unorganised working class was formed, so new banners were unfurled. At unveiling ceremonies conducted by the heroes of the hour, Tom Mann, Ben Tillett, John Burns, Tom McCarthy, a new form of militant imagery was revealed. Gone for the most part were the mottos of conciliation; now was the cry for social change, solidarity and brotherhood. 'Union and Victory' proclaimed the motto on the banner of the Amalgamated Stevedores' Labour Protection League (page 42). It had been daubed upon a piece of sailcloth and carried throughout the daily parades during the strike; now it was no longer a slogan, but a statement of fact. The solidarity of the Australian 'wharfies' who had collected and sent more than £25,000 to the strike fund was commemorated on the banner by the painting of two dockers, one British, the other Australian, clasping hands in unity with only the lion and kangaroo as symbols. Even more aggressively militant was the banner of the Export Branch of the Dockers' Union: 'We will fight and may die but will never surrender' was emblazoned on their colour. The illustration was that of a Herculean docker wrestling with the serpent of capitalism, 'This is a holy war and we shall not cease until all destitution, prostitution and exploitation is swept away.' This was the voice of a new kind of trade unionism and it required a new style: that style was to be dominated by the socialist art of Walter Crane and the commercial art of George Tutill. Crane was already famous as an illustrator of children's books, an artist of the pre-Raphaelite school and a wealthy man. Influenced by W.J. Linton, engraver and Chartist to whom Crane was apprenticed in 1859, the writings of John Ruskin and John Stuart Mill, he had been converted to socialism by William Morris after reading his pamphlet on *Art and Socialism*. Crane followed Morris into the Social Democratic Federation around 1884 and placed his talent at the disposal of the movement. There was hardly a progressive or socialist cause that did not make use of his art and scarcely any aspect of design for the movement that Crane did not

undertake. Membership cards (page 114), logos (page 111), cartoons (page 8), invitation cards (page 174), posters (page 162), and illustrations (page 142). His non-sectarian socialism enabled him to design the prospectus for the Communist Louise Michel's International School as readily as he undertook to design a banner for the Irish Nationalists.

It was Walter Crane's cartoons, his black and white illustrations and engravings, many of which were drawn for socialist journals like *Clarion, Justice* and *Commonweal*, that shaped the imagery of socialism on trade union banners for thirty years from the early 1890s until well into the 1920s. His 'Triumph of Labour', drawn in 1891 to commemorate the first International May Day in 1890, which he dedicated to the 'wage workers of all countries', formed both the inspiration and the basis for design on countless union banners. The cartoon had been given pride of place on the front page of *Commonweal*, set amid the latest serialised chapter of *News from Nowhere* by William Morris. 'International Solidarity of Labour', 1889, 'The Workers' Maypole', 1894, and 'A Garland for May Day', 1895, all became established favourites for banner illustrations. The militant Workers' Union formed by Tom Mann on May Day 1898 used Crane's cartoons as the fundamental design for nearly all their branch banners from Chichester to Ipswich. General workers, builders, dockers, miners, all turned to Crane's inspirational imagery for the adornment of their banners. To have an even further-reaching effect upon art and design for the cause of labour was Walter Crane's 'Angel of Freedom', a symbol of working class emancipation that was adapted in a hundred ways, copied and imitated throughout the labour movement and still survives until today. The figure, a winged female angel, was the subject of a major painting by Crane entitled *Freedom*, exhibited at the Grosvenor Gallery exhibition in 1885. The subject proved disturbing to the gallery owner and Crane records that 'Sir Coutts Lindsay began to show me the cold shoulder and from giving me prominent places in his gallery gradually shelved my works.' The painting was inspired by Swinburne's poem, 'The Eve of Revolution', and Crane originally conceived the symbol in the 1860s. In the poem, a winged figure clad in flowering drapery and wearing the *bonnet rouge* rescues humanity, symbolised by a youth, chained and guarded by a king in armour and a cowled priest, a ready subject for a socialist artist. Crane likened his angel to 'a vision breaking into the sunshine of spring'. His angel was to become a ready symbol for labour, heralding the future sunshine of the co-operative commonwealth.

Crane himself used the winged and draped female figure again and again, using a variant of it for his beautiful and famous banner produced for the Electrical Trades Union, 'Light and Liberty', in 1898. The figure recurs in his engraving of the 'Triumph of Labour' and his cartoon, 'International Solidarity of Labour', where she presides over a world of united workers, hands clasped in solidarity. In 1899 May Day in London was celebrated by a huge festive gathering at Crystal Palace where the highlight of the evening was a gigantic set piece in fireworks by Brocks, reproducing the solidarity image, a masterpiece of pyrotechnics that thrilled the vast crowd. In 1900 Crane again adapted his figure in a painting entitled *A Stranger* which he created as a protest against the imperialist Boer War. Here the winged figure is seen hovering over the world, holding an olive branch of peace. Crane's refusal to be enmeshed in the jingoism of the time led to his resignation from the Fabian Society.

George Tutill, the great banner-making company with studios at 83 City Road, London, used Crane's cartoons as ready references for centre paintings on hundreds of trade union banners. In 1921 the National Amalgamated Workers' Union banner showed the angel as the figure of trade unionism handing the key of organisation to Labour to unlock the gate to economic emancipation. About the same time, Crane's solidarity cartoon was used to adorn the Shamrock Branch banner of the National Builders' Labourers' and Constructional Workers' Society. Even when not faithfully copied, Crane's female figures in flowing robes wearing red Phrygian caps graced innumerable banners over the years, an image of heroic and visionary form, both guardian and prophet. Tutill's had no need to copy Crane's work for they employed many talented and creative artists, Tutill himself having exhibited at the Royal Academy in 1847. They were merely responding to Crane's immense popularity as the artist of socialism, meeting a market demand. Tutill's were in no way committed to the labour movement but regarded it as a valuable source of commercial work. Trade union banners were woven and painted alongside banners for Sunday schools, temperance societies, Rechabites, Oddfellows, Foresters and Ancient Gardeners, the imagery of any one likely to be plagiarised to suit the needs of another. George Tutill had started his working life as a fairground showman in the 1830s when travelling showmen painted their own fascias to boxing booths, sideshows and roundabouts. It was the baroque ornamentation, fairground lettering and overall style that Tutill carried to the imagery of nineteenth century trade unionism. Early photographs of country fairs like the St Giles Fair in Oxfordshire show the remarkable similarity of the huge canvas painted fascias of the sideshows to trade union banners, even to the corner cameos that Tutill featured so often in his work. Tutill had painted his first trade union banner while still working with a travelling fair and the fairground influence was to remain on trade union banners, even after the Second World War.

Crane designed relatively few banners himself, those for the Electrical Trades Union, the Bristol branch of the National Union of Gasworkers and the Carlisle branch of the Social Democratic Federation among them. His influence, however,

on banner painting was enormous, rivalled only by Tutill, whose company produced more trade union banners than any other firm in the world.

Beyond the commercial production of banner designs are to be found some charming examples of amateur and professional banner painting, though in relatively small numbers. The banner of the Amalgamated Society of Railway Servants for Scotland (page 46) is a fine example of naive banner painting. By contrast, the banners of the National Union of Agricultural Labourers and Rural Workers (page 43) and the Central Labour College (page 50) are 'homemade' banners with the professional touch. The artist who painted the Mulbarton banner is unknown but it has a quality of lettering and design that is all 'arts and crafts' and surely the work of a professional painter. The Central Labour College banner is the design of the well-known socialist artist, Frank Horrabin, but is given a homespun look by the sack-like material used and the embroidery of Winifred Horrabin, Rebecca West and Winifred Blatchford. Banners made for single issue campaigns, slogan-waving messages, rarely have artistic merit and are of interest as relics of past battles rather than form. 'Tunnel Shelters' (page 54) and 'Arms for Spain' (page 55), made by those taking part in the struggle or bought from a local signwriter at the lowest possible price, are images as transitory as the processions in which they were carried. It is the issues on which the campaigns were fought that create images in the mind: ARP, the bombing of the London docks, refugees, the years of left wing anti-fascist activity that gripped a generation. Such banners remain as memory joggers.

Commemorative pottery is designed specifically to recall the past and act as an ever-present reminder of notable events. Apart from royal occasions, marked by millions of mugs, the British have been moved to celebrate wars, pit disasters, cricket scores, Acts of Parliament, buildings, bridges, actresses, politicians and highwaymen by the transfer of printed images onto jugs, plates, bowls and mugs. People have been applying decoration to pottery since the first clay was moulded and fired but it was the son of a printer who revolutionised the pottery industry by inventing a process of transferring print to earthenware. It was in 1756 that John Sadler, a Liverpool potter, the son of Adam Sadler, a printer, together with Guy Green, succeeded in transferring a print to earthenware. Prior to that, the slow, highly skilled art of hand decoration had been the only means of embellishing pottery. The industrial revolution had reached out to touch the most ancient of crafts, making it possible for the factory worker to replace the artist craftsman in the production of large runs of decorated ware. By the 1770s printers and engravers were established in Liverpool, the Potteries, Bristol and in other towns and cities where large quantities of earthenware were being produced. Even so, there was no reason or demand to commemorate events of which hardly anyone had heard. For the most part, people lived in isolated rural communities, largely uneducated and subject to the subtle censorship of the squirearchy telling them only such news as was considered good for them. It was the nineteenth century development of communications, railways, macadamised roads, the penny post, newspapers and education that for the first time enabled the populace to have any real knowledge of national affairs. With the growth of industrial capitalism came urbanisation, as people deserted the villages to work in the Bastille-like mills and factories of the cities, creating a densely packed, dispossessed working class but one which at least had access to those who could read, travel and disseminate news. Potters now grasped the opportunity to use printed transfers to turn their wares into a persuasive and commemorative medium.

Early images of working class struggle are to be found on the jugs produced to commemorate and condemn the Peterloo massacre (page 59). It was on 16 August 1819, that 60,000 men, women and children gathered there to hear their hero, Henry (Orator) Hunt, give voice to their demands for reform. They had marched in the sunshine from the outlying districts of Manchester, Middleton, Rochdale, Oldham, Stockport, Pendleton and Bury to St Peter's Field, ablaze with colour, bands and banners, singing and dancing, a massive but peaceful demonstration of popular protest. They left a bloody battlefield, cut down by the sabres of the Yeoman Cavalry, little businessmen playing soldiers at the behest of government. The marches converging on Manchester were a pageantry of working class imagery. Contemporary accounts capture the scene: '. . . forty women and the colours were handsome, "No Corn Laws", "Universal Suffrage"'. . . 'The banners flashed in the sunlight, other music was heard, it was that of the Rochdale party coming to join us – we met – and a shout from ten thousand startled the echoes of the woods and dingles.' 'The procession was arranged with bands of youths in front wearing laurels . . . then came the band and colours, Unity and Strength, Liberty and Fraternity.' The white silk banner of the people of Oldham, the white and green silk banner of Chadderton, twelve feet by nine feet, the inscription on the banner of the Royton Female Union, 'Let us die like men and not be sold like slaves.' The Oldham and Royton banners were accompanied by two hundred women dressed in white. From the Saddleworth, Lees and Mossley Union came a banner bearing figures of Justice, 'holding the scales and two hands clasped', 'No Boroughmongering', 'Taxation without rep-resentation is tyrannical.' Scattered among the marchers of the various contingents were red peaked caps held aloft on poles, the Phrygian-shaped caps that had been used as symbols of liberty by the revolutionists in France and said to have originated as a symbol of the manumission of a slave in Roman times. It was a symbol that was

seized by nineteenth century trade unionists and socialists as an image calling for the emancipation of labour.

What of the people themselves? 'They were haggard looking men certainly, but the majority were young persons, in their best Sunday suits, and the light coloured dresses of the cheerful, tidy looking women relieved the effect of the dark fustians worn by the men.' 'They were full of humour, laughing and shouting and making fun.' 'I saw boys and girls taking their father's hands in the procession.' It was against this gathering of working class families that a hysterical magistracy unleashed a sabre-wielding yeomanry, their swords newly sharpened for the affray.

The jugs produced after the massacre bear witness to the outrage: one depicts the charge of the Manchester and Salford Yeoman Cavalry with the inscription 'Murdered on the plains of Peterloo', another carries a transfer print showing the cavalry riding over fallen victims and carries the verse,

> The scripture cries out life for life,
> And God ordained it so,
> We'll not forget to pay the debt
> Incurred at Peterloo

The jug that carries the message 'Bad luck to the Manchester butchers' (page 59) also testifies that in the days before photography few apart from those

Designed by J.F. Horrabin as a greetings card from himself and his wife Winifred.

who had seen him could have known what Orator Hunt looked like. The jug that purports to carry his likeness in fact shows Commodore Bainbridge of the United States Navy! The potter simply used a handy print of the sailor assuming that, as the original had been intended for export and few had actually seen Hunt, the deception would pass. Another jug that does carry a true likeness of Hunt also bears a portrait of T.J. Wooler, editor of the radical news sheet, the *Black Dwarf*, and carries the inscription 'To the memory of the unfortunate sufferers of Manchester'. Just how far the radical sympathies of the makers of these jugs extended is hard to say but the items they produced are valuable relics of working class struggle.

Two other areas of popular agitation were to provide potters with further opportunities of producing propaganda pottery – the Reform Act of 1832 and the revival of the demand for the repeal of the Corn Laws. The Reform Act resulted in the widespread production of jugs and mugs featuring portraits of Althorp, Brougham, Grey and Russell, the main protagonists for reform. Taking commercial advantage of national celebrations it was sufficient to stick the word 'Reform' on a milk jug (page 59) to boost the sales of ordinary kitchen-ware. Many of the pieces produced carry a cartouche of laurel leaves encircling the 'clasped hands' symbol, but they should not be mistaken for relics of trade unionism for it was also the symbol used by the political unions. Some of the pieces produced were elaborate in design, featuring drawings attacking the 'Rotten borough system' with the Tory cabinet lampooned, while Whig leaders wield the axe of Reform. For potters, it was to become the most widely celebrated event in the history of political commemorative pottery.

The Anti-Corn Law Association which grew out of a meeting of free-traders held in Manchester in the autumn of 1838 provided another chance for potters to board the popular band wagon. The League had a wide following because it attacked monopoly and privilege and appealed to the self-interest of both the working and middle classes, offering the prospect of cheap food. The potters adorned their wares with 'Free trade' and 'Cheap corn', adding likenesses of Richard Cobden and John Bright, firmly establishing the practice of celebrating heroes by firing their portraits into pottery sealing their place in history. Almost a century later a vainglorious leader of Labour, Ramsay MacDonald, commemorated himself (page 61) by giving away plates bearing his image to his faithful supporters.

Perhaps the greatest single source of commemorative pottery directly associated with the labour movement is the anniversary plates, cups and saucers, bowls and jugs produced for the co-operative societies. Nearly all the pieces were made at the Co-operative Wholesale Society's own pottery works at Longton, Staffordshire, opened in 1886. As the turn of the century was reached, many co-operative societies were approaching their fiftieth anniversaries, reflecting the upsurge of co-operation that followed the Industrial and Provident Societies Act of 1862. Between 1864 and 1867 over 200 new societies were registered each year. The number of pieces produced in celebration of silver, gold and diamond jubilees is impossible to estimate, but as there were over 1,400 societies with comings of age to mark and the Longton works was decorating commemorative ware for over forty years, the figure must be enormous. The majority, like the fiftieth anniversary jug for the Stratford Co-operative and Industrial Society (page 62), are stamped with the co-operative 'wheatsheaf' symbol and the motto 'Labour and Wait', the latter taken from 'A Psalm of Life' by Henry Wadsworth Longfellow. From the Daiseyfield Industrial Bees Co-operative, who ordered commemorative plates in 1902 to mark the opening of their new premises, until the Longton works ceased individual requirement production in 1939, bread plates and tea-pots, milk jugs and cups carried the celebratory message of co-operation into millions of working class homes.

Since 1980 a new impetus in commemorative pottery produced directly for the labour movement has been created by Lou Kenton, an amateur potter, socialist and print worker. His first effort, a mug commemorating the lock-out of printing trade unions by Times Newspapers Ltd in 1979 (page 64), was so successful that it has been followed by a steady issue of plates, mugs, ashtrays and cups marking trade union anniversaries and strikes as well as notable events for the wider labour movement. The Greenham Women's Peace Camp, GLC Peace Year, Marx's centenary, the one hundred and fiftieth anniversary of the Tolpuddle Martyrs and the People's March for Jobs (page 64) are among some of the pieces produced in runs of thousands during the past five years. Coincidentally, a tenuous link with the past is maintained, the manufacture now being carried out by Crown Winsor at Longton, a co-operative-owned enterprise. If bolder and brasher than commemorative pottery of earlier years the tradition is in direct line, the historic miners' strike of 1984 being recorded on plates and mugs just as the Durham miners marked their strike in 1892. Friendly society loving cups, bowls for 'Wilkes and Liberty', jugs for the Lancashire Weavers' Union and plates to remind us of the Tolpuddle Martyrs are all of a piece, part of the radical tradition and an important field of working class visual history.

Symbols create identity; they denote purpose, signal unity and create for the member of an organisation a sense of belonging. Repeated use makes for easy recognition and gains wide acceptance. Badges, emblems, membership cards and certificates confirm common aims and give a feeling of pride. At least one old trade unionist is known to have had his union emblem cut into his tombstone. Among early trade unionists a membership card bearing the arms and title of the trade acted as a passport to employment as the unionist tramped from town to town in search of work. The tramping card of the Amalgamated Society of Tin-Plate Workers (page 108) in 1868 guaranteed beer, bed and breakfast and 1s. 8d. a day for eighteen days while the tramping member sought employment. It would be produced at the appropriate 'house of call', a public house where the local Society met, and be signed by the landlord or secretary of the branch or lodge. The card opened the way to immediate fellowship among his brother workers in the craft and they would do their best to help him find employment in a 'legal' shop, i.e. a trade union workshop paying the agreed rate for the job. The United Society of Journeymen Brushworkers' card in 1845 bore the arms of the trade and had pages inside to log the journey of a member as he tramped a specified route around Britain, covering 1,210 miles from London back to London, taking in Norwich, Manchester, Liverpool and Exeter. The whole journey to be covered in four months!

Henry Broadhurst, the Stonemasons' MP, wrote, 'My trades unions had relieving stations in nearly every town, generally situated in one of the smaller public houses. Two of the local masons are appointed to act as relieving officer and bed inspector. The duty of the latter is to see that the beds are kept clean, in good condition and well aired . . . When a mason on tramp enters a town he finds his way to the relieving officer and presents his card. On this card is written the applicant's name and last permanent address. In addition he carries a printed ticket bearing the stamp of the last lodge at which the traveller received relief.' A worker might travel to a town where he had heard there was a job only to find that no more hands were required. He would show his card to a Society man who would endeavour to collect what he could for him, offer to share his home for the night and see him safely on his way the following morning. There was no shame in tramping; all sorts of trades

supported members trudging around the countryside in search of work. It has been estimated that in 1879, a year of trade depression, over 5,000 engineers, masons, ironfounders and tailors took to the road with trampcards in their pockets. During that year, the printers paid for 366,000 miles of tramping, a distance of fourteen times around the world!

What of the wayward member who might take relief and then work in a non-union shop? His name would be published to the trade to be reviled by his brothers, the houses of call closed to him and he might face expulsion from the union. The earliest of trade unionists had no doubts as to the sort of creature that would betray his workmates. In 1792 the Cordwainers gave this definition, 'What is a scab? He is to his trade what a traitor is to his country; though both may be useful to one party in troublesome times when peace returns they are detested alike by all . . . He first sells the journeymen and is himself afterwards sold in turn by the master, till at last he is despised by both and deserted by all. He is an enemy to himself, to the present age and to posterity.' In 1819 the Preston Tin Plate Workers made a handwritten list of 'four rats in Preston' and a circular issued by typographers in 1849 names a man who took relief and then entered a 'rat hole', a shop that did not abide by union conditions. In 1812 the Hatters are known to have barred their houses to 'foul men'. On the back of the second report of the Bookbinders' Consolidated Union is a blacklist of men throughout the country who refused to observe the union rules, headed by the representation of a 'rat'. In small closed crafts, the outlook for a scab would be bleak indeed.

Membership cards, like tramping cards, were a means of checking and control, the weekly contributions carefully entered and signed, the details transferred to the Society's ledger, benefits recorded, changes of address and employment noted. They were also the precursors of emblematic imagery, the engraved 'true sign of the trade' preceding the emblems and certificates of membership and service. Along with the appropriated and adapted forms of the guild arms came the mottos of craft unionism, jealously guarding their representation of the trade. The card of the King's Lynn Society of Brushmakers' arms bore the inscription 'May our trade in love and unity ever flourish, to keep those out that would our rights demolish.' The Operative Stonemasons and the Staveley Society of Brushmakers in 1815 both proclaimed, 'In peace and unity may we support our trade and keep out those that would our rights invade.' The cards carrying the bearings of the trade would be finely engraved, not only for decoration and trade identity but to dissuade forgers. As trade unionism developed in the mid-nineteenth century, the cards became, on the whole, less decorative and more functional in design. An exception was the London Society of Compositors which from 1907 opened the design of its card to annual competition among its membership. The first competition brought over one thousand entries, the design submitted in proof form displaying a high standard of craftsmanship. Over the years the designs reflect the changing fashions in graphic design, moving from art nouveau on early cards to art deco in the thirties.

The Social Democratic Federation, founded in 1881 as the Democratic Federation by Henry Mayers Hyndman, was fortunate in having both William Morris and Walter Crane among its membership. Morris designed the first card for the Democratic Federation, an ornate design featuring an oak tree spreading its leafy branches and incorporating the motto 'Educate, Organise, Agitate'. When the movement positively embraced socialism, becoming the Social Democratic Federation on 4 August 1894, its new membership card was designed by Walter Crane (page 114). Crane's design illustrated a tree bearing heavy fruit, its roots firmly planted in the fertile soil of 'socialisation of the means of production, distribution and exchange', with two workers, male and female, wearing caps of liberty: the man representative of 'production', holding a spade, the woman, 'distribution', holding a wheel and both holding fast to the banner of the SDF. The Marxist party, although aided by the financial support of Hyndman and Morris, both wealthy men, depended on the meagre resources of its supporters to fund its political activities. To finance elections, the party canvassed for penny contributions to its 'war chest', issuing receipts in the form of red stamps, printed with the unequivocal slogan 'Penny nails in the coffin of capitalism' (page 114).

Red stamps at a penny each were also receipts for the weekly contributions stuck onto the membership cards of the National Unemployed Workers' Movement (page 97). Founded in 1920 to combat the despair and poverty of the growing number of workless, the Unemployed Workers' Movement organised to fight back instead of starving in silence. The sight of thin and ragged men, wearing their war medals, standing in the gutters singing for pennies or selling matches had been a familiar sight in London and other cities since 1918; now the red membership card of the NUWM became a symbol of resistance. The movement organised the first of their national hunger marches on 17 October 1922 and followed with a series of spectacular demonstrations aimed at drawing public attention to the plight of the unemployed and to their demand for 'Work or full maintenance'. An ex-serviceman showed the spirit generated by the movement and the symbolic value of the card when he wrote,

> When you are down and the world seems hard,
> Don't despair, be on your guard,
> And just take out that small red card,
> – Be organised.

Penny stamps as a means of fund raising and publicity were used in 1928 when the Labour Party launched its 'Labour's bid for power' fund (page 113) as part of a campaign to raise £100,000 to fight the 1929 general election. 15,000 receipt books were distributed to the labour movement and the pennies received contributed towards the £50,000 that was achieved and the subsequent election victory for the party. In 1939 the Surrey Spain Foodship Appeal (page 116) successfully sold penny publicity stamps as part of their target fund of £5,000 to stock a ship with food to be sent to Spain to relieve hungry refugees from Franco's war. Penny stamps seem to have been an effective form of fund raising among working class organisations, combining a realistic contribution with a propaganda message.

From birth to death, each of us collect some certificates charting our progress through life, confirming achievement, membership or service. In the iconography of the labour movement, certificates have their place, marking membership, celebrating anniversaries or commemorating notable events. Among the most beautiful certificates of all are the membership and birthday certificates designed by F.J. Bourne for the Socialist Sunday Schools movement. Bourne, a pioneer socialist and a secretary of the Gateshead branch of the Independent Labour Party, joined the adult section of the Socialist Sunday School in 1903. Biographical details of his life are scarce but there is evidence of his all-round artistic talent, musical, literary and graphic. He suffered a deformity and was a diminutive figure, under five feet in height, who moved about with the aid of a crutch and a stick. By all accounts he loved children and had the gift of being able to teach them with love and affection, described in a tribute to him published in the *Young Socialist* in 1913 as 'handling children as a gardener does a beautiful plant'. Jim Simmons, a ninety-two year old veteran socialist who was a close friend of Bourne, wrote to say that he was 'loved by everyone'. As a superintendent of the Tyneside and District Union of the Socialist Sunday School he is remembered as a 'quiet and lovable comrade' who was known to the children as 'Uncle Fred'. Simmons writes that Bourne, who played and taught the piano, was a collector of Northumbrian folk songs, which he taught to the children, and that he also contributed a song of his own, 'Sing, Let Us Sing', to the Socialist Sunday School *National Tune Book*.

He excelled as a teacher, using his ability as an artist to enthral children as he illustrated his talks by drawing on the blackboard. Together with T. Hedley of the Gateshead Public Library he drew up a comprehensive syllabus and a list of books for the use of teachers in the Socialist Sunday Schools. His work as an artist is something of a mystery; Simmons writes that he used to produce advertisements for a local store, using his niece as a model to wear the dresses he had to illustrate. The quality of his work on the certificates and for the postcard he produced for the *Young Socialist* (page 140) leaves no doubt that he would have made an ideal illustrator of children's books, yet apart from the certificates his work appears to be unrecorded. Bourne lived alone and according to Simmons had a hard life. When he tried to trace Bourne in later life he found him in a home for men in a building that was once a workhouse. He had devoted his life to the cause of socialism and appears to have ended as a victim of the society he strove so hard to change into a more equitable, peaceful and loving system. The final epitaph comes from Jim Simmons, who writes that he 'was a brave and kindly man'.

In contrast to Bourne, the artist unknown, the certificate for the Women's Co-operative Guild (page 73) was drawn by a distinguished and successful Glasgow-born artist, Muirhead Bone, who achieved fame as an etcher and dry-point engraver. From 7 members in 1883 the Guild grew to 10,000 by 1897, 50,000 by 1920 and to nearly 90,000 at its peak in 1939. The pioneer Co-operative women overcame considerable social difficulties in building the organisation at a time when most working class women were tied to a treadmill cycle of housework and children, keeping a home together on starvation wages. For a woman to leave the housework for a few hours or to go out to a meeting after finishing work at mill or factory was socially unacceptable to most men. As Margaret Llewellyn Davies, who became the General Secretary of the Guild, put it in 1889, the position was summed up by the northern expression, 'Let my wife stay at home and wash my moleskin trousers.' Nevertheless, the Guild grew into a powerful socialist, feminist movement involving tens of thousands of married working class women in regular political activity. The Guild did pioneer work on questions of vital importance to women, campaigning for the provision of birth control, abortion, nursery schools, free school dinners, maternity clinics and family allowances. On wider issues, they championed the cause of peace and burned with a vision of equality, justice and co-operation. Muirhead Bone's symbol of the woman with the shopping basket represented the only economic power many women had, the power to decide where to spend their husbands' wages. Together with the 'divi' it was the only money they controlled. The symbol was incorporated in the design of a banner for the Guild in 1933 (page 175) and the total effectiveness and relevance of the image is demonstrated by the fact that it is still in use today.

Fifty years of service in the trade union movement invariably brings a free life-membership card, a coveted fifty years badge and often a certificate to record the event. The certificate produced by the Amalgamated Society of Woodworkers (page 71) in 1928 for presentation to veteran members presented a design problem, for many members had come into the union having served their time in other unions in the trade before the amalgamation. The difficulty was cleverly overcome by Arthur Mostyn, an artist well known in the labour movement, who depicted a finely proportioned archway, each stone of the portal bearing the name of one of the unions that made up the Society, from the General Union of Carpenters and Joiners founded in 1827 to the Scottish Cabinet Makers formed in 1918. The keystone of the arch was, of course, the Amalgamated Society of Woodworkers. The presentations were no dull branch-night affairs; monologues, singing, piano playing and stand-up comics enlivened the evenings, with humorous and sometimes moving stories of the trade from long ago being related by the long serving recipients of the certificates.

The history of early trade unionism is evoked by the 'box with three locks' (page 123), a reminder of the days when combinations of working people were held to be illegal and their funds had no protection under the law. Unable to deposit funds with banks they held to the old practice of the guilds and friendly societies by keeping their funds secure in a box with three different locks, each key held by a different person. As nearly all the early trade unions met in club rooms at public houses, the landlord invariably kept one key, the other two being held by officers of the unions, usually the general secretary and the treasurer. In 1806 the clubhouse of the London Brushmakers was at 'The sign of the Craven Head' in Drury Lane where they would meet on the last Wednesday in every month. The Society's articles stated, 'That a box with three different locks and keys shall be provided: each steward to keep a key and the landlord of the meeting house the other.' The box combined the skills of carpenter and blacksmith, strongly bound with wrought iron and of considerable weight. The weight was important so that it could not easily be lifted and for the same reason of security it was usually kept upstairs. The articles of the Society further provided that 'the landlord shall provide a room, with every necessary accommodation, on each meeting night, or to be fined 2/6d. for each neglect, and shall if required give security for the box and its contents.' Should an unscrupulous officer embezzle the funds the union had no redress in law and small unions were known to collapse when someone absconded with the money. The Operative Society of Masons in 1834 narrowly survived when the Grand Corresponding Secretary, seeing the union defeated in a strike and convinced the union was going down, helped himself to the remaining funds and disappeared with £35. 3s. 9½d. Grand Master and Grand Tiler heard of the treachery with dismay as the total funds from all the lodges only amounted to £54. 15s. 4½d. Happily the tragedy stimulated the union into renewed activity and they survived. In the same year, the Grand National Consolidated Trades Union heard that the Worcester delegate had embarked for Sydney and 'God knows how much of the money he has taken along with him'. Fortunately, there was little dishonesty and the unions grew in financial strength, though even this posed problems; John White, the founder of the 'Old Mechanics', remembered how in the 1840s he had hidden as much as £6,000 up the chimney of his house in Manchester.

Many of the boxes were elaborately decorated with the Society's coat of arms rather in the style of naval officers' sea chests. The box of the Glasgow Ropemakers' Friendly Society was painted with arms and kept in the custody of the president who was elected annually. Until the 1860s the tradition was maintained of solemnly transporting the box through the streets of Glasgow to the house of the new president, with the procession of Ropespinners headed by a piper.

It was not until the Trade Union Act of 1871 that union funds finally came under the protection of the law, though with the current practice of fining trade unions and sequestering their funds, a return to the box with three locks could yet regain favour. Union funds provided not only for tramping relief, strike or unemployment pay, but also made provision for sickness, old age and death. The friendly society or burial club aspect of trade unionism was vital in an era before social security and offered a safeguard against the final ignominy of poverty, a pauper's funeral. The rules governing the payment of mutual benefits were strict: in the 1820s the Falkirk Society excluded anyone 'defiling themselves with unclean women' while the Manchester Order of Bricklayers in 1829 not only excluded 'any member found fighting' but 'combined economy with Puritanism' by stopping the sick pay of any member whose disease was caused by 'wrestling, leaping, racing, football, acts of bravado, drunkenness or immoral conduct', a rule not repealed until 1908! The same enforcement of morality could also apply to members' widows, the 1861 rules of the Tin Plate Workers' Trade Society stating that a widow whose husband had not received benefit could nominate any of her children if 'she does not marry again and maintains a good moral character'.

For funerals, the unions would not only pay a death benefit to the widow but might provide the necessary trappings for a decent burial. The rules of the Dublin Bakers in 1838 provided for all that was needed for the laying out of the dead: 'three large linen sheets and tablecloth, six candlesticks, a snuffer and a snuffer's tray'. The Dublin Woodworkers, as befitting their craft, provided a magnificent carved wood bier, painted in black, scarlet and gold. The London Plumbers would delegate members to act as mutes and 'two members to stand at the door of a departed member on the day of a funeral'. The Dublin Housepainters obliged members living within one mile of the city to attend a member's funeral, instructing them to appear 'clean and neatly dressed and not disgraced with liquor' on the penalty of a sixpenny fine. In the London docks, where many Irish worked, the Stevedores' union would loan widow's weeds (page 121) free of charge and the union banner draped with black crepe would be carried at the head of the cortege, the bearers wearing black sashes.

In the late Victorian era funerals grew to become elaborate demonstrations of grief and scores of trade union banners from the period carry poignant scenes of bereaved widows and orphaned children; 'Do you hear the children weeping, O my brothers' ran the inscription on the banner of the United Society of Boiler Scalers and Stoke Hold Labourers, with scenes of union brothers consoling widow and children. Havelock Wilson, the Secretary of the National Amalgamated Sailors' and Firemens' Union, complained in 1889 that the burial of members with full union honours had got out of hand. A band and instruments were purchased together with marine uniform for the bandsmen and all branches in the immediate vicinity would be called upon to take part in the ceremony. Possibly with exaggeration he claimed that funerals would cost up to £200 and said, 'We had one official in London at this time who could honestly claim a medal for funerals. He had one nearly every week.'

The National Union of Railwaymen have more of the 'We provide for the orphans of our members' genre of banners (page 46) than any other union and although present society has abandoned the grand ritual ceremony of Victorian funerals, trade union banners are still carried at funerals of prominent members or when they have died in particularly tragic circumstances. When Yorkshire miners, Joe Green and David Gareth Jones, were killed whilst on the picket line during the 1984 miners' strike, their funerals were headed by their lodge banners as the president and general secretary joined relatives to lead thousands of miners and their families who followed the coffin. At miners' galas and annual picnics, the tradition of draping a lodge banner with black if there has been a fatality at the colliery during the year is still maintained.

Death is starkly depicted on the poster, 'The "Military" Practice of the Rebels', designed by an unknown artist in protest against the fascist bombing of civilians in Spain during the Franco rebellion (page 170). A dead child lies tagged and numbered, silent witness to the atrocity. The war generated hundreds of posters, powerful graphic pleas for the defence of the Republic, as artists joined in the struggle against fascism. In Britain, the Artists' International Association, founded in 1933 by Cliff Rowe, Misha Black, James Boswell, James Fitton and Pearl Binder, attracted hundreds of artists to mobilise 'the international unity of artists against Imperialist war on the Soviet Union, Fascism and Colonial oppression'. By the time of the fascist attack on the Republican government of Spain in 1936, the AIA had over 600 members, including many leading artists of the period, Augustus John, Dame Laura Knight, Muirhead Bone, Duncan Grant and Vanessa Bell among them. It was the Artists' International Association who made a banner for the British Battalion of the International Brigade, designed by James Lucas and embroidered by Phyllis Ladyman, the clenched fist symbol on the banner pole being sculpted by Betty Rea. In December 1936 the Association mounted an exhibition, 'Artists help

Spain', to raise funds for a field kitchen for the International Column in defence of Madrid. Some idea of the popular support aroused is understood by the artists who donated works, including Pissarro, Epstein, Paul Nash and Eric Gill. It was amid this enthusiasm and desire to do something that Felicity Ashbee, the daughter of Charles R. Ashbee, founder of the Guild of Handicraft, was drawn into the popular front movement against fascism. Felicity Ashbee came from a celebrated, talented middle class family where she had enjoyed the benefit of private education, servants and foreign travel, yet like so many other intellectuals from the privileged strata of British society in the thirties she became deeply involved in the left wing movement with anti-fascism as the central issue. Trained in the fine arts and a Royal Academician she joined the large number of talented artists, the famous and the unknown who painted banners, hoardings and posters for Spain, May Day and the cause of peace. Her poster 'Famine in Spain' (page 169) was one of three she designed for the National Joint Committee for Spanish Relief. It is perhaps the best of her posters, poignant, haunting, the gaunt faces a precursor of the hollow-eyed drawings by Vicky in his post-war pleas for the hungry of the Third World.

The Artists' International Association brought a new vitality to the art of Labour, working in every medium. Artists like Nan Youngman and Priscilla Thorneycroft painted giant hoardings – 'Spain fights on – send food now'. Edith Tudor-Hart used her camera to photograph the poor, people at work and scenes of everyday life, her images being used for posters, book jackets and pamphlets for left wing organisations. Peter Peri produced a sculpture, *Aid Spain*, a mother looking with dread to the skies and protecting her child. At a meeting held at the Albert Hall to raise money for the Basque children, Picasso made a drawing for the programme, Peter Kapp designed the cover, J.B. Priestley wrote a foreword and Paul Robeson sang to the audience.

The activity reached out to involve working people in making their own visual propaganda. In the East End of London, Norman King and a group of socialist artists set up a workshop in a church hall to teach workers how to make banners, posters, murals and leaflets. The poster 'Propaganda Art' (page 168) is a good example of the vigorous graphic form that the people created in support of working class unity. Reproduced by a simple silk-screen process it is remarkably similar in character to the poster art that spontaneously erupted from the Atelier Populaire during the student revolt in Paris, thirty years on.

The posters of the labour movement offer a visual history from the earliest days of trade unionism to the present-day struggles of labour against the excesses of the most reactionary British government of the twentieth century. From the simple wood-block, black and white posters of the early nineteenth century to the full-colour lithographed posters of today, a graphic pictorial record is presented of the fight for social justice by ordinary working people. The 1815 poster for the firm of Butterworth Brooks (page 160) conceals an attempt to introduce non-union labour, the familiar accusation of impeding new technology being levelled at the strikers.

Printed in Hebrew, the poster for the Amalgamated Society of Tailors in 1889 (page 161) is a reminder of 'the good old days', when poor Jewish immigrant tailors went on strike for a reduction in working hours to ten and a half hours a day, from eight in the morning till eight at night with a break for breakfast and at mid-day! Earlier that year, Will Thorne had led the gasworkers in a successful battle to reduce their hours from twelve to eight a day, a triumph enshrined on their union emblem which featured a clock with the hands set at eight and headed boldly 'Eight hours labour'.

The call for an eight-hour working day had come from the First International in 1865 and was reiterated at the congress of the Second International held in Paris in 1889, when the resolution was passed that '. . . on one appointed day the toiling masses shall demand of the state authorities the legal reduction of the working day to eight hours . . .' The day chosen was 1 May. Interesting relics of the trade union struggle for the eight-hour day are the watchcases, some of which may date from the 1860s and bear the inscription 'We require eight hours for work, eight hours for our own instruction and eight hours for repose.' Despite the huge advance in technology and the machinery of mass production, most factory workers still labour for eight hours, the demand for shorter hours being greeted by government and employers alike with the same horror expressed when the call for an eight-hour day was made a hundred years ago.

Unemployment and hunger in the 'midst of plenty' was humorously treated by the Social Democratic Federation and trade union leader, Harry Quelch (page 164), in an election poster from the early part of this century. The artist is unknown but the illustration that suggests that even monkeys would not tolerate the injustice suffered by the working class accords with Quelch's own views. Speaking during the general election campaign of 1910, he said of the British working class, '. . . it is certainly more completely imbued with bourgeois ideas, less conscious of its own subject position as a class than any other working class I know.'

Humour was used to devastating effect by Frank Horrabin to attack Philip Snowden's National Government budget of 1931 (page 167) giving the lie to 'equality of sacrifice' when the Chancellor cut the weekly amount paid to an unemployed worker from 17s. to 15s. 3d. The use of humour as a weapon of political propaganda on official posters of the labour movement is rarely seen today, although it still surfaces in the poster art produced for local trade disputes. An exception was the poster produced by the Kent miners during the 1972 strike (page 172). Drawn by Con Connolly, the poster was so popular that it was circulated nationally. The capacity to joke during adversity is deeply rooted in the culture of the British working class and is evidenced by the witty slogans and satirical drawings that appear on the homemade posters and placards that appear during any local trade union dispute. Norman Tebbitt, Secretary of State for Employment in 1982, became the butt of working class humour when he lectured the 3,000,000 unemployed, suggesting they should emulate his father who 'got on his bike and looked for work'. Thousands of button badges were worn, a drawing of a bicycle combined with the catch phrase from a popular television series, 'Gis a job' (page 39), making a reply as sharply as any political speech.

A classic among Labour Party posters in serious vein is John Armstrong's brilliant poster for the 1945 election campaign, 'Now Let Us Win the Peace', cleverly using the V for Victory wartime symbol to Labour's advantage. In fact, it was only one of eight posters designed by Armstrong for the campaign, the artist working flat out for a week to meet the deadline. Those who now suggest that Labour did not expect to win the 1945 election should acquaint themselves with the colossal amount of publicity and propaganda material produced for the campaign and the scale and efficiency of the distribution.

At a time of acute shortage of materials and labour at the end of a devastating war, the Labour Party skilfully organised the production of 2,000,000 sixteen-page pictorial booklets, 2,000,000 leaflets, 1,000,000 policy pamphlets, 1,000,000 'Election Specials' and 400,000 posters, apart from 500,000 copies of the party manifesto, 'Let Us Face the Future', speakers' handbooks, speakers' cards and 900,000 other pamphlets. The campaign sub-committee carried out the huge undertaking by calling in professional designers and publicity experts who supported the party, enlisting the help of the printing trade unions and mobilising the Constituency Labour Parties to help with distribution. Wartime regulations on transport were still in force and the party had to make representation to the Ministry of Transport to ensure rail deliveries of the huge mass of material. It was co-operation between the TUC, the trade unions and the Labour Party plus the willing and freely given help from professional designers, journalists and publicists that helped carry Labour to election victory. To infer that power was given to Labour on the whim of a war-weary electorate seeking change is to ignore the programme for sweeping social change on which the party fought the election, the co-operative effort of the whole movement to spread that message and the strength of Clement Attlee's leadership. It is to ignore also the decades of selfless work by tens of thousands of trade unionists and socialists to whom socialism was more than a cross on a ballot paper.

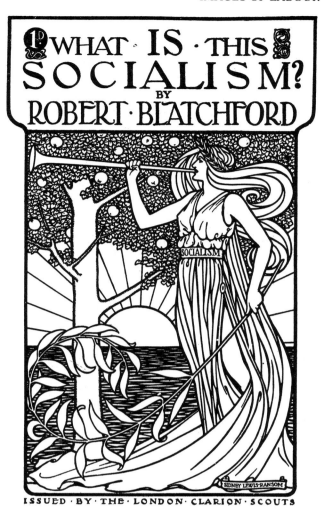

Sidney Lewis-Ransom's cover design for a Blatchford *Clarion* pamphlet.

The evangelical spirit of those who 'preached' socialism shines from the images on any amount of printed ephemera, pamphlets and publications. The postcard of the horse-drawn Clarion van recalls the selfless devotion of the 'vanners', the men and women who travelled from town to village, spreading the gospel of socialism. The *Clarion* was first published on 12 December 1892, founded by four journalists from the *Sunday Chronicle* who wrote under peculiar pen names, Robert Blatchford (Nunquam), his brother Montague Blatchford (The Insect), Edward Fay (The Bounder) and Alex Thompson (Dangle). The first issue sold 40,000 copies and within a few years had moved up to the steady circulation of over 80,000. Sales of the paper were given a boost by the publication of Robert Blatchford's *Merrie England*, a book which argued the case for socialism, sold 750,000 copies at the first rush, eventually selling over 2,000,000. The *Clarion* became more than a newspaper; it became a fellowship. There were no rules or formal organisation, simply the comradeship of those who supported the paper. Readers gave loyalty to advertisers, buying their boots, bikes and soap from those who supported socialism. In 1894 the first Clarion cycling club was formed in Birmingham and clubs soon sprang up all over the country bringing fresh air and socialism to the two-wheeled gospellers who pedalled into the countryside at weekends and peddled *Clarion* at the same time. By 1896 came the first of the Clarion vans, horse-drawn caravans equipped and provisioned to enable the 'vanners' to travel for weeks on end carrying the message of socialism to outlying districts and villages. The gipsy-like life was seldom romantic; while the speaker may have been well received in some towns, elsewhere there was open hostility. Bruce Glasier told how touring with the van at Maybole he held 'an open air meeting much disturbed by drunk men' and was 'much disturbed by the filthiness of their remarks'. Robert Tressell (the pen name of Robert Noonan) in his great novel of working class life in the building trade, *The Ragged Trousered Philanthropists*, described the visit of a van to 'Mugsborough'. 'As soon as the crowd saw it, they gave an exultant cheer, or, rather, yell, and began running down the hill to meet it, and in a few minutes it was surrounded by a howling mob. The van was drawn by two horses, there was a door and a small platform at the back and over this was a sign with white letters on a red ground, "Socialism, the only hope of the workers".' In the story, the van is stoned and run out of town, an experience not unknown to vanners in real life, but then Noonan's story was drawn from life and the Clarion van had been to Hastings, the 'Mugsborough' where the 'philanthropists' lived and worked. The first of the Clarion vans was a simple conversion of a farmer's wagon, but later they were purpose built and named after pioneers like Caroline Martyn, Enid Stacy and William Morris (page 150). The Morris van, made in 1914, was a mobile tribute to labour, with a dozen exterior carved mahogany panels designed by Walter Crane and an ornate headpiece lettered 'Socialism' crowned with a rising sun. A small example of Robert Noonan's work as a decorator survives in the form of one section of a mural he painted in 1905 for St Andrew's Church, Hastings. The remainder of the mural was destroyed when the church was demolished in 1970, the surviving plaster panel being rescued by the action of Noonan's biographer, Fred Ball, and his friend David Haines.

The Workers' Cry (page 144) was a less successful attempt to produce an evangelising newspaper of labour. Founded by Frank Smith, a former Commissioner in the Salvation Army, the paper was launched on 2 May 1891 with a policy of 'Justice for all, privilege for none and equal rights for all women workers'. The paper ran for only twenty issues. Frank Smith, the father of Salvation Army social work, was converted to socialism during the upsurge of the new unionism of 1889 and the unemployed demonstrations of 1890. Smith, already deeply concerned with the alleviation of the distress of the poor, led a number of street protests and ended up in prison for his sins. His paper, the title barely removed from the *War Cry* of the Salvation Army, was subtitled 'Advocate of the claims of the Labour Army'. As a symbol, Smith simply adapted the crest of the Salvation Army, replacing 'Blood and Fire' with 'Truth and Right', abandoning the 'Crown of Glory' and replacing it with the Statue of Liberty and disposing of the crossed swords of holy warfare in favour of a pick-axe and two spades.

If his plagiarism was blatant, his sincerity was in no doubt. A close friend and confidant of Keir Hardie and a member of the Independent Labour Party, he stood for Parliament no less than twelve times before finally winning a seat in 1929 at the age of seventy-six!

The pre-eminent image of labour, the Red Flag, as symbol and song is recalled by the picture of James Connell on his pamphlet, 'Socialism and the Survival of the Fittest' (page 141). A rebel and a poacher throughout his life, Connell wrote the battle hymn of socialism after hearing a speech by the Social Democratic Federation pioneer, Herbert Burrows. Variously attributing the Great Dock Strike of 1889, the Paris Commune, the Chicago Martyrs and the Russian Nihilists as the deeper source of his inspiration, he wrote the first two stanzas and the chorus while travelling on the top deck of a bus between Charing Cross and New Cross. To his eternal grief, A.S. Headingley (Adolphe Smith), an SDF leader who had served as an ambulance man during the Paris Commune, changed the tune from the original, sung to 'The White Cockade', to 'Tannenbaum', an old German Roman Catholic hymn. The 'Red Flag' was first published in *Justice* in the Christmas issue of 1889 and quickly became as popular as the 'Marseillaise' and the 'Internationale' as a revolutionary hymn. 'Tho' cowards flinch', so Ramsay MacDonald in 1925 made a determined effort to replace the 'Red Flag' as the song of Labour, saying, 'We still want a great Labour song' and prompting a competition in the *Daily Herald*. Three hundred entries were received but not one approached the passion and inspiration of Jim Connell's masterful contribution to the imagery of socialism. The *Daily Herald* of 1925 was far removed from Lansbury's *Herald* of 1918 (page 143) that could publish a front page during the war with the massive headline, 'Keep the Red Flag flying, and call for a Soviet Great Britain'. In the muddled folklore of the labour movement the old *Herald* is still spoken of with affection by trade union and Labour leaders to whom its left wing policies would have been anathema.

Socialist opposition to the First World War is recalled by the concert programmes (page 180) produced by conscientious objectors held in Dartmoor Prison. Most were members of the Independent Labour Party and the No Conscription Fellowship (page 52) who remained true to their socialist principles and refused to support a capitalist war. The division in the British labour movement was wide, with many pioneer socialists and trade unionists supporting the war, among them Hyndman, Blatchford, Tillett, Clynes and

Thorne. It was the ILP that responded to the declaration of war with a manifesto of internationalism declaring, '. . . out of the darkness and depth we hail our working class comrades of every land, across the roar of guns we send sympathy and greetings to the German socialists.' It was that spirit which led to the 'Red Flag' being sung in Dartmoor Prison to the fury of the jingoists outside.

The throwaway printed scraps of labour history help to give substance to past struggles, won or lost, names, imagery and typography stamping the period as clearly as any date. A ticket for a fund-raising bazaar for the SDF, season's greetings from the Federated Postmen of Sheffield, a resolution by the London Society of Compositors in support of a strike of music hall artistes that included Marie Lloyd and 'Little Tich'. A grubby twopenny receipt issued by London cabbies during a strike, a Herald League ticket to hear Jim Larkin 'raising the fiery cross' in support of the locked-out Dublin workers, a sixpenny collecting ticket for the relief of the wives and children of striking miners. As surely as London bus tickets once marked the stages of a journey they chart the progress of organised labour.

Leaflets, the basic propaganda weapon of any striving group, have greater depth, outlining the argument for the issue of the day. They too, in language and typography, conjure life into past battles: the Salvation Army accused by the woodworkers of 'philanthropic sweating', the campaigns to provide school meals for hungry children, Churchill and Jarrow, code words in the mythology of labour, the Russian Revolution of 1905, a hunger march of 1925. Some ring familiar as history repeats itself − a 'right to work demonstration' in 1906; some present a surprise − a meeting of the Civil Service Socialist Society, with Tom Mann urging the government servants to 'Organise, Organise, Organise, Fight, Fight, Fight', an exhortation to inspire the civil servants at GCHQ seventy-five years on. The persecution of two socialist schoolteachers, the persecution of a single policeman, the judicial murder of two anarchists: episodes that present snatches of history, stimulating further inquiry. The yellowing sheets create images of men and women huddled together, drafting and redrafting, desperately trying to arrange a few words to attract and convince, each leaflet the result of a decision to 'do something', the hoped-for outcome to be some form of action.

In contrast to expendable print, photographs, even snapshots, are taken to be kept as reminders, the instant preservation of a moment past. They survive as visual history to be studied and read as carefully as letters and minute books, a library of images to complement the printed or written word. A photographic archive is an important primary research source, yet it needs to be approached with circumspection for a photographer may have all the prejudices of a partisan biographer. Yet, however a picture may be contrived, it has something to impart to the careful researcher, if it is only the way

in which the photographer or subject wishes it to appear. Fox Talbot viewed the people who worked on his estate with a feudal benevolence; Dr Barnado sought to wring hearts and pennies; mum at the seaside snaps enjoyment; an employer may photograph his staff and machinery to depict power and possession while the borough engineer attempts documentary evidence. All are valid as social history, from the box Brownie snapshot to the studio pose or the commercial daily work of a photojournalist. Linked with careful research they buttress the evidence of the written word and add to our understanding of that which has happened.

The photographs taken by John Galt for the *Daily News'* Sweated Industries Exhibition in 1906 (pages 151 and 152) have the very stench of poverty. In squalid, bug-ridden, overcrowded hovels, children were robbed of childhood and women worked to exhaustion for pennies. No work was too dirty, too tedious or too obnoxious to escape the homework net that enmeshed the sick, disabled, widowed, orphaned and simply poor. Clementina Black's account of match-box making for Royal Swan Vestas is a description of an infinite and tedious hell with 10,368 pieces of chip and paper being assembled for half a crown. These were the 'People of the Abyss', the submerged poor who scarcely avoided starvation while working seventy hours a week. Unorganised and unrepresented they were defenceless and vulnerable, easy prey for the sweater.

A rare episode in British trade union history, the use of direct action by organised labour for a political end, is recalled by the picture of ammunition boxes and guncarriage wheels stowed in the hold of the *Jolly George* in 1920. Intended for shipment to Poland for use in the war on the young Soviet Union, the ship was prevented from sailing by the refusal of London dockers to handle the cargo. The action was fully supported by the TUC and the Labour Party who warned the government, 'The whole industrial power of the organised workers will be used to defeat this war.' Faced with the determined stand of the labour movement, the government abandoned support for the war and the story of the dockers and the *Jolly George* became a legend of working class power.

The power of direct action by trade unionists is also captured in Cliff Rowe's mural panel of electricians pulling the fuses of the Albert Hall in 1918. Rowe, a founder of the Artists' International Association, was commissioned by the Electrical Trades Union in 1954 to paint a series of mural panels illustrating scenes from trade union history to adorn the walls of Esher Place, the ETU's college. One of the subjects decided upon was the action of electricians in support of the right of the *Daily Herald* to hold a meeting at the Royal Albert Hall. The meeting had, in fact, been agreed by the management who then cancelled it at four days' notice when thousands of tickets had already been sold. Among the supporters applying for tickets was J.W. Muir of the ETU. Told that the meeting was cancelled by order of the management, Muir replied, 'We'll stop that little game.' The following day, electricians removed the main fuses and other trade unions gave support, instructing taxi drivers, bus and train drivers to refuse to stop at the Albert Hall or at South Kensington. The management was forced to give in and 12,000 trade unionists packed the hall to hear George Lansbury, who said, 'If only the toilers could realise that all power lies in their hands, and, realising that, would use their power to assist each other upward to a better life, how much quicker we should reach our goal.'

Rowe himself does not hold his five paintings for the ETU in high esteem but they are powerful and telling reminders of key struggles in the history of trade unionism.

137 years earlier, on 21 April 1834, 30,000 trade unionists, dressed in their Sunday best, fell in behind the banners of the Grand National Consolidated Trades Union at Copenhagen Fields, London, to call for the release of the Tolpuddle Martyrs. Lined in regimental order behind thirty-two standards they watched Dr Arthur Wade, chaplain of the Metropolitan Trade Unions, in scarlet hood and full canonical dress set off to present a petition bearing a quarter of a million signatures to the Home Secretary, Lord Melbourne.

On 21 February 1971 the TUC held a massive march and demonstration against the Conservative government's Industrial Relations Bill, legislation aimed at curtailing the rights of trade unions. Onto the streets of London, paraded alongside tens of thousands of posters, placards, badges and banners made for the occasion, trade unionists also carried their old and historic banners recalling past struggles for trade union rights. Among the 140,000 that marched against the Bill were some trade unionists wearing sashes, reminders of the early days when regalia was a vital part of the pageantry and identity of trade unions. Dug out from dusty banner boxes, the old banners and sashes recalled the splendour and colour of our forebears as they marched for fundamental rights, creating images of labour, unfaded by time.

To greet the Chartists, Peter McDouall and John Collins, on their release from prison in 1840, the people gathered in Manchester, led by 'Two marshalls on horse back with green scarves and green and white favours'. Behind a portrait of McDouall, 'The tyrant's foe', came 'twenty committeemen with staves, scarves and favours'. Following were 'eight young women dressed in white, wearing green and white favours' and carrying 'four splendid garlands'. At a Reform League demonstration in London in 1867, the trade unions turned out in force, led by members of the Farriers, 'horsemen wearing top-boots, scarves and cockades'. From the south came the Amalgamated Engineers, the Ironfounders, the Plasterers and 'several Lodges of Operative Masons wearing their aprons'. The West End Cabinetmakers were there with banner and band, their motto reading 'Bright Cabinetmakers wanted: No Adullamites need apply.' Then came the Amalgamated Carpenters and Joiners, 'Deal with us on the square, you have chiselled us long enough.'

In the Preston Guild procession of 1882 the parade was led by the Tin Plate Workers and Gas Fitters, who had gained the privilege by ballot. Two trumpeters clad in ancient costume preceded the 'beautiful banner displaying the interior of a workshop', the marshalls carried 'silver mounted staves and were adorned with regalia'. The Saddlers' and Harness Makers' banner was led by 'four lads in jockey's costumes, complete with white unmentionables and pink smocks, also being booted and spurred'. Plumbers and painters were headed by a banner displaying the motto 'Love and Obedience' and the painters' art was illustrated by a lurry on the side of which were the painters' arms, crest and emblem. The Steam Engine Makers were there with 'four girls in white representing Faith, Hope, Charity and Plenty together with a model locomotive valued at two hundred pounds.'

The first May Day demonstration in London, 1890, was led by the 'aristocrats of labour', twenty-five farriers 'right gallantly mounted on sprightly steeds, the riders wearing blue and white sashes and smoking cigars'. They were escorted by two outriders, one of whom wore 'a green coat and a cap of liberty, the other a red Garibaldi jacket'. The Ladies' Tailors' Union bore a banner with an unexplained device, a 'Stag of magnificent head jumping a fence'. The 'West End Tailors wore black frock coats with a fresh flower in the buttonhole and tall hats.' It was no rabble but a confident army of working men and women that took to the streets that day, the dull grey cobbles of the London roads warmed by the brilliance of shimmering silk and lit by the heraldry of labour.

If time has seen an end to the trade union use of regalia, some of the old forms of imagery linger on. The first banner has appeared, perhaps incongruously, bearing the image of a micro-chip. The new images will appear on video recordings, tapes and future means of electronic communication; the need, however, for presence and identity remains, as does the need for working people to combine together to protect their economic and social interests. Art is not static but changes with society. Walter Crane, the moulder of nineteenth century labour imagery, wrote, 'Art is not a revolving kaleidoscope of dead styles, but in its true sense, in a vital and healthy condition, is the spontaneous expression of the life and aspirations of a free people.'

It is the irrepressible creative and ever developing art that springs from work and working people that will shape the future images of labour.

Walter Crane's design for the children's page of the *Young Socialist*.

BADGES

The demand for more and more men to die or to be mutilated in the mud of Flanders fortuitously provided women with the opportunity to enter craft industries that were previously closed to them. The colossal requirements of the armed services for machines and munitions were met only by allowing women workers into the engineering industry. For many of the women, it was also their introduction to trade unionism.

On the afternoon of Saturday, 20 May 1916, nineteen women welders working on aircraft production met at Notting Hill to consider forming their own trade union. The proposal to establish the Society of Women Welders was made by Margaret Godsal and supported by Violet Willis. It was enthusiastically received by the women and a committee was chosen from women working at Sopwith's, Napier's, Safe Bros. and Menn's. Without funds or premises they turned to other women's organisations for assistance and were given financial help by the London Society for Women's Suffrage and the Union of Women Optical Glass Workers. They were offered the share of an office with the Society of Women Motor Drivers and organisational advice from the Women's Trade Union League. They also had a discussion with the Amalgamated Society of Engineers, but rejected the suggestion of Mr Swales, the London and District

Secretary, that they should change their name to the Society of Women Oxyacetylene Welders, Finishers and Braziers!

Upon formation they immediately entered into negotiation with the management of the larger factories for an increase in pay from 8d. to 9d. an hour, pointing out that men were paid 1s. an hour for similar work. With persistence, the women won their claim and strengthened the union with recruitment from smaller factories. The membership figure is uncertain but it is doubtful if it ever reached 1,000. The end of the war meant the end of the factories of war and by 1919 most of the members of the Society of Women Welders were unemployed. The financial difficulties created placed the union in a position where it was no longer able to continue and on 26 July 1919 a final meeting of the Society was held in London. There was an offer from the London Society for Women's Service to form a welders' group within the Service but this was rejected as the LSWS was not a trade union. The women hoped to 'hold together the machinery of our organisation in readiness for re-starting on trade union lines,' but the future offered little hope. On 8 August 1919 the union issued a final circular urging working members to join any other appropriate trade union. The Society of Women Welders was ended.

Amalgamated Society of Farriers, 1905

National Amalgamated Society of Male
and Female Pottery Workers, 1906

Postmen's Federation, 1891

Municipal Employees' Association, 1894

London and Provincial Union of Licensed
Vehicle Workers, 1919

National Amalgamated Union of
Labour, 1889

'No badge – no bus' is emblazoned on the banner of the Acton branch of the London and Provincial Union of Licensed Vehicle Workers, 1913, recording a notable victory for one hundred percent trade unionism. While membership cards give an effective record of dues paid and are easily checked against the register at branch meetings, a badge provides ready identity on the shop floor or at the factory gate. Some unions have used their badges to signify that a member is in benefit, paid up to date, as illustrated on the 'December clearance 1914' badge of the Licensed Vehicle Workers. Quarterly control badges were issued by a number of the new unions in the 1890s: the National Union of Dock Labourers, Rule 12, Clause 14, stated the badge was '... during the current quarter the property of the union and shall be issued to new members and all members clear on the books at the end of the financial quarter ... At the end of the quarter the old badge shall become the property of the union branch.' The badges were numbered 1-4 and carried the branch ledger number on the front with the branch number marked on the reverse.

Faced with the task of maintaining union membership in an industry of casual workers and a glut of labour, the NUDL rules stated, 'Each member of the union shall be supplied with a badge. He shall when seeking employment prominently display his badge, and on demand of any member of the branch or district, produce it for inspection.' Wearing the badge might also invite the open hostility of management and members would wear their badge as a button on jacket or waistcoat, behind the lapel or on a belt. The NUDL realised the difficulties and added in their rules, 'the enforcement of this clause is not compulsory on branches as in the cases where branches are comparatively weak and it could not safely be enforced.'

Other unions also adopted the quarterly badge, the Quay Porters of the Amalgamated Warehouse Workers' Union operating the system until 1921. The Mersey Quay and Railway Carters' Union used a half yearly badge and laid down fines for anyone 'lending, pledging or selling' their badges: 'For the first offence any sum not exceeding £1 and for any future offence any sum not exceeding £5 or the option of the Committee may be suspension or expulsion.' For the most part, badges were symbols of recognition to be worn with pride by the union member, making them part of a fraternity. The design usually incorporated some part of the union emblem or carried a symbol of the trade. The National Union of Gasworkers and General Labourers did, in fact, reproduce their union emblem in full colour on an early button badge but the tiny reproduction is barely legible.

The Amalgamated Society of Farriers settled for part of their emblem, using a horse's head surrounded by a horseshoe, while the Amalgamated Society of Male and Female Pottery Workers selected an urn as the symbol of their craft. Many unions were content with 'the clasp of brotherhood the world o'er', the handshake of unity, friendship and mutual help together with the union title and motto or the date of establishment.

The new unionism that grew from the Great Dock Strike of 1889 saw new trade unions being formed week by week. Along with the rule book, a banner and badges were first priorities to announce their arrival and proclaim their presence. The Dock, Wharf, Riverside and General Workers' Union badge carries the motto 'Each for all, all for each,' the National Union of Gas and General Workers the motto 'Unity, Fidelity, Love', which was adopted at a meeting of 2,000 gasworkers in Victoria Park on 20 May 1889 at a meeting chaired by Will Thorne. The militant

1. Dock, Wharf, Riverside and General Workers' Union, 1889

2. The Workers' Union

3. Transport and General Workers' Union, 1922

4. National Union of Gas and General Workers, 1889

5. National Amalgamated Seamen's and Firemen's Union, 1888

6. United Operative Plumbers' Association of Great Britain, 1865

7. United Builders' Labourers' Union, 1889

Workers' Union, formed on May Day 1898 with Tom Mann as President, produced an elaborate lapel badge for its delegate conference depicting a male and female worker, hands clasped in unity, distinctly demonstrating the change of direction from the traditions of the older craft unions. In 1929 the Workers' Union was to amalgamate with the Transport and General Workers' Union that itself had grown out of the Dockers' Union. The National Amalgamated Seamen's and Firemen's union, formed in 1888 by J. Havelock Wilson, chose a lighthouse and sailing ship to adorn its badge, leaving no room for the union's apt motto 'pull together'. The motto on the badge of the United Operative Plumbers' Association of Great Britain, 'Defence not defiance', reveals the early origin of the union, founded in 1865 when craft unions were anxious to prove that they represented no threat to government and the law but merely sought to protect the trade. In 1869 George May, the Corresponding Secretary, writing to his members explained, 'We can take up our motto without fear that we are united to protect but not combined to injure.' The United Builders' Labourers' Union, another of the 1889 unions to organise non-craft workers, simply settled for title, date of foundation and the symbolic handshake for their badge.

Many thousands of badges have been manufactured for British trades unions and a comprehensive collection from any one of them will cover the complex history of amalgamations, breakaways and sectional interests. The imagery, while of necessity simpler than the intricate designs of emblems and banners, is still a rewarding source of study, as are the mottos. 'Educate, Organise, Control', the motto of the Amalgamated Engineering Union, is hard to better as a concise expression of political intent. The National Union of Railwaymen still use a variation of Karl Marx's clarion call from the *Communist Manifesto*, 'Workers of the world unite'. The Electrical Trades Union stood for 'Light and Liberty', using Walter Crane's angel of freedom as its symbol.

In design and mottos, badges display a miniature history of the development of trades unionism, charting the existence of long defunct unions, from Chimney Cleaners to Stick and Cane Dressers. The badges mark anniversaries, length of service, office, commemorate victories, strikes, lock-outs and struggles lost. They have been struck in silver and gold, made of laminated paper (Cabinet Makers' Trade Union) and celluloid-covered paper and metal. There are presidential badges three or four inches in length with suspended bars reminiscent of military

1. Amalgamated Engineering Union, 1851

2. National Union of Railwaymen, 1913

3. Associated Society of Locomotive Engineers and Firemen, 1880

4. National Union of Public Employees, 1928

5. National Union of Mineworkers, 1945

6. National Union of Boot and Shoe Operatives, 1890

7. National Union of Agricultural Workers, 1912

8. Electrical Trades Union, 1889

9. Union of Construction, Allied Trades and Technicians, 1971

medals and minute lapel badges that seem to have been designed for discreet city wear. The variety and number of trade union badges is unknown but runs into thousands and they represent one of the important facets of labour imagery.

The dates given to the badges illustrated are from the date of adoption of the title shown on the badge.

The first button badges were produced in America in 1896 and were made possible by the invention of celluloid some twenty years earlier. Patented by Whitehead and Hoag of Newark, New Jersey, they were first used as free gifts in cigarette packets as an alternative to cigarette cards. The Americans were quick to see the value of button badges for electioneering and they were used in the McKinley versus Bryan Presidential Election the same year they were invented. Button badges were still rare in Britain at the turn of the century and although some were made for the Diamond Jubilee of Queen Victoria and to mark the victory of Britain in the Boer War, they were both made in the United States and imported. It was not until the machinery was bought from America that the first British-produced badges were made, sometime during the first decade of the twentieth century.

Among the earliest British political button badges were those for the first of the two General Elections held in 1910, produced for the Liberal and Labour candidates in the North East by the *Northern Echo*, the Liberal and progressive halfpenny morning daily. Thirty-two candidates were supported by the paper and the badges were sold at 1s. for a card of sixteen, direct from the offices of the *Echo*, or at 1d. each by newsagents. The first four illustrated portray Thomas Summerbell, Sunderland, Harold Elverston, Gateshead, Pete Curran, Jarrow, and John Taylor, Chester-le-Street, all candidates for the cause of Labour. Elverston and Taylor won their seats but Summerbell and Curran were among the thirty-eight Labour candidates defeated in a total of seventy-eight constituencies contested by Labour.

The button badge for Herbert Burrows, the Social Democratic Federation pioneer socialist, may have been produced at the same period but was made in the South, being manufactured by Merchant's Portrait Company of Kentish Town Road. The badge of Jimmy Maxton, the Clydeside rebel who became leader of the Independent Labour Party, carries a portrait of him taken in 1919 and was probably made for the election of that year when Maxton was elected to Parliament for the first time as member for Bridgeton.

SSS is the red-flag button badge of the Socialist Sunday Schools movement, founded in Battersea in 1892 and vigorously promoted in Scotland by Keir Hardie, Archie McArthur and Caroline Martyn. The movement aimed to provide a socialist education for children, offering a moral and ethical alternative to Christianity. Unlike the Sunday schools of the Anglican Church, the movement opposed war and preached that 'the wealth of the world is produced by labour and should be shared, each according to his need.' The basis of the movement was love and justice, and the movement argued that the private ownership of the means of production was a breach of moral law. By 1912 more than 12,000 were attending Socialist Sunday Schools, where adults and children sat, studied and learned together. A close link developed between the SSS and the Independent Labour Party and the declining membership of the Socialist Sunday Schools movement after 1935 paralleled the decline of the ILP. In 1965 the movement ceased to be known as the Socialist Sunday Schools and became the Socialist Fellowship.

The PPU badge is that of the Peace Pledge Union, founded in 1934 by Canon 'Dick' Shepherd as a non-party pacifist organisation. Shepherd wrote to the newspapers and asked those who opposed war to write to him on a postcard with the pledge, 'I renounce war and will never support or sanction another.' The response was so great that he felt compelled to form an organisation to represent the tens of thousands who replied to his appeal and formed the Peace Pledge Union.

Thomas Summerbell Harold Elverston Pete Curran

John Taylor Herbert Burrows James Maxton

With the cross, the swastika and the hammer and sickle, the symbol of the Campaign for Nuclear Disarmament must rank as a major image of universal recognition. It was designed by Gerald Holtom a few weeks before the first Aldermaston march in 1958. Holtom's explanation of the emblem is that it is the semaphore signal for ND, nuclear disarmament. Secondly, the broken cross means the death of man, while the circle represents the unborn child. It represents in total the threat of nuclear weapons to all mankind. Designed as a black and white logo, it was first made into badges by Eric Austin of Kensington CND who made them in pottery, reasoning that if the nuclear holocaust came, the badges would survive the fire as a memorial. Since then, millions of badges and representations of the CND symbol have been reproduced throughout the world, making it a world-wide sign of peace campaigners in all lands. The adapted symbol, produced for the great anti-nuclear demonstration of 1980, is the work of Peter Kennard, who graphically used a perspective form of the original design breaking a cruise missile as his image for the day of protest.

The Medical Aid Committee for Vietnam was formed in June 1965 at a meeting in the House of Commons with John Rankin, MP, as Chairman, Lord Boyd Orr as President and Professor Dorothy Hodgkin, OM, FRS, as Vice President. The meeting was held on the initiative of Dr Joan McMichael who had been involved in Spanish Medical Aid in 1936 and had been Secretary of China Medical Aid for a short period in 1938-39. At first, aid was sent to the Red Cross Society in the National Liberation Front areas of South Vietnam where the US bombing was heaviest. With the American decision to bomb North Vietnam, the Committee extended its aid to include the North.

'Vietnam' and 'napalm' are words to recall the horror of one of the fiercest conflicts in the history of man. The photograph of a young girl, running naked and burning with blazing napalm

sticking to her body, was shown on television around the world and perhaps did more to make people aware of the horrors of American air attacks on that little country than any other image of the war. The burning flames of war were used to powerful and telling effect in a poster design by Ken Sprague, 'Tell Johnson, Stop the Bombing', produced after the first American air attack on Hanoi. Later, in Sprague's studio, the poster design was adapted by Mick Daniels to provide the graphic red and white badge of Medical Aid for Vietnam.

May Day 1940 was the fiftieth anniversary of 1 May as a day of international working class demonstration and celebration. The idea grew from the congress of the International Association of Working Men (the Second International) held in Paris on 14 July 1889, the hundredth anniversary of the fall of the Bastille. The decision to set aside 1 May as a day upon which the workers of the world were to fight for the eight-hour working day was influenced by the American Federation of Labour who had already decided on 1 May 1890 as a day of demonstration. Following speeches from the American delegates, the congress adopted the resolution:
The Congress decides to organise a great international demonstration, so that in all countries and in all cities on one appointed day the toiling masses shall demand of the state authorities the legal reduction of the working day to eight hours, as well as carrying out other decisions of the Paris Congress. Since a similar demonstration has already been decided upon for May lst, 1890 by the American Federation of Labour at its Convention in St. Louis, December 1888, this day is accepted for the international demonstration. The workers of the various countries must organise this demonstration according to the conditions prevailing in each country.

Socialist Sunday Schools, 1892   Socialist Fellowship, 1965   Peace Pledge Union, 1934

Campaign for Nuclear   Medical Aid for Vietnam, 1965   Campaign for Nuclear
Disarmament, 1958   Disarmament, 1980

The conditions prevailing in Europe in 1940 were hardly conducive to jubilee celebrations. Britain and France were at war with Germany. The most ardent supporters of May Day demonstrations, the communists, did not support the war due to the Nazi-Soviet non-aggression pact and the subsequent broadcast from Moscow that proclaimed, 'There is no doubt in the minds of the Soviet people that this war is an imperialist and predatory war for a new redivision of the world, a robber war kindled from all sides by the two imperialist groups of powers.'

The Communist Party marched under the banner of the May 1st Committee with the central slogans 'End the millionaires' war', 'Hands off the land of socialism', 'One hundred percent trade unionism' and 'Higher wages now', while the Labour Party refused to co-operate and held its own separate May Day demonstration. Eight days later, German panzer divisions crossed the frontiers of France.

In January 1941 the Communist Party's policy of 'a people's peace' and a 'people's government' was given voice at an enormously successful convention when 2,234 delegates from various organisations from trade unions to tenants' associations, representing 1,200,000 people, met at the Free Trades Hall, Manchester. The convention attracted a number of well-known public figures, among them the Reverend Mervyn Stockwood (later Bishop of Southwark) and actor Michael Redgrave. The BBC attempted an act of censorship, demanding a number of broadcasters withdraw their support or be suspended. Protests against the threat came from Vaughan Williams, Rose Macaulay and others and the BBC climbed down. Herbert Morrison, the

Home Secretary, was on safer ground and in some panic at the turn of events banned the *Daily Worker* under Defence Regulation 2D nine days after the convention. The first session agreed to elect a National Committee and adjourned until recalled. Before this could happen, the convention and Communist Party were overtaken by events of greater import.

1 May 1941 again saw the Communist Party active on the May 1st Committee. While the button badge confined itself to the simple statement, 1 May 1941, the printed programme attacked Labour and trade union leaders who had taken their place in the government to 'bolster up decaying capitalism', and complained that compulsory fire watching, industrial conscription and the abolition of strikes had reduced the working class to industrial serfdom. By now, London and Coventry had experienced the full effects of the Nazi blitz. On Sunday, 22 June 1941 Hitler launched his all-out attack on the Soviet Union.

Within months Soviet badges were worn with pride, the Hammer and Sickle united with the union flag, and communist shop stewards a leading force on joint production committees to boost output in Britain's war factories. The Joint Committee for Soviet Aid co-ordinated the activities of five organisations working to send medical aid and supplies to the Soviet Union. Morrison lifted the ban on the *Daily Worker* and the BBC gave full coverage to a huge meeting at the Central Hall, London, with the title 'Allied Greetings to Soviet Russia' under the chairmanship of Earl Lytton. At a meeting of 7,000 workers at the Empress Hall concerned with Anglo-Soviet friendship,

greetings were received from Frank Phillips for the BBC, Arthur Bliss for music, Laurence Olivier for stage and cinema, L.A.G. Strong for literature, Sir John Boyd Orr for science, J.R. Scott (AEU) for industry and George Allison, the manager of Arsenal football club, for sport. From the battlefields came cables of support from General MacArthur, General Wavell, Marshall Timoshenko and others. With a display of ballet dancing from members of Sadler's Wells and a bayonet charge from the Scots Guards, the meeting ended with pledges of Anglo-Soviet friendship: 'Long live the Alliance of the Russian and British Peoples.' In the words of Winston Churchill, 'Let us go forward together.'

The popularity of button badges that boomed with the rise of pop culture in Britain in the sixties has continued to grow, millions being produced every year. Increasingly used as a form of campaigning publicity for every conceivable cause, the speed and cheapness of production has made the button badge an ideal vehicle for slogans and instant propaganda, transforming a person into a walking advertisement, a self-proclamation of affiliation. From the battle of the poorly paid night cleaners, led by May Hobbs, to the battle of Saltley Gates, led by Arthur Scargill, the public have been able to express open support, or opposition, to any political or industrial cause by pinning on a badge within a few days of the event; on a small scale, badges appear within hours.

Sometimes, as with the case of the ASTMS badge 'A Woman's place is in her union' or the 'Keep music live' slogan of the Musicians' Union, the publicity is fringe support for a sustained objective. The Association of Scientific, Managerial and Technical Staffs borrowed their slogan from a visiting delegation of American trade unionists from the Confederation of Labour Women in 1979, some of whom were wearing badges carrying the slogan. Apparently first used by the American Garment Workers' Union during International Women's Year in 1975, the British union saw the motto fitting neatly into a current campaign to recruit more women and to persuade women members to stand for office in the ASTMS. Designed by Maurice Herson, 10,000 were made. For the musicians, who have

campaigned for the use of live entertainment since electronics first posed a threat, the slogan 'Keep music live' is more than a catchphrase, it is union policy. The slogan was first used on branch stamps; it was later printed as car stickers and eventually as button badges. Thousands were distributed during the 1980 strike of BBC musicians who fought against the disbandment of five staff orchestras.

During the height of the 'Fares Fair' campaign in support of the GLC policy of cheaper fares to promote the wider use of public transport, the 'Save London Transport' badge was one of the most popular in London. Designed by Sid Brown using the familiar London Transport logo to carry the message, the badge was sold by the *Morning Star*, 25,000 being issued in the first wave. Later the design was used by the GLC, who continued to issue them throughout the campaign.

The Conservative government's Industrial Relations Bill aimed at restricting the rights of trade unions, by law, brought massive opposition from the whole British trade union movement. In a united demonstration in London on 21 February 1971, possibly the largest demonstration since the Chartists led working men to demand the vote, a seven mile long march took place with the central theme, 'Kill the Bill'. With a parade of banners on a scale that few people could have witnessed before, 140,000 working people from all parts of the country marched in protest against the proposed anti-union legislation. Led by the General Council of the TUC, the lead banner proclaimed, 'If it is a crime to fight for a better life – we are guilty.' Along the route thousands bought and wore the badges with the message of the day, 'Kill the Bill'.

The 1972 miners' strike, their first national stoppage since 1926, was a fight for higher wages, to win a minimum wage of £26 per week for surface workers and £28 per week for underground workers. The strike, in which flying pickets were used by the miners for the first time, was marked by the solidarity action of other workers. Railwaymen refused to cross picket lines, thereby halting the movement of coal from the collieries. At Saltley Coke Depot, Birmingham, 10,000 engineering and building workers left work to join the miners' picket to stop the removal of 100,000 tons of coke by scab lorry drivers. Faced with

the united action of the miners and factory workers, the police closed the depot. Arthur Scargill, at that time a little known delegate from Woolley colliery in Yorkshire, established his reputation as an organiser during the 'battle of Saltley Gates'. Addressing a mass meeting after the closing of the gates, he said, 'There can be no doubt it was this act of solidarity and class understanding from the Birmingham workers which was vital in winning this battle.' In a rally at Trafalgar Square, miners from the continent and workers from London joined the miners in a great demonstration of international solidarity, thousands buying and wearing the simple black and white solidarity badge.

The three badges 'I didn't vote Tory', 'People's march for jobs' and 'Gis a job' are all of a piece. The General Election of 1979, giving a Conservative victory, prompted the *Morning Star* publicity manager, Sid Brown, to say to himself, 'Well, at least I didn't vote Tory.' That was it – he set out the lettering, ordered 1,000 badges and sold them in two days. Within two months the newspaper had sold the amazing number of 137,000 badges to those who wanted to make it publicly clear that they were not responsible for Tory power. The most notable achievement of the new government, led by Margaret Thatcher, was to increase unemployment to a record figure of well over 3,000,000. The 'People's march for jobs' badge was designed by Anna Aubrey and was only one item in a range of publicity material carrying the symbol during the march of 500 unemployed men and women from Glasgow to London (see page 64). 'Gis a job', with the drawing of a bicycle, combines a catchphrase and a symbol that were a humorous riposte to the tragedy of mass unemployment. Speaking at a Conservative Party conference on 15 October 1982, Norman Tebbitt, the Secretary of State for Employment, said, 'I grew up in the thirties with an unemployed father; he did not riot, he got on his bike and looked for work and he kept on looking until he found it.' The absurdity of the implication that more than 3,000,000 people should be pedalling around Britain in search of non-existent jobs was not missed by the labour movement. When the Minister visited factories he was sure to be greeted by trade unionists cycling around the plant, and his speeches would be greeted with shouts of 'On your

bike, Tebbitt'. The phrase 'I can do that, gis a job' came from a popular BBC television series, first shown in October 1982, 'The Boys from the Blackstuff' by Alan Bleasdale. Set in Liverpool, the focus of the programme was Yosser Hughes, an unemployed asphalt worker played by Bernard Hill. As the unemployment figures in the real world of Britain in 1983 rose week by week, so Yosser's catchphrase, 'I can do that, gis a job', became as familiar as any of Tommy Handley's one-liners from ITMA during the grim years of the war. The button badge with the bike typifies the humour of the British working class in adversity. Unemployment is no fun for the unemployed, but tactless and unthinking politicians have always been a target for barbed jocularity.

The production of badges to mark anniversaries and notable events is a well established tradition in the history of the trade union movement. The tendency is to ignore the amalgamations and changes of name over the years and to reach back to the earliest origins of a union as a starting date for celebration.

The National Amalgamated Stevedores' and Dockers' Union was formed in 1872 as the Amalgamated Stevedores' Labour Protection League with its headquarters at the Wade's Arms in Jeremiah Street, East London. One of the oldest of the unions associated with work at the London docks, the stevedores strictly controlled admission to the union, giving preference to sons of stevedores. In 1881 the Stevedores' Committee actually passed a resolution that no-one under eighteen could be admitted except on this hereditary principle. Like many small closed unions, the largely Irish membership regarded their union not only as a means of trade protection, but as a social club, with the planning of the annual outing complete with band, banners and fireworks taking up a disproportionate amount of the union's time. In 1922 the union linked for a brief period with the Lightermen, Watermen and Bargemen, to become the National Amalgamated Union of Stevedores, Lightermen, Watermen and Dockers. In 1932 the union adopted the title of the National Amalgamated Stevedores' and Dockers' Union . It survived its centenary by only ten years, the coming of containerisation and the reduction of dock labour forcing it to

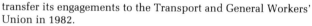

1.

2.

3.

1. National Amalgamated Stevedores' and Dockers' Union, 1872-1982

2. United Society of Boilermakers and Iron and Steel Shipbuilders, 1834-1934

3. Trades Union Congress, 1868-1968

4. National Union of General and Municipal Workers, 1924-1974

5. National Association of Operative Plasterers, 1860-1960

6. Tolpuddle Martyrs, 1834-1984

7. Miners' Federation of Great Britain, 1926

8. Associated Society of Locomotive Engineers and Firemen, 1924.

9. National Union of Mineworkers, Kent Area, 1972

4.

5.

6.

7.

8.

9.

transfer its engagements to the Transport and General Workers' Union in 1982.

The Boilermakers' centenary in 1934 marked the forming of the original combination, the Friendly Boilermakers' Society in Manchester in 1834. The union declared as its motto 'To humanity, nothing hostile' and closed its monthly meetings with a prayer, 'Almighty dispenser of mercy, grant that as we meet and constitute here on earth a lodge of friendship, we may so meet in heaven, to constitute a lodge of happiness, through Jesus Christ our Lord. Brothers, I declare this lodge to be legally closed.' Whether or not there is a lodge of the Friendly Boilermakers in heaven must remain uncertain, although it continued to flourish on earth. In 1852 the union expanded to become the United Society of Boilermakers and Iron Shipbuilders. By 1891 it had grown further and become the United Society of Boilermakers and Iron and Steel Shipbuilders. In 1953 it became known as the United Society of Boilermakers, Shipbuilders and Structural Workers and further amalgamations in 1962 made it the United Society of Boilermakers, Blacksmiths, Shipbuilders and Structural Workers. There was one final change in 1963 to the Amalgamated Society of Boilermakers, Shipwrights, Blacksmiths and Structural Workers before it became the Boilermakers' Section of the General Municipal, Boilermakers' and Allied Trades Union in 1982.

The Trades Union Congress celebrated its centenary at Blackpool in 1968. The first Congress was held in Manchester, where thirty-four delegates represented 118,367 members and elected George Potter of the Working Men's Association as its first General Secretary. At the 1968 Congress 1,051 delegates assembled from 160 unions, representing 8,725,604 trade unionists.

The General and Municipal Workers' Union fiftieth anniversary congress badge commemorates the forming of the National Union of General and Municipal Workers in 1924. Three unions amalgamated to form the NUGMW, the National Union of General Workers, the National Amalgamated Union of Labour and the Municipal Employees' Association. The General Workers traced their origins to 1889 as the National Union of Gas Workers and General Labourers founded by Will Thorne. The National Amalgamated Union of Labour was also formed in that year and the Municipal Employees' Association in 1894. The

GMWU chose to celebrate the great amalgamation and ignore the founding dates of the older unions.

The centenary badge of the National Association of Operative Plasterers carried a crude representation of the union's 'arms' freely borrowed from the Worshipful Company of Plasterers, incorporated by charter in 1500. The date of 1860 is generally accepted as the founding date of the union, a delegate conference being held in Birmingham in March of that year.

The gold and black badge issued by the TUC to mark the one hundred and fiftieth anniversary of the transportation of the Tolpuddle martyrs was designed by the socialist artist, Ken Sprague. A reminder that trade unionism is still the subject of government prejudice and opposition is made with the slogan 'repeal anti-union laws', a reference to the 1984 Trade Union Act restricting secondary picketing and providing for legal action against unions involved in industrial disputes, preparing the way for latter-day martyrs.

The miniature copper-coloured miner's lamp is a relic of the great lock-out of miners and the General Strike of 1926. After the surrender of the TUC to the government, the miners fought on for six long months against the demand of the coal owners to cut wages and lengthen working hours. In the days before social security the hardship was intense for the miners and their families as they fought to avoid starvation. The lapel lamps were sold by the Miners' Federation of Great Britain at 1s. each, the money being donated to the Miners' Wives' and Children's Relief Fund.

The 1924 badge, or watch fob, was made to celebrate a victorious strike of engine drivers. Following a National Wages Board finding that meant worsened conditions of service, members of the Associated Society of Locomotive Engineers and Firemen came out on strike in January 1924 and won their demands in a dispute marked by solid backing for the union action. The National Union of Mineworkers, Kent Area, badge commemorates the national strike of miners from 8 January to 28 February 1972 in a fight for higher pay. The dispute saw mass picketing of power stations and the innovation of 'flying pickets' in a dispute that ended in victory for the miners. Many miners saw the victory as a redress of the humiliating defeat of 1926 when the Conservative government backed the mine owners in starving the men back to work.

BANNERS

The magnificent silken banner of the Amalgamated Stevedores' Labour Protection League is both a proclamation of birth and a commemoration of victory. 'Union and Victory', the slogan daubed upon a simple piece of sailcloth and carried throughout the Great Dock Strike of 1889, was emblazoned upon the banners of the emergent unions at the end of the strike, not as an expression of hope, but as a statement of fact, a vindication of faith, a cry of arrival. The clasped handshake of friendship between the old world and the new is more than an acknowledgement of the financial aid given to the strikers by their Australian brothers, it is a symbol of a new working class unity, a unity born from the struggle of the poorest, the casual labourers of the London docks.

The strike was the awakening of the 'men on the stones', the dockers who were subjected to the daily cattle market at the dock gates. Ben Tillett, whose tiny union, the Tea Operatives' and General Labourers' Association, kindled the flame of revolt, described how the contractors would walk up and down picking and choosing the strongest men from the crowd. Desperate to obtain even a few hours' work they would fight and trample each other to catch the foreman's eye. The casual work for which the hungry men fought was paid at 4d. or 5d. an hour. Encouraged by the successful strikes the previous year of the match girls at Bryant and May's and the gasworkers at Beckton, the ill-fed, downtrodden dockers rose without warning to paralyse the world's largest port. The so-called unskilled had joined the army of organised labour.

The demands of the men included the raising of wages to 6d. an hour, 8d. for overtime and a reduction in the number of 'call-ons' which kept the men hanging around the dock gates, sometimes the whole day in the wet and cold.

Divisions in the docks were tightly drawn, not only between employer and employed but between worker and worker, between skilled and unskilled, between the aristocrats of labour like the watermen and lightermen whose jobs were handed down, father to son, and the rootless casual labourer striving to sell his muscle to avoid starvation. The Great Strike that started with a meeting of a handful of men at Wroots' Coffee House on 12 August 1889, smashed at that division as stevedores, boilermakers, coal heavers, ballastmen, deal porters, carpenters, painters and lightermen joined the casual labourers as they marched from their slums and alleys from east of the Aldgate Pump to the very heart of the capital of the greatest Empire. Their daily sallies into the city grew into pageants of solidarity as the ragged army with red rags on poles and fish heads on pikes was reinforced with the banners of the organised unions. They flew in silver, gold and crimson splendour above a stalwart battalion of watermen, freemen of the river, marching proudly in long scarlet coats, pink stockings and velvet caps with huge pewter badges on their breasts. Led by the band of the Stevedores' Union, 50,000 men followed bearing a variety of homemade emblems, the docker's dinner and the sweater's dinner, the docker's cat and the sweater's cat, skiffs mounted on wheels, the coalies in wagons fishing for coppers with bags tied to the end of poles. Bringing up the rear were the bass broom dressers, themselves locked out for forming a union, carrying their bass brooms like lictors. The impact upon the metropolis was enormous and contributions to the strike fund eventually reached £48,736. 2s. 1d., more than £25,000 coming from collections taken by Australian dockers, a staggering sum in 1889.

The banner of the number six branch of the Amalgamated Stevedores' Protection League pays visual tribute to the solidarity of the Australian dockers. It also records the date of the amalgamation, the original union, the Labour Protection League, having been formed in 1871 by John Caulfield, a docker, Patrick Hennessey of the Land and Labour League and Charles Keen, Secretary of the English Council of the International Working Men's Association. The twelve feet high banner was made by the London firm of George Tutill and is painted in oils upon an embroidered silk background woven on Tutill's giant Jacquard loom.

Poverty, rotten housing and wage slavery were not exclusive to the cities. While the density of slums and the plight of the poor were readily visible to the casual observer, the tyranny of the countryside was often concealed by natural beauty. The farm labourer and his family were victims of a myth of idyllic thatched cottages, the honest ploughman and the roast beef of old England. The reality was life in a rural hovel, a tied cottage with eviction as the farmer's whip. While the dockers struck for 6d. an hour, a waggoner was lucky to receive £18 a year and a 'strong dairy girl' could expect no more than £8. An 'overtime' rate was unknown. Daily fare was likely to consist of

tea, bread and vegetables with occasional bacon. If the landed gentry shot pheasant and grouse by the hundreds of brace, woe betide the poor labourer caught snaring a rabbit for his hungry children, for the game laws were ferocious in preserving the beasts of the field for those with fat stomachs. Like his brothers and sisters in the cities the reward for a lifetime of toil for a farm labourer was too often the workhouse.

The banner of the National Union of Agricultural Labourers and Rural Workers remains as a testimony to the courage of the scattered and often isolated labourers who stood up to farmer, squire and parson and demanded that the labourer should be 'worthy of his hire'. The origin of the banner remains an enigma for the style of painting suggests the work of a talented artist and not the work of a local signwriter or even a commercial banner company like Tutill's or Kenning's. Even the lettering and colouring have an aesthetic beauty rarely found on trade union banners. The banner was probably made in 1919, for the union was not known as the Agricultural Labourers and Rural Workers until 1910, previously being the Eastern Counties Agricultural Labourers' and Small Holders' Union, formed in 1906 by George Edwards. An extant photograph shows the banner being carried

to Wicklewood workhouse in 1923 on a march to claim outdoor relief for farmworkers, but no records of the design and manufacture of the banner have been traced. For many years it lay in a garden shed in the village of Hethersett, near Mulbarton in Norfolk, until it was discovered in 1976 by Wilfred Page, an official of the National Union of Agricultural Workers.

The Poplar Labour League, formed in 1892, was originally known as the Poplar Labour Election Committee and was one of many such groups formed in the 1890s to secure for working people direct labour representation on administrative and governing bodies. In the days when MPs were unpaid, Parliament was a hobby for the wealthy, another means of buying power. Likewise with local government, employers did not pay working men and women to take time off to sit on the Board of Guardians, the LCC or any other local representative body. The League preceded the Labour Representation Committee and played a crucial role in the development of Labour in government by providing wages funds for elected members.

The Poplar Labour League grew from regular Sunday morning meetings held outside the East India Dock gates by Will Crooks. Competing with the nearby public house for his Sunday audience, Crooks' powers of oratory held a big enough crowd over a long period for the meetings to become known as 'Crooks College'. A journeyman cooper, Crooks had spent time in the workhouse as a child, been unemployed, known personal tragedy in his family life and shared with the poor the helplessness, degradation and despair of poverty. The first executive of the Election Committee consisted of representatives of the London Trades Council, the Engine Drivers' and Firemen's Union, the Philanthropic Coopers' Society, the East London Plumbers' Union, the Federated Trades' and Labour Unions, the Gasworkers' Union and the Revd H.A. Kennedy. It was a success from the start. Crooks was elected to the LCC to join other Labour stalwarts like John Burns, Ben Cooper of the Cigar Makers' Union, Harry Gosling of the Watermen's and Lightermen's Society and George Dew, secretary of the Workmen's Cheap Trains' Association. The League paid Crooks £3. 10s. 0d. a week and thought it worth every penny, as shown by this excerpt from the first annual report, 'The return of Will Crooks to the London Council marks an epoch in the life of industrial Poplar. From time immemorial this hive of industry has been represented by employers of labour and wealthy capitalists. Their record is now broken. Labour has awakened.'

Many other unions subscribed to the wages fund through their local branches, including the London Saddle and Harness Makers' Society, the Amalgamated Society of Engineers, the Municipal Employees' Association, the Postman's Federation and the Amalgamated Society of Railway Servants. Individuals sympathetic to Crooks and the cause of Labour also sent occasional contributions, the names of Mrs Bernard Shaw, Dr Clifford, Sidney Webb and Canon Barnet being among those recorded.

The League paid Crooks his wages until 1903, when he was elected to Parliament and received £200 p.a. from the trade union fund. Even then they made a small annual payment for the expenses inseparable from being a Member of Parliament. The banner of the Women's Branch of the South Poplar Labour League is a symbol of the determination of poor working people to be represented on every form of government by those of their own class.

The Northampton branch banner of the Social Democratic Federation is one of only three SDF banners known to be extant, the other two being those of the Carlisle and Burnley branches. Founded in 1881 as the Democratic Federation by Henry Mayers Hyndman, the organisation soon adopted an uncompromising socialist policy and on 4 August 1884 changed its name to that of the Social Democratic Federation.

The SDF took its socialism onto the streets, establishing regular weekly open-air meetings to preach the gospel with evangelical fervour, competing with temperance and religious organisations for converts to the cause. At the outset, the Federation was led by well-to-do middle class socialists, from the top-hatted Hyndman, who had played first class cricket as an amateur for Sussex, to William Morris, who poured his money as well as his talent into the cause of social revolution. Hyndman himself described a curious scene in the Strand, 'with Morris in his soft hat and blue suit, Champion, Frost and Joynes, in the morning garments of the well-to-do, several working men comrades, and I myself wearing the new frock coat in which Shaw said I was born, with a tall hat and good gloves, all earnestly engaged in selling a penny socialist paper.'

Nevertheless, the SDF carried the message of socialism, unflinching in the face of considerable hostility to every part of the land. It gave leadership where none had existed and became a platform for a generation of socialists whose names are immortalised as pioneers of the labour movement, attracting working men as well as middle class intellectuals in a momentous struggle against social injustice.

The Northampton banner of the Social Democratic Federation, made by Tutill's, captures the idealism of the movement with its full length figure of Justice and its series of mottos, repeating the word 'Justice' three times in its visual cry of hope to an oppressed and exploited working class.

'A meeting will be held at the Winchester Arms, Southwark Street on Sunday, December 3rd (1871) to further the objects of securing ten hours for a day's labour, payment for Sunday duty and weekly payment of wages. Chair to be taken at 6 o'clock. Please inform your mates and solicit them to attend.' Printed on tiny slips of paper, four inches by two inches, in order not to attract the attention of the employers, this was the message passed between railwaymen that led to the forming of the Amalgamated Society of Railway Servants. Despite the justified caution of the founders (there was an early proposal for a secret sign and a password) the railwaymen found a substantial ally in Michael Thomas Bass, MP, a wealthy brewer and an important shareholder in the Midland Railway Company. With his support, including the financing of the Railway Service Gazette, the

union gained credibility and by 24 June 1872 held its first delegate conference at the Sussex Hotel, near Fleet Street. Sixty-two pioneers attended, though notable by his absence was the delegate from Scotland, despite the offer of Mr Bass to pay his fare and expenses. This was unfortunate and his absence may well have led to the separate formation of the Amalgamated Society of Railway Servants for Scotland in August of the same year. The union existed until it amalgamated with the ASRS in 1892, thus placing the making of the Scottish banner within the period 1872-1892. The homemade banner has a naive charm that is direct and honest both in mottos and character. The outer border is stencilled onto linen strips while the illustration and lettering are handpainted. By contrast, the Hither Green branch banner of the National Union of Railwaymen is the product of a commercial banner company. It is a classic of the 'we care for our widows and orphans' style of banner imagery that was popular with the old ASRS and remained as a recurring theme until the Second World War. The scene of a branch official, complete with sash of office, money bag and cheque, making the payment on behalf of the union can be found in various forms on railway trade union banners from the 1890s to 1939. The emphasis on orphan care was not without good reason for the railway industry produced a regular annual toll of fatal accidents among its workers. In the early days of private railway companies and infant trade unionism, destitution was the family fate if the breadwinner was killed at work. Their plight was aptly described by F. Harcombe, a goods guard on the Taff Vale railway company, when asked by a Royal Commission, 'What is the custom with regard to compensation to a man if he is killed leaving a widow?' he replied, 'I believe the compensation they receive is a nice coffin.' The men had no claim upon the railway companies in law, and in 1874, when 788 railwaymen were killed at work, the General Secretary of ASRS, F.W. Evans, told a Parliamentary Committee (1876) 'the life of a railway servant was of less value than the life of a horse.'

Because of the appalling number of accidental deaths among railwaymen, often due to unreasonable, long hours and consequent fatigue, the union fought vigorously for improvements in safety and took action to help the widows and orphans. Small lump sums were paid by all the early railway

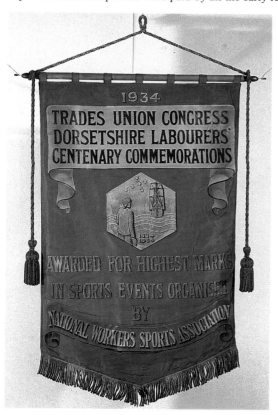

societies to alleviate the distress and some managed to make weekly payments to widows.

The National Union of Railwaymen was formed in 1913 by an amalgamation of the Amalgamated Society of Railway Servants, the United Pointsmen's and Signalmen's Society and the General Railway Workers' Union and many old banners were overpainted with the new national name. The Hither Green banner was made by George Tutill's and was probably ordered upon the amalgamation.

1934 marked the centenary of the prosecution and subsequent sentence of transportation to Botany Bay for seven years of six poor agricultural labourers from the Dorset village of Tolpuddle. Their crime was the forming of a trade union, the Friendly Society of Agricultural Labourers. George Loveless, the most articulate of the Tolpuddle Martyrs, said, 'We were uniting together to preserve ourselves, our wives and our children from utter degradation and starvation.' The answer of the wealthy landowners, the local magistracy and the government was prison hulks and penal settlements. Passing sentence, the judge, whose name is recorded by history and forgotten by men, said, 'It is also for the sake of offering an example and a warning.' The example was ignored, the warning unheeded, by men and women of immense moral courage who built a democratic trade union movement of more than 1,000 trade unions and almost 5,000,000 members in the next 100 years.

The TUC under the leadership of Walter Citrine marked the centenary of the Tolpuddle Martyrs in splendid style. Six model cottages for aged agricultural workers were built at Tolpuddle, each named after one of the martyrs. A commemorative book was produced that included contributions from George Bernard Shaw, Sidney and Beatrice Webb, G.D.H. Cole, Stafford Cripps and Harold Laski, with drawings by Low, Will Dyson and Frank Horrabin. A four-day programme of celebrations was held at Tolpuddle with football matches between England, France and Belgium, a tennis tournament, brass band concerts, a new play *Six Men of Dorset* and a grand pageant. Representatives of labour came from twenty-one nations and the British trades unions paraded with their historic banners in a blaze of colour and triumphal celebration.

The sporting events were organised by the National Workers' Sports' Association, a body formed in 1930 to encourage, promote and control amateur sport and recreation among working class organisations. It received the official support of the Labour and trade union movement, being represented at the inaugural conference by H. Elvin of the TUC and F.O. Roberts of the Labour Party, and was affiliated to the Socialist Workers' Sports' International formed at Ghent in 1913. In 1934 the individual membership of the National Workers' Sports' Association was just under 7,000 with additional trades union affiliation. The Association President at the time of the centenary events was Arthur Henderson.

The bannerette, awarded for the highest marks in the sports events, reproduces the Tolpuddle medallion, struck to perpetuate the memory of the centenary. The medallion design was open to competition and the panel of judges included the distinguished artist and engraver, Eric Gill (who carved the memorial tombstone to James Hammett, the only martyr to be buried at Tolpuddle), Frank Dobson and G.T. Friend. The winning design came from a professional badge designer, E.J. Fey of Birmingham, who had trained at the Aston Technical School. It depicts a manacled figure looking at a receding ship that has carried him into exile, beneath a sky lit by the Southern Cross. The bannerette was made by George Tutill's, as was the centenary banner of the National Union of Agricultural Workers and brought to light an interesting fact. Asked for their union cards by the diligent member of the NUAW placing the order, Tutill's had to admit that having made the majority of trade union banners since 1837, they were a non-union firm! The staff subsequently joined the National Union of Tailors and Garment Workers.

Behind the symbolism of the 'clasp of brotherhood the world o're' and the red rose of Lancashire lies the red, raw and bloody history of cotton and the industrial revolution. It is a familiar history of child labour, of children from seven years of age working thirteen hours a day, of women operatives working to within a week of childbirth and returning to work ten days later. It is a record of humid, ear-deafening, filthy working conditions, 'weavers' cough', greasy clothes and hunger. It is a twentieth century story too, of child half-timers robbed of childhood and education alike, of smashed looms and derelict factories, of 'cotton cancer', wage cuts, long hours for low pay and the whip of unemployment. Behind the proud banner of the Wigan Cotton Operatives is the reason for the founding of the union in 1829: unfettered, avaricious, rapacious industrial capitalism.

The union did not register as a Friendly Society until 1865, for there were years of concerted efforts by united mill owners to force down wages, years of lock-outs and strike breaking with the union being driven out of existence, only to rise and rise again. It is a history of a fight by cotton workers, mill by mill, town by town, district by district, to build a powerful trade union. From 1865 the history is one of amalgamation and mergers as the Wigan Cotton Operatives joined with the Wigan Cardroom and Mule Spinners and others to grow in numbers and strength.

The embroidered and painted banner of the Wigan Cotton Operatives was made between 1925 and 1930 when the industry was operating more than 700,000 power looms. It was passed to the National Museum of Labour History when the union finally went out of existence in 1974, with the continued decline of the industry. The few hundred members left in the union transferred to the Bolton and District Textile Allied Workers' Union and subsequently became part of the present Amalgamated Textile Workers' Union, formed in 1975.

'That in view of the persistent attacks and misrepresentations made by the opponents of the Co-operative Movement in Parliament, and in local administrative bodies, the Congress is of the opinion that the time has arrived when Co-operation should secure direct representation in Parliament and on all local administrative bodies.' It was this resolution moved in the name of 104 co-operative societies at the Co-operative Congress of 1917 that led directly to the formation of the Co-operative Party. The idea was not new, for as early as 1897 an attempt was made to persuade Congress to seek direct Parliamentary representation when the movement was under a boycott attack by private traders, but it was government prejudice against the co-operatives during the First World War that finally precipitated the move.

In 1914, when the war began, the movement already had over 3,000,000 members and was growing apace. As the war continued, food shortages, profiteering and inept distribution combined to create increasing hardship among the civilian population, especially among the poorer of the community. Instead of looking to the co-operative movement for assistance in planning and distribution, they were pointedly rejected. G.D.H. Cole observed, 'The Government, so far from showing any appreciation of the potential value of the movement as an instrument of war-time control, treated it with stupid neglect. Control where it was imposed was placed almost always in the hands of private trading interests.' The private business interests which also dominated the appellate tribunals on military service brought continual accusations of discrimination from co-operative bodies. One society alleged that of its 102 employees, 99 were obliged to enlist. The government further aroused the wrath of the movement when it ignored previous practice and applied income tax liability against the co-operatives, basing their calculations upon a formula that militated against them because of their continued expansion. To compound matters,

the Prime Minister, Lloyd George, refused to receive a deputation from the Co-operative Union to discuss their grievances but agreed to receive a deputation from the Jockey Club!

It was 1918 before the first Parliamentary seat was contested by the Co-operative Party in the Prestwich Division of Manchester, the bye-election being caused by the elevation of the sitting Conservative to the peerage. The Co-operative Party candidate was Henry J. May, secretary to the Joint Parliamentary Committee and a well-known personality in the movement. Although he did not gain the seat, May polled 2,832 votes against a coalition candidate vote of 8,520. The first Co-operative MP was A.E. Waterson, elected for Kettering in the General Election of 1918, and the Party reached its peak of Parliamentary representation in 1945 when twenty-three Co-operative MPs were elected.

The Bethnal Green Co-operative Movement does not appear to have taken root before the formation of the London Co-operative Society in 1920 although there is mention of no less than seven societies founded in Bethnal Green between 1830 and 1833. Thereafter there is no mention of societies in Bethnal Green for decades, although others appeared on the fringes of the Borough, there being a North Bow Society in 1875-1877, and a Tower Hamlets Society founded by the Guild of Co-operators in 1882, though this had apparently disappeared by 1896. The explanation for the lack of early success in Bethnal Green may be that it lacked the stable and skilled working population that provided the foundation for so many nineteenth century societies.

The Bethnal Green Co-operative Party seems to have been formed in around 1928, though as the records are missing it is unverified. The banner of the party was unfurled by Harry Tate, the local secretary, at a small ceremony held in the Labour Party rooms in Bethnal Green Road on 4 July 1957. Presented by the Political Committee of the London Co-operative Society, the banner was subsequently paid for by the running of a football tote by the local party members and a competition based upon the 'What a life' cartoon by Wilkinson that used to appear in the *Daily Herald*. The banner was regularly carried on May Day marches in London until the Bethnal Green party became part of the Tower Hamlets Co-operative Party.

The Central Labour College was founded on 2 August 1909 by a small group of young working men. It represented a revolutionary and intellectual challenge to established educational practice, to seek to create a college supported by the labour movement and offering an education to meet the needs of the working class, to understand and challenge capitalism. The first resolution passed at the founding conference read, 'that this Conference of workers declares that the time has now arrived when the working class should enter the education world and work out its own problems for itself.' The path to independent working class education had been opened.

There were earlier attempts to provide educational opportunities for workers, the Workers' Education Association had been formed in 1903 and Ruskin College, Oxford, which claimed to be a Labour College, had been founded in 1889. The essential difference was that they offered an education that was politically neutral and non-partisan. The CLC held that 'education provided by the capitalist ruling class must, by definition of their class interests be designed to further those interests.' The need was for 'the belief in the power of the working class to work out its own emancipation.'

During the twenty years of its existence, the Central Labour College produced many future labour and trade union leaders from its students. Among those who benefited from trade union scholarship to the College were Aneurin Bevan, A.J. Cook, Idris Cox, Ness Edwards, James Griffiths, Frank Hodges, Lewis Jones and Will Lawther. The College also attracted talented and devoted socialists who were prepared to give of their time and ability to further the cause of working class education. Two such people were the Horrabins, Winifred and Frank. It was Winifred Horrabin who designed the Central Labour College banner in 1912. Born in 1887 at Pitsmoor, Sheffield, as Winifred Batho she was educated at a local elementary school, the Central Secondary School, and then the Sheffield School of Art. Winifred was film critic for the *Manchester Evening News* and throughout her life contributed articles and reviews to the Labour press from the days of the *Clarion* and *New Leader* to the *Daily Herald* and *Tribune*. The banner with its beautiful art nouveau lettering and decoration is embroidered onto a homespun material, giving an arts and crafts movement feel to the finished article. The symbolism includes a cap of liberty surmounting the old motto of the Social Democratic Federation, 'Educate, Agitate, Organise'. The torch of learning is itself comprised of a fasces stem, the symbol of the power of unity. Although signed with the initials of Winifred Horrabin, she was apparently helped in

her embroidery of the banner by Rebecca West, the writer, and Winifred Blatchford, the daughter of the socialist writer, Robert Blatchford.

The banner of the National Council of Labour Colleges was designed by Winifred's husband, James Francis Horrabin, in 1922. Born in Peterborough in 1884, he was educated at Stamford Grammar School in Lincolnshire and then at Sheffield School of Art where he met his future wife. Frank Horrabin was a gifted artist and in all probability the inventor of the strip cartoon. He worked in the art department of the *Sheffield Telegraph* from 1906 to 1909 and was art editor of the *Yorkshire Telegraph and Star* before leaving for Fleet Street, joining the *Daily News* in 1911. In 1922 Wilson Pope, the editor of the *Star*, asked for a comic strip about office girls and 'Dot and Carrie' were born, a strip that Horrabin was to produce for the next seventeen years. Among his other cartoon characters was Mrs Mopps, the office charlady. Editor of *Plebs*, the Labour College monthly, Labour MP for Peterborough, map artist and illustrator, Horrabin was a versatile artist and dedicated socialist. The banner was first carried in the May Day march of 1922, J.P.M. Millar, the Secretary of the NCCL, being one of the bearers.

The No More War Movement grew from the No Conscription Fellowship, a movement prompted by Lilla Brockway in 1914. It was at her suggestion that her husband, Fenner Brockway, wrote a letter to the *Labour Leader* in November 1914, asking all who were determined not to fight to send their names to Mrs Brockway so that co-ordinated action could be taken if conscription was introduced. Replies came in from Cornwall to Scotland demonstrating that not everyone had succumbed to the jingoistic fervour that had greeted the declaration of war. Early in 1915 a provisional committee of Fenner Brockway, Clifford Allen, J.H. Hudson and the Revd Leyton Richards met to discuss ways of organising resistance to conscription. In July it was decided to create a network of Fellowship Branches all over the country and W.H. Chamberlain was given the organisational task.

The subsequent passive resistance to the war is one of countless stories of individual heroism in the face of public opprobrium, persecution, imprisonment and ill treatment. It is hard to imagine the passionate spirit of blind patriotism that gripped a nation to the extent that it did in Britain during the First World War. The Bishop of London declared that 'khaki is the garment of the faithful', the veteran trade union leader and socialist, Will Thorne, founder of the Gas Workers' Union, friend of Eleanor Marx and Frederick Engels, rushed to join the West Ham Volunteer Force and was given the rank of Lieutenant Colonel, parading himself in full martial array complete with spurs. Young women hounded able-bodied young men to their deaths by taunting them with 'white feathers', symbols of cowardice, Bertrand Russell was removed from his lectureship of Trinity College, Cambridge, and the *Daily Mail* led in the vilification of 'conchies' while publishing headlines like 'Haig is killing Germans'. It is doubtful if Haig ever killed a single German, though he was unquestionably responsible for the deaths of tens of thousands of British troops. The harassment of war resisters, both private and public, was petty and vicious, unreasoning and calculated.

Those who aroused the greatest hatred from the military authorities were the absolutists, those who not only refused to fight but refused to engage in work which might be of help to the war effort. James Brighthouse, a young war resister, was put into a narrow pit, twelve feet deep, with two feet of water in the bottom and left there for four days. Thirty absolutists were sent to France, court-martialled and sentenced to be shot for refusing to obey orders on active service. When Professor Gilbert Murray secured an interview with the Secretary of War on behalf of the men and told him the objectors were to be shot, Lord Derby replied, 'And quite right too.' It was only on Murray's intervention with the Prime Minister that the sentence was commuted to ten years' penal servitude.

The main thrust of opposition to the war came from the Independent Labour Party, supported by the British Socialist Party, though other objectors ranged from Buddhists and Christadelphians to the New and Latter House of Israel and Jehovah's Witnesses.

Lloyd George maintained his vindictive attitude towards the absolutists until months after the Armistice, the last resisters being released in July 1919. The last meeting of the No Conscription Fellowship was held in November 1919, presided over by Clifford Allen and attended by 400 delegates. Fourteen months later, the No More War Movement was founded at a conference held at the Penn Club, London, with a provisional committee of Miss T.W. Wilson, Bertram Appleby, H. Runham Brown, Fenner Brockway, F. Fincham and Wilfred Wellock, with W.J. Chamberlain as Chairman and Beatrice Brown as Secretary. The Declaration signed by every member read:

War is a crime against humanity. I am therefore determined
1. Not to take part in any war, international or civil.
2. To work for total disarmament, the removal of all causes of war and the establishment of a new Social and International order based on the pacifist principle of co-operation for the common good.

The movement spread all over the country, gaining the support of socialists, co-operators and trade unionists and embracing such diverse characters as Professor Harold Laski, Dr Hugh Dalton, Margaret Llewellyn Davies, Hamilton Fyffe, Ben Turner and John Hill. It flourished as the British section of War Resisters' International and finally merged with the Peace Pledge Union in 1937. By then, the emergence of fascism and the Spanish Civil War caused some to doubt their absolute pacifism. Fenner Brockway wrote, 'Faced with the issue I did not hesitate. I wanted the Spanish workers to win.' Bertrand Russell was also to agree that Nazism had to be resisted by force. Others remained firm in their belief that killing people is wrong in any circumstances. That they did not have to suffer the harsh treatment endured by conscientious objectors during the First World War when the second great conflict finally came, was due to the resolution, courage and public influence of those who joined the No Conscription Fellowship, the No More War Movement and won the right to say 'Never Again'.

'Against fascism, against war', that was the slogan of the Left Book Club from the moment of its inception in May 1936. Founded by the publisher, Victor Gollancz, in association with John Strachey and Harold Laski, the aim of the club was to be both educationalist and propagandist. Printing large numbers of brightly orange bound soft cover books at half a crown each, the club grew to a peak of 57,000 members organised into 1,500 study groups.

With the rise of fascism, particularly with Franco's attack upon the Spanish Republic, the club became a catalyst for the left. A powerful advocate for the People's Front, the club organised mass rallies throughout Britain, packing the platforms with a range of speakers from Conservatives to Communists who saw the need to halt fascism by united action. Robert Boothby, David Lloyd George, Stafford Cripps, Richard Acland, Harry Pollitt and the Dean of Canterbury, all spoke at LBC rallies. The enthusiasm of Gollancz permeated the clubs, the social as well as the political side of life flourishing in the years preceding the Second World War as the club organised rambles, plays, garden parties, seaside outings and summer schools. There were specialist groups like the London Art Students, Paddington Railway Workers, the Clarion Cycling Club and even the office of the *Manchester Guardian*. The actors' group included Sybil Thorndike, Michael Redgrave, Beatrix Lehmann and Miles Malleson.

Club members bought a book a month, each a new title selected or commissioned by the Club. The first to appear was *France Today and the People's Front* by the French Communist Party leader Maurice Thorez in May 1936, the last in October 1948, *The Meaning of Marxism* by G.D.H. Cole. The impact on socialist education over the twelve years was enormous. A generation of left wing socialists were nurtured on Strachey's

The Coming Struggle for Power while Ellen Wilkinson's *The Town that was Murdered*, the story of Jarrow, is a textbook indictment of capitalism. Orwell's *Road to Wigan Pier* sold 40,000 copies and although the Labour Party never officially supported the Left Book Club because of its involvement with the communists, Attlee wrote for them *The Labour Party in Perspective*.

The Carshalton banner of the Left Book Club reflects the wider purpose of the Club, 'by speech and pen to make men more enlightened'. If Carshalton seems an unlikely base for an active LBC group, it is an indication of how deeply it reached into British Society. The brightly coloured books, stamped 'Left Book Club, Not for sale to the Public', are an integral part of the history of the left in the 1930s and are remembered by many with affection. With Britain threatened by fascism and war, Pollitt, speaking at a LBC rally, voiced the thoughts of many when he quoted Lenin: 'We have only just obtained the opportunity of learning. I do not know how long this opportunity will last. But every moment we have free from war we must devote to study.'

The signing of the Nazi-Soviet Pact on 23 August 1939 was the beginning of the end. The Club lost direction, the Popular Front was never achieved and the declaration of war on 3 September 1939 meant that the main aim of the Club had been lost.

A bestseller published by the Left Book Club in 1938 was *ARP* by J.B.S. Haldane, and it provided the basis of a substantial campaign for civilian protection in the event of air raids upon Britain.

The Nazi-Franco attack upon Guernica in 1936 provided the first real experience of modern aerial bombardment when in little more than two and a half hours, 1,600 people were killed and some 900 wounded. A combination of the dropping of small high explosive bombs (including packets of hand grenades), incendiaries and the ruthless machine gunning of the terrified civilians as they ran for safety effectively destroyed the town and martyred the inhabitants. It was easy to project the consequences of unleashing full-scale bombing raids upon the cities of Europe.

J.B.S. Haldane, a Fellow of the Royal Society and a popular communist scientist, wrote that the Germans were building 500 aeroplanes a month and that we could expect an attack to be mounted by successive waves of planes dropping their bombs almost simultaneously. At an average of one and a half tons of bombs to each plane, a squadron would drop 400 tons in half a minute. This would kill an estimated 8,000 people and wound another 15,000 and could be repeated several times a day! Oliver Simmonds, President of the Air Raid Protection Trust, said, 'In each week, Britain might have 100,000 killed and 200,000 wounded in air raids . . . it would be possible for Germany to drop 3,000 tons a day.' The need for bombproof shelters for the civilian population of Britain was seemingly self-evident.

Drawing on the experience of Spain, Haldane looked to the shelter tunnels of Barcelona which were brick-lined labyrinths fifty or sixty feet below the surface and capable of sustaining a direct hit from the size of high explosive bombs in use at that time. Deep, bombproof shelters were needed if the population was to be adequately protected and Haldane proposed a two year plan of construction. He put the cost of such a project at £400,000,000 claiming that London alone required 1,000 miles of tunnels to give adequate shelter to 5,500,000 people.

The National Government were not surprisingly opposed to the building of deep shelters on such a scale, though of course they were quick to provide such shelter for themselves and their administration. The Communist Party was prominent in the campaign to give air raid protection to working people and contrasted the provisions being made by the rich to protect themselves with the lack of any real policy to shelter the inhabitants of the crowded tenements of our major cities.

Sir John Anderson in charge of ARP was caustically referred to as the Minister of Casualties and the corrugated iron shelters named after him derogatorily described as 'steel dog kennels' and 'tin cans'. In the confusion of the preparation for war some of the Anderson shelters that had to be dug into the ground and covered with earth were delivered to East End homes where the gardens consisted of small concrete back yards. One mum remarked, 'It comes in useful to cover the mangle.' Some local authorities under Labour control drew up elaborate schemes for deep shelter protection but none succeeded in gaining government financial support.

While the projections of the scale of air attacks upon Britain proved to be fortunately exaggerated (the total number of people killed by all forms of air attack was approximately 60,000, of whom about half were killed in London, and about 86,000 were seriously injured), the communists were right in predicting that it would be the densely populated working class districts that would suffer most. The first major air attack on London, 7 September 1940, caused widespread destruction among the small terraced homes of the dockside boroughs of West Ham and Stepney. Although the Anderson shelters proved to give effective protection from almost everything but a direct hit, the tenement dwellers remained without adequate shelter. As the blitz got under way in 1940, the deep shelter campaign entered a second phase with a demand for the London underground stations to be opened as public shelters. The campaign was successful and seventy-nine stations were opened for use as deep shelters.

The campaign in Britain for 'Arms for Spain' was a demand for the democratically elected government of Spain to be allowed the right to defend its people aganst a military fascist rebellion that was supported by Hitler and Mussolini. That the Spanish Government could not buy arms on the open market was due to the British Government's policy of appeasement towards the fascist dictators, in this instance operating under the title of 'non-intervention'. The result was that the Spanish Government had to scrounge for weapons and supplies to resist the fascist generals who from the very beginning enjoyed the military support of Germany and Italy. Within a few days of the insurrection on 18 July 1936, the first German planes were in Morocco to fly in the élite troops of the Spanish Foreign Legion and Moorish mercenaries to the mainland. Italy followed by sending Franco twelve Savoias-81 bombers and a few days later on 5 August the German battleship *Deutschland* delivered six Heinkel HE-51 fighter planes, complete with crews and supplies, to the rebels at Cadiz. The supply of men, arms and supplies from the fascist powers to their fascist ally, General Francisco Franco, had started and was to continue throughout the conflict.

The aim of Britain and France to prevent the spread of war to a wider Europe led them to sponsor a Non-intervention Committee to prevent arms from reaching either the Spanish Government or the rebels. Although both Italy and Germany accepted the principle together with other European nations, including the Soviet Union, the fascist governments never ceased to send practical aid to the fascist insurgents. The result was that during the crucial early stages of the war, when the Spanish Government needed to arm its people to crush the revolt, they were deprived of the legitimate right of a sovereign nation to buy arms for its defence. Meanwhile, the rebels strengthened by the troops, airmen, planes, tanks and artillery from Italy, Germany and Portugal, secured their positions. So blatant was the support of Hitler and Mussolini for Franco that the Soviet Union warned the Non-intervention Committee that they would not be more bound than other signatories and on 8 October began loading the first freighters to sail from Odessa with supplies for the Spanish Government. The British Government and the chairman of the Non-intervention Committee, Lord Plymouth, did their utmost to whitewash the fascist powers and ignore the overwhelming evidence of their military intervention. In the end, the whole world knew and any pretence at concealment was abandoned.

The Republican Government of Spain was inadequately prepared to meet military aggression so strongly supported by foreign governments. The government forces and their supporters, the volunteers of the International Brigades, never had the necessary arms to combat the modern planes, tanks and guns of the enemy. While Hitler took the opportunity to try out his 88mm guns, (to be used so effectively during the Second World War), perfect dive bombing terror techniques and rotate his troops to give them battle experience, the republican forces fought back with primitive and out-of-date weaponry. Some of the rifles used by the volunteers were single shot, loading one round at a time; there were battles fought with rifles dating back to 1890. It was a monumental task to organise each brigade to be equipped with the same kind of guns that accepted the same ammunition. Soviet aid never matched the logistical support given by the fascists, and volunteers from all countries never equalled in numbers the divisions of regular troops sent by Italy.

The British Labour movement rallied to the cause of Republican Spain and the banner 'Arms for Spain' made by the Poplar Labour Party is evidence of the opposition to the policy of fascist appeasement pursued by the Chamberlain Government.

Formed in 1921, the Young Communist League lays claim to be the first autonomous political organisation for youth in the history of the British labour movement. There had been earlier organisations formed to provide socialist education for the young, the Socialist Sunday School movement founded at the end of the nineteenth century being the largest, though that catered for the lower age group of seven to fifteen years. In 1920 the Young Socialist League, led by Harry Gilbert and James Stewart, established study classes in economic and industrial history for young workers and in the same year the Young Labour League was formed. The latter body, whose first President was Frank Hodges of the Miners' Federation, was inclined towards the Labour Party, though it had no official link. In 1921 the two groups merged to form the Young Workers' League and later in the year further merged with the International Communist Schools' Movement. After a referendum of branches, the Young Communist League of Great Britain was set up in October of the same year. The YCL, as it was usually called, was under the political direction of the Communist Party but organisationally independent and had its own paper, the *Young Communist*.

For members of the YCL, trade union membership was obligatory and the movement soon decided to base itself 'where the young workers are to be found, i.e. the factories, workshops and mills.' If somewhat sectarian, the YCL campaigned to improve the lot of young people, calling for a minimum wage, the raising of the school leaving age to sixteen, the elimination of night work for youth, the provision of free meals for school children and the granting of full political rights to youth in the armed forces.

Many future trade union, Labour Party and Communist Party leaders served their political apprenticeship in the YCL, especially during the 1930s when the fight against fascism dominated the political arena. When the victory march to Victoria Park Square was held to celebrate the famous battle of Cable Street that stopped Mosley's fascists from marching through London's East End, it was the band of the YCL that headed the procession.

The homemade banner of the North London Branch (Hackney) was probably made in the late 1920s or early 1930s and reflects the confidence of youth. It leaves no doubt as to their ultimate goal, communism, and the red star and hammer and sickle proclaims their identity with the first socialist state, the Soviet Union.

Life and work in Britain's docks following the Second World War was a turbulent period of strikes and labour disputes, the vast majority of them unofficial. Between 1947 and 1955 350,000 working days were lost and from 1960 to 1964 there were 421 strikes, 410 of them unofficial. The Transport and General Workers' Union led by Arthur Deakin which represented eighty-five percent of the workers in the industry did not support any of them. It was this gap between the official leadership and the men at work that contributed to the unofficial rank and file Port Workers' Committees and Liaison Committees that developed in the post-war period.

The reasons for the continual unrest in the docks were complex and became the subject of a series of surveys and enquiries into labour relations, conditions of work and trade union organisation. Eventually, in 1965, the Government set up an authoritative enquiry headed by Lord Devlin. One of the recommendations of the Devlin Report was the creation of an official shop stewards' movement based upon the various companies for whom the men worked, a scheme devised to bring an end to the unofficial rank and file movement existing at the time. This was accepted by the unions but immediately caused further conflict between the dockers and their union officials. In 1949, at the Biennial Delegate Conference of the Transport and General Workers' Union, Deakin had carefully and cleverly succeeded in winning support for a motion 'That no member of the Communist Party shall be eligible to hold an office within the Union, either as a lay member or as a permanent or full time officer.' This proscription was still in force when the dockers voted in 1967 to elect their official shop stewards. The problem was that a number of those standing for election were well-known communists. Docklands, like mining communities, were close societies with strong traditions of class loyalty and militant trades unionism bred from years of hard and dangerous work coupled with insecurity and bitter poverty. This tradition of loyalty did not desert them when it came to the vote. Dockers from one company after another voted for candidates who had been leaders of the unofficial liaison committees, some of whom were also communists. In the London docks, these included Vic Turner, Micky Fenn, David Timothy, Ted Kirkby, Danny Lyons, Jack Dash and Bernie Steer. Some were members of the National Amalgamated Stevedores' and Dockers' Union, which did not operate the ban on communists, but others were members of the Transport and General Workers' Union, which did. While the constitutional arguments from the London Docks Group of the T & GWU continued, confrontation was avoided by a decision of the executive of the T & GWU, now led by Frank Cousins, to

ROYAL GROUP OF DOCKS
SHOP STEWARDS
COMMITTEE
ARISE YE WORKERS

recommend support for a removal of the ban at the next rules revision conference in 1968.

One of the stewards elected to the Royal Group of Docks was Bernie Steer, a communist. It was Steer who was given the job of producing a banner for the newly formed Shop Stewards' Committee and who coined the slogan 'arise ye workers', an echo of the opening words of the 'Internationale'. The slogan was agreed by the other stewards on the committee and the banner was made by Diana Cameron, the wife of a seaman, for a total cost of £20. The banner was carried on May Day marches, solidarity demonstrations and protests until the docks were finally closed and the committee disbanded in 1980.

Grunwick, like Upper Clyde Shipbuilders, Roberts-Arundel and Saltley Gates, is a name to be inscribed upon the battle colours of post-war British trade unionism. It was an heroic strike started by six immigrant workers who had never before been on strike or had even been members of a trade union.

Employed by the film processing company, Grunwick, a slow simmering discontent against low pay, compulsory overtime and autocratic management finally boiled over on 20 August 1976 during the hottest summer for a hundred years. Within eight days of the first sacking and subsequent walk-out, the strike had trade union recognition. Within weeks it had TUC support and in months it had national and international trade union support and was debated in the highest courts in the land.

At the time of the dispute, the starting pay for a process worker at Grunwick's was £28 for a forty hour week. Overtime was compulsory and the management screwed the last ounce from every worker. If overtime was compulsory, it was also necessary in order to obtain a living wage, the national industrial average at that time being £76 per week. This at a time when the previous year's profit for the company was over £200,000 and managing director George Ward owned eleven racehorses, paying his trainers £60 per week!

The workers in the mail order department where the strike began were mainly Indians from Uganda, Kenya and Tanzania and the majority were women. Poorly paid, first generation immigrants to Britain, women workers without trade union experience were perhaps unlikely material for a strike that was to last almost two years. Yet, within weeks, the diminutive figure of Jayaben Desai clad in her colourful sari, confronting police and management on the picket line was to become a national figure in the press and on television.

The strike was precipitated when Michael Alden, manager of the mail order department, pre-emptively sacked Devshi Bhudia for slow work. He was joined by three fellow workers who walked out with him. Later that day Mrs Desai and her son Sunil also walked out following an argument over compulsory overtime. Her parting words to Michael Alden were a classic piece of invective, 'What you are running here is not a factory, it is a zoo. But in a zoo there are many types of animals. Some are monkeys who dance on your finger tips, others are lions who can bite your head off. We are those lions, Mr Manager.'

So they were. The strike developed into a battle for the reinstatement of 137 strikers and for trade union recognition. Thousands of trade unionists mobilised to join the mass pickets, 20,000 arriving to give support on 11 July 1977. Three government ministers joined the picket line, Shirley Williams, Denis Howell and Fred Mulley. In November seven Labour Members of Parliament joined the picket, including Neil Kinnock. Despite such support, the workers could not break the Grunwick management and the strike was finally abandoned on 14 July 1978.

The banner of the strike committee was the first of the Grunwick banners to be made and was carried in the 1,400 strong march around Willesden in support of the strike. It was designed by a young Indian worker from Grunwick by the name of Jayandi and painted by him and Vipin Magdani, a member of the strike committee. According to Magdani, Jayandi had some art experience which is evidenced by the similarity of the design to the work of the Russian artist, El Lissitzky. In particular, the banner design strongly resembles the Lissitzky poster, 'Beat the whites with the red wedge', designed in 1920. The banner bears the initials of the Association of Professional, Executive Clerical and Computer Staffs and the Transport and General Workers' Union, the two unions involved in the dispute.

CERAMICS

On English commemorative pottery perhaps no more poignant inscriptions are to be found than those carried on the creamware jugs that were made to mark the massacre of peaceful citizens at St Peter's Field, Manchester, on 16 August 1819. 'Bad luck to the Manchester butchers' is a curse from the past to remind all who strive for liberty of the dreadful carnage ordered that day by the judiciary in the name of law and order. The demands of the reformers inscribed upon the jug illustrated would seem to be reasonable enough: 'No Corn Bill, Universal suffrage, Annual parliaments, voting by ballot, Bill of rights and Habeas-Corpus'. To the government, supported as it was by the armed services, the Church, the universities, the landed gentry and the unreformed municipalities, such demands from the unrepresented masses were mischievous, dangerous and revolutionary.

The meeting to endorse the popular demand for enfranchisement was planned to take place a week earlier, being advertised in the *Manchester Observer*: 'The public are respectfully informed that a meeting will be held here on Monday, the 9th of August, 1819, on the area near St. Peter's Church to take into consideration the most speedy and effectual mode of obtaining radical reform in the Commons House of Parliament, being fully convinced that nothing less can remove the intolerable evils under which the people of the country have so long, and do still, groan; and also to consider the propriety of the unrepresented inhabitants of Manchester electing a person to represent them in Parliament and adopting Major Cartwright's Bill. H. Hunt in the chair.'

On learning of the advertisement, Lord Sidmouth, the Home Secretary, wrote immediately to the Lord Lieutenant of Cheshire urging the utmost vigilance on the part of the magistrates and instructing them to give notice to the Yeomanry Cavalry to hold themselves in readiness for any call for support or assistance they may receive from the bench. The Manchester Cavalry promptly sent their sabres to the cutler to be sharpened.

A week later the magistrates proclaimed the proposed meeting illegal. Seeking legal opinion, the reformers were advised that the intention of choosing representatives contrary to the existing law 'tends greatly to render the proposed meeting seditious.' Heeding the advice, the reformers cancelled the meeting and carefully revised their programme. They petitioned the three main officials of local authority to summon a meeting 'to consider the propriety of adopting the most legal and effectual means of obtaining reform in the Commons House of Parliament.' This was refused and notice was therefore given, signed by 1,300 inhabitants that a meeting would be held in St Peter's Field, on Monday, 16 August at 12 o'clock and that Henry Hunt would take the chair.

It was Hunt that the people wanted to hear. 'Orator Hunt' was an imposing and charismatic figure, over six feet in height, well dressed, quick witted, able to handle a large audience and always shrewd enough to keep within the law. He crowned his appearance with a white hat that was to become a symbol of radicalism in the way that Ben Tillett's wide brimmed hat was to become a symbol of the new unionism eighty years later. Hunt had been born the son of a wealthy Wiltshire farmer in 1773 and led a turbulent private life. In politics his record bore greater scrutiny. He presented the earliest petition to Parliament for Women's Suffrage, fought for reform, campaigned for the ballot and universal suffrage and for the repeal of the Corn Laws. It was to hear Hunt speak for liberty that more than 60,000 poor working people and their families marched into Manchester from the outlying districts, bands playing, banners flying and the red caps of liberty held aloft.

The first contingent was led by Samuel Bamford, the radical weaver, a procession of more than 6,000 men, women and children. In the forefront were youths wearing laurels, then came representatives from the various districts, behind them the band and the colours. The banners bore mottos, 'Unity and Strength, Liberty and Fraternity, Parliaments Annual, Suffrage Universal' and amid the banners a red velvet cape inscribed 'Libertas'. Bamford wrote of his contingent as 'a most respectable assemblage of labouring men, all decently though humbly attired.' As the column moved off, banners flashing in the summer sun, the music from another party could be heard, the Rochdale procession of 10,000, the women and children singing and dancing as they made their way through fields and woods. The Oldham contingent joined with the Chadderton section at Bent Grange at nine in the morning, the green and white silk banner of Chadderton measuring twelve feet by nine. The Oldham banner was said to be the most beautiful of all, made of pure white silk and emblazoned with mottos, 'Universal suffrage and annual Parliaments', 'Election by ballot', 'No Combination Act', 'Oldham Union'. In contrast to the drab clothing of the men, the Royton banner was escorted by 200 women dressed in white, their banner proclaiming 'The Royton Female Union', 'Let us DIE like men and not be sold like slaves'. The banner of the Saddleworth, Lees and Mossley Union was jet black and bore the inscription 'Equal representation or death' and illustrated the figure of justice with her scales and the clasped hands of unity. Both the Royton and Saddleworth banners were to be captured later that day by the Yeomanry and produced as 'evidence' against the reformers in the trial at York the following year.

The processions wended towards the city, a bystander recording, 'I never saw a gayer spectacle, the young persons in their best Sunday suits and the light coloured dresses of the cheerful tidy looking women relieved the effect of the dark fustians worn by the men.'

By one o'clock, St Peter's Field presented an astonishing scene, for there in the heat of an August day had gathered the largest assembly of people ever gathered together on English soil. The estimates varied from Hunt's extravagant claim of between

180,000 and 200,000 to the figure of 30,000 given by a short-sighted magistrate. The *Manchester Observer* reckoned it at 153,000 while *The Times* gave both 80,000 and 100,000. The certainty was that it was a radical triumph.

As Hunt made his way on a barouche into the field, the banner of the Manchester Female Reformers flying alongside the coachman, a great roar arose from the multitude, banners were hoisted and waved and the massed bands played 'See the Conquering Hero Comes'. Surrounding St Peter's Field the magistrates had deployed under the command of Lieutenant-Colonel Guy l'Estrange, the officer commanding the Manchester district, a veritable army. He had four squadrons of cavalry of the 15th Hussars comprising about 600 men, several hundred men from the 88th Foot, and several squadrons of the 31st Foot. He backed this with a detachment of the Royal Horse Artillery with two six-pounder guns and the full strength of the amateur Cheshire Yeomanry Cavalry, at least 400 men, and three troops of the Manchester and Salford Yeomanry Cavalry, another 180 men. In addition some 400 special constables were on duty in the town.

It was in this position, the vast crowd ringed by the military and the Yeomanry, that the magistrates decided to arrest Hunt, sending the cavalry onto the field at a gallop and halting in some disorder. Hunt, who had only just started to speak, saw their approach and said, 'Stand firm, my friends, you see they are in disorder already. This is a trick, give them three cheers.' The cavalry moved to the hustings, sabres flashing in a path of chaos and panic as people were trampled, crushed and cut as the soldiers made their way towards the wagons that served as platforms. Hunt was arrested and urged the crowd to remain calm as he descended from the wagon of his own accord. Others were dragged brutally from the high wagons and Mrs Fildes of the Female Reformers found her white dress caught on a nail; tugging frantically to free herself she was 'slashed across her exposed body by one of the brave cavalry'. The Manchester Yeomanry Cavalry left the escorting of Hunt and his associates to the special constables while they turned their attention to smashing the wagons and seizing the banners. In the mêlée of dust, noise, heat and shouts, l'Estrange was ordered by the magistrates to disperse the crowd. In a few moments the Hussars charged onto the field. Now all was confusion as the packed mass stumbled and struggled to escape the rearing horses, trampling hooves and hacking sabres. Heads were split and bones smashed as young and old desperately sought escape from the bloody ring. As they fled carrying their wounded, children screaming, blood running, they were harried and pursued into the nearby streets by a berserk cavalry drunk on blood and imagined glory.

By two o'clock St Peter's Field was quiet, littered with broken banner poles, bonnets, shawls, a child's shoe and the moaning wounded and silent dead, bundles of slashed and trampled citizens that had met in peace to ask for the right to vote. The Yeomanry had dismounted and stood wiping their sabres. The law had been enforced. Fifteen were dead, including a two-year old boy, some 500 were injured and most were afraid to seek medical aid, fearful of further prosecution.

In the outcry that followed, Shelley composed the *Mask of Anarchy*, writing to his publisher, 'The torrent of indignation has not yet done boiling in my veins.' In his poem he castigated two cabinet ministers, Viscounts Sidmouth and Castlereagh:

> I met murder on the way
> He had a mask like Castlereagh.

and

> Like Sidmouth next, Hypocrisy
> On a crocodile came by.

His verses ended with a fighting call:

> Rise, like lions after slumber,
> In unvanquishable number!
> Shake your chains to earth, like dew,
> Which in sleep had fallen on you!
> Ye are many – they are few.

If some, like Shelley and Bamford, were moved to genuine protest in verse, others seized the moment for profit and transfers were hurriedly applied to jugs to convert them to commemorative pieces. Such is the jug illustrated, for the portrait is not that of Hunt but of Commodore Bainbridge of the United States Navy! Originally made for export to America, the manufacturers worked on the assumption that few people would have known what Hunt looked like and that as the originals had been sent to America, they would never be seen in Britain. Other Peterloo jugs feature heroes of the 1812-14 British-American War using them as a stand-in for Hunt. Some jugs were specially produced to commemorate the massacre and are remarkably radical in content. One mentions the radical newspaper *The Black Dwarf*, and others leave no doubt as to the dreadful role of the cavalry. One illustration depicts 'a spirited print of a single cavalryman with upswung sabre riding down a single woman'.

Another Peterloo jug carried a transfer print showing the cavalry riding over the fallen victims at Peterloo and across the sprawled victims a banner bearing the caption 'Murder'. Below the print is a rhyme:

> The scripture cries out life for life,
> And God ordained it so,
> We'll not forget to pay the debt
> Incurred at Peterloo.

It is surprising that the makers were not indicted for incitement. While most of the Peterloo commemorative pottery extols the virtues of Hunt, the champion of liberty, it is left to the commemorative medal to carry the most apt inscription of all, a verse from Psalms:

> The wicked have drawn out the sword,
> They have cut down the poor and needy
> and such as be of upright conversation.

Another form of practical commemorative pottery is the gin flasks of brown stoneware made in the likenesses of reform leaders. Most of these were made by Doulton and Watts of Lambeth or the Belper pottery run by Joseph Bourne. The flask illustrated is impressed with the name of the manufacturer as Belper and Denby, Bournes Potteries, Derbyshire. About 1800 William Bourne took over the small coarseware pottery of Blood, Webster and Simpson at Belper and carried on the manufacture of ginger beer and spirit bottles using clay from a local bed.

reform, it is revolution.' To the radicals, the Bill did not go far enough in meeting their demands for universal suffrage though the eventual passing of the Bill was met by national jubilation. It was met too with jubilation by the manufacturers of commemorative pottery, who rushed into print and production with mugs, jugs and bowls carrying a myriad of transfers marking the event. The 1832 Reform Bill became the most commemorated political event in nineteenth century British history. Most of the pottery carried likenesses of the four main Whig protagonists for the Bill, Althorpe, Brougham, Grey and Russell, though complex illustrations are plentiful enough. Some mugs and jugs carry the likenesses of the Whig leaders laying the axe of reform to the rotten borough system while it is energetically defended by the Tory Cabinet. Another depicts an elaborate tree hung with placards reading 'Rotten borough system' and 'You take our lives when you take away the means whereby we live' and is encaptioned 'The old rotten tree'. On one side of the tree, the four Whig leaders lay the axe of Reform to the roots of the tree while the Tory Cabinet endeavour to prop up the tree.

The milk jug illustrated does not carry a maker's name and was just one of the many popular pieces marketed to cash in on a national celebration.

Roughly centred on a willow pattern design, the circular stamp of the Honley Mechanics' Institute is another example of 'instant' commemorative ware. Made in Staffordshire during the 1830s, the stamp has been superimposed on an existing pattern to provide the small Yorkshire town's Mechanics' Institute with a suitable piece of pottery to adorn the dressers of its proud and ambitious members.

The first Mechanical Institution was founded in London in 1817 by Timothy Claxton, a mechanic, and lasted only three years. The idea was revived in 1823 by Thomas Hodgskin and J.C. Robertson, the joint editors of the *Mechanics' Magazine*. Hodgskin was a friend of Francis Place (the radical tailor and former chairman of the London Corresponding Society) and soon enlisted his help in raising funds from trade unions and his political acquaintances. The working men were suspicious that the Institute would be controlled by their employers for their own ends and the wealthy were afraid of the consequences of the spread of education among working men. Lord Grosvenor, when approached for a contribution, said he had a strong desire to assist the institution but he also had some apprehension that the education the people were getting would make them discontented with the government. Place replied with assurance, 'The people are already discontented with the Government, and that although teaching them would not remove their discontent,

The Reform Bill of 1832 was the occasion for the production of a series of bottles incorporating likenesses of various reform leaders together with slogans such as 'The true spirit of reform', 'The People's Right' and 'The second Magna Carta'. The reformers featured were the Whig leaders, Grey, Brougham and Russell, not the radical leaders who had fought so consistently for a reformed Commons. The Brougham cordial bottle would have held gin, the term cordial being used in the warm and friendly sense of the word. Whatever Brougham may have done to deserve his immortality as a gin flask, he should also be remembered for his part as Lord Chancellor in supporting the prosecution of the Tolpuddle Martyrs.

The demand for reform was not halted by the brutal response of the government to the Manchester reformers and the public voice over the next decade grew louder and more assertive, culminating in the great Reform Bill of 1832. The Bill, passed by a Whig government, was opposed by the Tories on the grounds that it marked the beginning of a revolution; every bishop except two voted against it and Wellington said, 'It is not

it would make them less disposed to turbulence.' At the first set of lectures in 1824, Place wrote of 'his joy at seeing eight to nine hundred, clean respectable-looking mechanics paying most marked attention to a lecture on chemistry.'

Lord Grosvenor need not have worried, for respectability was surely laid as the keystone of the Institute. Those who joined were the élite of labour, skilled artisans, the printers, engineers, joiners, the workers who ate meat, vegetables, fruit and dairy produce, who paid substantial dues to craft trade unions and whose eyes were set on self-improvement rather than social revolution. Hodgskin, who in 1825 published a pamphlet entitled *Labour defended against the claims of Capital*, an able attack on the existing system of producing wealth, was opposed by Place when he applied for the lectureship in political economy at the Institute in 1827. From the mid 1830s, when the Honley plate was made, the emphasis on study moved from science and economics to meet the needs of a new membership of clerks and shopkeepers who wanted to share the culture of their superiors, the middle class. Within a decade, the Institute was offering popular lectures, classes on phrenology and holding soirées. The Institutes grew from 55 in 1831 to 1,200 by 1860 with some 200,000 members. Moral restraint and self-help was the message and Engels had early perceived the uselessness of Mechanics' Institutes as a force for working class education when he wrote, 'Mechanics' Institutes offer classes in that brand of political economy which takes free competition as its God. The teachers of this subject preach the doctrine that it does not lie within the power of the workers to change the existing economic order. The proletariat is told that they must resign themselves to starving without making a fuss. The students are taught to be subservient to the existing political and social order.'

It was as a vehicle for social climbing without disturbing the social order that was the true stamp of the Mechanics' Institutes.

1929 was the first general election in Britain to be held under complete adult suffrage. The result gave Labour 288 seats to the Conservatives' 260, but still did not give Labour a majority in the Commons. For Ramsay MacDonald the election was a personal triumph, being returned for Seaham with a majority of 28,794, the largest recorded in the election. On 4 June Stanley Baldwin placed his resignation in the hands of the King and the following day MacDonald was sent for and agreed to form a government; for the second time he was Prime Minister, having formed the first minority Labour government in 1924.

To his constituents at Seaham, MacDonald said, 'Make no mistake about it, it is not going to be all beer and skittles, especially for me.' It would have made a suitable epitaph for his tombstone, for in little more than two years he was dead as far as the Labour Party was concerned, having betrayed the movement he had helped to build, presiding over a cabinet of Tories and Liberals as Prime Minister of a National Government. That the souvenir plate presented by him to the East Fulham Labour Party survives is remarkable, for the memory of the betrayal lives on in the Labour movement to this day. In Durham the miners, who idolised him, painted out his portrait from their lodge banners and his name was vilified whenever socialists gathered. Photographs and portraits were removed from party rooms and unceremoniously dumped, his pamphlets consigned to dustbins; he was as Judas to his disciples.

Just for a handful of silver he left us,
Just for a ribbon to stick in his coat.

Although illustrating the historic cottages of the Tolpuddle Martyrs, the late nineteenth century plate is of no real political significance. Made especially for the china shop of J.T. Godwins situated in High West Street, Dorchester, the plate is little more than a tourist souvenir of cheap scrivener, made at a time when local topographical scenes were popular subjects for gift china. The transfer print was just one of a series of Dorset views printed for plates, mugs, bowls and dishes directed at the tourist trade. Nevertheless, as a 'present from Tolpuddle', the recipients of the plates were reminded that behind the scene of rural bliss lay a social injustice that will never be forgotten.

The development of the co-operative trading movement since its inception by the Rochdale pioneers in 1844 brought a spate of jubilee and coming-of-age anniversaries in the early part of the present century. Between 1864 and 1867 200 new societies a year were registered under the Industrial and Provident Societies Act. Apart from the elaborate public celebrations staged to mark the jubilees and twenty-first anniversaries, most societies chose to record their achievement by the issue of some form of commemorative pottery. The Co-operative Wholesale Society had already entered the business of crockery manufacture in 1886 under the management of John Rhodes and by 1889 the business had grown sufficiently to warrant the building of a substantial factory at Longton, Staffordshire. The factory mainly produced kitchen crockery, which was a main selling line in the household departments of local societies, but in 1898 a decorating department was added and before long there were twenty workers using three kilns. Lithographic transfers bought in from specialist printers were added to the ware, designs being made to order. With 1,400 different societies approaching celebratory dates, the CWS began to produce mugs, jugs, teapots and bowls bearing prints of premises, pioneers and local landmarks, whatever a society chose to order. It was possible to print as few as 500 on an economic basis so that even the smallest societies could commemorate their foundation.

The Stratford Co-operative and Industrial Society, known locally as 'the stores', was founded in the upper rooms of Easy's Temperance Coffee House in Stratford Broadway by a small group of railwaymen and friends. The immense junction and railway works of the Great Eastern Railway Company dominated Stratford and at the second meeting only men from the railway workers were invited. The society was formed to 'raise by the voluntary subscription of the members a fund for better enabling them to purchase food, firing, clothes and necessaries by carrying on in common the trade or business of general dealers.' Four weeks later a little shop was acquired on the corner of Falmouth Street and Maryland Street, open two evenings a week. By the time of the Stratford Societies' Jubilee, there were thirty-six branches from Bow to Wanstead.

The scene on the commemorative jug shows Stratford Broadway with horse-drawn vehicles and open-topped tram and bears the stamp of Longton on the base with the Co-operative motto 'Labour and wait'.

James Keir Hardie, the pioneer, prophet and most loved of all British socialists, was born on 15 August 1856 in the village of Legbrannock, Lanarkshire. His arrival could hardly have been a cause for rejoicing in the tumbledown, mud-floored, one room cottage that his mother, Mary Keir, shared with her mother and two younger sisters, for another to live in the overcrowded room and another mouth to be fed was calamitous. To compound the difficulties of the family, the baby was illegitimate, the father William Aitkin, a miner, having disowned his son.

Mary Keir christened her son James after her own father and returned to her work in the fields, a sinner and outcast struggling to keep her widowed mother, her sisters, baby and herself from starvation. Hardie recalled his first memory as 'hot tears falling'. After three years, Mary married David Hardie, a ship's carpenter and moved to Govan to live in a single room near the Napier's Shipbuilding Yard and to make a new life. What sort of life it was, can barely be imagined. Mary had two more children, wages were low and the family lived in abject poverty that was to become seared into the mind of young James Keir Hardie and to remain with him throughout his life.

There was no compulsory schooling and Hardie, who had started casual work at the age of six, worked regularly from the age of seven. His first job was as a message boy with the Anchor Line Steamship Company. He then transferred to the brass finishing shop to be apprenticed to the trade but had to abandon the opportunity on learning that the first year of the apprenticeship was 'without wages'. He then obtained a job at a printers in the Trongate at half a crown a week but once again had to leave because his parents could not afford to apprentice him. He next worked as an errand boy for a baker's shop and at the age of ten had his first experience of being sacked. The incident was traumatic and formative and is best described in Hardie's own words.

The year 1866 was nearing its close. Owing to a lock-out in the shipbuilding yards on the Clyde, my father had been out of employment for nearly six months. The funds of the Union were so exhausted that the benefits were reduced to 1s. 6d. and 2s. a week. I was the only breadwinner, being employed by a high-class baker in Lancefield Street, Glasgow, for 3s. 6d. a week. My hours were from 7 a.m. to 7.30 p.m. – 12½ hours each day. I was the eldest of a family of three, and the brother next to me was down with fever, from which he never recovered, though his life dragged on for two years thereafter. As most of the neighbourhood had children, they feared coming into the house because of the danger of contagion, and my mother, who was very near her confinement, was in delicate health.

It was the last week in the year. Father had been away for two or three days in search of work. Towards the end of the week, having been up most of the night, I got to the shop fifteen minutes late, and was told by the young lady in charge that if that occurred again I would be punished. I made no reply. I couldn't. I felt like crying. Next morning the same thing happened. I could tell why, but that was neither here nor there. It was a very wet morning, and when I reached the shop I was drenched to the skin, barefooted and hungry. There had not been a crust of bread in the house that morning.

But that was pay-day, and I was filled with hope. 'You are wanted upstairs by the master,' said the girl behind the counter, and my heart almost stopped beating. Outside the

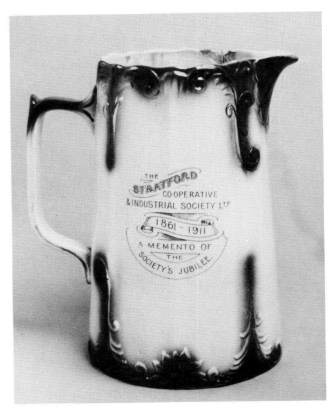

dining-room door a servant bade me wait till 'master had finished prayers'. (He was noted for his piety.) At length the girl opened the door, and the sight of that room is fresh in my memory even as I write, nearly fifty years after. Round the great mahogany table sat the members of the family, with the father at the top. In front of him was a very wonderful-looking coffee boiler, in the great glass bowl of which the coffee was bubbling. The table was loaded with dainties. My master looked at me over his glasses and said in quite a pleasant tone of voice, 'Boy, this is the second morning you have been late, and my customers leave me if they are kept waiting for their hot breakfast rolls. I therefore dismiss you, and, to make you more careful in the future, I have decided to fine you a week's wages. And now you may go!'
I wanted to speak and explain about my home, and muttered out something to explain why I was late, but the servant took me by the arm and led me downstairs. As I passed through the shop the girl in charge gave me a roll and said a kind word. I knew my mother was waiting for my wages. As the afternoon was drawing to a close I ventured home and told her what had happened. It seemed to be the last blow. The roll was still under my vest, but soaked with rain. That night the baby was born, and the sun rose on the first of January, 1867, over a home in which there was neither fire nor food, though, fortunately, relief came before the day had reached its noon. But the memory of these early days abides with me, and makes me doubt the sincerity of those who make pretence in their prayers.

His next employment was heating rivets in Thompson's Shipyard for half a crown a week where he worked in a scaffold with another boy. The lad fell off and was killed and Hardie's mother, frightened by the accident, refused to allow him to return.

Life in Govan was now so hard and miserable for the family that they decided to return to Lanarkshire and settle in the mining village of Newarthill. It was here that Keir Hardie's association with the miners began when he started work at the pit as a trapper, the boy whose job it was to open and close a door which kept the air supply for the men in a given direction. For several years he rarely saw daylight during the winter months, down the pit by six o'clock and not leaving again until half past five, six days a week and a half day on Sundays. The work for a boy of ten was cold, lonely and eerie, the underground silence being broken only by the sighing of the wind and the drip, drip of water, the darkness relieved by the fluttering flame of a single lamp. The simple fireclay lamp was given by Keir Hardie to Caroline Martyn, founder of the Socialist Sunday School in Glasgow, as a memento when she was a student at Glasgow University. On her death she left the lamp to Charles Scott, who owned a shop in Union Street, Glasgow, and was known locally as the 'top-hatted socialist'. On his death, his widow gave the lamp to Mr and Mrs McDonald of Paisley. When Mr McDonald died, May McDonald donated the lamp to the Trade Union, Labour and Democratic History Society, having cared for it for half a century.

In 1815 John Doulton risked his life-savings of £100 by investing in a small riverside pottery in Lambeth, South London. With his craft skill, drive and personal ambition, the pottery thrived and was to make a major contribution to the development of the studio pottery movement as well as the more practical contribution to public health by the manufacture of drainpipes and sanitary ware.

By the 1830s, trading as Doulton and Watts, the company began to produce its first commemorative wares in the form of the figure-shaped salt-glazed spirit flasks. From the Lambeth factory came a succession of jugs, mugs, figures, busts, tobacco jars and teapots to mark wars, anniversaries, coronations, sporting and political events. Doulton's first suffragette figure was in the form of an inkwell modelled in coloured stoneware by Leslie Harradine in 1906. 'Votes for Women' was a movement subjected to derision and hostility by both government and the popular press of the day and Harradine joined in the mockery by depicting his suffragette as an ugly virago with arms folded in defiance.

The distance of time often brings consensus and respectability to radical causes of the past and the Royal Doulton figure made in 1978 is of this genre. Designed by sculptor William K. Harpur, the figure this time is that of a 'chocolate box' heroine. It was not produced to mark any special anniversary of the suffragette struggle for the franchise but as a commercial saleable figure. The passing of seventy years has brought the gloss of glamour to an essential human right.

An old tradition in commemorative pottery was revived as a result of the lock-out of printing trade unions by Times Newspapers Ltd. in 1978. Following the year-long dispute, during which no copies of *The Sunday Times, The Times* or any of its supplements, *Literary, Educational* or *Higher Educational* appeared, the Joint Liaison Committee representing the seven unions involved issued a victory jug to mark the end of the struggle.

The idea came from Lou Kenton, himself a copy reader at the *Financial Times*. Kenton was born in the East End of London in 1908, the son of an immigrant Jewish tailor who had been forced to flee from the pogroms in Russia in 1905. Growing up amid the hardship of the immigrant struggle for survival and acceptance in London's poorest quarter, the young Lou Kenton became a socialist and began a lifetime of work for the labour movement. In the late 1930s he became editor of the *Printer* and assistant secretary of the Printing and Allied Trades' Anti-Fascist Movement. When General Franco led the fascist uprising in Spain, Kenton joined the courageous band of volunteers for the British section of the International Brigade, where he served as an ambulance driver.

His interest in pottery started in 1974 at an age when most men have retired. From a tiny pottery at the end of his garden he made and fired his first commemorative item, the Times Challenger mug. The idea was received with enthusiasm by the unions who had taken part in the dispute and asked Kenton to make a thousand! So successful was the venture with the Times mug that a flow of orders began to overtake Kenton's cottage industry. To produce large quantities from his home was impractical, so he turned for help to a newly formed co-operative in Stoke, Longton Ceramics. It was a co-operative of workers, trade union, town council and Co-operative Bank, set up in 1981 after the firm of Shaw & Copestake had gone into liquidation. Working from home, Kenton organised the design and production of commemorative ware for trade union centenaries, strikes, GLC Peace Year, Karl Marx's centenary and the Greenham Common Women's Peace Camp, all made at Longton Ceramics. His largest order to date came for 20,000 mugs to mark and raise funds for the 'People's march for jobs' in 1983. The idea for the march was put forward in November 1980 by Barney Williams, President of the Liverpool Trades Council, who called for backing by the official labour and trade union movement supported by broad democratic and community organisations. A National Organising Committee was formed comprised of the Regional TUCs, the Scottish and Welsh TUC and representatives of ten trade unions who planned a forty-two day march from Glasgow to London as a trade union protest against mass unemployment which had passed the 3,000,000 total.

Under the chairmanship of Ron Todd of the Transport and General Workers' Union, the NOC planned and co-ordinated the forty-two day march in considerable detail. With an upper limit of 500 official marchers, provision was made for medical care, social security and unemployment payments, feeding, accommodation, marshalls, transport, publicity and town events culminating in a final demonstration in London on 5 June. The unemployed marchers were chosen by each of the Regional TUCs to represent a broad cross section of unemployed workers. Unemployed they may have been, but they were not the unsuitably clad marchers with holes in their boots that were such a familiar sight in the 1930s. Trade union funds ensured that adequate and distinctive clothing with all necessary accessories and equipment was provided for the unemployed marchers. Starting from Glasgow, the march to London gathered support from feeder marches joining the main body from Land's End, Liverpool, Newcastle, Keighley, Hull and Great Yarmouth. Warmly greeted through 129 cities and towns (though the conservatives of Harrow declined to meet them), the Scottish contingent led the final procession into Hyde Park after nearly 1,000 miles of walking, secure in the knowledge that the journey home would be by train, paid for by the National Union of Railwaymen.

Designed by Anna Aubrey, the logo for the People's March for Jobs reproduced on the mugs was already a familiar sight throughout the land. Printed on button badges and T-shirts worn by the marchers and their supporters and painted on their banners it had been publicly displayed throughout Britain. The logo is similar in design to that used by the United Automobile Workers for their 'March for jobs and justice' to Washington in 1981.

CERTIFICATES

I found my first Ragged School in an obscene place called West Street, Saffron Hill, pitifully struggling for life under every disadvantage. It had no means: it had no suitable rooms: it derived no power or protection from being recognised by any authority: it attracted within its walls a fluctuating swarm of faces – young in years, but youthful in nothing else – that scowled Hope out of countenance. It was held in a low-roofed den, in a sickening atmosphere, in the midst of taint and dirt and pestilence: with all the deadly sins let loose, howling and shrieking at the doors. Zeal did not supply the place of method and training: the teachers knew little of their office: the pupils with an evil sharpness, found them out, got the better of them, derided them, made blasphemous answers to Scriptural questions, sang, fought, danced, robbed each other – seemed possessed by a legion of devils. The place was stormed and carried over and over again: the lights were blown out, the books strewn in the gutters, and the female scholars carried off triumphantly to the old wickedness.

The words are those of Charles Dickens recording his first visit to Field Lane School, off Holborn Hill, and the account is fact, not fiction. These were the children of one of the worst slum areas in London, street arabs, the product of gutter poverty, considered too ragged to be allowed into any Sunday school.

It was John Pounds, a compassionate and crippled cobbler from Portsmouth, who, in 1835, first gathered little groups of outcast children together in his workshop, teaching them to read while he continued with his repairs, who inspired the foundation of the Ragged School Union in 1844. An evangelical mission for Christianity, the schools had to cope with social problems caused by the deprivation and poverty endemic among their pupils. Apart from scripture, the Ragged Schools gave refuge to the destitute, bread to the starving and baths to the filthy, combining spiritual zeal with Victorian charity. Samuel Smiles' book, *Self Help*, was widely used as a teaching text in the Ragged Schools and the elementary education was supplemented by work and domestic training suitable for the children of the industrious classes. Boys were set to wood chopping, formed into shoe-black brigades, sent to training ships and emigration farms while 'fallen females were rescued from the path of sin' and taught the domestic skills necessary to a good servant or wife – cooking, sewing and knitting.

The extent of absolute poverty among working class children is reflected in the claim that by 1871, not less than 300,000 children had been taught in Ragged Schools. At the time of the passing of the Education Act in 1870, the schools had 440 paid teachers and thousands of voluntary helpers. The movement attracted support from wealthy philanthropists, among whom were Quentin Hogg, Judge Hughes (author of *Tom Brown's Schooldays*), Sir Walter Besant and Sir Robert Carden. Dr Barnado was a Ragged School teacher and conceded 'my own rescue work sprang out of the Ragged School.'

Among the pupils was William Southgate, father of Walter Southgate, a joint founder of the Trade Union, Labour, Co-operative, Democratic History Society. William Southgate's certificate from the Ragged School Union was given from the school in Dove Row, Haggerstone, East London, in 1868, the family having moved to the city from Norwich in the early 1860s.

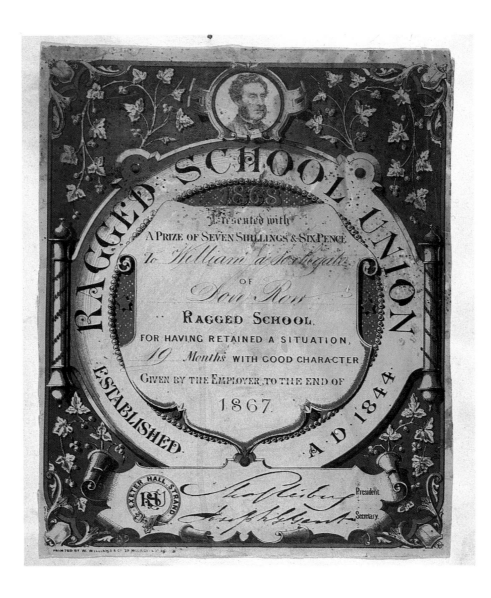

The certificate carried a prize of 7s. 6d. for having held his job for nineteen months with 'good character'. As William Southgate was born in 1853, he must have been working from the age of twelve, if not younger. The education served him well, though the religious instruction did not lead him to Christianity but rather to become a follower of the radical atheist, Charles Bradlaugh. Southgate was never a socialist, but had read Henry George and in the evenings after his day's work as a quill-pen cutter would hold forth in his local four-ale bar on the evils of landlordism and the need for nationalisation of the land.

The certificate bears the portrait and signature of Lord Shaftesbury, the President of the Ragged School Union, who devoted his life to the alleviation of distress among the poor.

'Daddy Time' was Keir Hardie. Writing in the first issue of his new paper, *Labour Leader*, on 31 March 1894, Hardie included a feature entitled 'Chats with the lads and lasses' by Daddy Time. With his compassion for humanity, children were always precious to him and he generated a natural warmth when in their company. He realised the value of teaching the moral values of socialism to the young in preparation for their future role as citizens of the socialist commonwealth and despite the enormous demands upon him in his political life, gave time to write especially for children. He wrote for them in the *Labour Leader* posing the question, 'Have you heard the story of Jack the giant killer? Well, I know where there is a whole castle of big, ugly, dirty giants . . . now hands up all those willing to fight the giants. All those who want to join send in their name and age.' Those who did were to have their names entered in a 'great big book' and as soon as he had received a thousand names they were to receive a card with their name upon it. When he had a thousand members they were to form an army called the 'Labour Crusaders'. The girls and boys who joined were to be Dames and Knights to fight the giants of Monopoly and Competition. In the issue of 26 May 1894 'Daddy Time' asked each Crusader to promise three things: first, to remember that men and women

were created to enjoy life; second, that everything which hinders men and women from enjoying life is wrong and sinful; third, that it is our duty to remove these hindrances. Letters from children came at a steady rate; one from Middlesborough told how they had a 'Cinderella Club' for slum children who were refused admission to Sunday School because they had no shoes or stockings. 'We issue eighty to one hundred tickets a week and give them a cup of tea and a bun and sing a Labour hymn.' 'Daddy Time' was drawn in the *Labour Leader* as a kindly Santa Claus type of figure, ringing a bell and accompanied by his dog, Toby. Children sent in drawings of Toby as well as poems, essays and criticism: 'We get the *Labour Leader* every week at the Labour Church but we have not seen our names printed yet.'

By 27 July 1895 the Crusader membership had reached over the thousand mark and seems to have been well established in many industrial areas. It was announced that the membership certificate was designed by Nannie Preston, 'a talented young lady artist', but it was not until early in 1896 that the certificate seems to have been ready for distribution. On 12 September 1896 the column became 'Chats with Crusaders'.

The Crusaders met on Sunday, usually in the afternoons, to sing socialist songs, like 'All for the Cause', 'England Arise', 'No Master', the 'Red Flag' and the 'Marseillaise' and to learn the principles of socialism expounded by the Glasiers, Bruce and Kathryn, Caroline Martyn, Archie McArthur and other pioneers of Labour. The schools spread throughout Britain and were to be found in most of the major industrial cities and the poor areas of London, including Canning Town, Dalston, Bermondsey, Walthamstow and Fulham. The teachers tried to bring some joy to the miserable lives of the children, organising rambles, providing tea parties and finding boots and clothes. A letter from the Salford school to the *Labour Leader* tells that 'we have a lot of ragged children among our scholars and I am trying to get some cast off clothing for them before winter sets in.' The driving force behind the 'Red Schools', as the opposition called them,

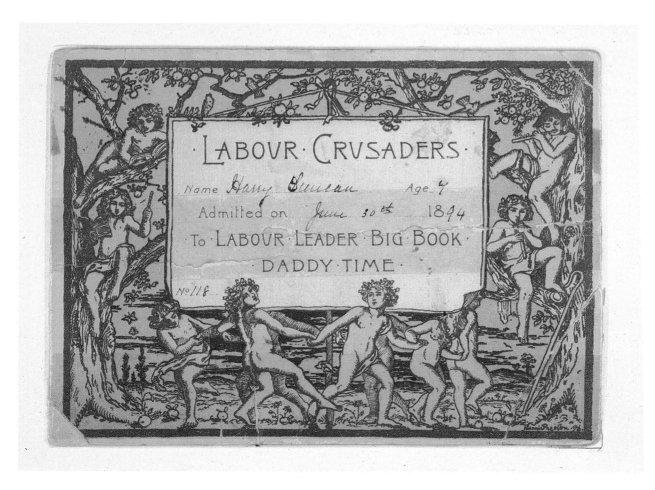

MINERS' PROTECTION SOCIETY.

AMICITIA · AMOR · ET · VERITAS

Presented to Mr.

by the Members of this Society in recognition of his Services as President

during the Year 190___

was common humanity, the need to teach children to love their fellows and fight injustice, to strive for a socialist society where none who were able to work would want. As Daddy Time wrote, 'Don't neglect the children, comrades, they are our successors and must be better fighters for the cause than we, their parents. Let's give them a chance to love the movement by enlarging their outlook on happiness.'

The origins of the Miners' Protection Society remains a mystery, unrecorded in trade union histories and never registered as a friendly society. Although the certificate allows for the date to be filled in between 1901 and 1909, the design is much older. The engraving of the illustration appears in the George Tutill catalogue of 1896 without the lettering at the head and may well have been a standard design used by more than one of the miners' organisations. Apart from early mining scenes and a clever centrepiece entwined with a colliery rope and basket, the image carries the allegorical figures of friendship, love and truth surmounted by the 'all-seeing eye'.

It is possible that the Miners' Protection Society was an employers' organisation, a benefit club formed to deprive miners of their rights under the Workmen's Compensation Act of 1880. The trades unions had fought for years to make employers liable for accidents at work caused by the negligence of management

and their case had been resisted by both Tories and Liberals. When the Act was finally passed, due largely to the tenacity of Henry Broadhurst, limited though it was, the employers sought ways to avoid their responsibilities. In a judgement made in 1882, in the case of Griffiths v. the Earl of Dudley, if 'a workman continued in employment after receiving a notice that he must forgo all his rights under the Act, and accept in lieu thereof, a claim on a Benefit Club to which the employer contributed, he was held to have entered into a contract to relinquish the rights given him by the Act of 1880.' Thus, the way was clear for employers to contract out of the Act and limit their liability in the case of death or injury.

The practice of contracting out of the Act was strongly opposed by the unions, especially by the miners, who suffered an appalling accident rate at their work. Keir Hardie summed up the attitude of the miners at the First Annual Conference of the Miners' Federation of Great Britain when he stated that an employer who contracted out 'was an enemy of the working class, and he should be stamped inside and outside of the House of Commons as a person unfit to be an employer. If a man thought more of his money than he did of the lives and limbs of his workpeople, he should be considered as one of the greatest pests in the country and to the human race.'

The image is a fine engraving of labour in the mining industry in the late nineteenth century and carries the familiar trade union scene of colleagues visiting a sick or injured brother. However, as Tutill was happy to adapt his work to suit any sort of Society, from Ancient Shepherds to True Ivorites, it is impossible to judge from the illustration whether the Miners' Protection Society was meant to protect the welfare of the miners or the purse of the coalowner.

The National Democratic League was formed on 27 October 1900 at a meeting of more than 600 held at the King's Hall, Holborn Restaurant. Sponsored by *Reynolds' Newspaper*, the object of the League was 'to democratise Parliament and thus place in the hands of the industrial classes the essential legislative instrument for securing drastic social and economic reforms.' The audience and the platform was representative of a wide spectrum of trade union, socialist, radical and democratic organisations and included many well-known figures. *Reynolds'*, announced as the 'official organ of the League', described the democrats who filled the hall as 'keen, buoyant, hopeful and at times merry'. Certainly there was much merriment when John Burns in his attack upon the composition of Parliament spoke of 'the snobbery, jobbery and robbery of the House of Commons'.

The meeting was chaired by W.M. Thompson, the editor of *Reynolds'*, and speakers included Tom Mann, pioneer trade unionist and the first Secretary of the Independent Labour Party, George Howell, the first Secretary of the London Trades Council, William Steadman, Fabian and a member of the Parliamentary Committee of the TUC, and Will Thorne, the Secretary of the Gasworkers' Union. Adopting the objects printed on the membership certificate, the meeting ended with three cheers for *Reynolds' Newspaper*, three for Tom Mann, three for the League and the singing of the 'Marseillaise'.

At the end of the first year of the League's existence, a membership of 10,000 was claimed, each paying a shilling a year and proudly holding the certificate signed by W.M. Thompson as secretary. The designer of the certificate with the strangely esoteric angel remains unknown. Aware of the propaganda value of the symbols of identity, the league adopted the colours of red, white and green, produced a badge which sold by the thousand, had a banner to fly at meetings and demonstrations and produced a song book, one edition of which was printed in Welsh.

The certificate survives as evidence of one of the many attempts by working people to win democratic representation in Parliament for all men and women.

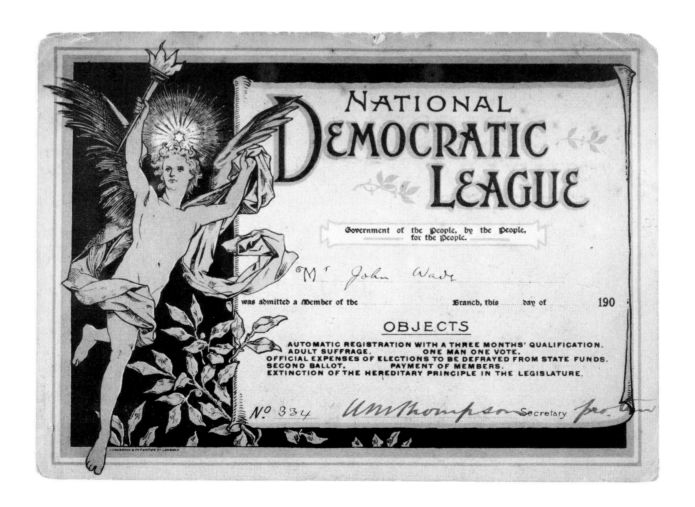

The Independent Labour Party celebrated its twenty-first birthday on 11 April 1914 with a 'Coming of Age' conference at Bradford, the same city where the inaugural meeting had taken place in 1893. Keir Hardie presided over the proceedings as he had done at that first historic conference and remembered clearly the comrades who had gathered there, the well-known and the less famous, Ben Tillett, Bob Smillie, James Sexton, Ben Turner, Bernard Shaw, Pete Curran, James Sims, Tom Smith, Alf Settle and scores of others. The programme at the first conference included demands for:

Abolition of child labour under fourteen years of age.
Legal eight hour maximum working day.
State provision for the aged, sick and disabled workers and for widows and orphans.
Work for the unemployed.

In his presidential speech Hardie said, 'In those days it was tenaciously upheld by the public authorities here and elsewhere that it was an offence against the laws of nature and ruinous to the State for public authorities to provide food for starving children or independent aid for the aged poor. Even safety regulations in mines and factories were taboo. They interfered with the "freedom of the individual". As for such proposals as an eight hour day, a minimum wage, the right to work and municipal houses, any serious mention of such classed a man as a fool . . . if today there is a kindlier social atmosphere it is mainly because of twenty-one years' work of the ILP.'

To mark the anniversary, a special 'Coming of Age' certificate was designed by Gordon M. Forsyth that reflects the internationalism that was central to the spirit and policy of the ILP. Workers of all lands are illustrated proudly marching along the road to the socialist commonwealth beneath the motto 'Socialism, the hope of the world'. The female figure on horseback is wearing a 'cap of liberty while her companion is draped in a red cape'. Forsyth was a painter, potter and stained-glass window artist who had studied at Gray's School of Art in Aberdeen and then won a scholarship to the Royal College of Art. His work was widely exhibited, including the Royal Academy, Glasgow Institute of Fine Arts and the Royal Institute of Painters in Water Colours.

St George's Hall, the venue for the conference, echoed the theme of the certificate, the bright colours of the flags of many nations draping the walls. The delegates, including many from overseas socialist parties, were greeted with an opening 'Song of Liberty' specially composed for the occasion by Dr Granville Bantock, played by the Kings Cross Prize and the Cleckheaton Victoria bands. The atmosphere was festive with a procession of Socialist Sunday Schools through the city, a dinner for foreign delegates, a grand carnival and a fancy dress competition. At the conference, Monsieur Camelmat, a veteran socialist from the Commune, addressed the delegates, as did Catherine Marshall of the National Union of Women's Suffrage Societies. The concluding speech came from Hermann Müller of the German Social Democratic Party, was given in German and translated by Sidney Webb.

Keir Hardie, whose signature as Chairman appears on the certificate together with that of Francis Johnson, Secretary, said, 'While I have anything to give, it shall be given ungrudgingly to the child of my life, the ILP.'

In 1928 the Amalgamated Society of Woodworkers decided that the society should officially mark its appreciation of the veterans of the union. To those members with fifty years continuous membership in any of the ten unions that had merged to make up the ASW it was decided to present a coloured jubilee certificate set in a frame a woodworker would be proud of, made of solid rosewood.

The design was created by Arthur Mostyn, well known in the labour movement, and depicted a 'finely proportioned archway, surmounted by a striking figure of labour, bearing the words at the top, Faithful Service', each stone of the portal

representing one of the unions that made up the Society, from the General Union of Carpenters and Joiners founded in 1827, to the Amalgamated Cabinet Makers and the Scottish Cabinet Makers, formed in 1918. The keystone of the arch is the Amalgamated Society of Woodworkers. Each branch was invited to send in names of men eligible for the certificate and the request brought an immediate response of almost 600 names.

The presentation ceremonies in the branches were warm and emotional as the veteran trade unionists expressed their thanks, looked back over a life with the tools and gave advice to the young. One of the first to receive a certificate was Brother William Henderson of Scarborough, aged eighty-nine, who brought his original membership card of 1859, signed by Robert Applegarth, to show to the branch. At Widnes Brother Arnold Young showed his card he had received on joining and told how he had been sacked for being in the union: his employer asked him did he 'belong to the club'? Young replied, 'Would you like to have a look at my card?' To which his employer replied, 'Neow! I want neowt to do with thee nor thee card, so tha can goo.'

Some responded to the presentation by making spirited speeches that belied their years, like Brother Brown of Coventry who, at over eighty, said, 'I am grieved to know that while millions are on the verge of starvation, the great combines are daily gambling with the people's food and making it harder to live. It will not get better but worse, until the young men and women fill the House of Commons with men like Brother Viant.' Apart from stirring and often humorous tales of the trade from years ago, the evening usually included some musical entertainment. At Bristol in 1929 it is recorded that 'Miss Burnett sang very sweetly, whilst Sylvia, comedienne and dancer, was a huge success.' Monologues, piano playing, humorous sketches and stand-up comics were intermingled with the presentation of watches, clocks, silver-topped canes and the coveted certificate. The end of the ceremony was invariably 'Boys of the Old Brigade' and 'Auld Lang Syne' as the stalwarts bid their brothers goodnight.

ginger in colour, as was the certificate; the badge carried a red 'G' in a capital letter and priced one shilling, 'to be worn by members only'.

From the 'Ginger shop' at 173 Hampstead Road, London, supporters could buy pamphlets, books, postcards of Labour leaders, the Ginger Club song book and gramophone records of the 'Red Flag' and the 'Internationale'. The club offered fraternal aid to any member of the club upon production of the certificate. From 5 March 1927 the front and back cover of *Lansbury's Labour Weekly* was printed on ginger-coloured paper and the readers urged to 'Give 'em ginger'.

On 9 July 1927 the paper announced a General Meeting of Club members to be held at Mortimer Hall, Regent Street, admission by badge or certificate. The paper was failing and the following Saturday saw the last issue of *Lansbury's Labour Weekly*. George Lansbury's ill health and the inability of the paper to win advertising revenue spelt the final demise not only of the paper but the club. The final issue carried a cartoon by Reginald Brill that showed a working man shaking hands with a person out of the picture, standing upon a road winding into the distance, with the caption, 'Goodbye, good luck, the road lies straight before you.'

As an epitaph the Ginger Club left an awful parody of the words of the 'Red Flag':

> The People's bread is Gingerbread
> The stuff that makes the Country red,
> And when the People's spirits sink
> We give 'em Ginger wine to drink
> Then wear the Ginger in your coat
> Whene'er you work or fight or vote!
> Let cowards seek a safer clime
> We'll give 'em GINGER every time.

'The Ginger Club' was a spirited attempt to inject unity and fight into a labour and trade union movement still shaken from the consequences of the miners' lock-out and General Strike of May 1926. Launched by *Lansbury's Labour Weekly* on Saturday, 11 December 1926, the first membership certificate was issued to A.J. Cook, Secretary of the Miners' Federation of Great Britain, and signed by George Lansbury as President of the Club. The Ginger Club combined serious intent with childlike humour in its efforts to rally support for the paper and the cause of socialism. Enrolment cost one shilling, the money being used to promote the sales of the paper, though this could have made very little difference to the precarious financial task of producing a weekly journal. Lansbury outlined the serious aim of those joining to become part of 'a movement to bring a spirit of fraternity and goodwill into the life and work of trade unionists, socialists, communists, anarchists – all who are working and want to work for the establishment of socialism in our time.' The Club organised the sales of socialist literature, especially *Lansbury's Labour Weekly*, supported the *Daily Herald* and organised social events embracing entertainment and propaganda.

Contributing to the serious discussion on the future of the movement was a weekly Parliamentary report from Ellen Wilkinson and articles by Raymond Postgate, G.D.H. Cole and Ben Turner. On the humorous side was the password of the Club, 'Ginger, you're barmy' and a weekly run of puns and jokes that were at the level of form one elementary school, e.g. 'Gentlemen prefer blondes, but WORKERS prefer GINGER', 'What's trumps – why Ginger Clubs' and 'You're a better man than I am, Ginger Din!' There were references to Ginger B. Shaw and H. Ginger Wells and a riposte to the Colman's Mustard Club, 'What is Labour's mustard club, why Ginger!' The Club issued a badge, square in shape because 'we stand foursquare to the enemy',

of whole heart cometh hope.

This is to Certify that *Gaadton Branch*
is enrolled a Member of the Women's Co-operative
Guild : a self-governing organization of *80,000*
Women, who work through Co-operation for the
welfare of the people, seeking Freedom for their
own progress, and the Equal Fellowship of men
and women in the Home, the Store, the Workshop
and the State.

Date. *March 1937*.

Eleanor Barton
General Secretary.

'What I want to know is, why are we held in such little esteem among men? Why is the feeblest type of man called an old woman? Why do our lecturers dislike to speak to a "parcel of women"? Why is "woman hearted" a term of reproach?' These rhetorical questions were put by Alice Acland in the 'Women's Corner' of *Co-operative News* early in 1883 and expressed her concern for the role of women in both the co-operative movement and in society. Editor of the 'Women's Corner' section of the paper and concerned with cookery, child care, needlework and the like, she saw the 'Corner' as a means to unify women within the co-operative movement.

Supported by Mary Lawrenson, who suggested through the 'Corner' in February 1883 that they should promote an independent body for instructional and recreational classes for mothers and single girls, the idea of a guild for women was mooted. The Women's League for the spread of Co-operation was launched and destined to grow into a powerful, radical, feminist movement, the Co-operative Women's Guild.

Early growth was pitifully slow, seven members by April 1883 and only 195 a year later. Women in most working class homes were tied to a treadmill cycle of housework and children, financially administered with starvation wages. To leave the housework for a few hours and to go alone to a meeting was socially unacceptable and the practicalities of taking on some administrative or organisational responsibility were often insurmountable. Margaret Llewellyn Davies who became the General Secretary of the Guild in 1889 referred to the northern expression, 'Let my wife stay at home and wash my moleskin trousers.'

Despite social constraints, the guild grew, matching the continued expansion of co-operative trading. The 'stores' and the 'divi' became an integral part of working class life and the guild offered young wives and mothers the opportunity for education and feminist action. The 'woman with the basket' became an essential part of the labour movement, working and planning for a peaceful, equal and co-operative commonwealth.

The symbol of the Co-operative Women's Guild was designed by Muirhead Bone, a Glasgow-born artist who achieved fame as an etcher and dry-point engraver. The figure of the woman with the shopping basket represented the only power women had, the power to decide where to spend their husbands' wages, and became one of the most widely reproduced images in the labour movement and is still in use today. The motto 'of whole heart cometh hope' is taken from *The Vision of Piers Plowman* by William Langland, *c.* 1330-1400. For the guildswomen the vision burned with justice, hope, equality and co-operation between all.

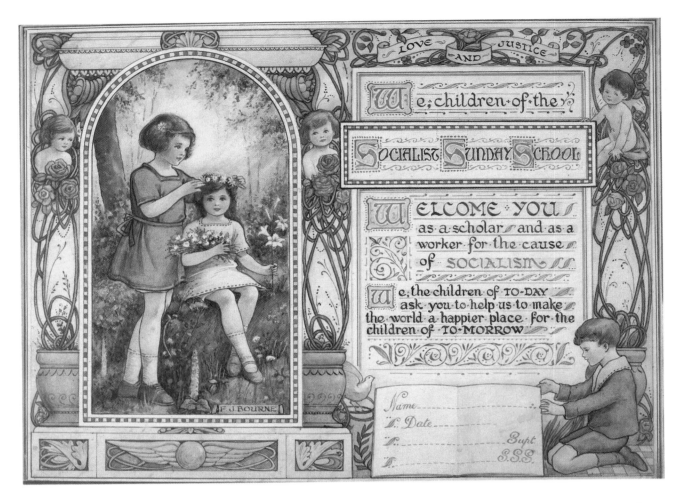

Socialist Sunday Schools preached the secular word of the religion of socialism. The origins lay in biting poverty, starving children and the need of socialists to explain to children their vision of a better world based upon love and human brotherhood. The first Socialist Sunday School may well have been the class given by Mary Gray on the second Sunday in November 1892 in Battersea. Mary Gray stated that the class arose from her experience while helping at a soup kitchen run by the Social Democratic Federation. She was brushing crumbs from the counter top at the end of the day when a small child came into the kitchen and said, 'Don't throw them away, missus, my sister would eat them.' The child was from the family of a dock labourer and she wondered how to explain to children the causes of poverty and unemployment. She discussed the matter with her husband and other members of the SDF but received little encouragement, though eventually they arranged for her to have the use of a room. At her first class there was but one boy and one girl, and the girl was her own daughter. She records telling them that she hoped this would be the start of a great movement.

About the same time the Clarion movement was forming Cinderella clubs for hungry children, meeting on Sundays, and the Labour Church movement, particularly in Yorkshire, was beginning to teach children socialist principles on Sunday afternoons. In Scotland, led by Caroline Martyn, Keir Hardie and Archie McArthur, the Socialist Sunday Schools movement gradually took shape and by 1901 had schools in most of the major cities and published its own monthly journal, the *Young Socialist*.

The movement was based on love and the emphasis was put on moral principles and service to one's fellows. The beauty and joy of nature was extolled and the exploiters of human labour and the despoilers of natural beauty condemned. The movement offered itself to working class families as an alternative to the doubtful social values taught at the Sunday Schools of the established church. The children became part of a socialist

family, 'named' instead of christened and with ten socialist precepts replacing the ten commandments. They reflect the values of socialist ideology and a humanist approach to life. They read:

1. Be friendly to your school fellows remembering that they will be your fellow workers in life.
2. Love learning which is the food of the mind.
3. Make every day worthwhile by good and useful deeds and kindly actions.
4. Honour the good, be courteous to all, bow down to none.
5. Do not hate or speak evil of anyone. Do not be revengeful, but stand up for your rights and resist oppression.
6. Do not be cowardly. Be a friend to the weak and love justice.
7. The wealth of the world is produced by labour and should be shared, each according to his needs.
8. Observe and think in order to discover the truth. Do not believe what is contrary to reason and never deceive yourself or others.
9. Do not think that because we love our own country, we should hate other nations or wish for war.
10. Work for the day when all men and women will be free citizens of the world and live in peace.

The movement had its own churchlike catechism of question and answer: 'What is our object?' Answer, 'Our object is to realise socialism', through eight questions and answers to be learned and remembered. Unlike the established church, however, the movement was anti-militarist; while Church of England children marched on Empire Day with regimental colours, socialist children marched on May Day with the red banners of socialism. The socialist schools issued colourful certificates of membership upon enrolment, each signed by the 'Superintendent'. It was Fred Bourne, a Socialist Sunday School Superintendent, that designed the illustrative certificate of

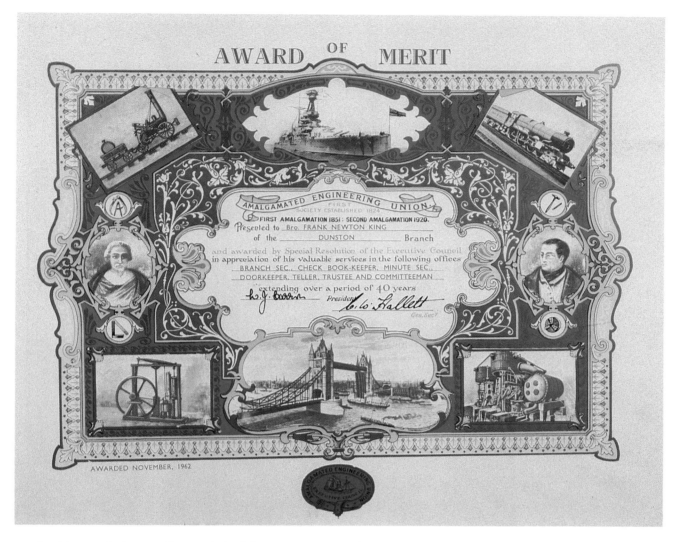

AWARDED NOVEMBER, 1962

membership, a work of extraordinary artistic ability. A man loved by the children he taught, he was known to them as 'Uncle Fred'. Less than five feet in height, he was crippled, moving only with the aid of a crutch and a stick. The children revelled in his talks, which he illustrated with chalk drawings on a blackboard while supported by his crutch. A collector of Northumbrian folk songs, he was an accomplished musician and he taught the children to sing the songs he discovered. Little is known of his life beyond the beautiful cars, certificates and drawings he has left as his monument to his love of life and socialism. He lived alone and gave his life to the cause of socialism through the ILP and the Socialist Sunday Schools movement. He died sometime during the 1930s in a home for men, the premises a former workhouse, tragic victim of the capitalist system he tried so hard to change.

'The VC of the ASE', the Victoria Cross of the Amalgamated Society of Engineers, was the trade name for the Certificate of Merit awarded for long and dedicated service in the Engineering Union. The certificate awarded to Brother Frank Newton King in 1962 for forty years of membership and branch office in the Amalgamated Engineering Union has the roots of its design in the earlier emblem and merit certificate of the old ASE.

Founded on 6 January 1851 by an amalgamation of the Mechanics' Friendly Union, the Society of Vicemen and Turners, the Millwrights' Society and the Steam Engine Makers, the newly named Amalgamated Society of Engineers ran a competition for the design of an emblem. The competition was won by a remarkable artist and engineer, James Sharples, who was rewarded with a prize of £5 for his superb allegorical and craft design. Sharples, one of thirteen children of a Yorkshire ironfounder, started work in the Phoenix factory in Bury. Hardly able to read or write, he developed his draughtsmanship by

drawing boiler designs in chalk on the factory floor under the direction of a foreman boilermaker. Sharples included in his prizewinning emblem the head of an ancient Greek, probably intended as a representation of Euclid, which also appears on the left side of the AEU certificate. He also depicted a Watt rotative wooden-framed engine which appears beneath the Greek head. The date and designer of the certificate remains unknown but the cameos of Stephenson's *Rocket*, the Watt rotative engine, the steam engine and the pair of engines for a twin screw vessel, all appear on the cover design of the *Amalgamated Engineer's Journal* in January 1901, albeit the steam engine of an earlier design than the King class Great Western Railway engine that is used on the AEU certificate.

The original certificate embracing some features of Sharples' 1851 emblem was designed in the last decade of the nineteenth century. An 1899 copy of the *Engineer's Journal* gives details of a presentation ceremony held at the Co-op Hall, Bury, at which a gold watch and a 'certificate of merit recently brought into use' was presented to Alderman T.S. Collinge by the Executive Council for thirty years' membership and service to the ASE in general and the Bury branch in particular. Such ceremonies, apart from the serious speeches, would include songs, recitals and piano-forte solos from fellow members and end with the singing of 'Auld Lang Syne'.

The Award of Merit certificate was re-designed in 1920 upon the amalgamation of the ASE with a number of other unions in the engineering industry to form the Amalgamated Engineering Union. Nevertheless, the certificate retains its direct link with the 1851 union, demonstrating the pride of its members in the products of their craft skills. Stephenson's *Rocket* established the possibility of high speed travel as distinct from low speed haulage, the battleship, probably HMS *Vanguard*, was the greatest of the 'Dreadnoughts', the *King George V* was the

The secret of our success has been our ability to unite men of diverse gifts, giving to each an outlet for his special talents.... The Socialist Movement is not for a day, but for all time.
Keir Hardie.

In commemoration of the Fiftieth Anniversary of the Labour Party

and recording the membership of —
A.S. KEMSHEAD
during the Jubilee year.

The foundations of a true Socialist Society must be laid in the hearts & minds of men and women. Socialists will be judged not by what they say, but by what they are.
C.R. Attlee.

culmination of locomotive development on the Great Western Railway and the marine engine was fitted to more large vessels than any other kind. Watt's rotative engine was the first to be used extensively for driving factory machinery and was a powerful influence on the spread of industrialisation. Tower Bridge, raised and lowered by steam machinery, was a symbol of London's commerce, the heart of the Empire at the time when British engineering products were renowned throughout the world.

The identity of the man on the right of the certificate remains a mystery. It is not William Allan or William Newton, the founders of the ASE, for they were both bearded. It is unlike Stephenson or Brunel and the only certainty is that he was an engineer of some note in either the industry or the trade union movement.

On 27 February 1900, 129 delegates assembled at the Memorial Hall, Farringdon Street, London, to 'devise ways and means for the securing of an increased number of Labour Members in the next Parliament'. The next Parliament came within eight months, the so-called 'Khaki' election held in the jingoistic atmosphere of imperial victories in South Africa, with the Labour Representation Committee fielding fifteen candidates and achieving only three successes, Keir Hardie, John Burns and Richard Bell of the Amalgamated Society of Railways' Servants. Yet, in less than half a century, the Labour Party was at the pinnacle of power, having won the General Election of 1945 by polling over 12,000,000 votes and winning 393 seats. Amid the euphoria of victory, bonfires were lit in the streets, people danced and old men wept at the joyful dawning of the millennium. When the House of Commons met, the newly elected Labour Members horrified the Tories by singing the 'Red Flag'.

Despite enormous legislation for social change, the gleam faded and preparations for the victorious celebration of the fiftieth anniversary of the founding of the Labour Party were overshadowed by the prospect of the General Election of 23 February 1950. When the national celebrations began on 2 February with an Eve of Conference Jubilee Reception and Dance at the Hammersmith Palais de Danse (tickets 4s., excluding refreshments), it required more than the music of Lou Praeger and Johnny Swiffen could create to lift the hearts of Prime Minister Attlee and his colleagues. By the time 27 February had arrived, exactly fifty years after the meeting at the Memorial Hall, the Labour majority in the Commons had been reduced to six, despite a record vote of more than 13,000,000.

The programme of events to mark the Jubilee included a Service of Thanksgiving and Dedication arranged by the Parliamentary Socialist Christian Group and held at Westminster Abbey, a concert at the Empress Hall organised by the *Daily Herald*, the publication of a history of the party, *Fifty Years' March* by Francis Williams, and the issue of a commemoration certificate. In the midst of the gloom that descended upon the Labour Party following the election results, it was fitting, though doubtless fortuitous, that the quotation from Keir Hardie printed upon the certificate included the words, 'The Socialist Movement is not for a day, but for all time.'

EMBLEMS

In the iconography of Labour, emblems, like banners, are visual symbols of identity, designed to give presence and create a sense of belonging. As the trade unions emerged to legality following the repeal of the Combination Laws in 1824, they looked for an imagery that would combine ready recognition with an impression of solid establishment and respectability. They turned to the craft guilds, readily appropriating their armorial bearings and Latin mottos, suitably adapted to meet their needs. They borrowed too from the allegorical imagery of the friendly societies, Freemasons and the Church. By combining these older and readily recognised symbols of craft, brotherhood and faith with their own illustrations of the workplace, they built up a complex and ornate style of graphic art, a tribute to labour as surely as any cathedral was a tribute to God.

In their efforts to acquire a readymade history and so strengthen their existence in the eyes of the community, they looked backwards to the biblical forefathers of their crafts as if to imply a direct descendancy, an unbroken link from the earliest times. The shipwrights laid claim to Noah and his ark, the masons to the building of Solomon's Temple, bricklayers to the Tower of Babel and the tailors to the making of the first suit of clothes for Adam and Eve. The Amalgamated Society of Paperhangers and Painters of Cork depicted St Luke painting the Virgin's portrait and proclaimed themselves 'Loyal brothers of St Luke'. It was left to the carpenters to make the most audacious claim of all, depicting Joseph on their emblem and declaring him 'the most distinguished member of our craft on record and the reputed father of our Saviour.' In a more secular search for

antecedents, printers looked to Gutenberg, Caxton and Senefelder, while the Steam Engine Makers' Society seconded Stephenson and Watt.

The masons were among the older unions, formed in 1831, and were quick to adopt rites, ceremonies and regalia as befitted their craft. The emblem of the Friendly Society of Stone Masons (GU) was designed by A.J. Waudby in 1867 at the special commission of the union. Waudby was an artist of some eminence, exhibiting at the Royal Academy during the 1840s and being the designer of emblems for the Amalgamated Society of Carpenters and Joiners, and the Operative Bricklayers' Society. At the top of the emblem Waudby has placed the 'all-seeing eye' of 'the omnipotent King of Kings, looking down and diffusing the rays of glory on all beneath, that never fails to light the path of the earnest worker and fearless spirit who believes in His almighty power.' There were those who saw it as the watchful eye of the General Secretary keeping close observance on the affairs of the union and especially upon the activities of the Treasurer! Beneath the eye is the true masonic coat of arms, flanked by the figures of Prudence with lips sealed and her bridle to restrain profuse and needless expenditure and Industry with her beehive, the emblem of industry. Set in four niches are the figures of Justice, weighing the issues with her scales, Temperance with her ewers of water, Truth with her mirror and Fortitude in resolute pose. The illustration of the building of Solomon's Temple, adapted from Raphael's Vatican frescoes, was opposed by the Hulme Lodge on the grounds that it was not 'according to scriptural writ. 1 Kings 6:7 reads "it was

of quarry stone already completed that it was built and as for hammers and axes or any tools of iron, they were not heard in the house while it was being built."' Their doctrinal submission was rejected, probably on the argument for artistic licence with Raphael on the side of Waudby. As well as an accurate depiction of masons at work on site constructing a church, the emblem includes the figures of Richard Harnott, the General Secretary of the union, and Thomas Connolly, the President. The emblem was so successful that the first 3,000 were quickly sold out at a cost of 2s. 9d. each (frames at 5s. and 7s.), though production problems delayed a reprint until 1872. The emblems would have been hung in the homes of members or in the pub rooms where the lodge held its meetings. In the home, the neatly framed and brightly lithographed emblem with its implication of ancient history was a 'connecting link with the other men in his trade and society' and for his wife a 'charter of rights in sickness and death'.

Card and Blowing Room Operatives are as much a part of the Lancashire cotton industry as beamers and twisters, little piecers and big piecers, clogs and shawls. The complexities of the varied processes peculiar to the world of cotton workers would take volumes to describe. So too would an account of the trades unions that sought to organise the cotton workers by trade, town and even individual mill. The unions would be numbered in hundreds as they formed, fell, re-organised, amalgamated and finally consolidated in a declining industry.

The first amalgamation of Card and Blowing Room Operatives took place in 1886 following a thirteen week long strike in Oldham in 1885 against a ten percent reduction in wages. The unsuccessful strike taught a bitter lesson and at its conclusion the existing societies in Oldham and district formed themselves into one province with one central authority and one central fund, with George Silk as General Secretary. At their first representative meeting in April 1886, George Silk was chosen as Chairman while William Mullins was made Secretary at a salary of 35s. a week. Mullins was to remain as Secretary until his death in 1920, leading the union during a long period of continued attack from the employers. It is Mullins' signature that appears on the emblem, which was probably designed around 1890.

The emblem's design provides a good example of the iconography of trades unionism in the new machine age, depicting the new technology of the period and the newly learned skills of the operatives.

Of the three main divisions in the cotton industry, spinning, weaving and finishing, the work of the Card and Blowing Room Operative is concerned with the primary stage. Bales of cotton are depicted being unloaded from sailing ships and the picture at the bottom left of the emblem shows a bale-breaking machine in operation in a cotton chamber. To the right is shown a further stage where the cotton is fed into a scutcher in the form of an unbroken fleecy sheet like cotton wool, where the cotton is cleaned without damage to the fibres. In the top left, the 'lap', as

the sheet is called, is fed into a carding engine which separates the fibres and removes most of the remaining impurities. Top right shows a further process in the carding room where two 'rovings' of cotton (thin lengths of cotton) are combined into one, and a second action produces finer and more uniform rovings. Much of the work was carried out by women and due recognition is given to their labour in three of the cameos. The motto 'Let us then be up and doing, with a heart for any fate, still achieving, still pursuing, Learn to labour and to wait' is from 'A Psalm of Life' by Henry Wadsworth Longfellow. The mottos in the lower shields, 'Honest labour bears a lovely face' and 'Labour shall refresh itself with hope', are both from Thomas Dekker, the English Renaissance playwright. Whether they were chosen by the executive committee of the union or offered as an acceptable suggestion by Alexander Gow & Co., the designers of the emblem, is uncertain. While hardly militant, they convey a certain stoicism in the face of a ruthless employer, the new cotton magnates, product of the industrial revolution and relentless pursuers of cheap labour.

To Machinists and General Toolmakers of Birmingham and District – a General Meeting will be held in the Board Schools, Oozell Street, on Tuesday evening, February 28th 1882, to report of the committee appointed to draw up Rules etc. of a Trade Society.

That simple press advertisement announced the birth of the National Amalgamated Society of General Toolmakers, Engineers and Machinists.

The small group of skilled engineers who had met two weeks earlier on 13 February at the Ivy Green in Edward Street to draw up the rules, announced that membership would be open to blacksmiths, fitters, engineers, turners, borers, planers, shapers, drillers, slotters, general toolmakers, bicycle, tricycle and sewing machine makers who 'for various causes were unable to join any other Society'. The last phrase was a clear reference to the exclusive and 'aristocratic' role of the Amalgamated Society of Engineers, who sought to protect their high wages and accumulated funds by careful control of

admission. The result was to deter further amalgamations and to encourage the formation of small specialist engineering unions like the National Society of Amalgamated Brassworkers or the extravagantly named Amalgamated Society of Kitchen Range, Stove Grate, Gas Stoves, Hot Water, Art Metal and other Smiths and Fitters. From bedsteadmakers to edge-toolmakers the unions proliferated.

The toolmakers did not seek to rival the ASE by militancy but concentrated on the 'friendly society' side of trade unionism by offering accident, funeral, superannuation and benevolent benefits. The executive council posed the question, as good trade unionists, 'Am I my brother's keeper?' and answered emphatically, 'Yes'. At the beginning this must have posed considerable problems for the first year's income was only £91. 0s. 0d.

The union's emblem, designed and printed in the early 1900s by Percival Jones Ltd. of Birmingham, places the emphasis firmly on the insurance benefits of trades unionism. The scene

entitled 'Donation' refers to unemployment pay, donation being the word widely used by trade unionists in the latter part of the nineteenth century for unemployment benefit. Such payments had replaced the old tramping benefits and the word was less demeaning than unemployment payment. The accident cameo is a reminder of the union's sick and injury pay scheme, vitally necessary in the days before any state system of social security. The illustration of the aged engineer seated in homely comfort with wife and cat extols the advantage of the union's superannuation scheme. This illustration was also used as the centre painting for the union banner. The emblem pays tribute to the workshop skills of its members and to great engineers past, Watt and Stanley. In all, the emblem captures the essence of the aims of the Society: mutual assistance.

Eventually, in 1920, the toolmakers joined eight other unions in amalgamation with the old ASE to form the Amalgamated Engineering Union.

The solid-looking emblem of the United Society of Boiler Makers and Iron Ship Builders was published as a black and white engraving in 1874, selling to members at 3s. 6d. per copy. Founded in 1834 as the Friendly Boiler Makers' Society, their first emblem was designed by their General Secretary, William Hughes, who was allotted the task of 'obtaining an emblematic design by which the Society could easily be recognised'. Hughes contrived a coat of arms with two hammer-holding smiths as supporters, a shield quartered depicting three aspects of boiler making and the clasped hands of friendship, crowned by the proper sign of the blacksmith, an arm embowed clasping a hammer. The two supporters stood upon a scroll bearing the motto *Humani nihil alienum*, 'to humanity nothing hostile'.

The 1874 emblem was the result of an open competition and portrayed the amalgamation of the Boiler Makers with the Iron Ship Builders. Beneath the figure of Justice, four cameos illustrate the friendly society aspect of the Society, covering sickness, accident at work, death benefits and superannuation. The emblem is signed by Robert Knight who became General Secretary in 1870, succeeding John Allen who had held the post from 1857. Knight had started work at the age of twelve as a trainee general engineer in his father's workshop. After a few years he left to travel the country in search of experience and seems to have succeeded as it is recorded that he worked as an angle iron smith on the building of the Royal Albert Bridge designed by the great engineer, Isambard Kingdom Brunel. He joined the Boiler Makers' Society in 1857 at the age of thirty-seven and was active in the fight for working class education, secretary of his local Co-operative Society, a regular churchgoer and a Sunday School teacher. He remained as General Secretary for twenty-nine years and helped establish the union as a stable and powerful force in the industry, as solid a structure as the edifice depicted on the emblem.

Stemming directly from the National Amalgamated Society of Operative House and Ship Painters, formed in 1873, which in turn became the National Painters' Society in 1885 and then the National Society of Painters in 1940, the Amalgamated Society of Painters and Decorators was constituted in 1961. The emblem is misleading for although the union did not become known as the Amalgamated Society until 1961, the design is much earlier. Close inspection reveals that the title is printed on very thin card, cut to shape and firmly pasted on top of the older title of the National Painters' Society, a sensible economy. The emblem was designed by C.J. Williams and to judge from the art nouveau figure of the woman artist, the traditional can of turpentine and the style of patterns on the wallpapers was produced in the 1890s or early 1900. Even older is the armorial bearing at the head of the emblem, this being freely borrowed from the Worshipful Company of Painter-Stainers, two guild companies that were united under that common title in 1502. The crest is a 'phoenix proper', a symbol of resurrection, and the supporters are 'panthers argent, spotted with various colours, ducally crowned, collared and chained'. The use of panthers may originate from a pun on the old English phonetic pronunciation as 'panters' (painters). The first and fourth quarterings of the arms are 'three escutcheons argent' (silver shields) and the second and third, a chevron between 'three phoenix heads erased', that is, torn off and left jagged. The Latin motto, translated as 'love and obedience', is also the guild motto and completes the trade union appropriation of the ancient imagery of the medieval craft guild of the Worshipful Company of Painters-Stainers.

As for the Amalgamated Society of Painters and Decorators, they merged with the Amalgamated Society of Woodworkers in 1970 who in turn combined with the Amalgamated Union of Building Trade Workers to form the Union of Construction, Allied Trades and Technicians in 1971.

LEAFLETS

'Get out a leaflet' has been an immediate response in the labour movement to a thousand crises, the ready means of protest against injustice, the quick call to rally support, the method of spreading the word for 'the cause'. Together with street oratory, leaflets have been the easiest and most direct method of communication with fellow workers. At the factory gates, on the shop floors, through household letterboxes, million upon million have carried the message of the moment. How many times have small groups huddled around a table, late into the night, debating every word, as a list of demands, a plea for support or an expression of outrage have been drafted for the printer? To flick through a collection of trade union and labour movement leaflets is to see a printed précis of the history of the struggle of working people.

pound per week and sixpence per hour overtime', and set off to march from firm to firm for support. The next day the men of Burts, Bradbury Agnew, Waterlow's and Cassell's came out in support of the demands. Help came from an unexpected source when George Evans, a member of the important craft union, the London Society of Compositors, and an active socialist, spoke at a strike meeting with such authority that he was appointed secretary of the campaign committee, the first task of which was to draft and issue the leaflet. As more firms backed the strike and the processions from Clerkenwell to Blackfriars, Waterloo and Fetter Lane, led by banners and bands, grew in size, other organisations gave their support, including the West Southwark and North Lambeth and the Deptford Radical Clubs. By 10 September most of the important companies had conceded to the

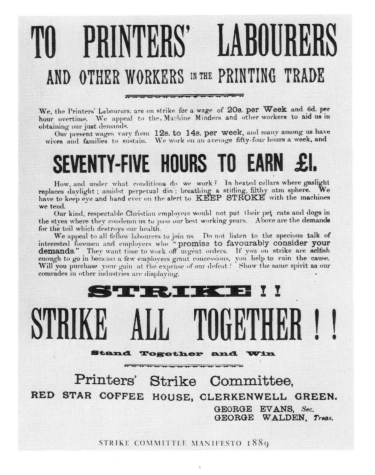

STRIKE COMMITTEE MANIFESTO 1889

In 1889, the momentous year of struggle by the 'unskilled', the printers' labourers walked out and drafted their manifesto for improved conditions and wages. What wages they were! 12s. to 14s. for a working week of fifty-four hours. To take home £1 on which to support a wife and children it was necessary to put in seventy-five hours of labour. What conditions they were in which to carry out that toil. The *Printers' Register* described the scene, 'usually an underground cellar, often only fit for the storage of coal. It is crowded with machinery. In many places there is no daylight, these men toil under the glare of gas light thrown on the boards. The heat is nearly always oppressive, in summer it is often intolerable. Ventilation is nearly always indifferent, in some the places stink (no other word is applicable) from the pollution of gas and the perspiration of men is so abominable that once experienced it can never be forgotten.'

The strike began at Spottiswoode's on 26 August when the men held a meeting on waste ground adjoining Old Farringdon Market. They fashioned a banner from two broomsticks and a couple of yards of calico, bearing the words, 'We demand one

demands; in other firms nobody returned without an increase in wages, though Spottiswoode's remained obdurate.

Early in February 1890 the first official meeting of the Printers' Labourers' Union was held and temporary offices were taken at the Red Star coffee tavern, Clerkenwell Green, with George Evans as the first General Secretary. A first priority was the need for a proper banner to announce the arrival of the new union and a banner fund was launched with a series of socials and concerts. The banner was unfurled the same year at a ceremony held at the Victoria Hall, the honours being performed by W. Steadman and W. Thompson. Feeling their strength, the union once again approached Spottiswoode's to pay the rate for the job. This time the firm complied but immediately provoked another dispute by sacking six men. Thus the union was born into struggle and continued in struggle to defend the living standards and working conditions of its members.

The name, Printers' Labourers' Union, was a misnomer, for the role of 'labourer' in the machine shop was to sheet feed the machine by hand at 800 to 2,000 per hour, an operation that

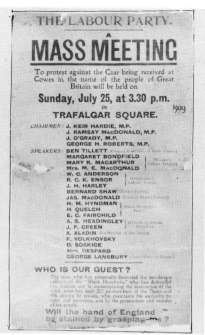

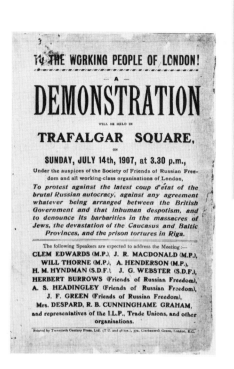

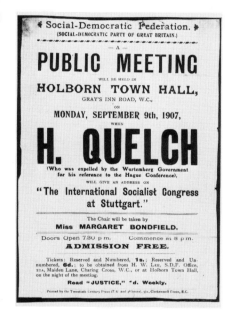

required strength, skill, experience and a good deal of nerve. Such a man was known as a 'stroker'. The work of a 'pointer' was even more demanding, as he was required to lay the sheets when working the second side so accurately that the points would enter exactly the punctures made when the machine was printing the first side. Eventually, in 1899, the name of the union was changed to the Operative Printers' Assistants' Society.

Harry Quelch, son of a Berkshire blacksmith, wage-earner at ten, shop boy, herd boy, factory worker, porter, Marxist, was given an ecstatic welcome when he returned to Britain after being peremptorily expelled from Stuttgart by the government of Württemberg. Quelch was attending the International Socialist Congress on 18 August 1907 as a representative of the Social Democratic Federation when he criticised the recent Hague Peace Conference by referring to the government they represented as a 'thieves' supper' who were 'exploiting and murdering the races of the earth'. The authorities accosted Quelch at a pre-Congress party and gave him ten hours to leave the country and he had no alternative but to part from his comrades and make the journey home. A thousand delegates from all the European countries together with socialists from America, Japan, Australia and South Africa had assembled in 'revolt against their rulers and determined to bring an end to the domination of the capitalist system.' 140 delegates came from Britain, including H.M. Hyndman, Keir Hardie, J. Ramsay MacDonald, Bruce Glasier and Alex Gossip. When the conference opened the German delegates expressed their deep regret at the expulsion of Quelch and placed an empty chair upon the table bearing the inscription 'Here sat H. Quelch, now expelled by the Württemberg Government.'

When the boat train arrived at Victoria, the crowd 'cheered for Quelch and groaned for the Wurtenburg Government.' He was greeted by Will Thorne and Jimmy Gribble, and the crowd, singing the 'Red Flag', swept him through the doorway and out onto the pavement. He was given a breakfast reception at the J.P. Restaurant where speeches were made and the owner of the restaurant refused payment for the meal.

Quelch, who refused to withdraw his remarks in Stuttgart, reiterated them in London, adding, 'There was no doubt about the rapacity of the powers represented at the Hague, every one of them had a bird or beast of prey as its emblem.' The meeting at the Holborn Hall, chaired by Margaret Bondfield (to become the first woman Cabinet Minister in Britain in 1929), was only one of a series held to welcome Quelch and report on the proceedings of the Congress.

The demonstration against the proposed entente between the Czarist Government of Russia and Britain, held in Trafalgar Square on Sunday, 14 July 1907, was organised jointly by the Independent Labour Party, the Social Democratic Federation and the Friends of Russian Freedom.

The first speaker, R.B. Cunningham Graham, denounced the Russian government as tyrannical, cowardly and bloodthirsty and called for a protest in the Commons by the small group of Labour members who supported the socialist cause. H.W. Nevinson followed, giving a vivid account of his recent visit to Russia and describing how he had seen political prisoners suspected of supporting the revolutionary risings being driven into prisons where they were to be hacked to death by the swords of the police. 'The prisons in Moscow were so full that prisoners were being shot to make room for more prisoners and schoolgirls suspected of distributing revolutionary propaganda were ordered to be stripped and flogged by the soldiers on the orders of the Governor General.'

T. Fisher Unwin, the well-known publisher, said that meetings were being held in almost every capital in Europe that day to denounce the cruelties of which the Russian autocracy had been guilty. He put the resolution that 'this meeting strongly protests against the agreement being arranged between the British Foreign Office and the Russian Government, believing that any such agreement would have the effect of strengthening the position of the autocracy against the Russian people. This meeting further protests against the coup d'état by which the Russian Duma was recently dismissed and the alteration of the electoral law by which it is sought to secure the election of a Duma that will be subservient to the autocracy. Finally, this meeting denounces the barbarities connived at by the Russian Government in the massacre of Jews, the devastation of the Caucasus and Baltic Provinces and the prison tortures in Riga and sends its heartiest good wishes to those Russians who are so nobly struggling to establish freedom and liberty in their country.'

Seconding the resolution, Will Thorne made the audience laugh by opening his speech with the words 'Friends, comrades and Russian spies'. Jack Williams of the SDF called for a march to the Foreign Office and, led by Williams and Hyndman, the march which included many women proceeded peacefully down Whitehall. When Williams mounted a parapet at the Foreign Office to put a resolution of protest to the marchers, the police pulled him down by his legs and waded into the crowd with fists and rolled capes. Mrs Despard was knocked down and even the pacifist George Lansbury was moved to try and rescue Williams from the attacks of the police. The banner of the Southwark ILP was snatched by the police and torn to shreds

and one of the poles was broken across Mrs Albery's shoulders. To the cry of 'Down with the English Cossacks', the marchers fought back with umbrellas and walking sticks, the thickest fighting taking place around the banner of the Bermondsey branch of the SDF. In the mêlée, Jack Williams escaped from the police by jumping onto a bus but was later summonsed. Two immigrant workers, one German, the other Russian, working in the tailoring industry, were arrested and later provided with bail by Fisher Unwin, who had chaired the meeting in Trafalgar Square.

'Philanthropic sweating' was the accusation made against the Salvation Army by the London Secretary of the Amalgamated Carpenters and Joiners in May 1907. S. Stennett had been keeping an exceedingly patient eye upon the activities of the London workshops of the Army for the past six years; now he had the evidence he sought. In a letter to *Reynolds' Newspaper* he described the plight of a joiner compelled to seek the assistance of the Salvation Army. A long spell of unemployment had finally compelled the unfortunate man to pawn his tools for bread; quite destitute he tramped to London and finally, being down and out, he took the advice of a friend and placed himself in the hands of the Salvation Army. He was given work at the Hanbury Street workshops and looked forward to earning a wage, redeeming his tools and starting normal life again. What he found was that he had to work from 6.30 a.m. to 6 p.m. each day with forty-five minutes for breakfast and one hour for dinner. The first week he received his board and lodgings estimated by the Army to be worth 9s. and 1s. in cash. The next six weeks he received 2s. in addition to his keep. The average wage for a joiner at that time was between £2. 5s. 0d. and £2. 10s. 0d. per week.

The exposure caused an outcry among trade unionists, especially when it was learned that the goods made by the

---

Salvation Army Sweating

**THE CAXTON HALL
LABOUR CONFERENCE
DEMAND AN IMPARTIAL
PUBLIC INQUIRY!**

The following is stated to be the difference in the Price paid for carpenters' labour at the Salvation Army Joinery Works, Hanbury Street, E. :—

    Salvation Army,   **Ordinary Firm,**

     £1 4s. 6d.   **£6**

(Other serious charges are brought against the Army by Mr. STENNETT, Secretary of the Carpenters' Union.

The 'Daily News' (July 21st) *says* :—

"*Sweated Labour breeds CRIME and PAUPERISM.*"

What do the Salvation Army soldiers

themselves say ?

A Demonstration of Protest against these Un-fair conditions will be held in Trafalgar Square 2nd or 3rd Sunday in September

1908

inmates of the Hanbury workshops were sold on the open market, undercutting prices.

The arguments were emotive. For the union, A.W. Harder, Chairman of the Joiners' Committee, said at a public meeting at Chandos Hall, 'The men were deprived of their liberty, penned in day after day, worked as many hours as the Army could squeeze out of them, paid a paltry wage and fed on a workhouse diet.' In defence, Colonel Moss of the Salvation Army said, 'The men are ragged and dirty, hopeless, they are fed and clothed by the Army and they are at liberty to find other employment. Are we to pay a fellow who is picked up out of the gutter the trade union rate of wages, or are we to give him what he is worth?'

The war lasted for years, the Salvation Army steadfastly refusing to understand that goods produced by cheap labour, undercutting trade union rates, were a threat to the living of craftsmen in the same area and could only lead to more destitution. Letters to the press, public meetings, pamphlets for and against, all were repeated shots in the protracted battle. The trade unions formed a United Workers' Anti-Sweating Committee composed of socialist bodies, trades councils and trade unions. The meeting advertised by the leaflet brought thousands to Trafalgar Square carrying banners with slogans 'End Salvation Army Sweating' and 'Close the Salvation Army Sweatshops'. Other towns and cities joined in exposing the conditions in their own workshops or 'Elevators' as they were known in Army jargon, public meetings of protest being held from Southport to Derby.

The Salvation Army refused to close the workshops on the grounds that they were saving destitutes from starvation. They were also providing themselves with the opportunity of saving their souls. The Army offered to restrict the making of goods to their own use, but this too was unacceptable to the unions although it provided the eventual solution as the war became one of attrition.

Perhaps the most damning indictment of the Salvation Army's methods was provided by the document that inmates of the Norwich 'Elevator' were obliged to sign before receiving help. It ran to seven paragraphs, the first of which read, 'I declare that being unable to find work elsewhere and being homeless, friendless and destitute, I have been admitted to the City Colony, to work only for my subsistence and shelter and that everything allowed me beyond this will be so allowed merely by the kindness of the Governor.'

At the Hanbury Street workshop the men sweated over fifty hours a week for 2d. an hour beneath the scriptural text 'Whatsoever thy hand findeth to do, do with thy might.'

'One pennorth of brawn and a halfpenny-worth of pickles form the daily dinner of thousands of children.' This extract from a report by Robert Sherhard on the life and work of children in Britain in 1905 was typical of what he found as he toured the country on his nationwide investigation. Women feeding babies on old bits of bread and cold potatoes while they themselves went without, children scrabbling for garbage from street markets, dinners of bread and marge, breakfasts of stale bread and rancid dripping, skimmed milk, red herrings, adulterated and rotten food – this and worse was the lot of hundreds and thousands of children. 'Starvation wages' was not a political catch phrase but a damning reality for millions of workers, men, women and children engaged in obnoxious, dangerous, excessive toil that did not pay enough to provide adequate food. The 'Farthing Breakfasts' of the Salvation Army, the soup kitchens of the Clarion Vans, the Cinderella Clubs, the Church Dinner funds, were all born of the need to feed starving children. Yet, despite the passing of the Education (Provision of Meals) Act in 1906, local opposition from Liberal and Tory Councils to the provision of school meals funded from the rates was conducted with ferocity.

Teachers facing barefooted, cold and hungry children in the classrooms were told that to feed them from the public purse would tempt parents to abrogate their responsibility to the state and that those who advocated school feeding refused to recognise this moral and social danger. That a government report in 1904 had stated it was 'the height of cruelty to subject half starved children to the process of education' was ignored. The

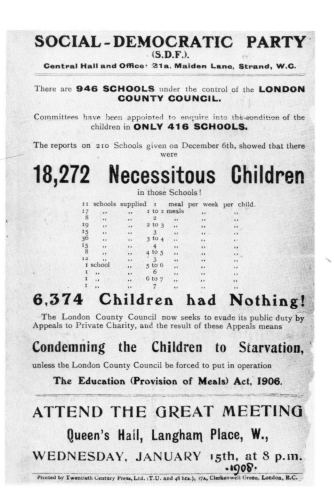

SOCIAL - DEMOCRATIC PARTY
(S.D.F.).
Central Hall and Office 21a. Maiden Lane, Strand, W.C.

There are **946 SCHOOLS** under the control of the **LONDON COUNTY COUNCIL.**

Committees have been appointed to enquire into the condition of the children in **ONLY 416 SCHOOLS.**

The reports on 210 Schools given on December 6th, showed that there were

18,272 Necessitous Children
in those Schools!

11 schools supplied	1	meal per week	per child.		
17 "	"	1 to 2 meals	"	"	
8 "	"	2	"	"	
19 "	"	2 to 3	"	"	
15 "	"	3	"	"	
36 "	"	3 to 4	"	"	
15 "	"	4	"	"	
8 "	"	4 to 5	"	"	
12 "	"	5	"	"	
1 school		5 to 6	"	"	
1 "	"	6	"	"	
1 "	"	6 to 7	"	"	
1 "	"	7	"	"	

6,374 Children had Nothing!

The London County Council now seeks to evade its public duty by Appeals to Private Charity, and the result of these Appeals means

Condemning the Children to Starvation,

unless the London County Council be forced to put in operation

The Education (Provision of Meals) Act, 1906.

ATTEND THE GREAT MEETING

Queen's Hall, Langham Place, W.,

WEDNESDAY, JANUARY 15th, at 8 p.m.
·1908·

Printed by Twentieth Century Press, Ltd. (T.U. and 48 hrs.), 37A, Clerkenwell Green, London, E.C.

FEED THE CHILDREN!

Under the Education (Provision of Meals) Act, 1906, the London County Council has power to levy a halfpenny rate to provide Meals for Children in Public Elementary Schools. This they have declined to do.

Charity is Inadequate.

Children are Starving.

A

TOWN'S MEETING

WILL BE HELD IN THE

TOWN HALL,
Mare Street, Hackney, ON

·Wednesday, February 5th, 1908,
AT 8 P.M.,

To consider this question and demand that the L.C.C. shall levy the Permissive Halfpenny Rate.

The Mayor (Alderman George Billings, L.C.C.)
WILL PRESIDE. SPEAKERS :

E. C. Fairchild,	Rev. G. B. Chambers,
John Stokes,	H. W. Inkpin,
E. Friend,	Albert Inkpin,
E. Crump,	O. H. Stephenson.

Printed by Twentieth Century Press, Ltd. (T.U. & 48 hrs.), 37A, Clerkenwell Green, E.C.

cry of the children was for food; the cry of the rich was charity. In a letter to *The Times* in 1907, Lords Rosebery, Rothschild and Avebury wrote in reference to a call for the LCC to use its powers to levy a halfpenny rate to provide school dinners, 'We do not think it fair that this burden should be laid on the general body of ratepayers . . .' and appealed to those with comfortable homes to 'make a voluntary offering towards the sum required and so avoid the composition of a rate which will probably entail consequences which those who watch the progress of Socialism cannot contemplate without the gravest misgiving.'

Fortunately for the hungry children the socialists continued to fight for the provision of free school meals wherever they had representation. The Social Democratic Federation tore to pieces the arguments of the Liberals and Tories that charity was adequately providing sufficient meals by publicising the facts and figures. In one small example, Bay Street School, Hackney, with twenty necessitous children, was providing only three meals a week!

In Bradford, where Fred Jowett, an ILP Councillor, had fought an election on the issue of providing at least one free meal a day as early as 1904, and won, the Liberals rallied the council to defeat the small Labour group, arguing that 'a moral principle was at stake: the principle of parental responsibility, the very bedrock of family life, religion and respectability'. Jowett was scathing in the long debate: 'I did not hear anything of these moral responsibilities when we voted £3,000 as a salary to the Mayor in order to hang bunting in the streets, and yet we are told of the moral consequences of spending £5,000 to feed hungry children . . . I will vote no money for the purchase of pictures, I will vote no money for any decorative purpose until the needs of the children have been met.'

Jowett's historic campaign led directly to the passing of the

1906 Act and was hailed by socialists as a precedent and a triumph. Keir Hardie sent him a prophetic message of congratulations saying it foreshadowed a time when the 'provision of school meals would pass into the common life of the people'. In October 1907 the White Abbey School, Bradford, became a dining centre for the first free meals, served to the children of Green Lane School by their headmaster, Jonathan Priestley (the father of J.B. Priestley) and his staff. The long fight for the funded feeding of children had begun, but it had far to go. By 1910 only one hundred authorities were providing school meals out of the rates and charity meals were still common. Bradford again set an example in the provision of meals during school holidays; until they did so, holiday times were also hungry times. It was not until 1945 under a Labour government that a full programme of school dinners and school milk was finally implemented.

Jarrow and Winston Churchill. It is doubtful if there are another two names that evoke such passionate anger and bitter memories in the Labour movement unless they are Tonypandy and Winston Churchill. By a quirk of history, the name of Churchill is obliquely linked with Jarrow on this torn relic of the Parliamentary election of 1906, before either had finally acquired the notoriety that was to weave their names deep into the folklore of British working class history.

The election for the Jarrow seat was a straight fight between the sitting member for thirty-two years, Sir Charles Mark Palmer, Liberal, and Pete Curran, Labour. Palmer was a millionaire shipbuilder and virtual owner of Jarrow; Curran, born of Irish parents, had started work at the age of ten and was an engineer and a committed socialist.

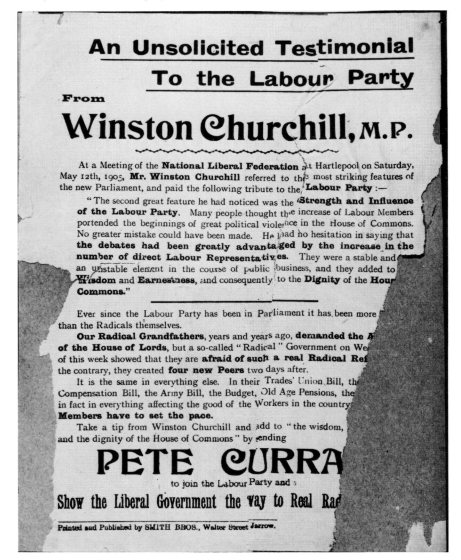

THE RAILWAY CRISIS.

UNDER THE AUSPICES OF THE

EAST END BRANCHES OF THE SOCIAL-DEMOCRATIC FEDERATION

—A—

MASS MEETING

ON THE ABOVE QUESTION WILL BE HELD IN

VICTORIA PARK,

On Sunday Afternoon, November 3, 1907.

Chair to be taken at 2.30 by A. A. WATTS

(London Society of Compositors).

THE MEETING WILL BE ADDRESSED BY

WILL THORNE, M.P.,

Councillor J. JONES   Alderman J. H. BANKS
(Gasworkers),   (Railway Workers),

W. J. PEARCE   **B. EDELSTEIN**   **W. WINDSOR**
(Sec. Mile End S.D.F.),   (Whitechapel S.D.F.),   (Sec. Bethnal Green S.D.F.),

JOHN SCURR   **E. CRUSE**   **W. J. REEVES**
(Shop Assistants),   (Toolmakers),   (Mile End S.D.F.),

Fellow Workers! This Meeting is called by Social-Democrats to express sympathy with the Railway Workers in their present struggle, and to lay before you the Socialist view of the whole system of exploitation by the Railway Companies of the country.

Stand by Your Class!

W. J. PEARCE, Secretary to the Committee, 100, Mile End Road.

Printed by Twentieth Century Press, Ltd. (T.U. & 48 hrs.), 37A, Clerkenwell Green, London, E.C.

To say that Palmer virtually owned Jarrow is not to exaggerate, for Jarrow was also known as Palmerstown and was in every sense a company town. The hospital was the Palmer Memorial Hospital, with a bronze statue of the man to remind the poor of their benefactor, the only libraries were in the Palmer Mechanics' Institute and even the church had a stained-glass window to his wife. The Town Hall had a Palmer portrait in the council chamber, the corridors were adorned with photographs of the Palmer Works, the streets of Jarrow were named after early managers and directors of the company and Palmers' general manager, company secretary and chief cashier were on the Town Council. Men worked for Palmer and stood up to him at risk of their livelihood. Jarrow was the epitome of free enterprise capitalism and Sir Charles Mark Palmer at the age of eighty-four did not intend to surrender his safe seat, his town, to any socialist agitator.

Pete Curran had helped form the Gas Workers' Union in the great struggle of 1889 and was a champion of the 'new unionism'. An early member of the Social Democratic Federation, he was an eloquent and persuasive speaker and immersed in the socialist and trade union movement. Among his diverse activities for the cause, Curran was Chairman of the General Federation of Trade Unions, a member of the Fabian Society, on the Executive Committees of both the Labour Party and the Independent Labour Party and a delegate to many International Socialist conferences. A delegate to the foundation conference of the Labour Party in 1900, Pete Curran's brand of socialism did not embrace the Lib-Lab alliance and he 'opposed Liberals as enemies of the working class posing as sympathisers'. His use of Churchill's remarks (as a Liberal MP) about the handful of

Labour Members was calculated to demonstrate the contradictions within the Liberal Party and persuade working people that the Labour Party was now the established political alternative to the Liberals.

Sir Charles Palmer, the benevolent capitalist who threw pennies to the children from his carriage during the election campaign, duly won the seat, but not without a strong fight by Curran who polled 5,093 votes to Palmer's 8,047 in the heaviest poll the town had known. Palmer had been returned unopposed in the two previous elections and the Conservatives again refrained from standing a candidate lest they should split the vote and allow 'an avowed socialist' to win. *The Jarrow Express* loyally reported before the poll that 'not one man who was getting his living in the yard dreamed of such a thing as opposing Mr Palmer . . . the old love and enthusiasm burns as brightly as ever and the battle cry today is as of yore, 'Palmer for Jarrow'.

Pete Curran fought an uncompromising campaign for socialism and said that he would not leave Jarrow until he had won it for Labour. He did not have long to wait, for in the following year Palmer died and Pete Curran took his seat as the Member for Jarrow alongside his two comrades from the Gasworkers' Union, Will Thorne and J.R. Clynes.

'The wages of sin is death, but the wages of the Great Eastern is starvation' was a railwayman's apt comment scrawled upon his ballot paper when voting in support of a strike for the 'Railwaymen's Charter' in 1907. The remark was prompted by the fact that earnings for railway workers had increased by only five percent since 1886, while wages for other industries had risen by up to twenty-nine percent. 100,000 railway workers,

LONDON TRADES COUNCIL

RIGHT TO WORK
DEMONSTRATION.

The State places heavy responsibilities upon its Citizens which can only be met by the FRUITS OF LABOUR, and punishes them by loss of citizenship or imprisonment when they are UNABLE to meet these responsibilities.

As the Workers must work in order TO LIVE, all Workers have a RIGHT TO DEMAND WORK.

CRIMINALS and LUNATICS ARE CARED for, FED, HOUSED, CLOTHED and GIVEN EMPLOYMENT by the State—for the STRUGGLING WORKLESS Workmen and Workwomen ALONE NOTHING practical is done.

"Society is divided into three classes— WORKERS, SHIRKERS, BEGGARS."

To which class do you belong? If the Working Class, join with your fellow workers in a demand that the GOVERNMENT SHALL ORGANISE THE UNEMPLOYED ON USEFUL AND PRODUCTIVE WORK.

---

thirty-nine percent of the industry, were paid less than £1 a week! The average wage for all grades was still a paltry 24s. 7d. Productivity and company profits had risen over the years while wages remained pegged often to subsistence level.

The disgraceful wages and long hours had led to a demand from branches for an 'all grades' campaign for higher wages, shorter hours and trade union recognition. Enthusiastic support was given by railway delegates to great conferences held in Birmingham, Glasgow and Dublin in the latter part of 1906. The demands of the men were modest enough, an eight-hour day for drivers, firemen, guards, shunters, signalmen and platelayers and a ten-hour day for other classes. The claim for drivers' wages was for 6s. 0d. a day, rising to 8s. 0d. after six years! It was the demand for union recognition, however, that brought the fiercest opposition from the autocratic directors of the privately owned railway companies. Sir Ernest Paget of the Midland Railway Company was typical when he said, 'The men are adequately paid,' and declined 'to allow any of their men to make representations as to grievances to be accompanied by anyone outside the company's own staff.'

Despite many attempts by the railway unions to meet the railway owners to discuss the claims of the men, all approaches were contemptuously refused. During the summer of 1907 calls for a strike grew in the face of the intransigence of the owners, and on 12 May of that year the unions staged mass demonstrations in support of the 'Charter'. In London 20,000 marched accompanied by twelve bands and banners flying. Throughout Britain, about 150,000 railwaymen took to the streets, the Railway Clerks' Association, the General Railway Workers' Unions, the Amalgamated Society of Railway Servants and the Associated Society of Locomotive Engineers and Firemen, united against the common enemy.

The result of the ballot for a strike, held in October 1907, was overwhelming in support of a stoppage. While the result of the ASRS vote was being announced to a huge rally at the Albert Hall (76,925 for the strike, 8,773 against), the Social Democratic Federation held a meeting of solidarity in Victoria Park with Will Thorne as the main speaker. All summer long, the SDF had put the socialist view of the conflict and had steadfastly supported the call for strike action.

At the last moment, Lloyd George, then President of the Board of Trade, sent for Richard Bell, the Secretary of the ASRS, who in an amazing about-face conceded that he would not press for union recognition if he obtained a satisfactory means of dealing with grievances and secured other improvements in hours and wages. The railway owners were off the hook for the time being, escaping official union recognition, though the conciliation scheme that was established laid the foundation for future trade union representation of the railway workers.

It was a dozen men led by 'General' Gibbon carrying a red flag that set out in the bitterly cold weather of January 1906 to march from Liverpool to London to demand the right to work. The now familiar phrase, first used by the French socialist, Louis Blanc, in 1848, was inscribed upon a yellow banner, carried in turn by the marchers as they headed towards the capital via Derby, Nottingham, Leicester, Northampton, Luton and St Albans. The small number was due in part to the requirement that only physically fit men were allowed to take part and that each had to be a bona-fide unemployed man appointed by his trade union. R.J. Gibbon, often referred to as the 'General', but elsewhere as 'Captain', was formerly of Lord George Sanger's circus where he was better known as Professor Valdo. An escapologist, Gibbon took with him on the journey a small handcart that carried his handcuffs, leg-irons and chains so that he could give street performances at the towns and villages en route to raise funds to provide for the marchers.

The march was made in appalling weather and despite the hospitality of trades councils and co-op's, the food and accommodation was often meagre and spartan. At Nottingham, by which time the number of marchers had grown to a hundred, they slept in the Co-operative Hall on straw covered with horse rugs provided by the Society. On 30 January when the march left Nottingham the men had a substantial breakfast, but after a day slogging along muddy roads, dinner at Loughborough is recorded as being bread, cheese and milk.

Many trades were represented by the marchers, including a cabinetmaker and a steeplejack, all denied the right to work. Perhaps the one non-unionist was J.H. Morley, a Christian Socialist, who joined the march at Manchester. Known in

Rochdale as 'the boy evangelist' he preached his way to London, addressing meetings in churches, halls and market squares to rouse support for the weary band.

At Leicester, cobblers mended the men's boots free of charge, while a police inspector poured out tea for them. The steeplejack told a reporter, 'Only one policeman on the route was rude to us, he shouted that we were a lot of loafers and other nasty things. We reported him and have since heard that he has been placed among the unemployed himself.' The march entered London on 8 February through Kilburn and Maida Vale in a hailstorm, trudging through mire, exhausted by the journey, to be met officially by Harry Quelch of The Right to Work National Council. After being entertained to tea by the Revd W.J. Potter of the Westbourne Grove Baptist Church, the men were taken to the homes of members of the Social Democratic Federation for the night.

On Monday 12 February 4,000 unemployed assembled on the Embankment led by a band from Poplar to escort the 'right to work' marchers to a meeting by the Reformers' Tree in Hyde Park. The speakers included Margaret Bondfield, Jack Jones, Fred Knee and Harry Gosling, but it was Jack Williams of the SDF who roused the crowd at the conclusion of the rally when he said thousands would walk the streets of the great city that night

without a bed or a meal and that thousands of little children would go to school on the morrow without any breakfast. 'Fight we must and fight we shall, and if we die, rather let us die fighting than die starving.'

The demand for the right to work was strongly supported by the London Trades Council, many of its leading members being actively involved in The Right to Work National Council. The leaflet was just one of many issued during the first decade of this century in support of the demand for useful public work for the unemployed.

Each year, from the time of his death on 3 October 1896 until the First World War, the anniversary of William Morris's death was marked by meetings of socialists in memory of their great comrade. The meeting that annually attracted the better known speakers was held in Hammersmith where Morris had led the Hammersmith Socialist Society from November 1890 and where he had lived at Kelmscott House from 1878.

The memorial meeting in 1909 followed a familiar pattern with tributes to Morris's contribution to socialism and art by men and women who had worked with him in the Social Democratic Federation, the Socialist League and the Hammersmith Socialist Society. 'No Master', a song by Morris, was sung by a few veterans of the original Hammersmith Socialist Choir and a Mrs Baker recited one of his socialist poems, 'The Day is Coming', including the famous verse,

> For that which the worker winneth
> shall then be his indeed,
> Nor shall half be reaped for nothing
> by him that sowed no seed

The meeting ended with the singing of revolutionary songs by the Willesden Socialist Choir and uplifted from the sadness of the loss of a good and talented friend they departed into the October twilight, the words of a funeral tribute from a Lancashire branch of the Social Democratic Federation in their minds and hearts, 'Comrade Morris is not dead, there is not a socialist living who would believe him dead, for he lives in the hearts of all true men and women still and will do so to the end of time.'

The Civil Service Socialist Society was formed in 1908, the inaugural conference being held at Chandos Hall, London, on 5 February of that year. Formed by Post Office workers, the Society originated from a number of small bodies, the earliest of which was the Postal Socialist League established in 1894. The Central Telegraph Office had a group known as the Pioneer Socialist Society and these two merged in 1906 to form the Post Office Socialist Society. This in turn joined with a number of other small groups to found the Civil Service Socialist Society.

The objects of the Society were stated as 'To educate the members of the Service in the principles of socialism, political action to be outside its province. Membership open to all Civil Servants providing (a) That they declare themselves socialist (b) That application be made on the official form, nominated by a member of the Society and elected by the local committee.' The subscription was agreed at 1d. per month.

Although the objects of the Society proscribed political action and were declared as 'largely evangelical', there was no doubt as to the left wing character of the Society. At an early meeting attended by some 900 postal workers, the speakers included Victor Grayson, recently elected as the first socialist MP and H.M. Hyndman, the Marxist leader of the Social Democratic Federation. The Society launched a monthly magazine entitled *Civil Service Socialist* which proclaimed 'the business of a socialist is socialism' and defined socialism as 'that system of society in which the land and means of production, distribution and exchange are collectively owned, their administration and control being exercised by the Democratic State in the interests of the entire community.' Edited by J.G. Newlove, the magazine claimed a circulation of 2,000 by the following year and the Society began to spread throughout the postal service and had thirty branches by 1908. At the first conference in 1908, the General Secretary, M.W. Beckess asked, 'Will any comrades in the Colonial Office who have not yet joined please let me have their names?' Coupled with the Central Committee of the Society sending 'May Day Greetings to their comrades in all countries', the Conservative Party became suitably alarmed. Questions were asked in the Commons, Tory members attributing sinister motives to its founders with the same mild hysteria that was to lead to the banning of trade union membership by civil servants employed at GCHQ by a Conservative government seventy-six years later!

About 1910 the movement became interested in the theories of the syndicalist movement and this no doubt prompted the invitation to Tom Mann to address the Society on 20 June 1910. This followed the participation of a large contingent from the Civil Service Socialist Society taking part in the May Day demonstration in London.

Tom Mann called his lecture 'London for Socialism' and spoke to a gathering of about 500 for one and a half hours. The meeting was chaired by Ben Tillett, who praised the work of the Society and said, 'Whether as postmen, clerks, inspectors, secretaries of high Government officials, we are all victims of the capitalist system.' Mann, who rose to speak to prolonged cheering, said he had generally found that civil servants, as a whole, considered themselves far too respectable to connect

themselves with anything like socialism, but he was glad to find a large proportion engaged as civil servants were not opposed to having a change of ideal. He spoke of those who thought that great changes could be made in the present system to benefit the workers, such as abolition of unemployment, the fixing of a minimum wage, etc., but pointed out that the incentive of the capitalist class was to make profit and that there could be no real benefit while the capitalist system remained. 'In spite of the increase in wealth, widespread poverty still exists, unemployment, overwork, female and child labour, sweating dens and the uncertainty of existence are increasing rather than decreasing.' He attacked the reformists, declaring, 'I am out and out, here and everywhere a social revolutionist – nothing will do but a complete change of the basis of society.' He continued, 'Many are now working seventy hours a week or more. The eight hours questions had been allowed to go to the wall. Where is the fight going on for better conditions? Not in Parliament or out of it. Children everywhere are dying of starvation, men out of work and foodless, passing the doors of warehouses that are stocked to the ceilings with the necessities of life. And where is the fight? The trade unions, instead of fighting the class war in earnest, are fighting only their stupid selves. They are bound up with agreements which, in their foolishness, they regard as sacred. Fancy an employer or an employers' federation that wanted to institute a lock-out in order to break the workers considering the terms of agreement!'

He concluded, 'The interest of the workers and of the employers are not identical, but diametrically opposed. Let the workers throw down the challenge and fight the battle for the emancipation of their class. Organise! Organise! Organise! Fight! Fight! Fight!' The meeting ended with a unanimous vote for industrial re-organisation on the lines he had outlined and the audience rose to sing the 'Red Flag'.

Despite the growth of the Society to all the main cities and postal depots of the country, the Society foundered with the advent of the First World War. The last issue of the *Civil Service Socialist* appeared in March 1915, and the Society soon disappeared. Nevertheless, the foundation for the building of strong trade unionism among government workers had been laid and the idea that trade unionism was for 'wage earners' only had been destroyed.

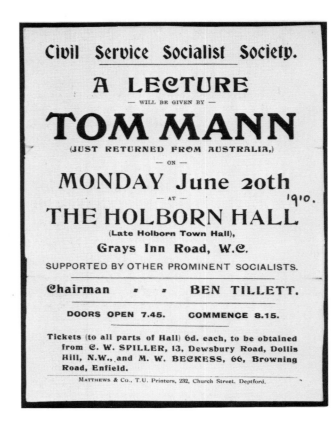

Civil Service Socialist Society.

A LECTURE
— WILL BE GIVEN BY —

TOM MANN
(JUST RETURNED FROM AUSTRALIA,)
— ON —

MONDAY June 20th
— AT — 1910.

THE HOLBORN HALL
(Late Holborn Town Hall),
Grays Inn Road, W.C.

SUPPORTED BY OTHER PROMINENT SOCIALISTS.

Chairman · · BEN TILLETT.

DOORS OPEN 7.45. COMMENCE 8.15.

Tickets (to all parts of Hall) 6d. each, to be obtained from C. W. SPILLER, 13, Dewsbury Road, Dollis Hill, N.W., and M. W. BECKESS, 66, Browning Road, Enfield.

MATTHEWS & CO., T.U. Printers, 232, Church Street, Deptford.

The meeting of representatives of the International Socialist Bureau held at Kingsway Hall, London, on 13 December 1913 was the culmination of a national campaign by the Independent Labour Party against the threat of war and conscription. Meetings were organised throughout Britain at the rate of twenty a week, with speakers like Bruce Glasier, Keir Hardie, Philip Snowden and Fenner Brockway putting to audiences of thousands the resolution 'That this demonstration of citizens having regard to the recent alarming growth in the foolish and wasteful expenditure upon armies and navies and the danger to the peace of the world thereby involved, declares its strong opposition to the agitation led by the National Service League and the armament interests in favour of making military service compulsory in Great Britain; further, realising that militarism, being an inheritance from the barbarism of the past, is in all its forms directly opposed to civic freedom and to the highest interests of the nation, and is alien to the true spirit of democracy, we rejoice at the decided anti-military attitude of the international socialist and working class movement and its growing determination to use the power of organised labour to combat the war spirit, and we call upon the organised workers and the Parliamentary Labour Party to resist by every means in their power the present alarming expenditure and particularly the proposed new blood tax of the militarist movement known as National Service.'

At Kingsway Hall the leaders of most of the socialist parties in Europe addressed the crowded meeting, fervent for peace and international working class solidarity against war. Emile Vandervelde, leader of the Belgian Labour Party, was the first speaker, rousing the audience with a speech of passion and eloquence that cast him as one of the great orators of his time. During his speech, the great writer Anatole France climbed onto the platform and Keir Hardie, chairman of the demonstration, allowed him to speak, saying, 'You have just listened to the most powerful pleader for human peace and freedom, now I am going to ask one of the greatest minds in the world to address you.' 'Socialism', declared Anatole France, 'stands not for poverty but riches, not for disorder but order. The world-wide Labour Movement is a beneficent giant, gentle yet terrible and strong, overcoming wrong and establishing right.'

Hardie's own speech was interrupted by a suffragette but he raised his voice and did not falter as women stewards of the Central London Branch of the Women's Labour League removed the disturber. Dan Irving spoke for the British Socialist Party and Herr Mockenbuhn, the German socialist leader, was given a standing ovation as he declared, 'The international socialist movement is the greatest safeguard against international conflict.' Jean Jaures, the French socialist leader, a thick-set man with shaggy hair, was greeted with an ecstatic waving of handkerchiefs and cries of 'Bravo'. One of the greatest of platform orators, he inspired the audience as he proclaimed the indissoluble unity of European workers. They left the hall with his passionate call giving way to the singing of the 'Marseillaise'. Within a year, Jaures was to be shot by a mad patriot and the

London Trade Unionists' Committee.

Burston School Strike!

A Village in Revolt!!   A Fight for Freedom and Justice!!!

A MEETING

WILL BE HELD AT THE

Bermondsey Town Hall,

Spa Road, Bermondsey,

On TUESDAY, FEB. 22nd, 1916,

for a Rally and Call for Unity.

Chair to be taken at 8 p.m. by

Dr. ALFRED SALTER, J.P.,

WITH THE ASSISTANCE OF THE FOLLOWING SPEAKERS:

MR. AND MRS. HIGDON

(THE VICTIMISED SCHOOL TEACHERS) and Children from the School of Burston

CASEY AND HIS FIDDLE

MR. H. B. WALKER
(Gen. Sec. Agricultural Labourers' Rural Workers' Union)

MR. WILL GODFREY
(National Union of Vehicle Workers)

MR. W CARTER
(Organising Sec. N.U.R.)

MR. J. BIRMINGHAM
(Organising Sec. N.U.R.)

MR. JOHN SCURR
("Herald")

MR. W. J. CRAGIE
(Bermondsey Branch N.U.R.)

Come and Hear for yourselves from Mr. and Mrs. Higdon and the brave women of Burston what they have suffered since April, 1914, and nobly struggled against the tyranny of Parson and Landowners!

LADIES ARE SPECIALLY INVITED!

Local Secretary: A. ROWLING,
183, Rolls Road, Bermondsey, S.E.

FROWDE & Co., Printers (T.U.), 244, Old Kent Road.

---

unity of the International Socialist Bureau torn to pieces by the mad chauvinism of the First World War.

The advent of the First World War did nothing to quell the strike of pupils and parents against the sacking of the headmistress and her assistant from the village school of Burston in the county of Norfolk. For this was not an educational squabble, but a fight against rural tyranny, against the old power of parson and landlord.

Annie Higdon and her husband Tom arrived at Burston to take up their new teaching posts on 31 January 1911. Both were gentle Christian Socialists who did not bow the knee to authority in the accustomed rural manner. Tom Higdon, born the son of a farm labourer, was himself active in the Agricultural Labourers' Union. Concern for their pupils and their parents, mainly poor agricultural workers, soon brought clashes with the school managers, led by the local parson, the Revd Charles Tucker Eland. Their efforts to improve the ill-lit, ill-drained, badly heated village school were provocation enough to a complacent church-dominated hierarchy, but when Tom Higdon organised the local farm labourers into the Agricultural Labourers' Union and led them to take power on the Parish Council, inflicting a humiliating defeat upon the Revd Eland (who polled nine votes), the end was surely nigh.

Allegations were made against the Higdons that they had lit a fire at the school without permission of the vicar who was chairman of the school managers, and that they had caned two girl pupils from Dr Barnado's Homes. The first allegation was true, the fire having been lit so that pupils could dry their wet clothes after having arrived soaked on a rainy morning. The second allegation was patently untrue. The outcome was the dismissal of the socialist teachers followed by a mass strike of the children, only seven attending school on the day following

the sacking. Arrangements were made to give lessons to the children on the village green and despite the prosecution of parents for the non-attendance of their children, the strike remained solid. Soon, the children were being taught in an old carpenter's shop in the village, and attracting trade union support for their resistance, the NUR donating forty-eight chairs. The parson, incensed by the wholehearted support given to the Higdons by the men, women and children of Burston, hit back by taking away glebe land of the blind owner of the carpenter's shop, Mr Sandy, and sending the churchwarden to plough up the land. An appeal to the Bishop of Norwich, secure in his palace and with an income of £4,500 p.a., elicited the advice to the poor blind man and two other villagers similarly treated to seek redress 'through legal tribunals'.

Trade union support for the strike spread, the leaflet publicising the meeting at Bermondsey being just one of a series held that week in Kentish Town, Paddington, Bermondsey and Leytonstone. The NUR organised a rally at Burston, two hundred railwaymen arriving by train with banners and bands, supported by the Agricultural Labourers' Union. 'Casey', the man with the fiddle, was Walter Hampson, first violinist of the Hallé Orchestra, who toured the country with his music and socialist propaganda while contributing a regular weekly article for the *Labour Leader*.

Eventually the trade unions raised enough money to build a school upon land given by the Parish Council, controlled by Tom Higdon and the farm labourers. The school stands alongside the churchyard, facing the village green and bears the carved inscription in stone 'Burston Strike School 1917'. Beneath are inscribed the names of the trade unions and societies that contributed to the cost. The official opening was held on Sunday 13 May, more than a thousand workers arriving by special train for the ceremony. The foundation stone was laid by George

LEAFLETS

Lansbury and among those present was Sylvia Pankhurst. The crowd then formed up to march to the rectory where they sang the 'Red Flag' and gave three resounding cheers for the teachers. Britain's first trade union school was open. Behind Annie Higdon's desk hung the banner of the National Union of Agricultural Workers, 'We sow the seed that feeds the world'.

As Tom Higdon remarked, 'I am a labourer's man and that's the top and bottom of it.'

The opening of Parliament on 13 October 1908 provided the opportunity for another militant demonstration by the Women's Social and Political Union in their fight for women's suffrage. 'Rush the Commons' was the call made by Emmeline and Christabel Pankhurst at a meeting in Trafalgar Square on Sunday, 11 October, while thousands of leaflets bearing the message were distributed to the crowd, and with considerable contempt for the law, to the police. Christabel Pankhurst declared, 'Let the men help the women to push their way into the House of Commons. The men need not be afraid of arrest, the women will take the lead.' The WSPU was incensed at the cabinet blocking of a private member's Bill put down by H.Y. Stanger, a Liberal MP, and resolved to force their way into the Commons to confront the government. The leaflets were pasted onto the doors of the homes of cabinet ministers and even on the gates of Holloway Prison. A 'votes for women' kite was flown over the Palace of Westminster and a specially chartered launch, decorated with banners and posters, steamed up and down the Thames attracting crowds on the bridges.

The police could not ignore the threat and an Inspector Jarvis was despatched to the WSPU offices in Clement's Inn to be met by Christabel saying, 'Have you seen our new leaflets?' and explaining that the word 'rush' was not large enough and needed to be in more prominent type! At mid-day on Monday, 12 October, a summons was served on Emmeline, Christabel and Flora Drummond which read, 'Information has been laid this day by the Commissioner of Police that you, in the month of October 1908, were guilty of conduct likely to provoke a breach

of the peace by initiating and causing to be initiated, by publishing and causing to be published a certain handbill, calling upon and inciting the public to a certain wrongful and illegal act, viz., to rush the House of Commons of October 13th. inst.' They provocatively declined to appear until 6 p.m. the following day and left for a meeting at Queen's Hall where they expected, and hoped, to be arrested on the platform. The police duly arrived and disappointed them by serving a notice of adjournment until the following morning. They again failed to appear the next morning, Emmeline and Christabel spending the day on the roof garden of the Pethick Lawrences' private flat while Mrs Drummond went about her business elsewhere. They duly presented themselves at Bow Street at 6 p.m. where it was too late for trial and bail was refused so that they could not join the 'rush' demonstration. Whilst the demonstration went ahead as planned, the three were imprisoned in some style, the Liberal MP James Murray sending beds and comfort from the Savoy Hotel, including an elaborate meal served by three waiters, the table decorated with tall candles, silver and flowers.

5,000 police, some mounted, cordoned off Parliament Square while police launches patrolled the Thames. Deputations of suffragettes made efforts to rush the lines but were easily repulsed, the police making no great effort to arrest any but the most determined. One woman, Mrs Travers Symons, did gain access to the House by asking to see Keir Hardie's private secretary. She then took advantage of her proximity to the chamber to rush onto the floor of the House during a debate on the Children's Bill, shouting, 'Leave off discussing the children and talk about the women.' She was removed and subsequently released, but in a trial, at which Lloyd George and Herbert Gladstone were subpoenaed as witnesses, Emmeline Pankhurst and Flora Drummond were sentenced to three months' imprisonment and Christabel Pankhurst to ten weeks'.

An interesting related event occurred at a meeting on unemployment held by the Social Democratic Federation in Trafalgar Square on Sunday, 11 October, when Will Thorne, MP, referred in his speech to the Pankhursts' call to rush the

WOMEN'S SOCIAL AND POLITICAL UNION,
4, CLEMENTS INN.

VOTES FOR WOMEN

MEN & WOMEN
HELP THE SUFFRAGETTES
TO RUSH
THE HOUSE OF COMMONS
ON
TUESDAY Evening, 13th October,
At 7.30.

Printed by St Clements Press, Ltd., Newspaper Buildings, Portugal Street, W.C.

Commons and said it would be futile to assail the Houses of Parliament as there was nothing in them worth the trouble. He told the crowd, 'If your wives and children are hungry, the best thing to do is to rush the bakers' shops.' Emmeline Pankhurst asked at her trial why Will Thorne was not in the dock and as a result he was duly charged with being 'Guilty of conduct likely to provoke a breach of the peace by advising and inciting in the course of a public speech the members of the unemployed to do a certain illegal act, namely to rush every bakers' shop in London rather than starve.' Sentenced to six months' imprisonment or to be bound over in sureties, Thorne offered to keep the peace, with two sureties of £50 from Pete Curran and James O'Grady.

From the Chicago anarchists to Ethel and Julius Rosenberg, American justice has been marred by political trials conducted amid state-generated hysteria and media hatred of minority groups.

The meeting held in Trafalgar Square on Sunday, 26 August 1928, organised by the International Class War Prisoners' Aid Association, was held to mark the first anniversary of the legal murder of Nicola Sacco and Bartolome Vanzetti, two poor Italian immigrants, sent to the electric chair on 23 August 1927. The meeting also continued the campaign for the release of two labour leaders, Tom Mooney and Warren Billings, who had already served twelve years of life sentences passed on them in 1916.

The case of Sacco and Vanzetti, accused of robbery and the killing of a security guard, had been a *cause célèbre*, joining such diverse figures as Stalin and Mussolini in pleading for clemency. Known as anarchists, Sacco, a shoemaker, and Vanzetti, a fish pedlar, were victims of racial prejudice and political hatred. As anarchists, they were enemies of the state. As poor Italians, they were aliens, described by the prosecuting attorney as 'regular Wops'. World-wide protests by liberals and radicals, including the British labour movement, asserted their innocence and pleaded for their release. Such was the power and volume of the international outcry and the tenacity of their own lawyers that

seven years elapsed before they were finally electrocuted. Bartolome Vanzetti's final letter bears eloquent testimony to their martyrdom. 'If it had not been for these things, I might have lived out my life talking at street corners to scorning men. I might have died unmarked, unknown, a failure. This is our career and our triumph. Never in our full life could we hope to do such work for tolerance, for justice, for man's understanding of man as now we do by accident. Our words – our lives – our pains – nothing. The taking of our lives, lives of a good shoemaker and a poor fish peddler – all. That last moment belongs to us – the agony is our triumph.' As Vanzetti was placed in the chair, he said, 'I am innocent. I have never committed any crime – some sins – but never any crime.'

By the time Sacco and Vanzetti were killed, labour leaders Tom Mooney and Warren Billings had already served eleven years on the alleged charge of bomb throwing. The incident had taken place in 1916 during a 'preparedness parade', a demonstration calculated to whip up jingoism in support of American entry into the First World War. Nine people were killed when a bomb was tossed into the parade. At the time of the outrage, the San Francisco Chamber of Commerce, who were supporting the parade, were engaged in a state of open and brutal warfare against the attempt of trade unionists to unionise factories in the State of California. Beatings, clubbings, shootings, even murder, were used to keep 'open shops' and smash the labour movement. Two of the most active fighters for trade unionism were Mooney and Billings, ready victims amid a campaign of patriotism and war hysteria.

The trial was held with prosecution witnesses rehearsed by the prosecuting attorneys and conducted with daily press conferences by the prosecution to a press that was solidly anti-trade unionism. Despite sound alibis they never stood a chance; Mooney was sentenced to death and Billings to life imprisonment. The sentences were met with world-wide protests by trade unionists and socialists, the workers of the newly formed Soviet state demonstrated at the American Embassy in Petrograd and rallies were held in all the major European cities. So strong were the accusations of perjury that the American President, Woodrow Wilson, requested an investigation. Despite the fact that the commission found considerable doubt existed as to their guilt, the only result was to commute the death sentence on Mooney to life imprisonment.

The march to the American Embassy announced on the leaflet never took place because of a police ban. The demand for the freeing of the two labour leaders continued over the years, but they were not pardoned until they had served sentences of twenty-four years, finally being released in 1939. Throughout the seemingly endless incarceration they remained true to the cause of labour. Mooney said, 'I have been fortified all through these years in prison by my faith in the movement which I serve in this outpost of the class struggle and by the consciousness that even though confined here I am an instrument of the workers' cause and a symbol of their struggle.'

They stood in the freezing winter rain, thinly dressed, most without topcoats, holed boots soggy in the muddy slush, unwrapping sandwiches of bread and marge from disintegrating newspaper. There were 6,000 of them, unemployed men and women lined up on the Embankment within sight of the Savoy Hotel where blackcoated waiters were serving four course lunches – another world. It was 23 February 1925, and the hungry men and women had gathered to march in protest against further cuts in unemployment benefits. Their leaders, George Lansbury, the champion of the poor, Ernest Thurtle, MP for Shoreditch, Wal Hannington, Secretary of the National Unemployed Workers' Movement, and Shapurji Saklatvala, Communist MP for North Battersea, were to go as a deputation to see the Minister of Labour to put the case for the workless.

1924 had raised the hopes of the unemployed with the election of a minority Labour government and the raising of benefits. The weekly scale had been raised from 15s. to 18s. for a man, from 12s. to 15s. for a woman and the allowance for dependent children was increased one hundred percent, from

MASS DEMONSTRATION

IN

Trafalgar Square

SUNDAY, 26th AUGUST

at 4.0 p.m.

to commemorate the Legal Murder of
SACCO and VANZETTI

and to demand the Release of Mooney and Billings, who have already been in an American Prison for 12 years on a framed-up charge

---

PROMINENT SPEAKERS

WORKERS! RALLY IN YOUR THOUSANDS

A march to the American Embassy will follow

THEY SHALL NOT BE FORGOTTEN !

Pugh (T.U.) at the Cromwell Press, Dawes 217 Road, Fulham

1s. to 2s.! Meagre as the improvements were they represented the good intention of the government and gave cause for expectation of better things to come. It was not to be – 1925 saw the Conservatives back in power and the immediate introduction of a new Unemployment Act under which benefit ceased to be a statutory right and became a privilege to be dispensed by the Ministry of Labour, who were invested with discretionary powers. The authorities could deny unemployment pay to an applicant who failed to prove that in normal times insurable employment would have been available. Pay could also be denied to an applicant that failed to prove he or she had made every reasonable effort to obtain employment. Just how such claims were to be substantiated was not explained.

The marchers moved slowly away towards Hyde Park, many with their toes protruding from boots that had parted from their soles. A contingent from Southwark bore a banner depicting a skull and crossbones, with the inscription, 'It is better to die than face starvation.' The banner of the Bethnal Green unemployed read, 'Down, but not out'. The *Daily Herald*, the only national daily newspaper to report the event, described the sight of the thin, hungry, poorly clad marchers as 'pathetic'. The leaders left to call at the Ministry where the Minister was not available to see them. Instead, they saw J.F.G. Price, the Chief Permanent Secretary, and for over three hours pleaded for the

quarter of a million unemployed who would be deprived of benefit. Their pleas went unheeded and the future was to be bleaker than they knew. The following month the Chancellor of the Exchequer, Winston Churchill, restored the pound sterling to the gold standard at the 1914 parity of US$4.4 to £1. Ahead lay the attack on the miners, rising unemployment, the yielding of MacDonald, Snowden and Thomas to the demands of the US bankers to cut unemployment pay, and the misery of the hungry thirties.

In October 1913 the *Police Review*, a journal founded by John Kempster in 1893 to champion the cause of the bobby on the beat, carried an advertisement announcing the formation of the Metropolitan Police Union. The officials were listed as John Syme, Secretary and Organiser, J. Gilbert Dale, a member of the Independent Labour Party, Mackenzie Bell, a former Liberal candidate, and J.R. Penfold, a boot- and shoemaker. The aims of the union were given as: 'To safeguard the police gainst official tyranny and injustice, to improve the conditions of the police service, to ensure equal chances of promotion, maintain just and efficient discipline, purge the service of corrupt and unworthy members and secure for the public honest and efficient police administration. Entrance fee one shilling, annual subscription one shilling.'

National Unemployed Workers Committee Movement
LONDON DISTRICT COUNCIL

MONSTER PROTEST

DEMONSTRATION

OF

London Unemployed Workers

WILL ASSEMBLE ON

VICTORIA EMBANKMENT
at 2.30 p.m., Monday, Feb. 23rd

A Deputation will proceed to the Ministry of Labour to protest against the disqualification from benefit of thousands of men and women throughout Great Britain.

GEORGE LANSBURY,
M.P.
WILL HEAD THE DEPUTATION

Unemployed Workers, Rally in your tens of thousands to protest against

Starvation

Reigate Divisional Labour Party.

Ex-Inspector

JOHN SYME

(JIX'S NIGHTMARE),

WILL ADDRESS A

MEETING of ELECTORS

AT THE

VICTORIA HALL,

HORLEY,

ON

WEDNESDAY, APRIL 17th, 1929.

Chair to be taken at 7.30 p.m.

Questions Answered.

COME AND HEAR THE TRUTH !

W. H. FITCH, PRINTER (T.U.), EARLSWOOD, SURREY.

The police force of 1913 exercised a military discipline, subjecting constables to harsh and stringent regulations and providing endless opportunities for martinet sergeants and inspectors to command their own petty tyrannies. Apart from a system of formal discipline where men could be reprimanded or fined, the real power lay in the threat of dismissal from the force and eviction from job security, uniform and pension to the outside world of mass unemployment, hunger and the hopeless task of seeking work with 'no character' to offer a prospective employer.

Syme had joined the police force in 1894 at the age of twenty-one. A quiet, respectable Presbyterian who had spent some years as an advocate's clerk in Scotland, he soon passed his police examinations and by 1909 was made an inspector. A petty incident brought him into conflict with his superiors and Syme began a lifelong fight against police injustice, beginning with his transfer from one station to another and culminating in his dismissal from the force in 1910 and a lifetime of public struggle to obtain a redress of grievance that lasted until his death in 1945.

Syme's union soon changed its title to the National Union of Police and Prison Officers and started a union journal, equipped itself with a banner and prepared to fight for a better deal for its members. Meanwhile, John Syme embarked upon a vendetta against Sir Edward Henry, the Commissioner of Police, in a spectacular series of threats and stunts to draw his personal case to public notice. He threw a brick through Lloyd George's window, a shell case through the window of 10 Downing Street, accosted the Prince of Wales, issued leaflets and pamphlets attacking high officials in the force and conducted a succession of public meetings. Such was the persistence, virulence and

single-minded obsession of his crusade that doubts were cast as to his sanity. His union removed him from office and disowned him as an embarrassment as he conducted his lone fight for justice. As the years passed, Syme went in and out of prison, responding to each sentence with hunger strikes and being released under the 'Cat and Mouse' Act. Between November 1921 and December 1922 he was released and re-arrested fourteen times. He publicly threatened to kill the king and after going to prison thirty times, was committed to Broadmoor in November 1924 where he stayed until July 1925.

Despite his eccentric, paranoiac or insane activities, his integrity won him many protagonists. George Lansbury said that keeping Syme in Broadmoor would drive him mad altogether. Ellen Wilkinson told a Trafalgar Square rally that Syme was in Broadmoor because he was a nuisance to officialdom, not because he was insane. A group of Labour MPs formed a committee to keep the case in front of the public and arranged a lecture tour on behalf of the Labour Party for him to speak on his hospital and prison experiences. Eventually, it fell to J.R. Clynes as the Home Secretary of the 1931 Labour Government to make the final official pronouncement on the case. In answer to a question in the Commons from Ernest Winterton, MP, Clynes announced that Ex-Inspector John Syme, in respect of his fifteen years' service in the Metropolitan Police, would be granted a pension calculated on his salary in the rank of inspector which he held in 1909, with appropriate increases payable since 1920 under the Pensions Increases Act. He was also to receive his arrears of pension amounting to £1,200.

Syme was not satisfied, contending that he should have been compensated for loss of his career prospects and he continued his lone and pitiful campaign until his death.

MANUSCRIPTS
&
RECORDS

Documentary evidence as provided by minute books, accounts and letters are central to historical research and our understanding of past events. The bound account book of the little Peckham and Dulwich Branch of the Social Democratic Federation provides an insight into the work of the branch from July 1893 to April 1889, stopping tantalisingly short of the upsurge of militancy that followed the Great Dock Strike of August 1889. The book records fifty-nine members of the branch, a figure that was to vary only slightly over the next seven years, new recruits being offset by resignations, those referred to as 'dropped out' and one case of expulsion. During one quarter it is written that 'four new members were made but seven utterly useless members will not appear in the books this quarter because they never put in any appearance, nor pay, nor given any reason for not paying.'

The accounts show a membership subscription of 1d. a week, a sum totally inadequate for the funding of the branch's political activity. Income was supplemented by collections, the sale of *Justice*, pamphlets, refreshments and tobacco. A tobacco licence was bought for 5s. 3d., a thoroughly worthwhile investment as the secretary's financial report makes clear, 'One of the most satisfactory items is that for refreshments and tobacco. One steward is developing into a capitalist of the most

virulent type. At the beginning of the quarter, seven shillings and sixpence was advanced to that office as capital. After providing for all necessary lighting and sundries for the hall, he has handed to the Secretary the substantial sum of £1. 3s. 2½d. in addition to which he has stock in hand to the value of three shillings and fivepence, while he still holds the original seven shillings and sixpence.' The Secretary pointed out that this represented a profit margin of three hundred percent and commented, 'If any comrade wants to know what capital is – ask the steward.' During the same quarter, the branch sold 555 copies of *Justice*, the weekly organ of the SDF, indicating a high level of street work. The Secretary for that period, 1893, was W.A. Woodroffe, a man with a droll sense of humour who reported to the branch that they had had a 'slight difference of opinion with the Landlord, which of course is natural'. As the landlord refused to carry out certain repairs to the hall, the branch took direct political action and stopped paying the rent. The question of premises was crucial and it is recorded that some members did not like political meetings held in private homes. The Secretary rejected that as an excuse for not attending meetings and said, 'If we are to wait for the first Monday morning under socialism for new premises, it is apparent we shall have to wait a considerable time yet.' Being pragmatic a 'new premises fund' was started and

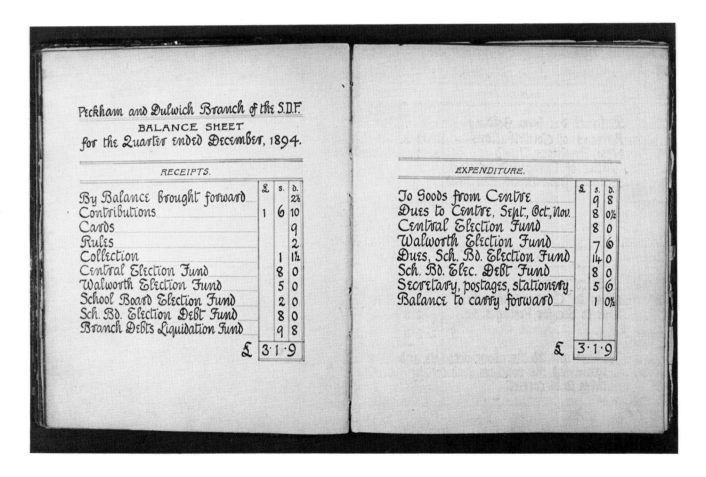

Peckham and Dulwich Branch of the S.D.F.
BALANCE SHEET
for the Quarter ended December, 1894.

RECEIPTS.	£	s.	d.
By Balance brought forward			2½
Contributions	1	6	10
Cards			9
Rules			2
Collection		1	1½
Central Election Fund		8	0
Walworth Election Fund		5	0
School Board Election Fund		2	0
Sch. Bd. Election Debt Fund		8	0
Branch Debts Liquidation Fund		9	8
£	3	1	9

EXPENDITURE.	£	s.	d.
To Goods from Centre		9	8
Dues to Centre, Sept., Oct., Nov.		8	0½
Central Election Fund		8	0
Walworth Election Fund		7	6
Dues, Sch. Bd. Election Fund		14	0
Sch. Bd. Elec. Debt Fund		8	0
Secretary, postages, stationery		5	6
Balance to carry forward		1	0½
£	3	1	9

of members have paid the levy of 4/-, and some, more; and it is now desirable that those who cannot afford 4/- should contribute "according to their ability." Those who have convictions will be impelled to make sacrifices for them.

Collections, amounting to 10/4½, have resulted chiefly from the efforts which comrade Dobson has made in our behalf at the Canal Head,—and members would do well to attend our Sunday-morning meetings more regularly. Tho' it may be our members have absented themselves from church recently, that affords no reason why the threepenny piece should not still be bestowed on a religious cause.

The items under the heading Expenditure need no comment; they might, however, well be larger in amount, so far, at least, as they relate to the Central Election Fund (2/6) and the School Board Election Fund (10/-).

Now turning our attention to the Assets and Liabilities account, the item "Balance due from Golding, 9/7," remains unreduced. A communication has been received from Golding, from which it appears

he looked forward to the time when the building would 'raise the status of our cause in Peckham' and be 'a local landmark of revolt against every form of social iniquity'. Within five weeks a 'few comrades had subscribed eight shillings and fourpence.'

Finance was a perennial problem. A debt of 9s. 7d. was incurred when the branch loaned £1. 6s. 1d. to comrade E. Golding 'to assist him acquire a small business'. Owing 9s. 7d. he decamped from his home in Brixton, an act of 'flagrant dishonesty' which caused much trouble and expense. Local elections, like the East Lambeth Schoolboard Election, put a tremendous strain on the precariously small income and required a levy of 4s. a member. To those who could not afford 4s., it was suggested in Marxist terms that they should contribute 'according to their ability'. There were a number of special funds run to finance the various political commitments of the branch; apart from the 'new premises fund', there was a 'lecture guarantee fund', a 'central election fund' and an 'International Congress Fund'. In minute amounts the finances of the branch are recorded in detail, 'two shillings for the placing of Justice in public libraries', a grant of half a crown to 'comrade Pearson's funeral', and a receipt of £1. 10s. 0d. from the Peckham and Camberwell SDF Stores, apparently a Social Democratic venture into co-operative trading in which the branch held three 2s. shares. Working class solidarity is reflected in the loan of 8s. to the Boot Trade lock-out fund, £2. 8s. 3d. 'having been disbursed for the support of the centre, Lansbury's and Dobson's candidates and other funds worthy of our restricted liberality.'

The picture that emerges from the carefully written pages is of a small, impecunious band of loyal and dedicated socialists struggling to make ends meet and to inspire political action. Exhortation to greater efforts mark every quarterly report: 'Members would do well to attend our Sunday morning meetings more regularly.'

Sometimes even the leadership wavered: 'A brief reference must be made to the candidature of Mr J.R. Lees, who called three delegate meetings, at all of which he failed to appear.' However, their spirit was indomitable and is encapsulated in time by the concluding remarks to the quarterly report of October 1894, graphically penned by the Secretary, William G. Killick: 'In conclusion, comrades, let our work be the measure of our faith in our conviction and ideals, always remembering that in the religion of socialism, "Faith without works, is dead."'

The ending of the Great Dock Strike in September 1889 did not bring peace within the docks. The Dockers' Union which had grown out of the strike was almost 20,000 strong, with Tom Mann as president and Ben Tillett as secretary. With such a mass membership, the leadership sought to tighten the organisation of the union and extend its influence on the activities within the dockyards. On 14 November workers at the Royal Albert Docks refused to hand over thirteen cases of furniture to a collecting carman because he did not hold a union ticket. Within a week carriers were being sent away from all the docks unless they were able to produce proof of union membership.

The first response of the employers at a meeting held on 26 November was to instruct the dock superintendents that if they failed to persuade the dockers to work with non-union labour, the men refusing to work should be paid off. This was further reiterated at a meeting of the London and India Docks Joint Committee when heads of departments were again instructed that men declining to work with non-union labour should be paid off and not re-employed 'until authority for doing so be obtained from the directors'. By 7 December the superintendent of the London and St Katherine's docks was reporting to his management his fears that paying off any men would lead to 'all the men at our wool warehouses turning out' and explaining that this would adversely affect the forthcoming wool sales.

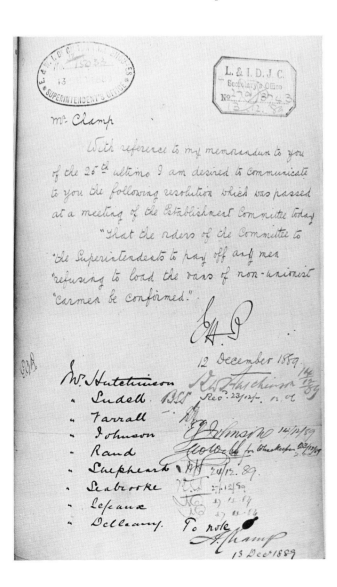

away having their dinner. 162 dockers walked out and within hours a telegram was sent from the Dockers' Union to the management which read, '162 men out from Victoria. Will not return until £3 are paid as fine by the men who loaded.' At this point there is a gap in the extant correspondence and it is uncertain if the fine was paid or on what terms the men returned to work. However, the dispute continued into February of 1890, when Cardinal Manning and Sydney Buxton, MP, who had been mediators in the Great Strike, again intervened. The union finally withdrew its demand that only union carmen would be loaded by the dockers, but wrested important concessions from the employers concerning the payment of piece work. The negotiations were confused at the last moment by a telegram to Cardinal Manning on 8 February from Tom Mann which read, 'I have declined to act on your advice.' It was a telegraphic error and should have read 'have *decided* to act on your advice.' The dispute was over.

Almost immediately another struggle began with the demand of the Dockers' Union that the foremen and permanent labourers should become members of the union. This was a battle the dockers lost and seriously affected their monopoly of dock labour and weakened their position for years to come. The union did, however, resist the attempts of the employers to engage non-union dockers, striking in defence of their right to check the union cards of men within the docks. The employers resisted at first, threatening to discharge anyone examining cards (letter reproduced). When the union displayed posters inside the warehouses concerning the examination of cards, the employers were furious, one director describing the action as 'a piece of impudence'. The directors took the view that the union 'should do its own work in its own time' but the real reason for their anger was that their attempt to introduce non-union labour and weaken the Dockers' Union was being thwarted.

Tom Mann's letter dated 10 December 1889 (first and last pages reproduced), written in his capacity as President of the Dock, Wharf, Riverside and General Labourers' Union to W.E. Hubbard, the Chairman of the Establishment Committee, was forthright and uncompromising, reasserting the principle of his members' working only with union labour, but making an exception for country firms and small businesses.

Hubbard replied, inviting Mann to meet with the superintendents, but Tom Mann was even more brusque, writing, 'It is those confounded superintendents and warehousekeepers who cause the difficulty and I don't want to talk to them.' The very next day the superintendents and warehousekeepers provoked a strike when they loaded goods onto a cart driven by a non-union carman while the dockers were

The letter sent by the dock police to the bosses (letter reproduced) reporting on Tom Mann's trade union activities away from the dock area clearly shows how concerned the dock owners were at the growing strength of the new union.

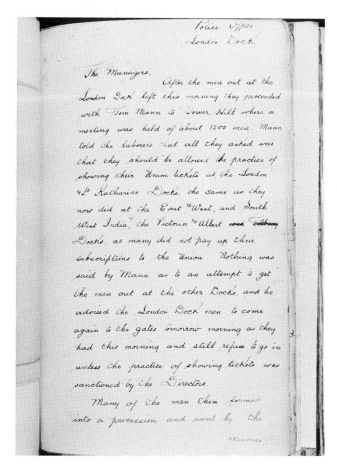

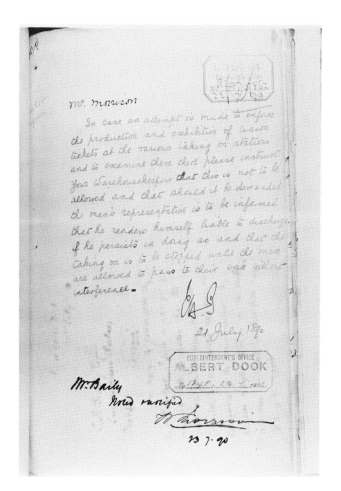

On 7 July 1906 Victor Grayson became the first member of Parliament to be elected as a socialist. He came as a thunderbolt from Colne Valley to Westminster at twenty-four years of age to take his seat among the representatives of the most deeply entrenched ruling class in the world. To mention Grayson in socialist circles today is to evoke set responses about his gift of oratory, his David-like victory for socialism and his mysterious disappearance in 1920. Such was his impact on the labour movement that even after seventy years his name draws admiration and provokes words like 'tragedy', 'sad loss', 'enigma', and speculation runs on what was and what might have been.

Born in Liverpool in 1882, the seventh son of a Yorkshire carpenter and a Scottish mother, he was educated at a board school, one of the schools set up under the 1870 Act to provide compulsory education for working class children. Apprenticed as an engineer for a firm at Bootle, he made his first contact with the ideas of socialism on the factory floor and led his first strike

at the age of eighteen. Grayson joined the Hamilton Road Mission Men's Debating Society, gaining his first experience as a public speaker – shy, stumbling words that could hardly have foretold the golden tongue that was to hold and move audiences all over the North within a few years. While making his way as a public speaker, from chairs, soapboxes and platforms of the local socialist group, he was noticed by a Unitarian minister who saw in him a preacher and who arranged for him to go to Liverpool University and then to Owen's College, Manchester, to study for the ministry. He duly went, but his mind and soul were committed to the preaching of the gospel of socialism; he was destined to preach not beneath a cross, but a red flag.

His stand as a socialist candidate in the election of 1906 for Colne Valley was as an uncompromising revolutionary socialist. Denied official ILP approval, Grayson fought and won with the help of a loyal band of local socialists and a mixed bag of supporting speakers including Conrad Noel, Ernest Marklew and Mrs Pankhurst. His election address made no concession to middle-of-the-road voters; it simply stated the socialist case and is worth reprinting:

I am appealing to you as one of your own class. I want emancipation from the wage slavery of capitalism.
I do not believe we are divinely destined to be drudges. Through the centuries we have been the serfs of an arrogant aristocracy.
We have toiled in the factories and workshops to grind profits with which to glut the greedy maw of the capitalist class.
Their children have been fed on the fat of the land. Our children have been neglected and handicapped in the struggle for existence.
We have served the classes and we have remained a mob. The time for our emancipation has come.
We must break the rule of the rich and take our destinies into our own hands.
Let charity begin with our children.
Workers, who respect their wives, who love their children, and who long for a fuller life for all:
A VOTE FOR THE LANDOWNER OR THE CAPITALIST IS TREACHERY TO YOUR CLASS.
To give your child a better chance than you have had, think carefully ere you make your cross.
The other classes have had their day. It is our turn now.
Albert Victor Grayson.

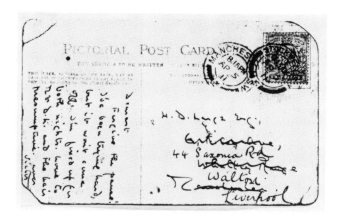

Hyndman, Blatchford and Quelch, although it was Grayson who filled the halls, preaching social revolution. To railway workers in Stratford, East London, Grayson said, 'We are on the brink of a great revolution. It is a revolution that need not mean bloodshed. I say "need not". I dare not say "will not".'

Yet the star flickered, dimmed and finally vanished. Grayson lost his seat in the General Election of January 1910 and although he continued to inspire through his writings and speeches, his personal life drifted to heavy drinking and profligate spending leading to bankruptcy. He followed Blatchford and Hyndman in their support for the war on Germany in 1914 and two years after the armistice in September 1920 he vanished. While drinking with a friend at the Georgian Hotel in London he was told by the receptionist that his luggage had been delivered to the Queen's Hotel, Leicester Square, in error. Grayson left, his whisky half finished, saying he would be back, walked out and was never conclusively seen again. Many theories have been advanced concerning his disappearance and as is the case with other famous missing persons there were sightings claimed in the years that followed, but none verified. An interesting explanation has been advanced by his biographer, Reg Groves, and his book, *The Strange Case of Victor Grayson*, is essential reading for the most detailed account of his life and last days.

Seven letters that were not available to Groves show an aspect of his life not previously considered by those who have written of the mystery. They were written between 1905 and 1911 to Henry Dawson, at various addresses in Liverpool and Manchester. (One letter and postcard reproduced). An undated letter reads:

> My stricken darling,
> Need I assure you although I have been out of your sight I have not been out of your mind. I agree with you that absence makes cowards of us all and is the thief of God's time, but you have no beastly right to rear yourself on your hind legs and baste me for cold hearted negligence other than a wretched paste-board with the nought conveying legend 108 McDonald Street inscribed thereon, I have had no communication from you. Month in and out I have pined in my windy garret and left the canker – sorrow – eat at my melancholy heart and whiten my damask cheek. Oft, oh how oft – have I opened my window and apostrophised the murky night in accents of bitter misanthropy. Many a belated wayfarer along Oldham Road has paused, startled and pricked his ears as he heard a deep rich voice telling the frozen sky that it didn't bite so nigh, as friend remembered not. And yet the while – you – the estranged and the supercilious were afar off, petulantly mouthing sapient proverbs like 'alcohol makes the heart grow fatty' and such rot. However, my heart's too full of Nestles No.1. brand to harbour a fancied grievance and I forgive you. It's the droop of your moustache that takes me; and anyhow, any man who's in favour of the nationalisation of the means of production, distribution and swap, needn't pass 238 The Katakombs in search of a friend. We'll burn a Player's Weight to old therapeina the wizened goddess of reconciliation and fondly lick one another's epidermis on the first convenient occasion. To blazes with miawling and grump. Set the thing you call your mind at rest. I love you as ever, with the same devouring passion and intensity and thickness. Your handwriting always pulls the stopper out of my heart and makes my affections to blubber and blub. Write by return and tell me when it will be possible to reassemble either at the Dinorwic Bower or elsewhere. I came home last Monday and have been ever since wandering joylessly in company with academic crustations from Brownlow Hill. I am here for about fifteen days more. I shall not visit Blair's until I hear from you.
> Thine till Plutus claims his own, and after.
>
> A.V. Grayson.

When the result was announced that Grayson had beaten the Liberal and Conservative, his supporters went wild. Millworkers in shawls, greasy engineers, children with red ribbons danced in streets and sang socialist songs. Workshops were draped with red streamers and the *Daily Express* reported, 'The red flag waves over Colne Valley.'

Grayson went to Parliament to speak for his people, though he held the exclusive club in a good deal of contempt. Speaking after his victory to the ILP in Manchester, he said, 'Revolutionary and unconstitutional means are needed to break up the stupendous mountains of tradition that prevail in Parliament. The men who expect real reforms from the modern Parliament with its musty procedure, its shibboleths and tradition, need a goodly share of optimism.' Outside Parliament Grayson became the most popular speaker in the labour movement, night after night addressing packed meetings of millworkers, railwaymen, building workers, engineers, and sharing the platforms with

Other letters to Dawson are signed 'thine ever', 'thine always', 'thine as ever' and 'thine lustily'.

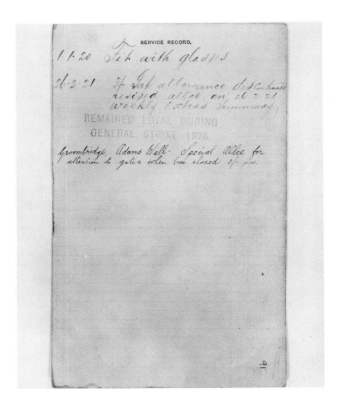

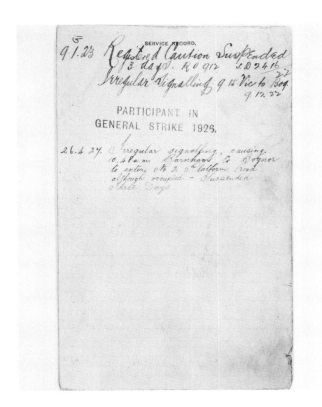

Perhaps it is easy to make too much of the endearments and grasp at them as a clue to understanding a secret side of Grayson's life. He had made enemies in high places of government and establishment and if there were other letters in similar vein in the hands of his enemies, flight may have seemed the only way to escape a final ignominy. The mystery remains to be solved.

When the General Strike began on 3 May 1926, in support of the miners, the railwaymen were among those chosen by the TUC to be in the first wave of the attack. The response of the railwaymen was a display of united action unequalled by any union during the nine days' struggle. Of 14,671 drivers on the London, Midland and Scottish Railway, only 93 reported for work. From the London and North Eastern Railway, only 94 men were available from 11,500. The Associated Society of Locomotive Engineers were virtually one hundred percent behind the strike, less than 50 out of 50,000 failing to respond to the call. The loyalty of the railwaymen to the unions and the TUC was made in the face of open letters from their employers that were intended to threaten the jobs of those who supported the strike: 'Your means of living and your personal interests are involved' (Great Western Railway); 'The Company desires to impress upon the staff that if they leave work in the manner indicated, they will be breaking their contract of service' (London and North Eastern Railway).

For the middle class, middle-aged men with their fairisle pullovers and plus fours, the government strike-breaking organisation, OMS (Organisation for the Maintenance of Supplies), provided them with a chance to realise their schoolboy dreams – to be an engine driver. Of course, they had long ago awakened from their dreams to the reality that being a stockbroker, insurance agent or a bank manager was a far more lucrative and cleaner way of earning a living, but here was a chance of a spot of jolly fun and a chance to teach those 'blighters on strike that we can do without them'. The attempt was not a success and some of the results were positively hair-raising. Driving a steam locomotive cannot be compared with driving a car and the understanding of the complex systems of signals, points, or how to keep a head of steam on a gradient was not to be acquired in a week. So tortuous was the progress of some volunteer-run trains, that the *Westminster Worker*, a strike bulletin, sarcastically announced that 'we understand luncheon cars are to be put on trains running between Westminster and Blackfriars'. The British Central Strike Committee ran to verse:

Early in the morning, per broadcast from London,
See the little puff-puffs all in a row,
D'Arcy on the engine, pulled a little lever,
Expansion of the boiler – UP WE GO!

While the Rt. Hons. were providing a stop-go service on empty lines, Winston Churchill's paper, *The British Gazette*, was misleading its readers with reports on the alleged success of the strikebreakers' efforts. On the fifth day of the strike, the headline ran, 'Vital services better each day', reporting that 3,000 trains ran the day before but omitting to mention that this was less than 10 percent of normal. By the end of the strike, the LMS was running only 3 percent of normal goods trains, the LNER 2 percent and the GWR 8.4 percent. The damage caused to the engines by their amateur drivers has never been calculated.

When the TUC called off the strike on 12 May the Prime Minister, Stanley Baldwin, said in his broadcast to the nation that he was 'a man of peace' who promised to secure 'even justice between man and man'. However, on the same day the government issued a statement that said, 'His Majesty's Government have no power to compel employers to take back every man who has been on strike.' The time for retribution had arrived. The GWR issued a circular to departmental managers that read, 'No man who is known to have taken a leading part in organising or carrying on the strike, nor any supervisor, is allowed to resume duty without explicit instructions from this office.' The terms offered by the railway companies were such that the railwaymen remained on strike for two more days while negotiations continued, but in the end were forced to accept humiliating terms that admitted that 'in calling a strike they committed a wrongful act against the Companies'. No guarantee of re-employment was given and after six months, 45,000 men, nearly a quarter of the membership of the National Union of Railwaymen, had not been re-instated. The service records of two men of the Southern Railway show how those who had taken part in the strike were marked men for the rest of their working days. The government promise that there would be no victimisation was worthless and the railwaymen suffered second only to the miners themselves as the employers took their revenge. For the blacklegs, the railway companies struck special medallions, gave engraved silver ashtrays and illuminated addresses of thanks. For the strikers, they marked their cards.

MEMBERSHIP CARDS & STAMPS

The Friendly Society of Tin Plate Workers was founded in 1798, changing its name to the Operative Society of Tin Plate Workers in 1805. After splitting into the Operative Gas Meter Workers and the Co-operative Society of Tin Plate Workers in 1846, an amalgamation in 1860 saw the formation of the Amalgamated Society of Tin Plate Workers. The Society was meeting regularly at Cogers' Hall, attached to the Old Cogers public house in Bride Lane, Fleet Street, by 1868 when the tramping card (illustrated) was issued.

The tramping, or travelling, system by which a member tramped from town to town in search of work was a trade union method of coping with unemployment. At each specified 'house of call', a public house, the local Society would mark the tramping card and provide supper, beer, company, bed and breakfast for the weary traveller. Weary he might well be; the Brushmakers' Society tramping route of 1829 covered forty towns spread over 1,210 miles from London back to London, taking in Norwich, Manchester, Liverpool and Exeter. The card stated, 'No tramp can become a receiver unless he has been all round in four months'! The tramping artisan occupied a bed that may well have been inspected and approved by the union secretary and drank beer for the good of himself and the house, the landlord usually allowing the Society the use of a clubroom for which he took no rent. The public house used by a union became a labour exchange where a 'vacant book' might be kept behind the bar with a list of jobs available at legal (union) shops.

The rule books of the Tin Plate Workers' Societies carefully set out the terms and conditions of travelling benefit. The 1885 rule book of the Tin Plate Workers' Trade Society allowed a free member (a fully paid-up member with one years' membership) 2s. 3d. a day for twenty days, Sundays included, while travelling in search of employment. The tramp had to move on within a specified time – in this case, six days in Manchester, Liverpool, Birmingham and Glasgow, three days in Newcastle and in all other towns two days. The 1868 card allowed 1s. 8d. a day for eighteen days whilst the tramping member sought employment.

It was not a case of a few Tin Plate workers tramping for work; all sorts of trades supported members trudging around the countryside in search of work. In 1879, a year of trade depression, the Amalgamated Society of Engineers had 7,000 of their 44,000 members out of work and issued 2,000 tramp cards. The Ironfounders fared even worse, more than 3,000 members being unemployed from a membership of nearly 12,000, with many taking out tramp cards. During 1878-9 the masons paid out £13,000 to their travelling unemployed and struggled to maintain their weekly subscription at 6d. It has been estimated that during 1879 over 5,000 engineers, masons, ironfounders and tailors took to the roads with tramp cards in their pockets.

There was nothing derogatory in being known as a tramp; you were merely a brother in search of work. A tramp would arrive at a local 'house' where the trade met and drank and would meet with his brother unionists. If his clothes or tools did not make him immediately recognisable, he could always give the sign of the trade. 'Providing you were in a public house . . . how would you act to prove if he were a friendly brother or not? I would take up my glass and act thus.' The Brushmakers' call was a little tune of five notes and the masons had a sign that would bring a fellow member down from a steeple.

The fraternity of the trade would do all they could to provide for a brother, perhaps best portrayed in an early emblem of the Friendly Society of Iron Moulders, where two men are seen in conversation saying:

Brother craft, can you give me a job?
If we cannot, we will assist you.

What of those who would not join the brotherhood? A handwritten list from Preston in 1819 gives a list of fourteen members of the Society of Tin Plate Workers; it also gives the names of four 'rats in Preston, Richard Crosdale, John Simpson, Thos. Barnes and William Tuill'. The preamble to the rule book of 1805 is quite clear regarding the definition of a rat:

A Rat is to this Trade, what a Traitor is to his Country, and although both may be useful to one party in troublesome times, when peace returns, they are detested alike by all; so when help is wanted, a Rat is the last to contribute assistance and the first to grasp a benefit he never laboured to procure. He cares only for himself, but he sees not beyond the extent of a day, and for a momentary and worthless approbation would betray friends, family and Country, in short he is a traitor on a small scale, he first sells the journeymen, and is himself afterwards sold in his turn by the master, until at last he is despised by both, and deserted by all. He is an enemy to himself – to the present age – and to posterity.

The founding of the Labour Church by John Trevor in 1891 was not an act of spontaneous creation. It was an evolutionary development of the socialist challenge to the role of the churches on social questions in a capitalist society. Tom Mann accused the established church of having 'persistently defended social customs and business proceedings that daily and hourly violated the first principles of brotherhood.' He was scathing in his attacks upon a clergy that fulfilled its social obligations by visiting a few worn-out drunkards and prostitutes while ignoring the millions who toiled and lived in poverty. Such challenges found responses from within the church, for not all the clergy saw their ministry as the defence of monopoly and privilege. As early as 1888 Stewart Headlam's Guild of St Matthew had presented a memorial to the Pan-Anglican Conference of Bishops, submitting 'that with the main contentions of the Socialist, the Christian is not only able, but bound to agree.' Some did not agree; a Methodist paper compared Headlam and the clergy who joined the socialists with Lot in the cities of the plain.

For John Trevor, the concept of a Labour Church preaching the emancipation of labour had been in his mind for some years. In June 1891 he wrote an article in the *Inquirer* on 'The proposed Labour Church' and said, 'The time is right for a new religious movement which shall unite together the forces of the two enthusiasms of our time – the enthusiasm for personal salvation

REGISTER NO. 175.]

AMALGAMATED

Society of Tin-Plate Workers,

LONDON.

Registered pursuant to Act of Parliament, 34 & 35 Vic., chap. 31.

"COGERS' HALL," BRIDE LANE, FLEET STREET, E.C.

*This is to certify that*_____

_____ *is a Free Member of*

*the above Society, and entitled to receive*_____

*Shillings per day for*_____ *to assist him*

when in search of employment.

All money advanced on this Card by any Society to the amount above stated, will be forwarded on application to the Secretary.

*Secretary*_____

*Address*_____

N.B.—Members are requested to return this Card within fourteen days after being filled up, or Member obtaining employment.

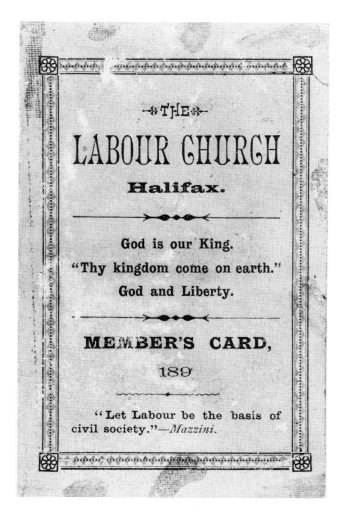

appeals especially to those who have abandoned the traditional religion of the day without having found satisfaction in abandoning religion altogether.' To those, like the Vic Feather household in Bradford, the Labour Church offered an acceptable socialist alternative to the established church. His mother, Edith Feather, took him to the Labour Church in Peckover Street, where the ILP was founded, and in place of a christening 'named him' without ceremony and said, 'Now I've done the right thing.' The services were, in effect, Sunday gatherings to listen to the best socialist speakers and sing socialist songs. The songs may not have been of great literary merit, usually sung to familiar tunes, but they expressed the spirit and passion of the religion of socialism. The hymn book included the 'Union Hymn' sung at the mass meeting of political unions in 1832 at Birmingham preceding the first Reform Act, the 'Red Flag' and poems by William Morris.

The movement declined within a decade, *The Labour Prophet* giving way to the less radical *Labour Prophet and Labour Church Record* in September 1895 with the Labour Churches slowly petering out of existence. There was still a Labour Church in Bradford in 1904, but it seems to have been a solitary survivor.

The Labour Church withered but its influence on the songs of the movement remained. In 1945 the author stood in the crowded assembly hall of West Ham Secondary School and joined in the singing of a hymn written by Ebenezer Elliot and published in the Labour Church *Hymn and Tune Book* in 1893:

> When wilt thou save thy people?
> O God of mercy, when?
> Not Kings or Lords but nations,
> Not crowns or thrones but men.

The Labour victory of 1945 heralded a new Jerusalem that would have uplifted the heart of John Trevor.

and the enthusiasm for social salvation.' Three months later in Manchester he collected £40 from sympathetic friends, printed thousands of handbills, formed a choir, printed hymn sheets and hired a band. On the first Sunday in October, the first Labour Church service was held and Ben Tillett and Robert Blatchford were booked to deliver the next two sermons. The theological foundation and the social basis of the new movement were expressed in five principles:

1. That the Labour Movement is a Religious Movement.
2. That the Religion of the Labour Movement is not a Class Religion, but unites members of all classes in working for the Abolition of Commercial Slavery.
3. That the Religion of the Labour Movement is not Sectarian or Dogmatic, but Free Religion, leaving each man free to develop his own relations with the Power that brought him into being.
4. That the Emancipation of Labour can only be realised so far as men learn both the Economic and Moral Laws of God, and heartily endeavour to obey them.
5. That the development of Personal Character and the improvement of Social Conditions are both essential to man's emancipation from moral and social bondage.

In June 1892 John Trevor started a monthly paper, *The Labour Prophet*, its illustrated heading proclaiming 'God is our King', and carrying regular articles by well-known socialists like Keir Hardie, Robert Blatchford and Pete Curran. Such was the spread of influence and support of the Labour Church that on 15 January 1893 a service was held in the St George's Hall, Manchester, in connecton with the ILP conference and was attended by 5,000 people. The chair was taken by Fred Jowett, President of the Bradford Labour Church, and speakers included Bernard Shaw, Keir Hardie, Edward Aveling and Robert Blatchford. Churches opened in Halifax, Birmingham, Barrow-in-Furness, Oldham and Leeds and at its peak the movement was active in almost thirty cities and towns.

John Trevor's Labour Church *Hymn Book* became the song book of socialism, the preface claiming that 'the Labour Church

Trade union membership cards were the key to trade union organisation on the job and the financial record of contributions at branch level. The ticket of the West Ham branch of the National Union of Corporation Workers, 1911, clearly defines its purpose as a contribution card, the dues being regularly collected once a fortnight at the Lord Raglan public house in Plaistow. The union was formed in 1888 as the LCC Employees' Association, becoming the Municipal Employees' Association in 1894 as the union extended its membership beyond the LCC to cover municipal workers in other towns and cities. The union split in 1907 and the National Union of Corporation Workers was formed, led by Albin Taylor. In 1928, with changes in the functions of the Boards of Guardians, it adopted the more embracing title of the National Union of Public Employees.

The 1923 membership card of the craft union, the Amalgamated Society of Woodworkers, Stratford branch, belonged to the author's father who maintained his membership throughout his working life, being made an honorary life member after fifty years of membership. 'Branch nights' were regarded as sacrosanct, the fortnightly dues being paid without fail for half a century, even during periods of unemployment in the 1930s.

The Amalgamated Engineering Union card is a shop steward's card that belonged to W. Johnston, who worked in the brass shop of Harland and Wolff Ltd., Belfast, in 1947. Inside, the procedure for dealing with shop floor disputes is clearly outlined from workers to foreman, shop steward and worker to shop foreman or manager, to works committee or district committee, to local conference and finally to central conference if the dispute remained unresolved. Most disputes are quickly resolved by stewards at shop-floor level and seldom go beyond negotiation with the production manager or personnel officer.

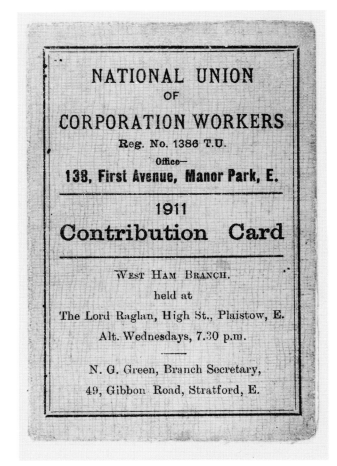

NATIONAL UNION
OF
CORPORATION WORKERS
Reg. No. 1386 T.U.
Office—
138, First Avenue, Manor Park, E.

1911
Contribution Card

WEST HAM BRANCH.

held at

The Lord Raglan, High St., Plaistow, E.

Alt. Wednesdays, 7.30 p.m.

N. G. Green, Branch Secretary,
49, Gibbon Road, Stratford, E.

Tom Mann returned to England from Australia on 10 May 1910, having been abroad for eight years, yet within two months he was producing *The Industrial Socialist*, a revolutionary monthly journal aimed at uniting workers into unions organised by industry. Learning from the French syndicalists and the American Industrial Workers of the World, Mann wrote, 'The curse of capitalism consists in this – that a handful of capitalists can compel hundreds of thousands of workers to work in such a manner and for such a wage as will please the capitalists. But this again is solely because of the inability of the workers to agree upon a common plan of action. The hour the workers agree and

act, they become all powerful. We can settle the capitalists' strike-breaking power once and for all. We shall have no need to plead with parliamentarians to be good enough to reduce hours as the workers have been doing for twenty years without result. We shall be able to do this ourselves, and there will be no power on earth to stop us so long as we do not fall foul of economic principles.'

Mann did not have to wait long before the chance of applying the theory of common action in practice. In July he had invited the transport unions to take part in a conference with a view to amalgamation or federation; at a second meeting in November a committee was appointed for drafting the constitution of the National Federation of Transport Workers. The first skirmish was fought against the rich International Shipping Federation who refused to employ any seaman who was a member of the National Sailors' and Firemen's Union. On 11 June 1911 dockers and seamen, all members of the Federation, struck for union recognition and such was the power and unity of the strikers that the autocratic shipowners who had refused to talk to the unions were forced to concede their demands. The lesson of solidarity was clear and on 28 June 4,000 Liverpool dockers came out, demanding recognition of the National Union of Dock Labourers. The city erupted into support as seamen, scalers, carters and finally railwaymen struck in support of the dockers. The government responded by sending two gunboats up the Mersey with guns trained on Liverpool and drafting in cavalry and infantry with fixed bayonets to confront the workers in the fiercest strike for many years. The workers remained unyielding and by 28 August all their demands had been met.

The campaign for amalgamations and joint action continued with some success, three railway unions coming together to form the National Union of Railwaymen in 1913 and the triple alliance agreement between miners, railwaymen and the Transport Federation being reached by 1914. In 1925 the alliance was used to effect in repulsing an attack on the miners' wages, a victory for the alliance that was dubbed by the *Daily Herald* as Red Friday. In fact, the mine owners and government used the temporary retreat to buy some time for the preparation of an all-out attack upon the miners, resulting in the lock-out and General Strike of 1926.

In the end, the Federation foundered after the defeat of the unions in the 1926 strike and formally dissolved in 1927. The membership card carries the logo designed for the Federation by Walter Crane, an Atlas-like worker carrying the world on his back with illustrations of sea and road transport on either side, contained within a wheel, the circular design a symbol of completeness.

National Transport
Workers' Federation

Federation Card
JUNE 30, 1914.

FOR QUARTER ENDING

220, Blackfriars Road, S.E.

President : H. GOSLING, L.C.C.
Secretary : ROBT. WILLIAMS.

Members of Federated Unions are requested to produce this Card, and request Members of other Federated Unions to do the same.

From 1907 the design for the membership card of the London Society of Compositors was open to annual competition by the membership of the union. The competition resulted from an outcry against one year's card which was described as a monstrosity and offended the craft pride of the display compositors.

The first competition brought seventy entries and was judged by Harry Whetton, the editor of *The British Printer* and a highly respected figure in the printing industry. Whetton's report on the competition praised the entries for their 'workmanship, good taste and pleasing effect' and he said that he did not 'remember a competition in which the average was so high, largely because there is scarcely a single sample devoid of some good points . . . significant of the standard of workmanship represented by the membership of the London Society of Compositors.' The entries were submitted anonymously under an entry number, and *The British Printer* simply records the winner of the first competition as '1,020', awarded the honour 'for an all-round, neat, useful, effective and workmanlike design'.

By 1915 Whetton's judge's report for the LSC trade card competition indicates a certain difficulty in selecting a winner, suggesting a sameness in design due to the constraints of the rules of the competition in terms of size, number of colours and copy. Nevertheless, he was still able to congratulate the competitors on their 'excellent workmanship' though this may have referred to the quality of the printed colour proofs which the entrants produced, rather than the effectiveness and style of the design. The entries were now submitted under a *nom-de-plume* instead of a number, the competition that year being won by 'Bona Fides' who was revealed as H.G. Blain, who worked at the Electrical Press in Fisher Street, just off the Kingsway.

In 1921 the trade card competition was won by 'Invicta', the alias of E.E. Parsons, who worked for E.G. Berryman & Son of Greenwich. The flowing lines of the art nouveau style of decoration framed medieval pioneers of the craft in a design described by Whetton as 'an illustration which may not be exactly a composing department subject, but an old-style compositor was also usually a pressman, so the whole design is appropriate.' The 1930 winning design from 'Elmore', A.E.

Feasey of the Edinburgh Press, Old Bailey, heralds the new, simple, clean approach to graphics that was to characterise the thirties. By then, the winner collected a prize of £5.

After the Second World War the competition prize still stood at £5, with a second prize of £1 and a third of 10s. The competitors had the added incentive of knowing that the order for the printing of 14,000 cards would be placed with the firm at which the winner was employed, a move calculated to please employee and employer alike.

1955 saw the last competition for the London Society of Compositors trade card, the first prize, now raised to £10, being won by B.E. Smith of the Curwen Press, Plaistow. The entries, judged by R.S. Hutchings, the successor of Harry Whetton as editor of *The British Printer*, were fewer than usual and there seems to have been a decline in craftsmanship, for a large proportion were disqualified for literal errors. The same year, the LSC amalgamated with the Printing Machine Managers' Trade Society to form the London Typographical Society. The competition continued until 1963 when the LTS amalgamated with the Typographical Association to form the National Graphical Association and the tradition was abandoned.

LONDON SOCIETY OF COMPOSITORS
7-9 ST. BRIDE STREET, LONDON, E.C.4

Mr. H. G. Palmer

No. 127   Entered 3-1912

Re-established in the Year 1848   1921   — Secretary —
T. E. NAYLOR

The strong traditions of craft skill and the pride of the 'comps' was exemplified by the quotation that used to hang in many a shop:

> Pause stranger, You stand in a Composing Room. Here, metal stamps called types are assembled by skilful hands into the master pattern from which the visible word is multiplied. Five hundred years ago the invention of moveable type opened a new epoch in the history of the human race, releasing the common people from the thraldom of illiteracy, it set their feet upon the road to self-government. You who travel that high road touch not without reverence these leaden symbols of freedom. Remember your incalculable debt to the compositor, who, in the proud servitude of craftsmanship, builds, word upon word, your stairway to the stars.

Labour's 'Bid for Power' fund was launched in April 1928 to counteract the immediate adverse effect of the Trades Disputes and Trades Unions Act (1927) and to raise funds in preparation for the General Election of 1929. Following the Conservative government's victory over the unions in the General Strike of 1926, the Tories were determined to exploit their power by punishing the trade unions and attacking the financial base of the Labour Party. Strongly supported by the National Confederation of Employers' Organisations, the government passed a punitive Act. General strikes were banned under threat of a two-year prison sentence, strikes by local government workers were made illegal, civil service unions banned from affiliation to the TUC, picketing restricted and the political levy clause of the Trade Union Amendment Act of 1913 repealed.

It was the latter legislation that was designed to deprive the Labour Party of a substantial portion of its financial support from the trade unions. The 'Provisions as to Political Fund' section of the Act meant that a trade union member had to give notice in writing of his or her willingness to contribute to the political levy in support of the Labour Party. The immediate result was to reduce the Labour Party's income from trade union affiliation fees by a third. This was because they lost the financial support of those who did not bother to contract in but had not previously chosen to contract out. Affiliation fees were also affected by a decline in trade union membership, which dropped by 1,327,208 from 1926 to 1928 among those unions affiliated to the TUC, as unemployment rose among the membership in mining, steel, engineering and shipbuilding. The total income of the Labour Party for the year ending 31 December 1928 was £57,654. 4s. 9½d., showing a drop in trade union affiliation fees of £15,000 from the previous year. It was from this position of recession that the Labour Party decided to fight back in a 'bid for power' in the next General Election. The fund was launched by Ramsay MacDonald, supported by the TUC, at a specially convened demonstration at the Kingsway Hall in an effort to ensure that

the campaign reached out to every supporter of Labour. 15,000 books of penny receipt tickets were printed at a cost of £140 and the collecting cards, stamps and money boxes went out to constituency Labour parties, trade unions and the various women's sections of the movement. Set against their average annual income, the £100,000 target represented a huge sum to raise by whatever means, and proved in the end to have been optimistic. Nevertheless, the loyal party members did raise almost £50,000 and spending only £40,000 on the election campaign succeeded in returning a Labour government, winning 288 seats to the Conservatives' 261 and the Liberals' 57. Although Labour formed the government, it did not have the overall majority needed to govern and the trades unions had to wait until the election of 1945 for the Labour government with a massive majority to amend the hated Trades Disputes and Trades Unions Act (1927).

> When you are down and the world seems hard
> Don't despair; be on your guard,
> And just take out that small red card.
> – Be organised.

The 'small red card' was the membership card of the National Unemployed Workers' Movement and the verse written by an ex-serviceman in 1922 reflects the fight back by disillusioned war veterans. Amid the mud and misery of the trenches the promises had been made by Lloyd George, whose Welsh rhetoric was intended to keep the men fighting for 'when it is all over', 'a land of milk and honey', 'fit for heroes'. The reality after a dilatory demobilisation was over 2,000,000 unemployed, existing on unemployment benefit of 11s. a week, begging from the Boards of Guardians and begging in the streets. The sight of thin and ragged men, wearing their medals, standing in the gutter singing for pennies, became a familiar sight in the great cities and the heart of the British Empire. In desperation, men busked for survival, 'playing the spoons', pushing barrel-organs, blowing mouth-organs, selling bootlaces and matches. Spontaneously, 'Unemployed Ex-servicemen's Organisations' were formed, some of them taking to the streets *en bloc* to beg for charity, a blind response to their rejection by the society for which they had fought. Among the unemployed were socialists and trade unionists who believed that the time had come to 'stop begging and start fighting'. In October 1920 a conference was held in Clerkenwell with delegates from twelve organisations of the unemployed and a London District Council of Unemployed was established with Wal Hannington as London Organiser; the demand was to be 'work or full maintenance'.

Supported by George Lansbury and the *Daily Herald*, a national conference of unemployed organisations was called, to be held at the International Socialist Club, City Road, London, on 15 April 1921. It was at this conference that the National Unemployed Workers' Movement was born, with Wal Hannington elected as the National Organiser.

From that time until the advent of the Second World War, the NUWM led an unrelenting struggle for work and maintenance at trade union rates. The movement challenged a succession of governments on their failure to provide work for all and kept the issue of unemployment before the public in a series of spectacular demonstrations of protest. They occupied employment exchanges, led mass entries to the workhouses, carried coffins to Downing Street, laid down in Oxford Street, invaded the Ritz Hotel, presented petitions, lobbied MPs and organised massive demonstrations of the unemployed. Of all the stunts that were devised to draw attention to the distress of the workless, it was for the hunger marches that the NUWM is best be remembered. The first of the national hunger marches set out from Glasgow to London on 17 October 1922, to gather men from other areas on the way and to arrive 2,000 strong for a mass demonstration in London on 17 November. The men were hungry and the march organisers lacked experience in such a venture. Some of the men took to the road without top-coats, let alone blankets and necessary kit. There were no food kitchens, no guarantees of food and shelter *en route*, no replacement boots and the summer was past. The men marched at times soaked to the skin in driving rain, without a hot meal, depending often on local goodwill for the bare boards of a cold hall to give shelter for the night. They endured because they were marching for their hungry families, and in doing so reached the emotions of a nation as they slogged through an awful English autumn to carry their message to the capital. They entered the city to a tremendous welcome from the people and the open hostility of the press, police and authorities. Led by a drum and fife band of the Barrow-in-Furness contingent, they gathered 70,000 sympathisers to march, ragged, weary and elated, through the city to Hyde Park.

Other hunger marches in the 1920s and 1930s were better organised, larger and won wider support from the official labour and trade union movement, but none asked more of the marchers than the first, none did more to awaken the people to the obscenity of unemployment and hunger in a rich and wealthy land.

The depth of commitment by members of the NUWM may be gauged by the oath they swore on joining the movement in those early days:

> I, a member of the great army of unemployed, being without work and compelled to suffer through no fault of my own, do hereby solemnly swear with all the strength and resolution of my being, to loyally abide by, and carry out the instructions of the National Unemployed Workers' Committee Movement, with the deliberate intention of pressing forward the claims of the unemployed, so that no man, woman or child suffers hunger or want this winter. Further, realising that only by the abolition of this hideous capitalist system can the horror of unemployment be removed from our midst, I here and now take upon myself a binding oath, to never cease from active strife against this system until capitalism is abolished and our country and all its resources truly belong to the people.

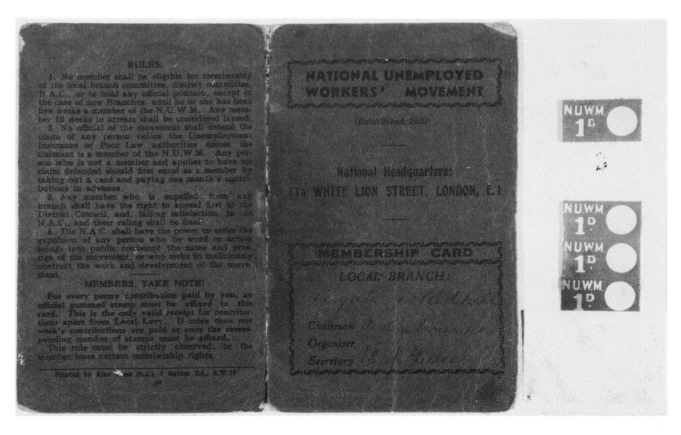

It was William Morris's pamphlet, *Art and Socialism*, published in 1884 that persuaded Walter Crane to the cause of socialism, a cause to which he remained true and which he served until his death in 1915. Crane wrote to Morris after reading the pamphlet, questioning some of his arguments and putting all that occurred to him against the movement. Morris wrote a full reply and, according to Crane, 'the result was that the difficulties disappeared and from the verge of pessimism as regards human progress, I accepted the socialist position, which became a universal solvent in my mind.' Morris had joined the Democratic Federation in January 1884 and had designed their membership card, headed, 'Liberty, Equality, Fraternity', illustrated with a leafy oak tree design, incorporating the motto 'Educate, Agitate, Organise'. Crane followed Morris into the Federation and dutifully followed him out again when the movement split and Morris established the Socialist League.

Crane put his remarkable talent as an artist at the disposal of the wider socialist movement and did not quibble at the divergencies of the various factions, from anarchists to communists. While remaining loyal to Morris, he was yet able to accept the offer to design the membership card of the Social Democratic Party (the SDF gradually referring to itself as a party around 1908). The design is typical of much of Crane's work for the movement, the tree planted firmly in the fertile soil of 'socialisation of the means of production, distribution and exchange' bearing heavy fruit while two workers, male and female, wearing the red caps of liberty, hold fast to the banner of Democratic Socialism.

After the split between the Hyndman and Morris factions in the SDF the financial problems of the SDF became more acute. The movement was supported by a few of the better off and Hyndman continued to subsidise the movement to some extent, but it still relied on its supporters for the funding of its weekly paper, *Justice*, and for the extra money always needed to fight elections. The Fulham Branch, whose members were mainly working men and women on lower wages, canvassed for penny contributions, giving receipts in the form of red stamps carrying the propaganda slogan 'Penny nails in the coffin of capitalism'. Election campaigns were fought on pitifully small sums of money, national speakers being paid only their fare money and being accommodated by local comrades, sharing not only their food and shelter, but sometimes having to share a bed. Harry Lee, a pioneer of the Democratic Federation, wrote, 'Only when a representative who was a workman went away for a week or longer was anything granted beyond fares, and then what he had would most certainly have made him a blackleg if there had been any such thing as a Union of Social-Propagandists.'

On 23 September 1937 the Republican Defence Ministry published a decree on the status and organisation of the International Brigade, the volunteer fighters for Spanish democracy that had come to Spain from all parts of the earth. Acknowledging the increasing pressure of the fascists, the decree formally recognised the International Brigade as an integral part of the Spanish Army, subject to the same regulations as other units. Bill Alexander, a commander of the British Battalion, wrote, 'The decree formalised what every volunteer had painfully learnt from one year's battle experience: organisation, discipline and trained leaders and soldiers were necessary to defeat the regular German and Italian units, the core of Franco's army.' Political conviction, dedication, courage and enthusiasm did not of themselves create a fighting force to match a regular trained army fighting with a plentiful supply of weapons and ammunition and in superior numbers to the Republican forces. The Brigade had to become part of the organised fighting force indigenous to Spain, the Republican Army. Volunteers for the International Brigade had to undertake to remain with them until the end of the war, with the Ministry of Defence deciding on requests for repatriation or leave outside Spain.

The British volunteers became part of the 35th Division commanded by 'General Walter' (Karol Swierczewski), a Pole who had seen service with the Red Army and who had distinguished himself during the fighting on the Cordoba front. The Carnet of Honour was given to those International Brigade volunteers that became part of the 35th Division. A map on the back cover of the card lists the 'actions of glory' and the names are evocative of the heroic battles fought by those who put their lives on the line for the defence of democracy and to halt fascism: Jarama, Brunete, Madrid, Guadarrama and, specially marked,

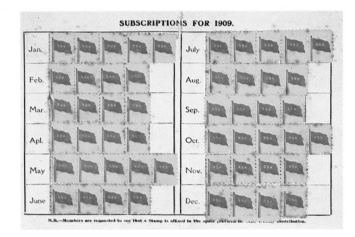

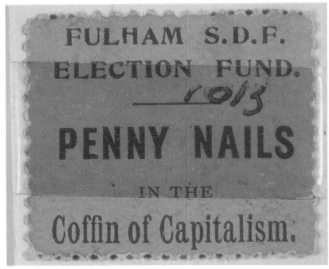

the Ebro river. The symbolic figure of the Spanish Republic has the addition of tears in her eyes as she overlooks a dead soldier. The citation inside the carnet reads:

> You are made an Honorable Combatant of the 35th Division of the Regular Popular Army, as a Freedom Volunteer. Through your actions, you have been, in our nation, a firm expression of the advance party of the Popular Front and Democracy in the World, in the struggle against invading fascism.
> The soldiers of the Division, all Spaniards, will never forget those who, with them, defended the independence of national soil, covering themselves with glory in the battles in which they took part.
> With our call of 'Long live the International Volunteers!', we affirm that the Spanish Republic will achieve its total independence.
> Spain, October 1938.

It was not until the death of General Franco in 1975, after thirty-seven years of fascist dictatorship, that Spain finally emerged to freedom and the surviving volunteers of the International Brigade were invited to return to march in celebration through the streets of Madrid and share the jubilation, the tears for freedom and the memory of all those who had suffered and died to make that freedom possible.

On 23 December 1938 General Franco launched his final offensive against the Republican army in Catalonia. With overwhelming military superiority, unchallenged control of the skies and backed with adequate transport and supplies, Barcelona fell and hundreds of thousands of women and children joined the stream of combatants fleeing from the terror and tyranny of the fascists. Daily accounts gave harrowing stories of the tragic fugitives, ill-clothed and hungry, making their way over the snow-clad Pyrenees to seek sanctuary within French borders. With half a million refugees on the move, the collapse of the transport system due to shortage of petrol, the bitter Catalonian winter and the chaos of war as the trekking columns were machine-gunned from the air, conditions of near famine existed in northern Spain.

FOOD FOR SPAIN

In the NAME of HUMANITY
we appeal to your
generosity to help
FILL THE FOOD SHIP

Surrey Food Ship Appeal

The National Joint Committee for Spanish Relief worked in Britain, bringing together groups from all over the country to alleviate the distress caused by Franco's aggression. In 1939 the Committee campaigned to send ships filled with desperately needed supplies of food, clothes and medical aid to the innocent victims. Local groups set about organising and raising funds to charter and fill ships and the Surrey Spain Foodship Appeal was just one of many in response to the call.

On 28 January 1939 an emergency meeting of representatives of sixteen Surrey Spain Relief Committees met at Epsom to plan their foodship appeal. Henry Fry volunteered to organise the collecting of food and money and a target of £5,000 was set to obtain milk, tinned foods, oils, fats, sugar, soap and clothing. A committee was formed that included the Mayor of Guildford, Robert Tribe, the Assistant Bishop of Guildford, The Very Revd Cyril H. Golding-Bird and many other civil and religious leaders from the county.

Support for the Foodship Appeal came from a wide cross section of the community. Cow and Gate Ltd. gave 1,000 tins of milk, Czechoslovakian refugees at Albury gave up their cigarettes and tobacco to donate a crate of milk, local grocers put tubs in their shops for gifts of food and a Spain Shop in the High Street, Guildford, was staffed by volunteers from the British Legion, the League of Nations' Union, the Left Book Club and the political parties. The penny stamps were only one of the many ways devised for raising the £5,000 as Surrey's contribution to a cause of common humanity.

OBJECTS

Evocative of a 1930s children's penny money box is the tin savings box for Royal Arsenal Co-operative Society checks. The history of co-operation in the area around the Royal Arsenal, however, stretches back to the eighteenth century when Woolwich shipwrights acquired their own corn mill in 1760. Further efforts at co-operative trading were made in 1805, with the forming of a co-operative butchers, in 1842 with the Co-operative Coal Society, and in 1851 when dockyard workers set up the Woolwich Co-operative Provident Society. A Co-operative Coal Society was launched in 1856 but all of these ventures followed early success with eventual failure.

It was not until 1868 when William Rose, a member of the Amalgamated Society of Engineers, raised the question of forming a co-operative society at his branch meeting that a lasting co-op was established in Woolwich. A week after Rose made his proposal, a meeting was held at the Lord Raglan public house; twenty members enrolled, five managers elected and £4. 11s. 0d. subscribed. Two weeks later with a capital of £7. 4s. 6d. a chest of tea was bought, 100 pounds of sugar and two crocks of butter.

The tiny shop opened on 28 November 1868 and sold goods to the value of £2. 4s. 9½d. on the first day. These early pioneers had to withstand the jibes and jeers of workmates at their modest trading endeavours and the open hostility of local traders. Nevertheless, after nine months of persistent work, trading profit stood at £13. 17s. 9d. and it was decided to adopt the Rochdale system of paying a bonus to customers on all purchases, the

keystone of co-operative trading. The society decided to register under the Industrial and Provident Societies Acts and drew up a set of rules based on guidelines issued by the Christian Socialists. They were submitted to the Registrar and, after some minor changes to the title, the certificate for the Royal Arsenal Co-operative Society Ltd. was issued on 17 February 1872.

The Society, firmly rooted among the working class, made steady and continual progress to become an integral part of the trading, manufacturing, cultural and political life of the community. A farm was bought, milk distribution arranged and the Society expanded into butchery, drapery, bootmaking, house building and printing. The visions and dreams became reality as new stores were built, a library opened, a rest home provided for employees and a Co-operative Hall made available for meetings and education. It proved, as Mr Maxwell of the Scottish Co-operative Wholesale Society said in a congratulatory speech, that 'by mutual help alone are the workers to be saved, and that the efforts of charity are useless and must fail to have any permanent effect.'

In order that members should receive their portion of the trading surplus in direct proportion to their purchases, dividend tokens were issued. These were made of tin and issued in various denominations of up to £1. Above that sum, brass tokens were used for £1, £2 and £5 and members were encouraged to save them in the bright red boxes bearing the RACS motto 'Each for all and all for each'. The 'tin checks' and 'brass checks' were used for more than half a century until the system was finally

discarded in 1960 in favour of the more sophisticated accounting method of giving a printed 'Climax' check against each purchase. This, in turn, was abandoned in 1970 when trading stamps were introduced.

For the generations between the wars, the 'divi' was an integral part of working class life, hardworking mums using the half yearly rebate to provide awaited necessities like new boots, clothes or the replacement of wornout hardware.

'Our aim is to create a genuinely Independent Labour Party to take charge of the revolution to which economic conditions are leading us, and its object is to build up the industrial commonwealth in which none will suffer want because of the overabundance of others.' With these words, Keir Hardie asserted the independence of a new force in British political life, a party of Labour free from association with the Liberals, the bitterest enemies of those socialists who stood for an independent party of the working class.

The opening conference was held at Bradford on 13 and 14 January 1893, an industrial city chosen for its radical traditions, a centre of the Labour Church and Labour Club movement, away from the middle class influences of the capital. Robert Blatchford declared at the conference, 'I regard Liberals and Tories as enemies of the people . . . I would consider it a stain on the Labour Party to have any dealings with the Liberals, I would as soon have dealings with the devil.'

To the pioneers of the ILP their movement was pledged to a socialism that meant more than 'the collective and communal ownership of all the means of production, distribution and exchange', the stated objective of the party: it was a humanitarian crusade. The 'commonweal' was practised with zeal as the missionaries of socialism travelled around the country sharing food and shelter with poor comrades, speaking at street corners night after night, at the beck and call of newly formed branches, never stinting in their efforts and never the question of financial reward. These were the new apostles preaching the brotherhood of man, the religion of socialism, each for all and all for each. To carry the message and fight elections cost money, and, for a working class party, that money could only come from themselves and the workers who supported them. In the General Election of 1895 Keir Hardie led twenty-eight ILP candidates in challenging the Liberals and Tories, but without success; all twenty-eight, Tom Mann, Robert Smillie, Keir Hardie and the rest, being beaten at the poll. The cost of fighting the election imposed an enormous financial burden, the election fund being raised by penny collections, though in some cases even wedding rings were pawned to meet the costs. The date of manufacture of the ILP collection box is uncertain. Its appeal for pennies 'To strike a blow gainst want and woe', for socialism, the commonweal, stands as a monument to the sacrifices of poor men and women for the cause of Labour.

One of Henry Fry's proudest acquisitions towards his jumbled collection of memorabilia was the table used by Thomas Paine for his writings in 1792. The authenticity of the relic seems in little doubt for it is documented in a biography of Paine by Thomas Clio Rickman, published in 1819. Paine and Rickman were friends for many years and Paine shared Rickman's home in London sometime before and during 1792 until leaving for France on 12 September of that year. The book also carries an illustration of the brass plaque that Rickman had inlaid into the table to commemorate its use by his friend. Rickman claims that Paine wrote his 'Letter to the Addressers', the second part of the 'Rights of Man', upon the table, as well as 'many other things he wrote at my house.' 'Letter to the Addressers' was first published in February 1792 and Rickman makes the extravagant assertion that 1,500,000 copies were printed in England.

By 1863 the table was in the possession of Clair James Grece, the town clerk of Horley, Surrey, and passed by descent within the family until it was bought for a purely nominal sum by Fry in 1965.

After the English revolutionary died in New York City on 8 June 1809, his bones were brought back to England in 1819 by William Cobbett. Fry tried for years to locate the final resting place of Paine without success.

The Victorian way of death was elaborate. At the time of the formation of the Labour Protection League in 1872, the forerunner of the Amalgamated Stevedores' Labour Protection League, a respectable funeral for a labouring man could cost six guineas, the equivalent of two months' wages. This would include a hearse with a pair of horses, mourning coach and pair,

elm coffin covered with black, inscription plate, use of a velvet pall, bearers and coachmen and attendant with black silk hatband – simple enough by the standards of the day. The price did not include the burial charges, gravestone, mourning wear for the family and the inevitable beer and ham sandwiches after the funeral.

Funerals grew in size, show and ritual in direct relation to the position in the social scale of the deceased, culminating in the final social acclaim, the size of the headstone, monument or tomb. For kings, queens, dukes and generals, funerals were a national pageant.

Although the working class could not hope to match their social superiors in their extravagance in death, a 'decent sendoff' was considered essential. For a working man or woman living on a weekly wage calculated by the employer to provide a bare weekly subsistence, while work was available, the cost of dying was an ever-present problem. For the working class, the ultimate humiliation was a pauper's funeral. In an age before social security, the trade unions were quick to offer 'friendly benefits' as an inducement to membership. In 1789 the Society of Bakers was formed in Dublin, the heading of the original document reading 'for the support of the sick and burial of deceased of said Society'. The Bakers also loaned out all that was needed for the laying out of the dead, the rules of the Bridge Street Society in Dublin in 1838 provided 'that the Society shall provide three large linen sheets and tablecloth, six candle sticks, a snuffer and snuffer's tray, and such other articles as they may deem necessary for the decent laying out of the dead.' The Dublin Woodworkers provided their members with a magnificent black Gothic bier while the Limerick Coopers offered £5 for the burial of a member and £4 for the burial of his wife. In England, many trade unions emblazoned their banners with graveside scenes, sorrowing widows and benevolent branch secretaries, cash in hand, to promote the benefits of membership. The Stockton branch banner of the NUR painted in 1914 showed a widow and four children at the grave of a dead 'brother' beneath the inscription, 'Do you hear the children weeping, O my brothers?' The late nineteenth century banner of the United Society of Boiler Scalers and Stoke Hold Labourers showed a similar scene but with the addition of a sympathising union representative at the graveside wearing his sash of office. So much emphasis was placed upon sick and death benefits by some of the craft trade unions that they were disparagingly called 'coffin clubs' by the new militant unions of the unskilled.

The widow's weeds, loaned by the Stevedores' Union free of charge to a deceased member's widow, would have been an invaluable contribution to ensuring the respectable and dignified public departure of a late brother. For an official or a long serving or popular member of the dockers' unions, the branch banner would be brought to the house to lead the cortège, the union officials wearing their sashes as a last mark of respect.

It was in 1913 that the Co-operative Wholesale Society produced the elaborately illustrated tin box to commemorate the jubilee of the Society. The portraits on the front are those of Abraham Greenwood of Rochdale, first President of the CWS, and John Shillito, a Halifax man who was President of the Society at the time of the Jubilee. The vast premises depicted on the lid are the Central Administrative Offices and Warehouses at Balloon Street, Manchester, first opened in 1869, while the side illustration shows the London Business Branch at Leman Street, East London.

First enrolled on 11 August 1863 as the North of England Co-operative Industrial and Provident Society Limited, the organisation commenced trading on 14 March 1864, and

achieved a turnover in excess of £50,000 during its first financial year. By the time of the Jubilee in 1913, the turnover was well over £30,000,000. The Society shortened its cumbersome title in 1867 by dropping the words 'Industrial and Provident' and further abridged the name in 1872 by dispensing with the 'North of England' prefix, arriving at the present name.

Formed as a bulk purchasing agency for co-operative societies, the Wholesale Society soon ventured into manufacturing, beginning with biscuit making at Crumpsall, Manchester, in 1873, and extended to cocoa and chocolate in 1874, clothing, 1890, cabinet making, 1893, printing and jam making, 1894, the manufacture of corsets, 1896, and went into the twentieth century with a wide range of consumer products. Insurance, banking and transport complemented the manufacturing base to make the Co-operative Wholesale Society a vital and powerful force in the commerce of the nation.

Abraham Greenwood was the chief founder of the Society, presenting his paper on 'Wholesale Agency' to a meeting of delegates from industrial and provident co-operative societies at the King Street stores, Oldham, on Christmas Day, 1862. Yes, Christmas Day, one of the few holidays allowed to working people and one of the few opportunities of gathering for a conference. The meeting resolved that 'all co-operative societies be requested to contribute one farthing per member to meet the expenses that may arise' in preparation of the plans for a central agency. The dedication, enthusiasm and tenacity of those co-operative pioneers may be judged from the fact that the follow-up meeting was held on Good Friday 1863, this time in Manchester.

John Shillito became President of the CWS in 1895 and held the position for nearly twenty years, leading the Society to celebrate its jubilee shortly before his retirement. Born at Upper Brear, near Halifax, in 1832, Shillito was apprenticed as a card wire drawer at the age of ten years. Self-educated at the Mechanics' Institute, he joined the co-operative movement in 1865 and devoted the rest of his life to the movement. He became a Fellow of the Royal Geographical Society and was a leading figure in the scientific and literary life of Halifax.

The two portraits of Greenwood and Shillito, pioneers of Wholesale Co-operation, printed on tin, mark more than a jubilee; they are a testimony to the power of working people to organise industry.

The box with three locks was to be found in almost every trade union branch in the early days of trade unionism. It was a simple means of safeguarding funds from embezzlement or protecting documents in the years when trade unions had no legal redress. As most union meetings were held in public houses, it was common for the box to be left in the safe custody of the landlord, who held one key, while the other two different keys would be held by two officers of the society, probably the treasurer and secretary.

The precaution was necessary, as more than one early trade union foundered as a result of a weak and unscrupulous member's absconding with the funds. The repeal of the Combination Laws had given working people the right to combine, but combinations in restraint of trade were still held to be unlawful and as such its funds were unprotected. An officer having sole access to the funds could, if he were so minded, embezzle them with impunity. It was not until the Trade Union Act of 1871 that trade union funds came under the protection of the law.

The tradition of the box with three locks belonged to the craft guilds and, later, to the friendly societies, and was another

piece of ritual and practice appropriated by the emergent trade unions. Contributions collected on the branch or lodge meeting night would be deposited in the box. The contribution, for example, of the Friendly Society of Ironfounders in 1809 was 'a shilling to the box'. Likewise, any tramping or sick benefits would be distributed directly from the box. To this day there are old trade unionists who refer to their claim for sick benefit as 'going on the box'. In the late eighteenth and early nineteenth centuries some unions chose their 'keymasters' or trustees on the system of rotation. The Journeyman Shoemakers of Edinburgh provided that the 'keymasters' be chosen by the roll, beginning at the top for the first keymaster, and at the middle of the roll for the youngest keymaster, and so on until the roll was finished. 'If any refuse the keymaster, he shall pay one shilling and sixpence sterling.' Many of the boxes were elaborately and beautifully painted with the society's 'coat of arms' and resembled the sea chests of naval officers in their lettering and decoration. The ancient box of the Glasgow Ropemakers' Friendly Society was painted with arms and kept in the custody of the president who was elected annually. Until the 1860s the tradition was maintained of solemnly transporting the box through the streets of Glasgow to the house of the new president with a procession of ropespinners headed by a piper, the ceremony concluding with a feast.

It was more usual for the box to be held without ceremony, in trust to a publican or union officer; fortunately for the growth of trade unionism, few betrayed the trust placed in them. Brewers, it seems, were held to be the friends of the union; when the United Society of Journeyman Brushmakers accumulated some £400 in 1831, they sought a safer repository than a box. Their solution was to take it to Whitbread's the brewers, and the minutes of the monthly delegate meeting on 29 June 1831 record 'Mr Farrington and Mr Salmon chosen trustees to invest the money with the Secretary in the Brewers' hands and that they be allowed 3s. 0d. each whenever they attend.' The banks could not be trusted, neither could the Post Office, for both were too close to a hostile government. John White, the founder of the 'Old Mechanics', one of the unions that came to be part of the new Amalgamated Society of Engineers in 1851, remembered how he used to change his lodging every few weeks to stop the 'constables from tracing his movements' and how, as treasurer of the union, he used to hide as much as £6,000 up the chimney of his house in China Lane, Manchester.

The box of the Banbury branch of the Amalgamated Society of Engineers dates from a time shortly after the founding of the union and was used for the safekeeping of the union funds and membership records.

The Wade's Arms, Jeremiah Street, Poplar, should have been preserved as a monument to the most significant strike in the history of British trades unionism, the Great Dock Strike of 1889. Once the strike got going, it was the headquarters of the Strike Committee, a scene of daily turmoil, 'the hub of the universe' as Ben Tillett described it, as the strike leaders and their helpers planned the fund raising, marches, demonstrations, appeals and argued the tactics of negotiation and dispensed relief to the strikers and their families. The Wade's Arms has gone, but a battered relic from the epic struggle survives, a leather bag used to carry money from street collections to be poured into the ice chest at the Wade's Arms that was used to store the coppers, the cash behind the relief tickets.

At first, the strikers had to tighten their belts and turn to the pawn shop as they speculated which would come first, starvation or surrender. It was not until the twelfth day of the strike as the loaded collection boxes began to come in from the city that the first distribution of bread and cheese was made, a move that did not please all the hungry men. An impossible situation developed at Wroots' Coffee House, the first headquarters of the strike, as thousands demanded a share of the money. It was Tom Mann who prudently decided that shilling relief tickets should be issued to be honoured by local tradesmen, for food and nothing else. On the first day of the scheme, 4,000 men waited outside and Mann pledged that every man should get his ticket if he would take his turn and bide his time. Planting himself in the doorway, his back jammed against one side of the frame, his foot up against the other, he allowed the men to creep in one at a time under his leg. For hour after hour Mann stuck at his task, his back rubbed raw, until every man received a ticket.

The headquarters were then moved to the Wade's Arms where Mann took charge of the relief work and began to organise it on a massive scale. Volunteers like Mrs Tillett, Mrs Burns and Eleanor Marx worked untiringly, stamping tickets and counting the farthings, halfpennies and pennies to pay the tradesmen when they presented their tickets. The ticket system ensured that relief could not be spent on drink; it also made recruits, for the relief committee only issued tickets against presentation of a union card. 20,000 union cards were issued at 2*d.* each during the strike and the distribution of relief tickets reached 25,000 a day, with a double issue on Saturdays. By the end of the strike, 440,000 tickets had been issued and all the tradesmen were paid in cash. More than £1,000 was raised by street collections, while over £10,000 came in from individual donations by post.

The bag held the pennies of the poor, given to help the poor, as 100,000 men refused to work until their claim had been met. The strike was a victory for organisation, with 16,000 pickets under captains, lieutenants and sergeants; it was a victory of solidarity, with skilled workers supporting the 'unskilled'; it was a victory for trade unionism as the organisation of non-craft workers spread to every industry.

PAINTINGS
PRINTS
DRAWINGS
&
SCULPTURE

A.J. Waudby's design for the emblem of the Operative Bricklayers' Society, produced in the 1860s, was described by him as 'being intended not merely to serve the purpose of a Trade Emblem, but to form an elaborate and interesting work of art'. The massive oak-framed oil painting (size 8ft x 6ft) which hung in the union's head office is unsigned, but almost certainly the work of Waudby, and is without question 'an interesting work of art'.

Dated 1869, it matches in style and design many features of Waudby's emblem and the Operative Bricklayers' Society's annual report for 1869 details expenditure of £115. 0s. 0d. to A.J. Waudby for the painting of a 'new flag'. Admittedly the painting cannot be described as a flag, but it is most likely that the original oil painting was made by Waudby to be copied by a professional firm of banner painters to form the centre panel of banners for the Society.

The design uses scaffold poles as a leading feature, according to Waudby who used them in his design for the union emblem, 'as being the most effective and appropriate object in the composition'. As with the emblem, the 'front' of the design introduces the tools of the trade. In addition to the use of two mottos familiar to trade unionists, 'Unity is strength' and 'Industry is the source of prosperity', there is an ambiguous part quotation from Proverbs 14:23, 'In all labour there is profit.' If the quotation is completed, 'but the talk of the lips tendeth only to penury', the meaning is apparent. Used only in part and on a trade union device, the retort is invited, 'Profit, yes – but for whom?'

The workshop scene, depicting gauge work, is surrounded by the three female figures of Architecture, Truth and Science and beneath are the familiar trade union cameos of injury at work, trade union compensation and concern for the family.

The date, 1869, is prefaced by 'London' to distinguish it from the Manchester Order of Bricklayers, the union having divided into two parts following the demise of the Friendly Society of Operative Bricklayers in 1848.

Painted in 1953 by J. Ashford, the origins of this oil painting of a railway worker and a little girl remain a mystery, for it has not yet proved possible to trace the artist or anyone who knew him. All that is known is that Ashford was himself a railway worker on the Southern Region who lived in Brighton and painted in his spare time. Like the work of so many worker artists who are Sunday painters, it has a humanity and natural warmth often sought and rarely captured in the work of professional portrait painters.

No artist has made a bigger contribution to the iconography of the labour movement than Walter Crane. From the moment of his conversion to socialism, joining the Social Democratic Federation shortly after William Morris in 1884, until his death in 1915, Crane gave freely of his enormous talent to the cause of labour, becoming in his own time the artist of socialism, a contribution that has yet to be surpassed and whose influence remains to this day.

Already famous as an illustrator of children's books, stained glass, ceramics and a painter of the pre-Raphaelite school, a wealthy man by inheritance, the strands that knitted together to bring him into the movement for social democracy were many. Crane himself acknowledges the influence of W.J. Linton, the Chartist engraver to whom Crane was apprenticed in 1859, the writings of John Ruskin, especially his 'A Joy Forever, and its Price in the Market', the works of John Stuart Mill, and the final catalyst, the pamphlet by William Morris on *Art and Socialism*. Like Morris, Walter Crane believed 'that work is a necessity of human life, not merely as a means to earn a living but for health and happiness.' Crane's work, his graphic and compelling imagery became the visual embodiment of the socialist message, his designs embracing virtually every form of decorative art, pamphlet covers, magazine headings, banners, badges, emblems, paintings, sketches and cartoons, all flowed from his brush and pen. His work was calculated to uplift and inspire, to pay tribute to labour and proclaim the coming millennium of the socialist commonwealth.

Crane designed a few banners for the Social Democratic Federation, the Gasworkers' Union, the Electrical Trades Union, the National Federation of Women Workers and the Irish Nationalists, but his drawings and engravings became the ready reference and inspiration for hundreds more. His 'Angel of

Freedom', originally included in his painting of 'Freedom' exhibited in the Grosvenor Gallery in 1885, was freely adapted on scores of trade union banners, his 'vision breaking into the sunshine of spring' changing to a vision breaking into the sunshine of socialism. His 'Triumph of Labour', produced in 1891 and 'dedicated to the workers of all countries', was reproduced in three languages and became the inspiration for an unknown number of banners until the 1930s, as did his cartoons of 'A Garland for May Day' and 'The Workers' Maypole'. His work attacked the Boer War, commemorated the Paris Commune, supported Greek freedom, marked Bloody Sunday and the death of Alfred Linnell. His non-sectarian approach to socialism enabled him to design for the Fabian Society, the Socialist League, the Herald League, the Independent Labour Party, for *Justice, Clarion, The Political World, Work, The Pioneer, Woman Worker, Free Russia* and *The British Esperantist*. He designed a seal for the Socialist Co-operative Federation of London, a firework display for a May Day demonstration at Crystal Palace,

Socialist Christmas cards, the cover of a socialist song book, the prospectus for an International School and, best known of all, his 'cartoons' for May Day. Crane's work became the recognisable imagery of international class solidarity while Crane himself became a people's artist.

The rare self-portrait pencil drawing was given to Henry Fry as a gift to TULC during an early exhibition at Outwood Church near Horley, Sussex. It hangs as a memorial, surrounded by the imagery of labour that became a central part of his life and work as an artist and socialist.

Esher Place, a residence of Cardinal Wolsey from 1519 until his downfall in 1529, was an improbable setting for a series of five murals painted by a communist artist for a national trade union. The house, standing amid landscaped grounds, was built upon a site given by William the Conqueror to the monks of the Abbey of St Leutfred's Cross on condition that two priests would stay at Esher and say masses for the souls of his predecessors.

The present structure, built on the order of a Bishop, William of Waynflete, in 1447, has been lived in by a series of wealthy notables from Richard Drake, the cousin of Sir Francis, to Thomas Lynch, one of the first colonists of Jamaica and the Right Honourable Henry Pelham, a corrupt and far from honourable Prime Minister.

It was in 1953, with Britain still recovering from the financial, material and human devastation of the Second World War, that the Electrical Trades Union led by a formidable executive, with Walter C. Stevens as General Secretary, bought Esher Place as a residential college for the training of shop stewards. The price paid was a bargain £23,000, hardly enough to cover the cost of the bricks, but 1953 saw Britain still in the grip of austerity and the cost of maintaining, heating, furnishing and staffing country mansions was a daunting proposition for a private family. Esher Place provided the union with an ideal college centre with thirty-five study-bedrooms, lecture room, board room, library, lounge, offices and leisure areas, including two squash courts, two saunas and billiard room. Set amid six beautiful acres (in which is the oldest tulip tree in England, planted in 1685), the acquisition established the union among the most progressive and far-sighted of trade unions in the 1950s. The union had been formed on 2 November 1889 at the Crown Hotel, Blackfriars Street, Manchester, and its first election was for a 'drink steward'. (For the historical record, the election was won by a Mr Brennan who polled eleven votes against nine votes for Mr Mellor.) Now the membership stood at over 200,000 and the ETU could claim to be 'a power in the land' in more than one way.

Walter Stevens, the General Secretary, is credited with the idea of commissioning the five murals depicting notable struggles from trade union history and providing the appropriate militant background for the training of shop stewards. To undertake the work he approached Cliff Rowe, a founder of the Artists' International Association and a loyal and respected member of the Communist Party. It was a sound choice, for Rowe was an experienced and talented painter, totally devoted to the cause of socialism.

Clifford Hooper Rowe was born in Wimbledon in 1904 and at the age of fourteen began his art education at Wimbledon School of Art. From there he won a scholarship to the Royal College of Art, a coveted prize for a young working class artist, but Rowe rebelled against the teaching, considering it to be 'out of date and reactionary', and after one year walked out to look for a job. He worked for two years as a commercial artist for a West End advertising agency, Saward Baker, and then left to freelance. By his own admission Rowe was not successful as a commercial artist but yearned to be a painter and like so many artists found himself impoverished and unable to afford canvas and paints. Whilst he lived through the reality of poverty, painting with bootpolish on newspapers, he was forced to see that money was a powerful factor in society, at the same time being contemptuous of political parties and attempting to solve his problems in his own individualistic manner. Unemployed, he was walking through Bloomsbury when he saw a poster in a small socialist bookshop advising workers to read. The poster was crude, and on an impulse Rowe offered to paint a new one for 7s. 6d. The bookseller agreed and Rowe, unknown to himself, had taken the first step on his road to socialism. A week later Pat Dooley, editor of *Irish Communist*, called on him and offered him a book jacket to design for a further 7s. 6d. It was a Marxist tract, and accepting the commission, Rowe diligently read the booklet that he had to illustrate. He was not convinced by what he read and argued the contents with Dooley, who then persuaded him to read the *Communist Manifesto*. It was a revelation to the young artist, who saw that in a capitalist society, art was a question of 'how much money'. It exposed the problem of money versus the quality of life. Rowe says, 'It solved so many intellectual problems about advertising and my work as a commercial artist that I felt the scales fall from my eyes.' He decided to go to Russia. Rowe sold some of his paintings and raised enough money to buy a ticket for a seven-day tour; he was not yet a communist but wanted to ignore the propaganda and go and see for himself, to see how an artist fared in the new society.

It was 1932 and Rowe left England in a crisis of capitalism, with rising unemployment, to find Russia 'in a hell of a state'. There were shortages of just about everything but the spirit of the people convinced him to stay and help as an artist. Rowe did not speak any Russian but discovered that first he must have a room; without a room, there was no employment for migrant workers. He found a room but still could not find a job, and he wandered the streets of Moscow until he saw a sign in English. It was the Foreign Workers' Publishing House and on the walls were covers of pamphlets he had designed for the Communist Party in England. They gave him a job and Rowe was free to paint, not for private gain but to help build a socialist society. The Red Army was a great patron of artists and they staged a huge exhibition in Moscow, including an international section for which they sought foreign artists so that each country would be represented by a native artist. Rowe was chosen to paint the English section, modestly admitting that he may not have been chosen on merit, but because he must have been the only English artist working in Russia! He was asked for a painting depicting some aspect of the class struggle and decided on a night scene of 'Hunger Marchers Entering Trafalgar Square', a painting of photographic realism that met the demands of Soviet art but represented a style for which Rowe had little sympathy. While working on the painting, he found himself immersed in political discussion with other artists, both Soviet and foreign. He was impressed by the lack of political division and the unity of thought that they should work together, for peace and against fascism. When the painting was completed, Rowe returned to England: 'I left only because I realised they did not need me. The class struggle was really going on in England so I decided to come back.'

Rowe wanted to create an international group of artists to work for peace and oppose fascism and social injustice, so he wrote to an old friend of his, Misha Black. The outcome was a meeting of a small group of artists at the top of an old building in Seven Dials and the foundation of the Artists' International Association. Within a year the Association had almost a thousand members, artists, musicians, actors, all giving of their talents to the cause of peace and liberty. James Boswell, Pearl Binder, James Fitton, Eric Gill, James Holland, Jack Hastings, Francis Klingender, A.L. Lloyd, and hundreds more, the well-known and the unrecognised, inspired groups of artists to work together producing posters, banners, paintings, drawings, supporting the hunger marchers, supporting Republican Spain, attacking fascist ideology and bringing a new approach to art that broke down barriers between commercial art and fine art, putting art to the service of the working class. All the time there was discussion about art, about socialist realism (which Rowe accepted for three years and then rejected) about content and form, abstract art, about Russia and Russian Art, experiments for a new socialist art. The organisation was loose and although the Artists' International Association had about a hundred Communist Party members, it was never a Communist Party organisation and was not constrained by the theoretical pronouncements on art by the Communist Party. Rowe has said that one must differentiate between the 'inner core' which was a small number of highly politically motivated people, many of whom were communists, and the large circle of people who contributed to exhibitions and who held different views about their work and society. At a period of broad popular opposition to fascism many Royal Academicians lent their names and work to the support of the AIA, Laura Knight, Muirhead Bone, Dod Proctor and Algernon Newton among them.

The AIA survived the war but did not survive the peace, losing its radical commitment and becoming a cosy club, an exhibition society without political direction.

Rowe no longer associated himself with the AIA but worked as an artist from his studio in Camden Town. When the Electrical Trades Union offered the commission to paint five murals for

Esher Place, Rowe was happy to accept the opportunity of using his talent in the service of a working class organisation. The ETU had a tradition as a patron of socialist art, having commissioned Walter Crane to paint their famous 'Light and Liberty' banner in 1898. Now Rowe was given the chance to record five episodes from trade union history as a permanent embellishment to the grandeur of Esher Place. The five subjects were chosen by the ETU: the Tolpuddle Martyrs, the General Strike, the Albert Hall black-out, and two ETU strikes, one in Bolton, the other in Fulham. Unfortunately, pressure was put upon Rowe to complete the murals for the official opening of the college and there was insufficient time to carry out research to ensure full accuracy in certain historical and costume details. Three of the murals were to be seven feet by twenty feet and Rowe decided to paint with a wax colour onto marine ply, working in sections in his Camden studio. He was used to the technique, if not to working on such a large scale. The size of the murals and their present location has made it impossible to photograph all the panels in their entirety and selected sections have been chosen to give some impression of the detailed work on each painting. The General Strike mural was painted without photographic reference but is surprisingly close to matching extant photographs of troop- and police-escorted convoys being driven by blacklegs from the London docks. If the Vickers machine gun seems overdramatic, it must be remembered that tanks from Wellington barracks were actually driven onto the streets to intimidate the strikers.

The Albert Hall mural illustrates a famous episode in the history of the ETU, when a meeting called by the *Daily Herald* to be held on 23 November 1918 at the Albert Hall was cancelled at four days' notice by the management. The official statement by the management read, 'In view of the demonstrations of a revolutionary character that took place here on the 3rd. and 4th. inst., on the part of Mr Lansbury's supporters, I do not think that

my Council will be justified, in their own interests, in allowing the meeting arranged for the 23rd. inst. to take place in the Royal Albert Hall. I am instructed to cancel the contract entered into by you on the 12th. inst., and to return your deposit.' The meeting referred to on the 3rd was held by the National Union of Railwaymen and the meeting on the 4th by the Labour Party. Both meetings were completely orderly, even the no smoking rule being observed. The sole act of a revolutionary character was that, due to the packed capacity of the Hall, some common trade unionists sat in the Royal Box! The manager, Hilton Carter, refused to meet with Lansbury to discuss the matter and Lansbury wrote to both the Home Secretary and Lloyd George, the Prime Minister. Lloyd George replied that 'the Albert Hall authorities are entirely free to make their own engagements' and said he could not interfere with their decision. Meanwhile, thousands of *Herald* supporters were applying for tickets and among them was J.W. Muir of the ETU asking for fifty tickets. Told that the meeting was cancelled by order of the Albert Hall manager, Muir replied, 'We'll stop that little game.' A few hours later F.J. Webb, the Secretary of the ETU, telephoned Hilton Carter and told him, 'If you don't allow the *Herald* to hold their meeting, we'll cut off your light.' Carter said, 'Is that a threat?'; to which Webb answered, 'No, it's a fact.' On Saturday morning ETU workers removed the fuses to the Royal Albert Hall and Ben Smith of the London and Provincial Union of Licensed Vehicle Workers instructed his members that no taxis would stop at the Albert Hall and that no buses or trains would stop at South Kensington. Hilton Carter appealed to the government (who, it is to be recalled, had no power to intervene) and the government appealed to Lansbury, who made it plain: no meeting, no light.

The Albert Hall management surrendered, the meeting was packed with 12,000 trade unionists and thousands were turned away. The *Herald* staff, J.R. MacDonald and Mrs Snowden were on the platform to hear Lansbury say, 'If only the toilers could

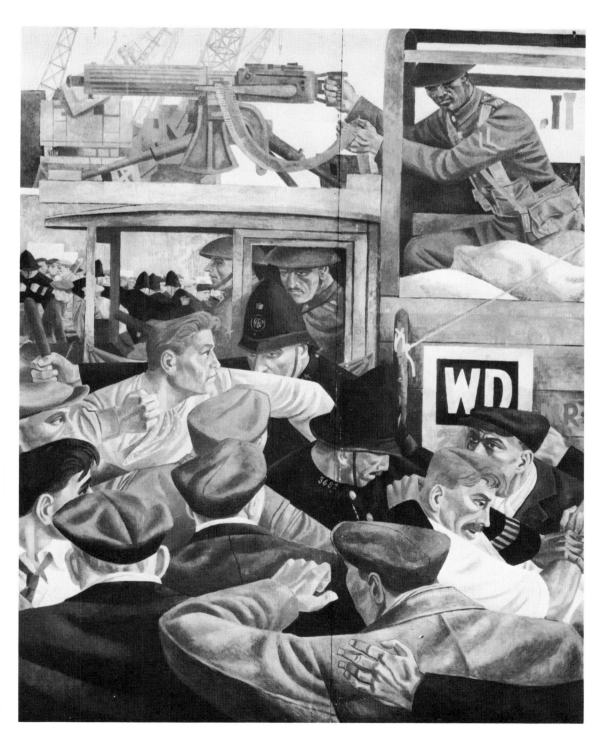

131

realise that all power lies in their hands, and realising that would use their power to assist each other upward to a better life, how much quicker we should reach our goal.' The ETU's pulling of the fuses was confirmed as one of the great victories for trade union solidarity and has become part of the legendary history of the *Daily Herald*.

Two smaller panels depicting successful local ETU strikes complete the series, which were hung on the lounge walls of Esher Place and unveiled in 1954. Rowe acknowledges the influence of the Mexican mural artists, Diego Rivera and David Alfaro Siqueiros, upon the style of the paintings but is dismissive of the importance of the ETU murals as works of art. Rowe said of them, 'They are not up to standard, they were too rushed. Would burn all the bloody lot, willingly!'

Whatever the debate upon the final artistic quality, the murals are a powerful representation of trade union struggle and occupy a significant position in the art history of the trade union movement. They remained at Esher Place until 1982 when they were removed and donated to the National Museum of Labour History.

Ken Sprague's lino cut, 'General Strike', is in sharp contrast to the social realism of Cliff Rowe's mural on the same subject, yet both capture the essence of the struggle between workers and the state.

Sprague was born on 1 January 1927, the son of an engine driver and a South London cardboard-box maker. He won a scholarship to the Bournemouth College of Art in 1940 and soon established himself as a radical artist. In a long and varied career, Sprague has been a baker's boy, mountaineer, a Udanik road builder in Yugoslavia, newspaper cartoonist, publicity manager of the *Daily Worker* and creative director of a left wing advertising agency. Add a short spell with George Summers' circus, four years in mining and you have a breadth of experience of life that is reflected in the diversity of his art. Drawing, painting, sculpting, pottery and print making have all been part of a prolific output of work for progressive and humanitarian causes spanning forty-five years.

His 'General Strike' lino cut was created in 1970 and subsequently reproduced as a screen-printed edition for 'Remember 1926', the fiftieth anniversary exhibition held at the Floral Hall, Covent Garden, in 1976.

Sprague's work has aroused controversy and public comment on more than one occasion: a poster designed for *Reynolds' News* was banned by London Transport, his poster for the Communist Party depicting the giant hand of a worker squeezing the life out of Edward Heath was condemned by Jimmy Reid and his series of posters and prints on Vietnam resulted in his being refused entry to the United States. Perhaps the greatest disaccord was caused by the publication of a folio of lino cuts entitled *Yours Fraternally* issued in September 1968, following the Soviet intervention in Czechoslovakia. Foreseeing the passion that would be aroused and the accusations that would be made, Sprague prefaced the folio of prints with a statement of explanation.

These prints will inevitably be called anti-Soviet, they are not, they are anti-tank, against those men who all too quickly rush in to solve the problems of our nuclear world by military action. There's a print about Big Brotherism and one about the heroism of youth. Another on the end of an era and a rise of protest symbolised by the clenched fist of the Spanish civil war and other demonstrations of the 30s. One of a ghastly womb that gives birth to a tank – to give birth to a tank . . .

There's one that says discussion is best when conducted between equals and another about those blinkered enthusiasts who see only the glorious young soldier (in traditional war memorial pose) but do not see the tank or the monstrous process of soldiering.

For people who find only references to Czechoslovakia in these pictures there's the three teardrops who conveniently forgetting Munich and more recent armed adventures of their own governments, see only in one direction.

These silk screened prints are, admittedly, simplified statements about complex politics. But somewhere in that complexity lies truth. It might help us to locate it if we began by putting military ideas in the dustbin.

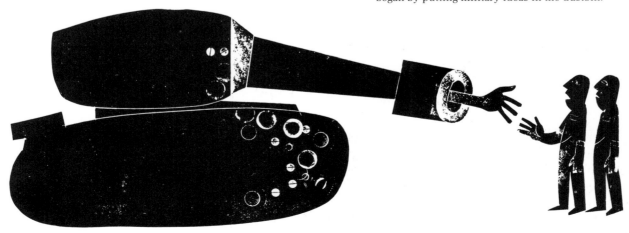

'A backcloth of British working class history' is how Maureen Scott describes her canvas painted especially for the National Museum of Labour History. Unveiled on 4 January 1976 by the Mayor of Tower Hamlets, Councillor Benjamin Holmes, the painting is one of a series of three. Of the other two, one portrays the struggle of the Chilean workers for democracy and is hung in the museum of the Amalgamated Union of Engineering Workers in London. The third, painted in memory of Kevin Gately, the young man killed as the result of a mounted police charge in Red Lion Square, London, during a demonstration against the National Front, hangs at Warwick University where Gately was a student.

Maureen Scott was born in Coventry in 1940 and after local primary school and grammar school, received her art training at Plymouth Art School. Despite the commitments of domestic and working life she has consistently painted throughout the years since leaving art school, working mainly in acrylics, painting scenes of industrial life and working class struggle. A frequent exhibitor, her panoramic scene of the history of British miners was purchased by the Museum of Modern Art in Utrecht and a series of her paintings on the unemployed are displayed in the Galerie Poll in West Berlin.

Her painting of British working class history is a sweeping scene of the major events in the record of the trade union and labour movement, from the strike of the Bryant and May match girls in 1888 to the feminist and black rights campaigns of the 1970s.

At the top left of the picture are depicted the men whom she says 'have given the British and world working class the field manual for final socialist victory', Marx and Engels. With them is William Morris, 'a man who clothed the science of struggle and class war with poetic insight.' In socialist realist style, two figures, male and female workers, dominate the struggle, standing before the banner of socialism and pointing the way to the final goal. Like Cliff Rowe, she admits to the influence of the Mexican revolutionary mural painters upon her work and openly regrets that she had never had the opportunity to travel and work in Mexico.

Scott believes that artists should stand side by side with all who serve the working class movement to 'feed the stream that will sweep all before it', to create a society which will give to the labourer the power to administer the products of his or her labour.

'Henry Mayers Hyndman, founder of the British Social-Democratic Federation, born 7 March 1842, died 22 November 1921' is the brief inscription on the Hyndman bust in the National Portrait Gallery, London.

To persuade the National Portrait Gallery to accept the bust, Rosalind Travers Hyndman, his second wife, used all the influence of their joint aristocratic origins. In a letter to the directors on 6 June 1922 she wrote, 'Members of the committee such as Sir James Frazer, Thomas Hardy or my husband's old and life-long friend, Lady St. Helier, will be able to assure you,

if there is need of assurance, that his fame in English history will increase and endure.' No mention was made of the well-known socialists on the Hyndman Memorial Committee of forty-five other names, including E. Belfort Bax, Will Thorne, George Lansbury, Herbert Burrows or George Bernard Shaw.

Hyndman was born in a house at Hyde Park Square, the grandson of a rich owner of slave plantations in Guyana. The family was linked on both sides with India through soldiers and administrators and his wife Rosalind was the grand-daughter of Bishop Ellicott of Gloucester. Despite the disadvantage of his wealthy background, Hyndman, the fox-hunting, cricketing oarsman, became the founder of the Democratic Federation, which in turn soon became the first English socialist organisation, the Social Democratic Federation, in 1884. In January of that year he had founded with Edward Carpenter, *Justice*, a socialist journal that was to have a profound influence on the development of the early socialist movement.

The memorial committee in 1922 decided to commemorate the death of Hyndman by the commission of a bust for presentation to the National Portrait Gallery and the endowment of an annual memorial lecture. The bust was the work of Edward Hill Lacey, a pupil of Howard Thomas and a young sculptor of great talent. Lacey made his plaster sculpture after two sittings with Hyndman and had it cast in bronze by E.J. Parlanti of the Art Bronze Foundry in Beaumont Road, West Kensington. He was persuaded by James Milner, the director of the Portrait Gallery, to cast it in dark bronze, advice which he accepted and which won the approval of Rosalind Hyndman. On 6 June 1922, before the presentation in July, Rosalind Hyndman wrote to Milner and requested permission for a duplicate bronze to be made which would remain in her possession. It is this bronze that is now held by the National Museum of Labour History. The only other impressions were the original plaster and two wax models.

The inscription to accompany the bust caused considerable debate. His wife suggested it should read simply, 'Henry Mayers Hyndman, the founder of English Social-Democracy'. Milner preferred to avoid the political claim and advance Hyndman's achievement as a writer, a suggestion that provoked a sharp reply from Rosalind Hyndman who wrote on 6 July 1922, 'About the inscription, I'm afraid the one you kindly suggest would make 9/10 of the committee and all his friends resort to 'Direct Action'. You see, even the most assuming Fabian, the most impudent communist, the most woolly headed worthy of the ILP would never deny that Henry Mayers Hyndman was the *Founder* of English Social Democracy. We would truly say, founder of English socialism.' She dismissed his literary claim to fame by continuing, '. . . only eleven books altogether of which the two best were written in my time. The pamphlets and the *Justice* writing, though often abominable, were only propaganda.' Rosalind Hyndman and the memorial committee won the argument and Hyndman was immortalised in an English bourgeois institution as the 'founder of the British Social-Democratic Federation'.

When he died at the age of seventy-nine, Hyndman left only £237, his considerable fortune having been given to the cause of socialist propaganda. The first memorial lecture, 'The Emancipation of South East Asia', based on his popular book, *The Awakening of Asia*, was given by R.W. Seton-Watson on 7 March 1923 at King's College, admission 2*s*. 6*d*. It must be questioned if any wage workers heard the lecture. Already Hyndman belonged to history.

George Lansbury, socialist, Christian, pacifist, was born on 21 February 1859 and died on 17 May 1940. Born at a time when no working man had the vote, no woman the vote, an age before compulsory education when children worked in the 'dark satanic mills' so damningly entitled by William Blake in Lansbury's favourite hymn, 'Jerusalem'. His life for Labour has filled many volumes, indeed, requires volumes to recount his life of service for the poor people he loved.

On Saturday, 15 July 1939 at a small meeting at Friends' House, Euston Road, a group of his friends and associates gathered to present him with a bronze bust of himself as a mark of their respect and appreciation in his eightieth year. Tributes were paid to him by Isaac Foot, Professor C.E.M. Joad, Barrow Cadbury, Lord Ponsonby, the Revd Henry Carter, Norman Bentvich, Canon C.E. Raven, Master of Christ's College, Cambridge, and J.F. Gilbertson, Mayor of Poplar.

It was a time when fascism in Europe was violating every concept of civilised decency and the threat of war pervaded every thought. Still Lansbury looked to the good in the hearts of men and in his speech of thanks said he 'did not believe there was any reason to despair.' He could not accept as certain the idea that humanity, even now with all the signs and portents, was going to rush, as it were, down the steep slope to destruction. Within a year he was dead, and his son-in-law, Raymond Postgate, wrote, 'Half his borough of Poplar laid in ruins, and of his own house in Bow Road, nothing would be left but a doorway and a door.'

The bronze was the work of Yussof Abbo, an Egyptian sculptor and himself a refugee from Hitler's Germany. Abbo spent months following Lansbury at public and private meetings to study and observe the character of the sensitive visionary, to sculpt more than a likeness – to capture the essence of the man. The bust was presented to the museum by Dorothy Thurtle, a daughter of George Lansbury and wife of Ernest Thurtle, Labour MP for Shoreditch.

PERIODICALS & PAMPHLETS

Liberty, a journal of anarchist communism, first appeared in January 1894, published monthly by James Tochatti, a quiet, studious tailor and a friend of William Morris from the days of the Socialist League. The first issue carried a manifesto that was a mix of anarchism and syndicalism and an article by George Bernard Shaw, 'Why I Am a Social Democrat'. The second issue in the 'Why I Ams' column was 'Why I Am a Communist' by William Morris. Tochatti, despite the destruction of Morris's Socialist League by the anarchists, remained on friendly terms with Morris and approached him in December 1893 to write an article for *Liberty*. During the past two years there had been a series of anarchist outrages on the Continent and Morris was reluctant to be associated with a group that embraced violence as a political means. His caution was clearly expressed in his reply to Tochatti's request on 31 December 1893.

I do not remember having promised to contribute to your paper, though I do remember promising to write a pamphlet for you. In any case, however, considering the attitude which some anarchists are taking up about the recent anarchist murders, and attempts to murder, I could not in conscience allow anything with my name attached to it to appear in an anarchist paper (as I understand yours is to be), unless you publish in said paper a distinct repudiation of such monstrosities. Here I might make an end, but since we have been in friendly association, I will ask you if you do not think you ought for your own sake as (I should hope) a person holding views which may be reasonably argued about to repudiate the use of means which can bring with them nothing but disaster to the cause of liberty. For your own sake and for those who honestly think that the principles of anarchy are right. For I cannot for the life of me see how such principles which propose the abolition of compulsion, can admit of promiscuous slaughter as a means of converting people.

Tochatti, who was not the most extreme of anarchists, gave Morris the repudiation he required and the article duly appeared in the February issue, a testimony to the generosity of Morris's nature. Later that year the article was reprinted as a pamphlet

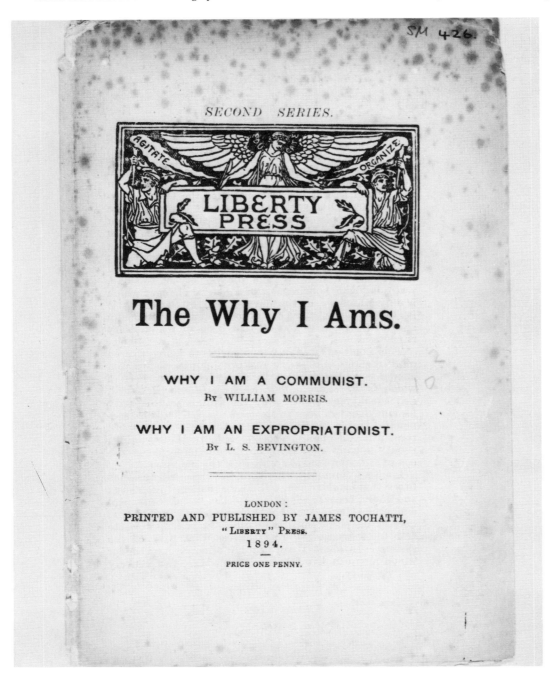

bearing the Liberty Press heading designed by Walter Crane. Oddly enough, although the Crane design appeared on the editorial page of *Liberty*, the cover was designed by W.M. Rowe, in a style that aped Crane's imagery, complete with a Marianne figure in flowing robes.

The last issue of *Liberty* appeared in December 1896.

The Socialist Labour Party emerged in 1903 from a divergent section of the Social Democratic Federation, adopting the name of the American Party led by Daniel De Leon, to whose ideas they broadly subscribed. Some of the old SDF pioneers were glad to see them go, Harry Quelch referring to them as 'this cursed De Leon-impossibilist leprosy' which had been 'working the very devil's mischief' in the Federation. The new party was mainly based in Scotland, especially on the Clyde, and in some sections in the North of England. It was doctrinaire and dogmatic, claiming to be 'the only Socialist Party in England and Scotland' (though it is not clear with whom they shared the honour in Wales), and insisted that enrolling members should sign an affirmative against six separate questions, e.g. question five,

Do you realise that all other political parties and factions thereof are necessarily the instruments of capitalist interests?

One of the first and most positive acts of the party was to buy a printing press on the instalment plan, and to enlist the help of some Edinburgh comrades who were printers to set up and compose their own monthly paper, *The Socialist*. The Socialist Labour Press, as it was called, rendered a useful service to the wider labour movement by the publication of educational pamphlets and the printing of Marxist classics. The press moved to Glasgow in 1912 and it was from there that the SLP issued the first of a new series in 1918, the centenary of Marx's birth. 'The Socialist Programme' was in fact an extract from a book written by John Spargo and summarised Marx's criticism of the 'Gotha Programme' and was used to defend the position of the Socialist Labour Party against the policies of the British Socialist Party and the Independent Labour Party.

'The tiniest magazine in the world' was how the first issue of *Young Socialist* was described by its editor and publisher Archie McArthur, when it made its first appearance in January 1901. He was probably right for it was little more than a typeset newsletter for Glasgow Socialist Sunday Schools. The heading of the first issue proclaimed its purpose as 'a magazine of love and service' and the third issue laid down a simple programme for young socialists: 'To build up the city of love in our own hearts, and so, by and by help to build it up in the world. To form the first beginnings of a world-wide union of socialist children, a socialist children's international of love and service.' By this time there were fifteen Socialist Sunday Schools in Britain, six of which were in Glasgow.

At the end of the first year the magazine was in financial trouble and was taken over by the Glasgow Socialist Sunday School Union to prevent its collapse. The heading for January 1902 stated, 'This magazine is owned by the Glasgow Socialist Sunday School Union and carried on by it in the interest of the socialist children of the country.' The following year, in January 1903, the magazine had its first pictorial front page with a heading designed by the Scottish pioneer socialist John Bruce Glasier, later to become the editor of *Labour Leader* and chairman of the Independent Labour Party. When asked what made him a socialist, Glasier would reply, 'Glasgow', a reference to the appalling slums and poverty that existed in the city.

By 1905 there were three SSS Unions, Glasgow, Yorkshire and London, with thirty-five schools attended by 1,643 children and 582 adults. Contributors to the magazine included Keir Hardie, F.J. Gould, Alex Gossip, Edward Carpenter and Ramsay MacDonald. A typical issue would include news from the Socialist Sunday Schools, letters from children and a political moralising story barely disguised as a fairy tale. Walter Crane designed the heading for the children's page in 1909. Poetry was always considered part of the movement and there would be quotes from socialist poets like William Morris and non-socialist poets like Tennyson, 'Live pure, speak true, right wrong, Else wherefore born?'

Although the circulation and the Sunday School movement grew steadily, the magazine was seldom out of debt. In 1910 it was taken over by the National Council of British Socialist Sunday Schools when its circulation was almost 3,000 and its deficit stood at £42. Within a year the circulation had climbed to 3,450 copies per month with a monthly loss of 30s. By a special drive, the National Council raised £180 by 1912 to put the magazine on a sound footing, but then came the First World War. Justice and love were not the watchwords of generals and politicians and there was open hostility towards those sections of the socialist movement that opposed the war. The outline of conduct for Socialist Sunday Schools stated, 'By constitution we are anti-militarist. Socialism and war never did walk hand in hand, one is the complete antipathy of the other.' Circulation figures are not available for the war years but the magazine

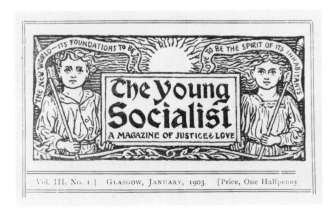

FOURTH EDITION.

SOCIALISM
— and the —
SURVIVAL OF THE FITTEST.

By J. CONNELL.

Author of " The Confessions of a Poacher," " The Red Flag," &c.

THE TWENTIETH CENTURY PRESS, LIMITED 164
(TRADE UNION AND 48 HOURS),
37, 37A & 38, CLERKENWELL GREEN, LONDON E.C.

20,000/6/10   **PRICE ONE PENNY.**

survived and continued to grow. In 1918 F.J. Bourne of the Tyneside and District Union designed a postcard to be sold for fund raising in place of the usual practice of selling artificial flowers. The illustration showed a 'massed procession of children representing all the nations of the world. Bravely and gaily at the head of the procession rides the banner of the children with its message of love and justice to all the peoples of the world.' The *Young Socialist* reproducing the design in its March issue said, 'With the peoples of Europe still grappling together in human conflict, our little pictorial peace message – written without words in the smiling and happy faces of these mingling children will come with prophetic meaning and appeal to anyone who is concerned either about what is happening today or with the brighter hopes that may emerge for humanity tomorrow.' Bourne's design reflects his care and love for children and his own quiet and gifted nature.

The *Young Socialist* survived the inter-war period and even emerged to continue after the Second World War, finally declining and ceasing publication in 1979, by which time the Socialist Sunday Schools Movement had become the Socialist Fellowship.

> In boyhood I quaffed with a passionate love
> The breath of the mountain and moor
> And hated the greed of the covetous Lord
> Who fenced out the weak and the poor.

This verse from the 'Old Poacher's Song' by James Connell expressed his lifelong hatred for the game laws of the rich, laws which he openly ignored throughout his seventy-six years. At one time he earned his living as a poacher and the experience was invaluable in his writing of two books published by the Humanitarian League, *The Truth About the Game Laws* and *The Confession of a Poacher*, the latter selling 80,000 copies. His pamphlet, 'Socialism and the Survival of the Fittest', was published in 1910 with an initial print order of 20,000.

Born in 1852 at Killskyre, County Meath, the son of a small farmer, he learned poaching as a boy from local labourers. His mother, a devout Catholic, wanted him to become a priest but Connell learned of socialism from a man called Landye and abandoned his Catholicism for the religion of socialism. Landye used to hold a political discussion on Sunday afternoons and would take his young disciples walking over the Dublin hills, shaping Connell's two loves, the countryside and socialism. His class-consciousness awakened by Landye and the terrible poverty of the Irish people, he joined the Fenian Brotherhood and when he came to England became a member of the British Executive Committee for the League.

Jim Connell, as he became known, joined the Social Democratic Federation and it was after hearing a lecture by Herbert Burrows that he was inspired to write the 'Red Flag', to become famous throughout the world as the battle hymn of socialism. According to Connell in an article written for *The*

Call, the publication of the British Socialist Party, he wrote the first two stanzas and the chorus on the top deck of a bus during the fifteen minute journey between Charing Cross and New Cross. The next day he completed the song and sent it to Harry Quelch, the editor of *Justice*. The 'Red Flag' first appeared in *Justice* in the Christmas issue of 1889 and was written to be sung to the lilting tune of 'The White Cockade', the song of the Jacobites. According to Jim Connell, it was A.S. Headingley of the SDF, a socialist who had been an ambulance driver for the Paris Commune, that changed the tune, a decision that Connell said broke his heart. He wrote,

> The only tune that ever has or ever will suit the Red Flag is the one I hummed when I wrote it – I mean The White Cockade [Connell specifically meant the original version], known to everybody in Ireland fifty years ago. Since then some fool has altered it by introducing mini notes into it, until it is now nearly a jig. A.S. Headingley took it upon himself to change the tune. May God forgive him, for I never shall! He linked the name with Maryland, the proper name of which is 'Tannenbaum', an old German Roman Catholic hymn.

George Bernard Shaw was to describe the 'Red Flag' as sounding like 'the death march of a conger eel', but presumably he had never heard it sung to the tune for which it was written.

Jim Connell variously gave the Great Dock Strike of 1889, the Paris Commune, the Chicago Martyrs and the Russian Nihilists as the sources for his inspiration for the writing of the 'Red Flag'. Some have said that he was influenced by a Chartist poet, Alfred Fennell, who published the 'Red Flag' in *The Democratic Review* in 1850. Its opening lines read,

> Tis in the Red Flag true republicans glory,
> Red is the emblem of Justice and Right –
> By martyr's blood dyed, whose names live in story,
> The victors, though fallen in liberty's fight.

In 1925 Ramsay MacDonald said the Labour Party were still looking for a great Labour song and the *Daily Herald* ran a competition to see if anyone could better the 'Red Flag'. 300 songs were sent in, but, in the opinion of the judges, not one was considered good enough to replace the 'Red Flag'. According to the late Norah Walshe, Jim Connell's only daughter, her father waited on the result and would have been heartbroken if his song had been replaced; it was his most important contribution to the labour movement.

Jim Connell wrote his own obituary, in which he said he was 'educated under a hedge for a few weeks', and was in turn, 'sheep farmer, dock labourer, navvy, railwayman, draper, journalist, a lawyer of sorts, and all the time a poacher'. Talking once to Wal Hannington, National Organiser of the Unemployed Workers' Movement, Connell asked him, 'Why don't you advise the unemployed to become poachers? There's plenty of good food to be grabbed on the big estates of the Lords and Dukes of Britain.'

Connell was a character, a striking personality, a big man with a sweeping moustache and, invariably, a flowing red necktie. He died a socialist and at his funeral in 1929, at Golders Green, his old comrade for forty years, Tom Mann, gave the valediction. George Hicks, representing the TUC, concluded the ceremony with the words, 'Farewell, glorious old comrade, Jim. We are glad you have lived. We are sorry you have departed this life.' As the coffin disappeared into the flames, the assembly sang the 'Red Flag' to the tune of 'Tannenbaum' and then to 'The White Cockade' – 'This song shall be our parting hymn.'

The Woman Worker was the official organ of the National Federation of Women Workers, founded by Mary MacArthur in 1906. The Federation filled a gap in the trade union movement, offering trade protection to women working in unorganised industries, providing legal aid, unemployment and sickness benefits, strike pay and negotiating strength. Within two years of its formation, Mary MacArthur had brought the membership to 2,000, organised in seventeen branches and affiliated to the TUC. The first issue of *The Woman Worker* appeared in September 1907 as a penny monthly but within a few months was being produced weekly, reaching a circulation of 20,000.

The paper was edited at first by Mary MacArthur, an indefatigable Scot, energetic, imaginative and courageous. Yet, MacArthur, the campaigning trade unionist and socialist agitator, working among the poorest, most exploited groups of women in Bermondsey, Cradley Heath and the Potteries, had come to socialism via the Primrose League! Mary Reid MacArthur was born in Glasgow on 13 August 1880, of wealthy parents, her father owning a chain of West End drapery stores. A conservative and a leading figure in the Primrose League, he educated his daughter as a 'lady' and she dutifully followed him into Conservative politics. Her conversion to trade unionism and socialism came when she was sent to report on a meeting of shop assistants for a Conservative newspaper, seeking a facetious article mocking the poor shopworkers. In Mary's own words, 'I went to a meeting at Ayr to write a skit on the proceedings. Going to scoff, I remained to pray. I became impressed with the truth and meaning of the Labour Movement.' The speaker was John Turner and the conversion must rank with Blatchford's conversion of the Countess of Warwick for the speed and completeness with which it was achieved.

The journal aimed 'to teach the need for unity, to help improve working conditions, to present a picture of the many activities of trade unionists and to discuss all questions affecting the health and interest of women.' Guest articles were written by notable figures in the labour movement, including Keir Hardie, George Lansbury, Margaret Bondfield and Pete Curran. J.J. Mallon contributed a series of pen portraits on women in the movement, among them Gertrude Tuckwell, Margaret MacDonald, Katherine Bruce Glasier and Mrs Despard.

Mary MacArthur became immersed in the campaign against sweated labour, an issue that overshadowed her work as editor, and she resigned the editorial chair at the end of 1908, saying, 'One cannot be agitator and editor at the same time, and I – well, it is not that I choose to be, but I *am* agitator first.'

The National Federation of Women Workers grew to 40,000 members and on 1 January 1921 became a separate women's section of the National Union of General Workers, *The Woman Worker* ceasing publication in July of that year.

The cover was designed by Walter Crane and the same illustration was painted on the banner of the National Federation of Women Workers.

The typographical cover of *The Herald*, from the point of view of design as well as intent, must stamp it as one of the most remarkable front pages ever printed by a British newspaper. The *Daily Herald* grew from a halfpenny strike sheet first published on 25 January 1911 to support the demand of printers who were locked out for asking that their working week be reduced to fifty hours, to become the daily expression of working class revolt. Although headed as a daily, the first issues in fact appeared on four days a week only but reached a circulation of 26,000 by the end of the dispute. At that point it nearly foundered, but Ben Tillett raised £300 to keep the paper alive and for the next eleven years it maintained an independent and revolutionary position.

Under the editorship of the syndicalist, Charles Lapworth, a brilliant staff moulded the character of the paper, supporting every strike, every militant rank and file revolution, attacking reformism and exposing political intrigue from Labour, Liberal and Tory politicians alike. In 1913 Will Dyson, the powerful Australian cartoonist, drew his famous 'Fantasy', a cartoon of Labour leaders at their devotions depicting them on their knees, bowing to a giant top hat, a drawing that infuriated the right wing of the Labour Party. The blazing flame of revolt burned brightest during the paper's support for the dock strike of 1912, its campaign for strikes and financial support for the families during the great Dublin lockout of 1913 and in support of the building workers during the lockout of 1914.

Under the editorship of George Lansbury, the *Daily Herald* opposed the First World War and in the jingoistic atmosphere of the times, with the Labour movement split, was compelled to appear as a weekly. The war was still on when the 'Red Flag' front page appeared and in a second leader, Robert Williams called for the creation of a British soviet: 'We may be satisfied with a Constituent Assembly. We should prefer an Association of Soviets, Workers' and Soldiers' Councils, have the shop stewards' movement and the rank and file in general enough courage and determination to give us a Soviet for Great Britain?' This was the *Daily Herald* that was loved and cherished to an extent that it became part of the muddled folklore of the labour movement that remembers it as the paper of the TUC. It was in 1919 that Lansbury and Tillett sought to interest Ernie Bevin in the paper and raise money from the trade unions, co-operative

THE HERALD

THE NATIONAL LABOUR WEEKLY

New Series, No. 932.   [Registered at G.P.O. as a newspaper. Postage U.K. newspaper rate.]   SATURDAY, JANUARY 26, 1918.   [PUBLISHED EVERY SATURDAY.]   ONE PENNY.

LABOUR

KEEPS THE

RED

FLAG

FLYING

societies and the Labour Party to save the paper from financial collapse. It was sold in 1922 to the official labour movement, but it was never the same paper again.

The Workers' Cry, an advocate of the claims of the labour army, was a short-lived socialist weekly first published on 2 May 1891 and closed twenty editions later on 12 September. The paper was the creation of the editor, Frank Smith, a leading salvationist who found his true salvation in the religion of socialism. Born in 1854, Smith was brought up in London, the 'Devil's Headquarters' as he used to call the city, and educated in 'the school of public house, sing-song, music hall and theatre'. His soul fired with the stage, he tried to earn his living as a minstrel and an acrobat before becoming a cabinetmaker and finding his vocation as an evangelist and social reformer.

Frank Smith found his first salvation when he saw a poster announcing that someone would 'sing and talk of God', and it was in a little hall in Chelsea that he discovered the 'religion of enjoyment' and joined the Salvation Army in 1879. Ever a showman, it is said that Smith won his first audience in Liverpool by riding a white charger through the streets on which he sat facing the tail of the horse, the crowd following and giving him a ready audience. In 1881 General William Booth called him to Headquarters and he was soon promoted to Major as Divisional Commander for London. In 1884 Booth sent him as Commissioner to the United States, where Major Thomas E. Moore had broken with the founder and taken most of the salvationists with him. Appropriating virtually the entire

organisation, Moore had copyrighted the original Salvation Army crest designed by Captain William H. Ebdon in 1879 and Smith, wishing to retain the familiar identity, avoided infringement by replacing the 'crown of glory' with the American eagle. Later, Smith was to adapt the crest yet again, the next time for the heading of his socialist newspaper, *The Workers' Cry*.

During his stay in America, Smith employed his skills as a showman and propagandist, drawing large crowds into street meetings and processions. He mixed with the very poor and became a social activist for disenfranchised black Americans and impoverished immigrants. Returning to England after a few years due to ill health, Smith took charge of the social wing of the Salvation Army and W.S. Stead has argued that it was 'experience gained by the social wing that caused General Booth to write "In Darkest England".'

Smith, always closer to the social wing of the Army than the evangelical, found himself in an England shaken by the Trafalgar Square riots of 1886 (the year before his return), the strikes of the Bryant and May match girls, the gasworkers and the London dockers, all events to move him closer to socialism. The Salvation Army had donated 5s. to the London Trades Council's match girls strike fund and Commissioner Frank Smith went further, inserting a paragraph in *War Cry* asking for 'any of our soldiers and comrades who thoroughly understand the manufacture of matches' to communicate with him. The outcome was the opening of a match factory in Lamprell Street, East London, in May 1891, employing one hundred workers with better pay and better conditions than prevailed elsewhere,

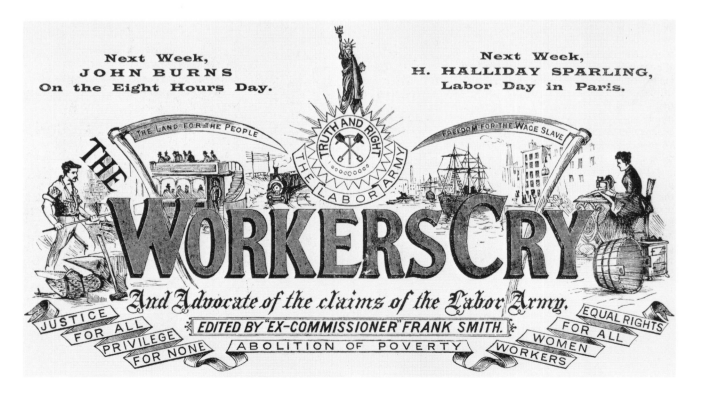

making phosphorus-free matches, the chemical that rotted the teeth and jaw bones of the Bryant and May girls.

However, by that time Smith, who had contributed so much to the work of relieving the distress of the poor in his work for the Army, had finally resigned in December 1890 and committed himself to the cause of social revolution. His paper, *The Workers' Cry*, recalls the title of the Salvation Army's own paper, *The War Cry*, and the Army crest had been changed by replacing the crown with the statue of liberty and the crossed swords of Christian warfare and the holy cross with a pick-axe and two spades. Smith had left the Salvation Army to build a Labour Army with the goal of the abolition of poverty, justice and equal rights for all, including women workers. His socialist creed was a mix of social reform, Christianity and revolutionary socialism.

If his paper did not last long, Smith did, becoming a Progressive Councillor on the new London County Council, a member of the Independent Labour Party and standing for Parliament twelve times before finally winning a seat in 1929 at the age of seventy-six! Frank Smith was the confidant of Keir Hardie, accompanying him on his visit to America, letting Hardie live rent free in his home in London and remaining his true friend and comrade until Hardie's death in 1915. According to Fenner Brockway, Frank Smith left an abiding memorial to the labour movement, a technique for collecting money at meetings. A genius at fund raising, he introduced the 'bidding system' into public meetings 'who will give ten pounds, let me have the first ten pounds – now the five pound notes', a technique later perfected by the communists, who developed it to a fine art at mass meetings.

The Railway Women's Guild conference of 1905 carried a resolution requesting the National Labour Representation Committee to form a National Women's Labour Committee. About the same time, Mrs Cawthorne, the wife of a Hull docker, wrote to Ramsay MacDonald, secretary of the LRC, asking him to set up an organisation of Labour women. From these two initiatives a meeting was held at the MacDonalds' home at Lincolns Inn Fields on 9 March 1906, which resulted in the formation of the Women's Labour League with Margaret MacDonald as president and Mary Fenton Macpherson as secretary.

The League campaigned on labour issues that directly affected women, sweated industries, feeding of schoolchildren, health and education, unemployment, labour laws and women's suffrage. Under the leadership of Katherine Glasier they took up the issue of industrial dirt and were among the earliest advocates of pithead baths. In 1910 the first issue of the *League Leaflet* appeared, a monthly issue supplied to branches at 6*d.* for 24 copies, post-free. The Women's Labour League grew in size and influence in public life and the *League Leaflet* reported in 1913 that 2,000 badges had now been ordered. In addition to the numerous leaflets issued by the League on political matters was a remarkably successful cookery book, *My Favourite Recipe, by Women of the Labour Party*, which sold thousands of copies at 6*d.* each.

By 1913 the *League Leaflet* gave way to a new, enlarged publication, *The Labour Woman*, first published on May Day of that year. The price of the paper was a ½*d.* and was available to branches at 9*d.* for two dozen and 4*d.* for every additional dozen. Posters were issued to branches, at the cost of 1*d.*, for display at newsagents and the editor wrote, 'It is the working women's paper and the working women will make it a power for good, a weapon in the fight for freedom, for happy firesides and noble citizenship.'

The January 1925 issue of *The Labour Woman* carried on its front page a wood engraving by the distinguished artist, Eric Gill, entitled 'First Aid'. Gill, born in 1882, was a sculptor, engraver, typographer and artist of international repute. He carved over a hundred figures or reliefs in stone, including the Stations of the Cross for Westminster Cathedral. The designer of the famous typefaces, Gill Sans and Perpetua, he produced over 750 works of inscriptional lettering for memorials, foundation stones and gravestones, including the memorial headstone for the grave of James Hammett, the only one of the Tolpuddle Martyrs to be buried at Tolpuddle. His engraving for *The Labour Woman* shows women struggling in the stormy sea of industrialism. The Liberal and Conservative capitalists have found a raft for themselves and stand smugly under their banner 'Safety First'. They have called in the police and military, who are depicted worshipping the capitalists, to look after their property. The Liberal clings to the police while the more militarist Tory has the soldier beside him. In the foreground the workers in the Trade Union and Labour movement have sent out their raft to bring the drowning to safety. The man hauls up Labour's flag, 'Justice First', the women stretch out their hands and pull the others in. 'It is a *man* hauling up the Labour flag,' wrote Eric Gill, for 'men are good at the theory of the thing – the women are fully occupied in giving first aid.'

Ellen Wilkinson's threepenny pamphlet, *Plan for Peace*, has the flavour of post-war Britain both in design and content. 'Red Ellen', to become Minister of Education in the 1945 Labour Government, was ideally suited to write on a planned society for she was the Member of Parliament for Jarrow, the 'town that was murdered' by free enterprise capitalism, and was famed and respected for her part in leading the Jarrow Crusade to London in 1936.

The content of the pamphlet made the point that the ultimate victories in the war were as a result of careful planning, that controlled team work and co-operation had provided the means to victory. 'Without a plan, there would have been no D-day for attack, no V-day for victory. Without a plan, British Tommies would have landed in Normandy to find their reserves of ammunition missing, British tanks would have been stranded without petrol. Planning was needed to ensure that no detail of success was overlooked.' The Labour Party believed this was a vital lesson that the people of Britain should grasp: 'There must be a plan for peace, just as there was a plan for war.' The events that followed the ending of the First World War were not forgotten; food prices had soared, only 700 homes were built in 1919 and there were over 2,000,000 unemployed by 1921. To working people, the fairness of food control, rationing, was obvious; the Tory way was to ration by the purse. With 4,000,000 homes destroyed or damaged by bombing during the Second World War, the need for a planned repair and building programme was clear. With the memories of the depression years of the thirties still fresh, the need to plan industry was obvious. 'Only with planning can we be sure of the future,' said Labour's 'Plan for Peace'. The message was clear: an early return to private enterprise would mean ex-servicemen without homes but mansions for the wealthy, the war worker unemployed and 'at the whim of the capitalist employer'; without controls on food prices and clothing, plenty for the rich and little for the poor. Labour put its plan as 'the same as the wartime plan – to meet the needs of the nation.' The pamphlet put eight points in Labour's immediate plan, a policy that won the overwhelming vote of endorsement in the General Election of 1945.

1. Public Ownership of the Coal and Power Industries.
2. Public Ownership of Inland Transport.
3. Public Ownership of the Iron and Steel Industry.
4. Public Supervision of Monopolies and Cartels, to prevent excessive prices and restrictive practices.
5. Power both for the Central Government and for Local Authorities to buy without delay any land, in town or country, required for any public purpose.
6. State action to get our Export Trade on its feet on condition that industry is efficient and go-ahead.
7. Priorities in the use of raw materials for vital industries, control of the prices of food and other essentials, suitable controls to ensure that homes for the people came before mansions, and necessities for all before luxuries for the few.
8. Better organisation of Government Departments and the Civil Service.

It was the policy that laid the foundation for the welfare state.

PHOTOGRAPHS

Photographs are visual history, to be read as carefully as minute books, to be scrutinised for incidental detail to help reveal the past. As the shutter closes, a glimpse of that which is gone is recorded by the action of light upon chemicals as surely as pen upon paper. A photographic archive is a research source, but it needs to be approached with the same circumspection as the culling of newspapers for fact, for the photographer has all the guile of a journalist, the prejudices of a biographer. Yet, taken and balanced with complementary material, it helps to provide an insight into yesterday. However contrived, each picture has something to impart, if only the way in which the photographer wished the subject to be seen, or how the characters wanted to be portrayed.

To select a handful of photographs from a collection of thousands, unless a random choice, is necessarily subjective. The following photographs have been chosen as representative, but remain a personal choice. The decision to include portraits was difficult, for it may be argued that they tell us nothing of the past, for although fashions change, the human face has not altered since light falling on silver salts produced the first image. Nevertheless, curiosity is satisfied to some extent by putting a likeness to a name and there is fascination in searching the image, however formally posed, for some sign of the inner force that formed the character. The portraits selected are figures central to the development of the labour movement towards the end of the last century, heroes of labour, their lives overlapping as they came from diverse backgrounds, each to help shape the form of the British labour movement.

William Morris appears as a friendly giant, the true eyes of an artist fixed in the middle distance, yet Morris saw further than most men, for he held the vision of a co-operative commonwealth where useful labour, art and equity would replace the horrors of industrial capitalism. It was a vision that produced not only *News from Nowhere*, but compelled one of the greatest artists of the nineteenth century to give so much of his time to the cause of smashing capitalism.

The picture of Will Thorne shows him as a young man, taken when he was working an eighteen-hour shift. This is Thorne who started work at six years of age for a rope and twine spinner in Birmingham, working from six in the morning till six at night for a half crown a week.

When Thorne married at the age of twenty-two, he could not sign his name for he had no education, but he founded the National Union of Gasworkers and General Labourers in 1889, winning the eight-hour day, pioneering the new unionism and choosing for his union's motto 'Union, Fidelity, Love'.

The press photograph of Ben Tillett is well known, for here is Tillett the orator in full spate, his famous wide-brimmed hat set back on his head, surrounded by a mass audience held by his persuasive speech. Like Thorne, Tillett started work early in life, labouring at seven years of age in a brickyard, then ran away to join a circus and at thirteen enlisted in the navy at the Oak Tavern in West Street, Bristol. The year was 1873 and it was a navy of sailing ships, of holystoning, the ship's rope and cutlass drill, a hard training that was to prepare Tillett for the tough task of organising London's dockers into their first trade union and waging the Great Dock Strike of 1889. Tillett helped Will Thorne to form the Gasworkers' Union and now Thorne helped Tillett to start the most significant strike in the 1880s.

The studio photograph of Tom Mann gives no indication of his origins, even the signature is not Mann's handwriting; winged collar, bow tie, watch chain and waxed moustache conceal Mann the revolutionary. Only the lapel badge of the Amalgamated Engineering Union, of which Mann was elected General Secretary in 1891, gives any indication of his association with the labour movement. Mann, another of the leaders of the Great Dock Strike, started work in 1865, at the age of nine. His description of his work in a mine at that age is worth recounting.

These air courses were only three feet high and wide, and my work was to take away the 'mullock', coal or dirt that the man would require taken from him as he worked away at 'heading' a new road, or repairing an existing one. For this removal there were boxes known down the mine as 'dans', about two feet six inches long and eighteen inches wide and of a similar depth, with an iron ring strongly fixed at each end. I had to draw the box along, not on rails, it was built sledge-like, and each boy had a belt and chain. A piece of stout material was fitted on the boy around the waist. To this there was a chain attached, and the boy would hook the chain to the box, and crawling on all fours, the chain between his legs, would drag the box along and take it to the 'gob' where it would be emptied. Donkey work it certainly was . The boys were stripped to the waist, and as there were only candles enough for one each, and these could not be carried, but had to be fixed at the end of the stages, the boy had to crawl on hands and toes, dragging his load along in worse than Egyptian darkness. Many a time did I actually lie down groaning as a consequence of the heavy strain on the loins, especially when the road was wet and 'clayey' causing much resistance to the load being dragged.

Behind the Edwardian figure is that boy, who grew to a life of revolutionary activity that did not cease until his death in 1941. A member of the Social Democratic Federation, President of the Dockers' Union, General Secretary of the AEU, General Secretary of the Independent Labour Party, founder of The Workers' Union and foundation member of the Communist Party of Great Britain were only some of the landmarks in his life of agitation for the workers of all lands.

Eleanor Marx was another of the band of socialists whose lives overlapped in the years of the upsurge of the new unionism. Ben Tillett wrote in his account of the strike:

Another of our helpers at headquarters, doing the drudgery of clerical work as well as more responsible duties, was Karl Marx's daughter, Eleanor . . . brilliant, devoted and beautiful . . . a Londoner by birth . . . she had lived all her life in the atmosphere of the Social Revolution. She lived with Aveling under very unhappy conditions, which did not, however, break her spirit, or cause her to waver in her devotion to the working-class·cause . . . she was also active in support of the efforts we were making to organise unskilled labour in the East End of London. She gave active help in the formation of the Gas Workers' Union, and, as I say, during our great strike, she worked unceasingly, literally day and night . . . Among those who live in my memory, Eleanor Marx remains a vivid and vital personality, with great force of character, courage and ability.

William Morris, Will Thorne, Ben Tillett, Tom Mann and Eleanor Marx, their lives linked in a common cause, left us more than their fading images to testify to their work for the emancipation of the working class.

An early Clarion van, the Caroline Martyn memorial, at a 'speaking stop' in Stratford, East London. The poster on the van gives the other meeting places as East Ham, Ilford and Barking and the painted slogan proclaims, 'There is no wealth but life.' The speaker is the stalwart Bradford socialist, Edward Hartley, a member of the Social Democratic Federation and a popular 'vanner'. Hartley was not a fiery speaker, he was a semi-professional elocutionist and had a quiet, conversational platform manner which he used to effect in dealing with anti-socialist hecklers. To the often repeated question, 'Where will you get the money from?' he would gently reply, 'From where it is, of course.'

The photograph was taken before the First World War and is believed to show the van in Angel Lane, close to the railway works and sidings of the Great Eastern Railway.

Sweated labour was never confined to sweatshops: it was in the homes of the very poor that the bloodsuckers leeched upon their most vulnerable of victims, women and children. The Sweated Industries Exhibition of 1906 organised by the *Daily News* gave a penetrating insight into the work and pay of the most exploited labour market of the capitalist system. It was in the squalid rooms of city slums that unknown thousands toiled weary hours for pennies, performing tortuous tasks, injurious to health, mind and happiness to ward off starvation with labour that had no minimum price. The committee and council, brought together by the *Daily News* to acquaint society with the evils of sweating, included the names of George Bernard Shaw, Keir Hardie, Herbert Burrows, Mary MacArthur, Clementina Black, George Lansbury, Mrs Despard, Robert Blatchford, Mrs Pethick Lawrence and many others dedicated to social change and social reform.

No labour-consuming task seemed too dirty, too tedious, too obnoxious, too big or too small to escape the homework net that enmeshed the sick, disabled, widowed, orphaned, helpless and simply poor. Fur-pulling, sack-making, mattress-stuffing, shirt-making, artificial-flower-making, coffin-tassel-making,

Bible-folding misery could all be consigned by the manufacturer or subcontractor to a tiny room in which a family of five, six or seven cooked, washed, slept, lived and usually died. Children were robbed of childhood by mothers working for a penny or twopence and hour, who, seeing their children hungry, could not resist the overwhelming temptation to add a few more pennies with the help of tiny hands. The children fetched and returned the bundles of work while their mothers laboured on, helped with work before and after school, working till they fell asleep, and fell asleep again in class the next day. Will Thorne's mother was a typical victim of the sweater; writing of his childhood Thorne said,

> When my father died I was the eldest of four children. Our poverty compelled my mother to take any work she could get. She made a contract with a manufacturer of hooks and eyes to sew these small articles on this card and the payment for this work was three halfpence per gross of cards, and my mother had to find her own needles and cotton. My elder sister used to help her, as well as looking after my two younger sisters. It was here I had intimate experience with sweated labour.

Clementina Black, investigating sweating, gave an account of matchbox making for Royal Swan Vesta:

> At first sight it is a pretty enough spectacle to see a match box made, one motion of the hands bends into shape the notched frame of the case, another surrounds it with the ready pasted strip of printed wrapper which, by long practice is fitted instantly without a wrinkle, then the sandpaper or phosphorous paper, pasted ready beforehand, is applied and pressed on so that it sticks fast. The finished case is thrown on the floor, the long narrow strip which is to form the frame of the drawer is laid upon the bright strip of ready pasted paper, then bent together and joined by an overlapping bit of the paper: the edges of paper below are bent flat, the ready-cut bottom is dropped in and pressed down and before the fingers are withdrawn they fold over the upper edges of the paper inside the top. Now the drawer, too, is cast on the floor to dry. All this, besides the preliminary pasting of wrapper, coloured paper, and sandpaper has to be done 144 times for 2½d. and even this is not all, for every drawer and case have to be fitted together and the packets tied up with hemp. Nor is the work done then, for paste has to be made before it can be used, and boxes, when they are ready have to be carried to the factory.

In twelve gross of boxes there were 10,368 pieces of chip and paper to be handled for half a crown!

Brush drawing was another devilish trade for the torment of the poor. The brush backs were given out ready drilled and the homeworker had to select a suitable number of bristles from a heap, fasten them securely in the centre with wire, and then with a sharp pull against the edge of the table, draw them through the hole. They were kept in position by a wire at the back of the brush and each row of bristles had to be trimmed with a large pair of shears fastened to a table vice. The women covered their fingers with leather but often the wire or leather slipped, making deep cuts into the fingers. To finish off the brushes, the backs had to be painted with lamp black that the women had to buy for themselves, but, when there was no money, soot from the chimney, boiled with water, would be used as a subsitute pigment. If the payment was comparable to slavery, as low as 3½d. for a dozen coarse scrubbing brushes, each with 100 holes, the greed of the employer did not end there. The materials were weighed when given out and had to be of equal weight when returned together with the clippings swept from the floor. If the sweepings were short, and a woman had no means of checking, a deduction would be made against a wage that rarely exceeded 8s. for seventy-two hours' work! Sack making and repairing was less tedious than matchbox or brush making, but was heavier, dirtier and often lower paid. Sacks would be given out for repair at 1½d. or 2d. a dozen, and a bundle might contain some with more holes than sacking. It was possible on a bad bundle for a woman to work all day and not earn 6d. Margaret Irwin of the Sweated Industries Council interviewed one woman who worked from six in the morning to seven in the evening and the highest week's pay she had ever taken was 6s. Making sacks of a smaller size

from large old sacks was another common form of homework, especially near the dock areas, where large numbers of sacks were used. Living rooms would be piled high with dozens of filthy sacks that had held anything from sugar to bonemeal. Irwin reported that the homes of sackmakers she visited were without exception vermin infested and that the sacks were often used in the winter as additional bed clothes.

Another means of adding to the infestation of a room was to fill it with straw for mattress stuffing. Here, the insects of the field mingled with their cousins from the town before they were thrust into the mattress, sewn in and sent to another poor home to provide nights of discomfort. For the poor who did not return all the materials given out in any of the numerous homework occupations, the employer could rely on the full support of the

law to administer punishment. 'We had no food', was the defence of a woman who pawned material given to her by her employer. 'The trousers had to be finished for twopence a pair and work consisted of putting on bottoms, the sewing of bottoms, pockets and flies and I had to find my own needles and thread.' To get food and light she pawned some of the material and then, unable to redeem it, was sent from her squalid room to prison.

The photographs of matchbox making, brush making, sack making and mattress stuffing were taken for the *Daily News* and are representative of the conditions in which the women and their families lived and worked.

With a baking tin for a palette, a young artist prepares a banner bearing a portrait of Harry Pollitt. The artist and the

demonstration for which the banner was made are not recorded, though it is likely to have been painted for a popular front event during the mid-1930s. If the likeness is thinner faced and squarer jawed than Pollitt appeared in life, it must be remembered that the artist was portraying a popular hero.

Born in the little textile village of Droylsden on 22 November 1890 into a working class home, Pollitt left school to work at the mill at thirteen years of age. Two years later he obtained a job at Gorton Tank, the great locomotive building plant of the Great Central Railway, and started his life-long membership of the Boilermakers' Society. From the earliest times his life was part of the labour movement; from Socialist Sunday School, Openshaw Socialist Society, Clarion Club, Independent Labour Party, from the Boilermakers' Society to the Communist Party, he lived and breathed the vision of socialism.

A founder member of the Communist Party of Great Britain and its General Secretary from 1929 to 1956 (with a break from 1939-41 due to a disagreement on the policy of the CP towards the war), Harry Pollitt was a name synonymous with revolutionary socialism. A skilful and talented orator, Pollitt brought thousands into the Communist Party with his ability to paint in words the hope, the future, the tomorrow of socialism. 'The gleam of socialism' he called it, a gleam shining with the warmth and sincerity that characterised his own humanity and made him a folk hero to tens of thousands of people, both inside and outside the Communist Party.

'Hands off Russia' was the call and the title of a national conference held in London on 18 January 1919, sponsored by the British Socialist Party, the Socialist Labour Party and the Industrial Workers of the World. The threat to the new Soviet Republic came from the British government, in particular from the Minister for War, Winston Churchill, who was eager to assist the Poles and the White Russians against the Red Army. Despite an assurance by Lloyd George in the House of Commons that the

government would neither encourage nor support an attack on Russia, there were many in the labour movement who knew that the government was quite prepared to offer aid to an attack upon the Bolsheviks. At the 'Hands off Russia' conference, the 350 delegates passed a resolution for a general strike unless the unconditional cessation of the Allied intervention was officially announced. The mover of the resolution was a young British Socialist Party delegate, Harry Pollitt.

As 1920 came, the tension over war on Russia increased and on 28 February the 'Hands off Russia' movement held their biggest rally yet, packing the Albert Hall to hear Tom Mann, John McClean and Robert Williams call for industrial action to stop any attempt to aid the war. In London's dockland, the agitation was continuous, with dock gate meetings, leaflets and personal discussion being used to win the dockers for direct action should any attempt be made to ship arms to Poland. Despite government denials rumours of munitions arriving at the docks were flying thick and fast and the dockers were urged to keep their eyes open for any signs of evidence, though with ninety miles of quay it was not as easy as some thought.

On 10 May the British press carried the news of the Polish capture of Kiev and the enemies of the Bolsheviks were triumphant. On the same day, the cargo ship *Jolly George* was in the East India Dock being loaded with cases marked OHMS, munitions for Poland. Angered by the duplicity of the government and influenced by the 'Hands of Russia' campaign, the dockers sent a deputation to Ernest Bevin, acting General Secretary of the Dockers' Union, who assured them of the union's full support if they refused to load or coal the vessel. Work stopped immediately and in spite of the pleas of the shipowner, the cargo was unloaded on 15 May, one munitions case bearing a little sticker, 'Hands off Russia'. As Pollitt said, 'It was only small, but that day it was big enough to be read all over the world.'

The labour and trade union movement was now aroused; when the dockers met at Plymouth a few days later, the first item on the agenda was an emergency resolution moved by Bevin, congratulating the London dockers on their initiative and calling on the whole labour movement to follow their tactics. Demonstrations were organised, the *Daily Herald* produced a special Sunday edition with the headline 'Not a man, not a gun, not a sou' and a manifesto signed by the leaders of the trade unions and the Parliamentary Labour Party warned the country against unnecessary war. At an emergency conference of the TUC Parliamentary Committee, the Labour Party Executive and the Parliamentary Labour Party on 9 August a statement was issued, warning that 'the whole industrial power of the organised workers will be used to defeat this war.' Councils of Action were set up everywhere and a deputation to Lloyd George made it clear that continued government support for the war on Russia would be opposed by the full force of the labour movement. No further attempt was made by the government to intervene in the conflict between Poland and Russia and the incident of the *Jolly George* has become a legend in the history of the British trade union and labour movement, a memorable victory.

The photograph taken by the Port of London Authority shows ammunition boxes and gun carriages stowed in the hold of the *Jolly George* before work stopped and the cargo was offloaded.

The photograph shows an unknown woman hunger marcher being arrested during a disturbance when the unemployed went to the House of Commons on 1 March 1934, a graphic illustration of the indifference of the National Government to the workless and hungry.

The national hunger march of 1934 was marked by police harassment and a determined effort by the government to brand the marchers as potential rioters. As 500 marchers, led by Harry McShane, set out from Glasgow, Sir John Gilmour, the Home Secretary, warned, 'The government will have to ask Parliament to grant such powers as experience might show to be necessary to deal with such demonstrations.' Two days later, Sir Thomas Inskip, the Attorney General, referred to the march and talked of bloodshed, saying the government would be bound to take steps to stop it. As the march made its way south, gathering

contingents from the main cities, they were subjected to irritating petty provocation by the police. In Birmingham where the marchers spent the night in the workhouse, the police stayed with them, 'in case of fire'! The Tyneside contingent was visited by the police and five marchers arrested for 'wife desertion' because their wives were claiming poor relief. As the marchers neared London, the Duchess of Atholl asked the Home Secretary if he would take suitable steps to prevent the hunger marchers from holding meetings in Trafalgar Square. In London, the offices of the National Unemployed Workers' Movement were under surveillance by police, and plain clothes detectives followed the leaders from meeting to meeting.

The attempts by the authorities to represent the unemployed marchers as dangerous persons led to the formation of a committee by a number of eminent men and women under the title 'Council for Civil Liberties', a body that remains as an independent watchdog on civil rights to this day. In a letter to the *Manchester Guardian* signed by fifteen, including C.R. Attlee, A.P. Herbert, Kingsley Martin and Edith Summerskill, the signatories warned that '. . . certain features of the police preparation for the present march – for example, instructions to shopkeepers to barricade their windows – cannot but create an atmosphere of misgiving, not only dangerous but unjustified by the facts. All reports bear witness to the excellent discipline of the marchers.' The response of the Home Secretary was to order the stand-by of 10,000 special constables and provincial police to be on duty as the marchers entered London. Meanwhile, two of the march leaders, McShane and Jones, met a hundred MPs at a special meeting at the House of Commons and won their support for a request that some of the unemployed should be heard at the Bar of the House.

On Saturday, 24 February 1,500 delegates were welcomed at Bermondsey Town Hall by the mayor to a conference being held in conjunction with the march, only to be told that the two main speakers, Tom Mann and Harry Pollitt, had been arrested for seditious speeches in the Rhondda Valley and could not be present. Mrs Tom Mann was cheered when she told the delegates, 'Leaders may be taken away, but new leaders must grow up.' In the meantime a letter was sent requesting a meeting with the premier, Ramsay MacDonald, signed by Aneurin Bevan, James Maxton, John McGovern, Tom Mann, Ellen

Wilkinson, Harry Pollitt, Wal Hannington, Alex Gossip, James Carmichael, John Aplin, John Figgins and Maud Brown. MacDonald was incensed and in an outburst in the Commons said, 'Has anybody who cares to come to London, either on foot or in first class carriages, the constitutional right to demand to see me, to take up my time whether I like it or not? I say he has nothing of the kind!'

In cold drizzling rain, led by the fifes, drums and bagpipes of the Scottish contingent, the marchers made their way into Hyde Park to be greeted by 100,000 workers from all parts of London. Under the grey skies with banners flying and spirits high, marchers, field kitchens, ambulances, police cars and bands intermingled as they wound through the streets to the park, cheered along by well-wishers and the curious alike. Here were the men from the Welsh valleys, the slums of Glasgow, the women who had marched from Derby, the workless from Britain's cities of Tyneside, Cornwall, Lancashire, Norfolk, Yorkshire and Nottinghamshire, carrying the message of the thirties, 'Down with means test', 'restore the cuts', 'down with the National Government'.

The protests did not end with the rally and the speeches; a deputation went to Downing Street, MPs were lobbied at the House of Commons, a petition was presented to Parliament, speeches of support in the Commons came from the Liberal leader, Sir Herbert Samuel, and the Labour leader, Clement Attlee. MacDonald remained intransigent; he would not meet the unemployed.

If A.J. Cook was the messiah sent to lead the miners from darkness to light, Herbert Smith was the rock on which they could all depend. The adopted son of a Yorkshire mining couple, his boyhood was toughened by the black, brutal life of a mining village in the 1870s, an existence dominated by pit clothes, pit gear, pit talk and pit disasters. At ten years of age, on a July morning in 1872, young Herbert left his home in Glass Houghton at five in the morning to walk the cobbled streets alongside his stepfather to the colliery and drop into the darkness of another world. His father was a coal getter and Herbert watched as muscle and skill swung together to rip from the veins the shiny source of power for which a million men toiled.

It is said that it is a boy who enters the pit and a man who returns, that he emerges from the bowels that ring with steel and choke with heat and dust stamped apart from other men. The mark of it was to remain with Herbert all his life. Pit, pub, working men's club, co-op and union, chapel and lodge were to be Herbert Smith's daily bread for all his days. His house became the centre of the village, men sought his advice, looked to him for help, about accidents, compensation, insurance, unemployment benefit, wages; he was dour, taciturn, crude, tough and he was on their side. When death came at the pit, he could be the gentle consoler, he was part of them.

The miners, first in his village, then his area and finally his industry, chose Herbert Smith to represent them, to speak for them; a working miner, a man with a cloth cap who was afraid of no man, of no rank, *especially* of no rank. For Herbert Smith real men did real work, and that meant mining. It was as President of the Miners' Federation of Great Britain that Smith went to the Prime Minister's room at the House of Commons on 30 April 1926 with a Special Negotiating Committee to argue the case against a cut in pay and an increase in working hours for Britain's miners. The negotiations started at eleven o'clock that morning and continued with intervals throughout the day. The miners' negotiating committee sat at a table facing the members of the cabinet on the other side. Herbert Smith, his cap tucked in his pocket, sat opposite the Prime Minister, Stanley Baldwin. The Home Secretary, Lord Birkenhead, was in evening dress,

ready for a dinner engagement. The old arguments were reiterated by both sides till at last the Prime Minister made it quite clear the miners' wages must be cut and their hours of work increased. Both sides looked to Herbert Smith for the miners' reply. As Smith looked at the starchly dressed, comfortable, complacent Tories opposite, he must have contrasted all that they represented with his people, of coal-heavy pit clothes, the tin bath in front of the fire, of old men with black lungs, of the 2,526 killed in two years of 1924 and 1925 and another 410,000 seriously injured. They worked for 9s. a day but the earls and lords who owned the pits said that was too much. So did their friends in the government. Herbert Smith slowly took out his dentures, wiped them with his handkerchief, replaced them, looked directly at the Prime Minister and said, 'Nowt doing'. Whether he genuinely had trouble at that moment with his teeth, or whether it was a carefully contrived expression of his total contempt for the pampered enemy opposite we shall never know. The next morning, the coal owners shut their pits; the greatest lock-out in British trade union history had commenced.

On 16 June 1938 the man who had been President of the Miners' Federation of Great Britain and Mayor of Barnsley died. It was the day of the Yorkshire miners' demonstration; the banners from every lodge were draped with black. Instead of their being carried to the great meeting they flew behind the coffin of Herbert Smith in a funeral procession to Castleford where he had worked for years. He went back to the colliery for the last time.

The iconography of the British labour movement has always held a place for heroes, men and women deemed to have played a special role in building or leading some section of labour. From pioneers like Keir Hardie and Tommy Ramsey to popular heroes of the day such as Nye Bevan or Arthur Scargill, trade unions have adorned their banners with portraits of those considered worthy of the honour.

The banners which were to be carried in a May Day procession in 1935 pay homage to five Christian Socialists and pioneers of co-operation. Between them, their contribution to the founding of Christian socialism and to education, law, literature and reform was enormous. John Malcolm Ludlow, 1821-1911, Thomas Hughes, 1822-1896, Charles Kingsley, 1819-1875, Edward Vansittart Neale, 1810-1892, and Frederick Denison Maurice, 1805-1872, were all founders of the Society of Promoting Working Men's Associations, combining their Christian idealism with practical help for working people based upon the socialist ideal of co-operation. Kingsley, the novelist famed for his writing of *Yeast* and *Alton Locke*, books that revealed the squalor in which the poor had to live, scathingly compared competitive business to the behaviour of pigs around a trough. For all of them, capitalism and Christianity were incompatible and they sought to promote brotherly co-operation in society to replace free competition.

When the landlord's bowler-hatted agent went from house to house to collect the rents from Livingstone and Stanley roads in Stratford, East London, in 1953, he was likely to be accompanied by a musical chorus: 'There he goes, twinkletoes, nothing to spend on repairs, I suppose' taunted the women and children to a street tune that was later to become immortalised in Lionel Bart's musical, *Oliver!* It was the sort of romantic cockney humour in the face of adversity that writers are inspired to invent. But there was nothing romantic about the dilapidated state of the Victorian terraced houses in which the people were forced to dwell. Years of neglect from private landlordism and the wartime blasting from Nazi bombing had reduced the once respectable homes to a shambles.

The fight-back against the squalid living conditions came from the tenants themselves who organised a Tenants' Defence League. They faced the shame of living in such slums by shaming the landlords and the Borough Council, inviting the press and

public to their own 'Ideal Home' exhibition. Far from the contemporary dream-homes featured at the *Daily Mail*'s exhibition in Olympia, they displayed the rotten floorboards, damp walls, windowless rooms, crumbling brickwork and hole-riddled roofs of their real world.

When their 'exhibition' brought sympathy, but no action, the campaign escalated into a rent strike, the tenants handing their rent each week to the local vicar for safekeeping. 'Twinkletoes' was told, 'No repairs, no rent.' The campaign became increasingly political, the Conservative government's Housing Repairs and Rents Acts which gave private landlords the power to raise rents on 7,000,000 working class homes provoking intense opposition. The tenants' committee, led by

Jimmy Glover, was strongly supported by the local Communist Party. Glover lived in one of the worst affected houses and local Communist Party secretary, Wally Barnes, was still living with his family in a Nissen hut after being bombed out during the blitz. Deputations went to local councillors, the sitting Labour MP, Arthur Lewis, and to the Sanitary Office of the council.

On 24 June 1954 the tenants claimed victory. Four demolition orders and twenty-three certificates of disrepair were presented to the rent collector when he made his usual call.

The photograph taken by a staff photographer of the *Daily Worker* shows a group of tenants in Biggerstaff Road triumphantly waving their certificates of disrepair. There are no men in the picture, for they were all at work.

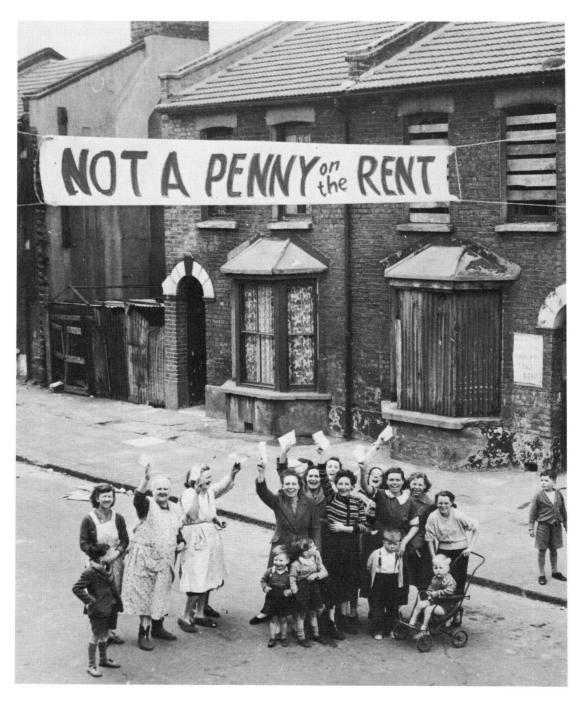

POSTERS

Early pioneers in trade unionism were the calico printers who in 1786 'turned out', that is, struck work, against the introduction of machinery and the taking on of more apprentices. The strike, at Mosney, near Preston, was led by a man called Walker who the employers complained 'went round the different print grounds to collect money to support the men out of work', an early example of working class solidarity.

Calico printing was originally confined to London where it was tightly controlled by the journeyman printers. The spread of the industry to Lancashire posed a threat to their high wages as the country districts made extensive use of child labour, undercutting the prevailing rates. When the Lancashire firm of Livesey and Company sought to raise the quality of their work by bringing experienced printers from London, they found that they also brought the experience of resolute trade unionists who sought to impose union conditions of work. The power of the union grew, imposing fines of from five to fifteen guineas upon members whom they termed 'knob-sticks', i.e. blacklegs, and restricting the number of apprentices to the trade. In 1808 the calico printers petitioned Parliament for a legal limitation to the number of apprentices, which was threatening their livelihood, and were in fact well received by the Select Committee. However, Sir Robert Peel, known in Lancashire as the father of the print business and whose own factories 'swarmed with boys', opposed the Bill in the name of individual freedom and carried the Commons with him. Peel went further and moved part of his business to Tamworth in Staffordshire to escape the restraint of the Lancashire union and introduced new machinery operated by 'apprentices'.

The poster issued by the Lancashire firm of Butterworth, Brooks and Company in 1815 tells much of the fight of the calico printers. It acknowledges the existence of the union and affirms the opposition of the employers to the combination of journeymen. The statement 'the usual wages will be given' conceals a familiar story in the struggle between capital and labour; it stands for the introduction of new machinery, cylinder printing in place of the old block process, with a consequent loss of jobs. The appeal for 'stout lads, young men or women

apprentices' was an attempt by the employers to break the ratio of apprentices to skilled craftsmen enforced by the union. It is a poster advertising for non-union, cheap labour.

Facts concerning the dispute are scarce, but in February 1815, one month after the poster was printed, an unstamped letter was received by the London Society of Brushmakers from calico printers asking for assistance. Records show that the Brushmakers paid the postage of 11d. and loaned the printers £10, free of interest. The following month, three calico printers walked to London from Manchester to explain their case to the Brushmakers. 3s. were spent on 'treating calico printers' and another 7½d. on 'attending to take voices'. This meant that the secretary of the Brushmakers' union went to the clubhouse to collect the tin box that had been passed around the trade to take votes on the issue of support. Made of tin with a leather strap, the box would circulate from shop to shop, being taken by a member wearing a coat with a large pocket for concealment. A little tune of five notes would be whistled, the 'Brushmakers' call' to summon the men and in passage or alley they would record their votes by dropping a token into the box. The property of an unlawful society, the tin box was unlawful, containing a terrible threat to employers: votes! The Brushmakers agreed to loan a further £10 free of interest and the accounts of the Brushmakers show that it was repaid by the calico printers eight years later in February 1823.

The firm of Butterworth, Brooks and Company was started by John Brooks, the son of a Manchester banker. In 1809 he entered into a partnership with a Mr Butterworth of Crawshawbooth, setting up as calico printers at the Sunnyside works, near Preston. John Brooks was an energetic and ambitious businessman who frequently drove to his works at five in the morning to greet any latecomers with 'Nah yo lads, don't you think yo could get up a bit earlier?'

The employers continued their policy of employing large numbers of apprentices as cheap labour and in 1830 came the great 'turn out' of the calico printers due to the hardship they were suffering. In a bitter dispute, the employers called in the troops against the strikers and, in one instance, John Brooks was

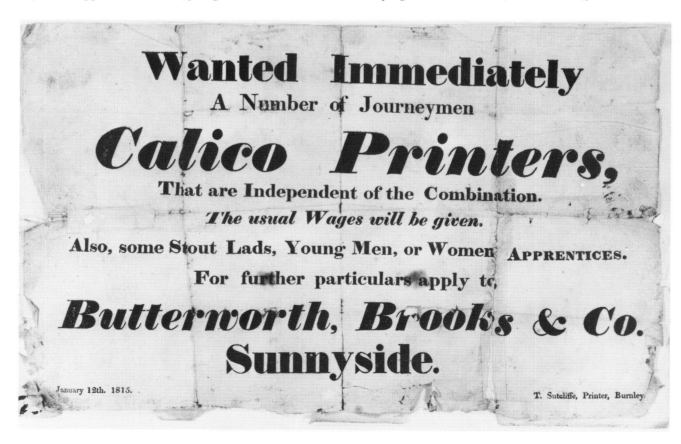

fortunate to escape with his life. Brooks had caused some of the striking calico printers to be brought before the magistrate at Haslingden, the Revd Gray. As Brooks and the strikers arrived at Haslingden, a group of workers lay in wait and chased Brooks, who was forced to seek refuge in a house at Spout House that was then besieged by the angry men. On the pretext of sending a little girl to the Bull's Head Inn for 'some barm' Brooks sent a message to the soldiers, who dispersed the crowd in all directions. The incident became part of Haslingden folklore and known as 'T Spaat Haase Feight'.

Such was the hardship endured by the apprentices that they petitioned the Master Calico Printers expressing their dismay at remaining apprentices for seven years and then being sacked when due the full rate of pay. '. . . we beg you to look at the critical state in which we are now involved. Our parents and children are starving . . .' Brooks appears to have been affected by the plight of his printers and by the 1840s was subscribing £100 a year to the Anti-Corn Law League, had joined with the Chartists and stood at Bolton as a parliamentary candidate. When he died in 1849, he was buried at Prestwich, his grave marked by a monument erected by the Anti-Corn Law League.

While the Great Dock Strike of 1889 held the attention of all London, another great strike was being fought, almost unnoticed, by the tailors of East London against the sweated conditions that imposed a hardship comparable to the lot endured by the dock labourer.

The influx of Jewish immigrants during the 1880s, victims of persecution from Poland and Czarist Russia, created new problems in housing and work in an already poverty-stricken area. The immigrants arrived for the most part penniless, many unable to speak English, free at last but vulnerable in the jungle of free enterprise. Small workshops proliferated in the rat-warren streets of Whitechapel and tailoring was the predominant industry. With a plentiful supply of unorganised, desperate, hungry labour. there was more undercutting than cloth cutting in the market of free choice. In his book, *East End Jewish Radicals*, Bill Fishman quotes Wilchinski to describe the 'greeners', the new, bewildered arrivals, making their way to the 'chazar mark' (pig market!), the open area near Black Lion Yard where the masters selected 'hands' from the assortment of hungry men:

TAILORS' STRIKE,
1889.

After five weeks' struggle, of Machinists, Pressers and Basters, the Master Tailors have accepted the following terms of the Men:

1. The hours of labour to be from 8 o'clock in the morning until 8 o'clock in the evening, with one hour for dinner and half-an-hour for tea.
2. All meals to be had off the work premises.
3. Only four hours overtime may be worked in a week.
4. Not more than two hours overtime to be worked in any one day.
5. The first two hours overtime to be paid for at the ordinary rate, and the second two hours to be paid for at the rate of time-and-a-half.
6. That the hour system be not introduced.

Signed on behalf of the Men,	Signed on behalf of the Employers,
LEWIS LYONS.	MARKS MOSES.
MORRIS ROSENTHAL.	ABRAHAM ROSENTHAL.
NOAH DAVIS.	S. ANSELL.
DAVIS LEVY.	M. GORDEMER.
LAZARUS GOLDSTEIN.	M. SYLVESTER.
SAMUEL JACOBS.	S. PHILLIPS.
MICHAEL FRENCHMAN.	J. VAN-COEVORDEN.
GODFREY STARGART.	
ALFRED LEEK.	

(Witness), SAMUEL MONTAGU, M.P.

October 2nd, 1889.

ALL MEN TO GO INTO WORK ON OCTOBER 6th, 1889, ON THE ABOVE TERMS.

October 3rd, 1889.   By Order of the Strike Committee.

'Many of them like myself, "greeners", willing to work at anything that would bring them the scantiest means of existence; some married with families and all with that enquiring, beseeching look, that half starved helpless, hopeless human beings possess . . . the majority . . . looked like so many unwashed corpses.'

Until he learned the trade, the single man might be offered board and lodging only, no wages at all. Wilchinski tells how he moved in with a tailor on such terms, the tailor occupying two rooms on a second floor, where he lived and worked with his wife and three children. 'The room we worked in was used for cooking also, and there I had to sleep on the floor. The wife helped as much as she could at the trade, besides doing all the work of the house and the children. A young woman worked the machine from eight in the morning till nine at night for three shillings a day, not very often making a full day's work . . . The master himself worked very hard indeed; and he himself told me that he had left the old country for the same reason as myself and that a few years previously he had been a cowkeeper and a dairyman, now he was a "tailor".'

So it was that the hope of the future was to own a sewing machine and be a 'tailor' employing a 'greener' and working him 'proper hours', from seven in the morning till nine at night. It was against this background that the Amalgamated Society of Tailors struck for a ten and a half hour day with not more than four hours' overtime a week. The non-organised Jewish tailors seemed to have rallied to the call of those employed by the large companies where there was trade union representation. Within two weeks, Lewis Lyons, the leader of the strike, announced that 10,000 men were out and that cabinetmakers and cigarmakers, two industries that had Jewish trade unions, were supporting the strike. Lyons said that if the employers did not surrender all the Jewish workers in the East End would leave work, which would paralyse the boot and shoe trade. The East End seethed with stories of the dockers' and the tailors' strike and Lyons and Wolf Wess, another of the strike leaders, followed the example of the

SOCIAL RE-CONSTRUCTION VERSUS
CAPITALIST CONSTRICTION,
A SOUVENIR FOR MAY-DAY, DEDICATED TO THE WORKERS OF THE WORLD

YOU CANNOT TRUST HIM
OR HIS RAG

PUT YOUR TRUST IN
BRITAINS FLAG

Vote UNIONIST

dockers in leading daily processions of their supporters, marching to Victoria Park and receiving fraternal support from guest speakers like Tom Mann, John Burns and Ben Tillett.

A joint meeting between the employers and workers lasted throughout the night of Thursday, 12 September, ending at 5 a.m. with the employers conceding the men's demands on hours and overtime. However, the employers would not ratify the agreement and the strike continued. The local MP, Samuel Montague, and Lord Rothschild were prevailed upon to act as mediators and to use their influence upon the masters to accede to the demands on hours and conditions. Montague donated £30. 10s. 0d. to the strike fund and Lord Rothschild gave £73. 0s. 0d. Trade unions rallied to support the strikers, the London Society of Compositors giving £10. 0s. 0d., the Amalgamated Society of Boot and Shoemakers, £10. 0s. 0d., the Mantel Makers' Co-operative Society, 7s. 2d., and the Dock Labourers' Strike Committee in a magnificent gesture of solidarity gave £100. 0s. 0d.

On Sunday, 29 September the tailors mounted a grand demonstration to Hyde Park, being joined by the Socialist League and the Social Democratic Federation, publicly exposing the employers for their duplicity. The following Wednesday, 2 October, the employers gave way, the agreement being signed by both parties and witnessed by Samuel Montague, MP, the next day. The posters proclaiming the victory and the terms of the settlement were printed in both English and Hebrew, the Jewish version being printed on the press of the *Worker's Friend*, the Jewish anarchist weekly.

Walter Crane's 'cartoons' were the popular art of the social-democratic movement, brightening the dreary walls of dingy meeting rooms, cheering cheerless homes and bringing the message of hope wherever a few workers gathered together to plan the social revolution. The imagery was always simple and compelling even when the drawings were elaborate. Capitalism was a serpent, a wolf or a dragon; the workers were men of Morris's England, labourers and craftsmen, strong and determined, ever ready to slay the monster of evil, the capitalist system. Socialism was a sunny future, the millennium, almost, but not quite within the eager grasp of a Phrygian-capped proletariat. The message of socialism was clearly spelt out, the co-operative commonwealth, 'production for use, not profit', 'public ownership of the means of life', 'no child toilers', 'solidarity of labour', 'the land for the people', 'work for all, overwork for none'.

The image of socialism bearing the torch, the banner or the keys of freedom was invariably a woman, Grecian robed, wearing the cap of liberty, sometimes graced with the wings of an angel, a heroine that was neither Britannia nor Joan of Arc yet encapsulated motherhood, beauty and courage.

Each May Day saw the publication of a specially drawn cartoon for one of the socialist papers, also issued as a poster print in black and white or sometimes in full colour. Their purpose was, as Crane explained, 'Directed to the embodiment of the principles of socialism and unmistakably inscribed with legends expressing the political aims and social aspiration of the party'. The colour poster, 'Socialist Re-construction versus Capitalist

Constriction', was drawn for the May Day issue of *Justice* in 1909 and sold as a souvenir by the Social Democratic Federation. In 1896 the Twentieth Century Press issued *Cartoons for the Cause*, a folio collection of cartoons and poems by Crane from 1886-1896 as a souvenir of the International Socialist Workers' and Trade Union congress held in London in 1896. In 1907, on the eve of the Third International Congress, the folio was republished extending the collection to cover a period of twenty years. The influence of Crane's art upon the iconography of the working class movement was immense and nowhere was it in greater evidence than upon the giant silken banners of the trades unions that had their golden age during the last decade of the nineteenth century. Crane's *Cartoons for the Cause* became a handbook for the banner painter, a ready reference of imagery, as dockers, gasworkers, miners, builders, seamen and railwaymen expressed their aspirations through the borrowed pageantry of 'The Workers' Maypole', 'The Triumph of Labour', or 'A Garland for May Day'.

Crane, undoubtedly influenced by William Morris, had a nostalgic and romantic view of England past and wrote, 'England was once not only "merrie" but beautiful – her people well and picturesquely clad: her towns rich with lovely architecture – life a perpetual pageant . . . the colour and fantastic invention in costume and heraldry; the constant show and processions, such as those organised by the craft guilds, full of quaint allegory and symbolic meaning . . . gay with flaunting banners . . .'

It was this utopian dream that Crane gave form, to shape the imagery of labour: heroic, idealistic, romantic. He painted an 'angel of freedom' that became a universal symbol for the cause, heralding the dawn of the socialist commonwealth, offering the key to emancipation. Crane likened his angel 'To a vision breaking into the sunshine of spring'. So it was, and working people throughout Europe grasped at the promise of a new life that would blossom like a flower in spring beneath the golden sun of socialism.

A month after the termination of the First World War, Lloyd George held his 'Khaki' election, facing an electorate elated with victory and intent on exacting punishment and reparation. As Prime Minister of the wartime coalition government, he saw his

In 1918 They Bamboozled You with a KHAKI ELECTION
In 1924 They Tricked You with a RED LETTER
This Time It's GOING TO BE RED, WHITE & BLUE
DON'T BE HOODWINKED
VOTE LABOUR

best chance of remaining in power by going to the nation and seeking endorsement for National Government candidates. To his fury, the Labour Party would have none of it and chose to fight the election as an independent party, fielding 363 candidates. To a people subjected to four years of jingo hysteria, Lloyd George used his eloquence to effect, castigating the pacifist leaders of the Labour Party, MacDonald, Snowden, Smillie and others. In an eve of election speech, with cavalier disregard for the inherent contradiction in his claim, he accused the Labour Party of being run by an 'extreme pacifist Bolshevist group'. The fact that other Labour leaders like Henderson and Clynes had been part of the wartime government was ignored. The Tories and Liberals united to attack the Labour Party and the electorate rejected Labour's programme, 'Labour and the new social order', in favour of a platitudinous platform of 'Make them pay', 'a land fit for heroes' and 'hang the Kaiser'. Of the heroes of the trenches, only 1,000,000 of the 4,000,000 eligible servicemen cast their votes, a large and unknown number never receiving their ballot papers. Labour won only 57 seats, all their candidates who had opposed the war being beaten.

In January 1924 Labour took office for the first time, with only 191 seats, dependent upon the support of the Liberals' 158 seats to combine against the Conservatives' 258. Labour had pledged in its election manifesto to undertake 'the resumption of free economic and diplomatic relations with Russia' that had been broken off following the revolution in 1917. Nine days after taking office, Labour accorded diplomatic recognition to the Soviet government. In April they commenced negotiations on an Anglo-Soviet treaty to settle the problem of pre-revolutionary debts, Czarist treaties and to conclude a commercial trading agreement. MacDonald was motivated not by a political affinity with Soviet communism, but by hard-headed practical consideration of peace, friendship and trade. The opposition from the right and the national press in Britain was predictable. Winston Churchill referred to 'the blood-dyed tyrants of Moscow', and the *Morning Post* claimed 'British interests are betrayed' and the paranoiac right could already see British MPs with 'snow on their boots'.

The treaties were not in the event concluded before the next election was called, the minority Labour government resigning after only eleven months in office over the pressing of an amendment in Parliament by the Liberals on the Campbell case. However, the Conservatives were determined to exploit to the full the scare of the 'red menace' and produced a poster showing Ramsay MacDonald turning his back on three downcast Britishers to greet two blood-thirsty looking Cossacks. The caption read, 'So this is socialism, vote unionist'.

While preparations were being made for the election, two emigré Russians, Alexis Bellegarde and Alexander Gumansky, both members of the anti-soviet Brotherhood of St George, forged a letter over the signatures of Zinoviev, President of the Comintern, Kuusinen, the Finnish Secretary of the International, and Arthur MacManus, a British communist and a member of the Praesidium of the International, addressed to the Central Committee of the British Communist Party. The letter gave secret instructions to British communists on support for the signing of the treaty, on bringing pressure upon the Labour Party and writing about 'armed insurrection', on the military section of the British Communist Party and the disaffection of the armed forces. The aim of the forgers was to prevent the signing of the treaty, as investment would strengthen the Soviet government and weaken the chances of counter-revolution.

The forgery was fed to the British intelligence service, Conservative Central Office, the Foreign Office and the *Daily Mail*. The *Daily Mail* splashed the story, 'Civil war plot by socialist's masters', 'Paralyse the Army and Navy', 'MacDonald would lend Russia our money'. The whole substance of the letter to the tiny British Communist Party of some 3,500 members was preposterous. Crude mistakes in the letter were obvious and were pointed out by MacManus and Zinoviev but neither the Conservative Party, the press, nor the Foreign Office were interested. MacDonald underestimated and mishandled the

Labour response and the newspapers had a red scare jamboree at the expense of the Labour Party.

On the eve of the election the *Daily Mail* printed, 'Get rid of your shifty Prime Minister'. On election day the *Daily Express* headline in red ink, howled, 'Do not vote red today'. The implication behind all the stories was clear: the Labour Party was manipulated by communists, a vote for Labour was a vote for Bolshevism. The Conservative poster gives a Conservative image of Labour, an evil-looking central European wearing a red scarf and carrying a red flag. Contrast the evil foreigner with the clean-cut Britisher and his trust in the British flag.

The publication of the forgery reduced Labour's Parliamentary strength from 193 to 152, a red letter day for the Tories, who won 411 seats.

The Zinoviev letter is not the only instance of last minute scare-mongering by the Conservatives to thwart the possibility of Labour electoral success. In 1931 the National Government led by Ramsay MacDonald and his new-found Tory friends attacked Labour's programme as 'Bolshevism gone mad' and warned the electorate that Labour would raid the workers' Post Office savings to pay the unemployment benefit that MacDonald and Snowden were planning to cut. In 1945 Winston Churchill attempted the biggest scare of all in an effort to win a general election. In a broadcast to the nation he warned that socialism would bring 'some form of Gestapo', a wild allegation that the voters chose to ignore.

Harry Quelch contested four Parliamentary elections, in 1898, 1902, 1906 and 1910, as Social Democratic candidate, his best result being at Dewsbury in 1902 when he polled 13.6 percent of the vote. It is uncertain for which of these elections the 'Monkeys' poster was printed, though it is likely to have been his last election when he was quoted as saying, 'The English working class is not less able, less intelligent or more stupid than

the working class in other European countries, but it is certainly more completely imbued with bourgeois ideas, less conscious of its own subject position as a class than any other working class I know.'

Quelch was born at Hungerford in Berkshire on 30 January 1858, the son of a blacksmith, and started work in an upholsterer's at the age of ten, from early morning to late at night. At the age of fourteen he left for London where he began work at Peak Freen's biscuit factory and afterwards at a skinyard and then a foundry. Quelch was gifted with the ability to learn languages and taught himself French, German and some Latin, reading voraciously the progressive literature of his time. He joined the Bermondsey Radical Club and gave his first vote to George Shipton, for many years secretary of the London Trades Council, when he stood as a labour candidate in 1880. Quelch read volume one of *Capital* in French and became an active member of the SDF. His life by now was dedicated to the cause of socialism and in 1887 he took part in the march on Trafalgar Square when it was closed to the people, the ensuing battle with the police and the death of Alfred Linnell battering it into history as Bloody Sunday. Quelch led his Bermondsey contingent through the police lines and though broken in formation got through without losing a man or a banner. In 1889 he founded the South Side Labour Protection League shortly after the Great Dock Strike and represented the union at the Trades Union Congresses of 1890, 1891 and 1892. Objection was taken at times by the labourers of his union to his socialism, but Quelch never wavered, saying, 'If you men, whose servant I am, think I am going to suppress the red flag for two pounds a week, you are mistaken.'

He became editor of *Justice* and chairman of the London Trades Council, resigning when the Council passed a vote of congratulations to John Burns on joining the Liberal Cabinet. In 1900 he was a delegate at the Memorial Hall conference which founded the Labour Representation Committee, but the SDF

made the mistake of seceding from the LRC, a move that Quelch strongly supported, a sectarian decision that isolated the SDF from the mass movement of Labour.

Nevertheless, the contribution of the self-taught country boy to the labour movement was considerable. When he died in 1913, 10,000 people attended his funeral. Lenin wrote of him, 'Quelch was in the front ranks of those who fought steadfastly and with conviction against opportunism and a liberal-labour policy in the British working class movement. True, isolation from the masses sometimes infected the British Social Democrats with a certain sectarianism. Hyndman, the leader and founder of Social-democracy in Britain, has even slipped into jingoism. But the party of the Social Democrats has fought him on this and over the whole of Britain the Social Democrats, and they alone, have for decades been carrying on systematic propaganda and agitation in the Marxist spirit. This is the great historical service rendered by Quelch and his comrades.'

The 'Revolution in Russia' to which the poster refers was the uprising of 1905 and the meeting at the Memorial Hall on 22 January 1906 was held to commemorate the St Petersburg massacre. Organised by the International Socialist Bureau, the meeting was one of a worldwide series of 'Red Sundays' held exactly one year to the day after Czarist police fired upon a peaceful demonstration in front of the Winter Palace in St Petersburg, killing about 1,000 people.

Socialists throughout the world met to condemn the brutality and oppression of the Czarist autocracy and to extend socialist sympathy and solidarity to the revolutionists in Russia. The platform at the Memorial Hall in London represented a broad section of the labour movement, embracing the Social Democratic Federation, the Independent Labour Party, the Labour Party, the London Trades Council, The Fabian Society and the Communist Club. The meeting was predictable in passing a resolution and notable for the reading of a long letter from Maxim Gorky by H.M. Hyndman. The resolution said that the meeting 'joins with the proletariat of the world in sending its message of sympathy and solidarity with the Russian people in their struggle against the forces of despotism and bureaucracy, and hopes that their efforts will shortly bring about the establishment of a politically free Russia, so that the Russian proletariat may be able to work out their social and economic emancipation relieved from the crushing burden of autocracy.'

Messages of support were read to the meeting from Will Thorne, who was unable to be present to chair the meeting, Walter Crane, and a number of far-flung branches of the SDF. The highlight of the gathering was the letter from Gorky, that began:

Comrades – The conflict against the mean oppression of poverty is a conflict for the liberation of the world from the net of coarse contradictions in which all men are fiercely and impotently struggling. You are manfully trying to break this net: your enemies are making determined efforts to entangle you still more securely in its meshes; your weapon is the sharp sword of truth, that of your enemies the crooked needle of falsehood. Dazzled by the glitter of gold, they slavishly trust in its might, and do not perceive with what steadily increasing brightness burns the great ideal of the union of all men in one comrade-family of free workers. Socialism, the religion of liberty, equality and fraternity, is as unintelligible to them as is music to a man who is deaf and dumb, or poetry to an idiot. When they see the mighty march of the masses of the people toward freedom and light, dreading a disturbance of their peace, trembling for their position as lords of life, they hide the truth even from one another and console themselves with the spectral hope of defeating justice. They slanderously describe the proletariat as a dark mass of hungry beasts whose one desire is to gorge large quantities of food and who are ready for the sake of a good hunk of bread to destroy everything with which they cannot fill their maw.

Religion and science they employ as instruments for holding you in servitude; they have invented Nationalism and Anti-semitism, venom with which they would poison your faith in the brotherhood of all men; even God exists for the bourgeois merely as a guardian of property. In Russia a revolution is bursting into flame, and they slander utterly the Russian proletariat, representing the workmen as a mere unconscious elemental force, a barbarous horde, ready to destroy, to wipe out completely all that exists, and incapable of creating anything but anarchy . . .

and continued after a lengthy résumé of the insurrection in Moscow with a declaration of faith in the final success of the revolution, concluding:

I declare that the Russian revolution is a cultural and constructive movement, the only movement capable of saving Russia from political dissolution. I declare that the bourgeoisie is impotent and incapable of constructive political work, and I further declare that the anarchy in my country is the work of a Government occupied solely with defence of its own interests, which have nothing in common with those of the nation.

All that I have here set down is truth, and will in due time be confirmed by history, if, that is, the hand of the historian be an honest hand and justice be his religion.

Long live, then, the proletariat as it goes forth to renew the whole world. Long live the working men of all lands who by the strength of their hands have built up the wealth of nations and are now labouring to create a new life! Long live Socialism, the religion of the future!

Greetings to all fighters, greetings to the workers of all lands, and may they ever have faith in the victory of truth, the victory of justice! Long live humanity fraternally united in the great ideals of equality and freedom!

'Labour Clears the Way' was issued as a four-sheet poster (size 60 inches x 40 inches) and as a one sheet (size 30 inches x 20 inches) by the Labour Party in 1910. The publication followed the constitutional crisis precipitated by the House of Lords' rejection of Lloyd George's Budget when they voted by 350 votes to 75 to reject the Finance Bill on 30 November 1909. At the heart of the matter was defence of privilege by wealthy Lords who did not wish to contribute to social reform.

Lloyd George called it a 'People's Budget', a 'War Budget' to wage war on poverty and squalidness. As a reforming budget it enjoyed the support of the parliamentary Labour Party, but the full effects of the radical nature of the budget were slow to dawn upon the Conservative benches. When they did awaken they waged a battle in the Commons that lasted seventy days and 554 divisions.

To carry out his programme, which included the introduction of old age pensions, Lloyd George needed an additional £16,000,000. His proposals hit the Lords with revolutionary force; income tax up by 2*d.* in the pound on incomes of £5,000 a year, a supertax of 6*d.* in the pound on incomes over £5,000, an increase of 6*d.* on whisky duty, new taxes on cars and petrol and certain land taxes. Crumbs from the rich to make provision for the poor. The Lords would have none of it. The Duke of Beaufort declared that he would like to see Lloyd George 'put in the middle of twenty couple of dog hounds'. For the first time in 250 years, the Lords rejected a Finance Bill; Asquith moved a resolution in the Commons declaring that the action of the House of Lords was 'a breach of the constitution and a usurpation of the rights of the Commons'. It was carried and the following day Parliament was dissolved and the General Election fixed for 14 January 1910.

Labour Party election leaflets and posters took up the issue of the House of Lords and were uncompromising in their

condemnation of the feudal system. 'The constitutional crisis is not merely a matter of political reform, the House of Lords is a fortified camp of anti-social privilege.' If the House of Lords was a fortified camp, Labour would show how to batter it down. Labour explained that the Tory Lords' policy of tariff reform would remove taxation from luxuries and impose them on food for the poor. They publicised the fact that one quarter of all the land in Britain was owned by 525 peers and exposed the capitalisation of the land as a result of community development. The Ramsden family bought the site of Huddersfield for £1,000 and was presently drawing a ground rent of £100,000 per annum from the citizens of the city.

The fight to restrict the power of the Lords was prolonged. Asquith won the election of January 1910, but only just. A constitutional conference failed and another election was held in December, the fight being on the issue of the House of Lords. The result was again a narrow majority for the Liberals, Labour winning 42 seats. The election victory still left the passage of the Parliament Bill to be resolved and die-hard Tory peers were determined to make serious amendments. This time, Asquith played his ace; the King had made a secret pledge prior to the December election to create the required number of Liberal peers to give a majority if opposition was maintained, the unionists

backed down and the government won the vote by a narrow majority on August 1911 with a majority of 17.

The Labour Party sold an astonishing 50,000 posters during the January election of 1910 in addition to distributing more than 5,000,000 leaflets and 800,000 manifestos. Despite reforms over the years, the House of Lords remains an undemocratic anachronism and will continue as such until the principle of hereditary power and patronage is totally abolished.

The 'Equality of Sacrifice' poster was a biting riposte to Philip Snowden's emergency budget of 10 September 1931. Following the treacherous formation by Ramsay MacDonald of a 'National' government two weeks earlier, Snowden was able to proceed with his proposal for cutting unemployment benefit, a proposal rejected by the majority of his cabinet colleagues of the Labour Government on 23 August 1931.

Snowden claimed equality of sacrifice, increasing surtax by ten percent and cutting the already pitifully inadequate unemployment relief by ten percent. In his budget speech he said, 'I have tried as best I could to spread the burden of the sacrifice as fairly and evenly as human ingenuity can devise.' He sat down at the end of his speech to the tremendous and sustained cheering of Tory and Liberal members, waving order

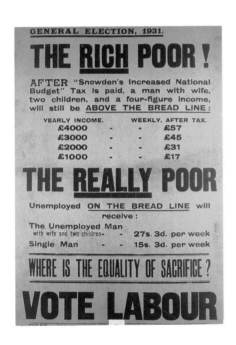

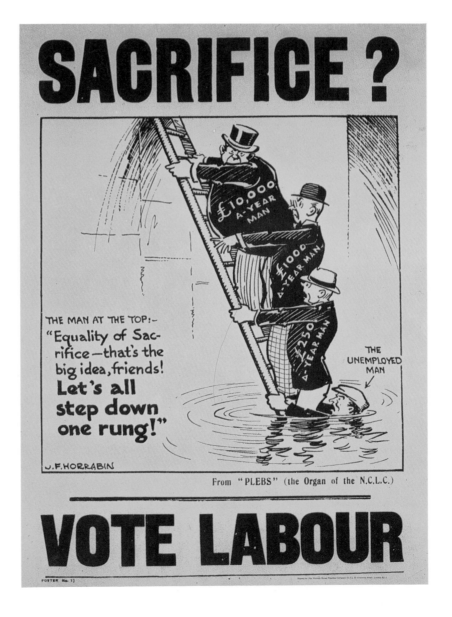

167

papers and handkerchiefs, for here was the solution to the current crisis of capitalism, to cut the amount paid to an unemployed worker from 17s. to 15s. 3d.

The government sought general powers by Orders in Council to eliminate discussions and by 12 November the 'means test', perhaps the most hated piece of legislation ever imposed upon the British working class, was in operation. Means test officers pried into the microscopic finances of impoverished families with extraordinary zeal. Women with newly-born babies were cross-examined on whether they were breast feeding their offspring, thereby saving on an allowance for milk! The depth of interrogation and the resulting misery burned into the heart of the working class and is remembered with bitterness three generations later. In three months, 377,511 people were denied benefit, a benefit to which they had paid their contributions. It was never a 'dole'.

The brilliant drawing by the socialist artist J.F. Horrabin first appeared in *Plebs*, the journal of the National Council of Labour Colleges, and was used as a poster during the election campaign of October 1931.

The value of poster art as political propaganda is clearly demonstrated by the powerful and telling imagery of the agitprop posters produced in the years following the Russian revolution of 1917. Made by young, unknown and often untrained artists enthused with the spirit of the revolution, they carried the message of the fight against famine and counter-revolution in simple graphic form to a largely illiterate peasantry. Reproduced in small numbers by simple stencil processes their crude amateurism has a strength and directness that reflects the political commitment of the artists.

The popular front agitation of the 1930s against fascism and war produced a similar spirit of involvement and purpose among artists in Britain anxious to give public expression to their political position. Impetus was given by the founding of the Artists' International Association in 1933, enlisting hundreds of

professional artists in a popular crusade against unemployment and the threat of fascism at home and abroad. With the Franco attack on Spanish democracy, the activities of the AIA in support of the popular front involved thousands of people in the production of banners, posters, leaflets, exhibitions, hoardings, murals and photographs. Groups of artists working together with untrained supporters produced an astonishing range of visual propaganda in support of working class unity.

In the East End of London in 1936 a group of left wing artists led by Norman King set up in a church hall to teach workers how to make their own propaganda material. On some evenings they had as many as seventy people busily painting banners, cutting stencils, printing posters and duplicating leaflets for marches, demonstrations and exhibitions.

On Saturday, 19 November 1938 Herbert Morrison opened an exhibition of their propaganda art at Christchurch Hall, Watney Street, presenting a display of tableaux, banners and posters produced by trade unionists with no special art training.

The poster advertising the exhibition was silk-screen printed in one colour from a hand-cut paper stencil. To those art critics who despised the use of art for politics, Eric Gill, the distinguished sculptor and engraver, replied, 'All art is propaganda, for it is all concerned with putting something across.' The trade unionists who worked in their spare time to make propaganda against fascism, war, unemployment and rack-rent landlords at the Watney Street Hall must have put their message across to millions of Londoners.

Two events in Britain in 1933 and 1934 reflected the growing support for pacifism and the rejection of war as a means of resolving international disputes. The first was the Oxford Union debate on 9 February 1933, when the motion, 'This House will in no circumstances fight for King and Country', was carried by 275 votes to 153. The second was the Peace Ballot of 1934, when over 11,000,000 people voted in an unofficial ballot on six questions concerning the League of Nations and disarmament. The vote was overwhelmingly in favour of the peace campaigners, more than 10,000,000 voting 'yes' to the second question, 'Are you in favour of an all-round reduction of armaments by international agreement?' In October 1934 Canon

Dick Shepherd invited those who cared for peace to send him a postcard: 'I renounce war and I will never support or sanction another.' Within a year, 80,000 cards were sent to him and the Peace Pledge Union was formed.

It was against this background that the Labour Party, pledged to support the League of Nations, issued their 'Stop War' poster sometime during 1935. It may have been in the early part of the year, when the party was led by the Christian pacifist, George Lansbury, or it may have been issued in response to the Italian fascist invasion of Abyssinia on 3 October 1935, an event that led a few days later to the resignation of Lansbury who could not support the Labour Party conference resolution calling on the League of Nations to '. . . use all the necessary measures provided by the covenant to prevent Italy's unjust and rapacious attack . . .' Another possibility is that it was designed and produced for the general election of November the same year.

What is known is that a Midland billposting company refused to handle the poster and that the Conservative Party Press Office, asked to comment on the poster, said, 'Rather bad taste, don't you think?' Within three years, the government issued 38,000,000 gas masks to the civilian population, including gas masks for babies!

Felicity Ashbee was one of four daughters born into a comfortable, celebrated, talented middle class family, splendidly housed in the Kentish countryside. It was a secure and privileged life of private education, servants, travel and the reflected achievements of her father, Charles R. Ashbee, founder of the Guild of Handicraft, and the more questionable fame of her grandfather, H.S. Ashbee, a wealthy merchant, linguist, bibliophile and voracious collector of pornographic literature.

Yet, by 1936, at the age of twenty-three, Felicity Ashbee was working with the Communist Party and giving her time and artistic talent to the cause of Republican Spain, anti-fascism and the socialist emancipation of the working class. Like Orwell, Cornford, Cauldwell, Nancy Mitford and so many other

intellectuals from the privileged strata of middle and upper class British society in the thirties, she was drawn into the struggle of the popular front movement against fascism. More than drawn, she was galvanised into action, her energies devoted to a crusade that was so obviously right, just, fair, against the clearly evil forces of fascism and capitalism. Ashbee herself described it as 'tantamount to a religious conversion'.

Trained in the fine arts, Felicity Ashbee had seen her oil paintings hung at the Royal Academy. Now, as a member of the Artists' International Association, she painted hoardings appealing for help for Spain, banners for May Day marches and posters for peace. A feminist before the word attained its present connotation, she penetrated a male domain by becoming a cartoonist. As an occasional illustrator for *Time and Tide*, she broke the relationship when they refused her cartoon on the Jarrow march.

Her involvement with the Communist Party was brief and had certainly ended at the time of the Nazi-Soviet Pact, but her commitment to anti-fascism remained firm and her work for progressive causes continued long after the rejection of the party card. The poster appealing for milk for starving Spanish children, designed in November 1937, is one of three she designed for the National Joint Committee for Spanish Relief in an attempt to alleviate the distress of half a million refugees from Franco's terror. It is perhaps the best of her posters, poignant, powerful, a precursor of the gaunt faces and helpless eyes to be drawn by Vicky in his pleas for the hungry of the Third World. Banned by the London Passenger Transport Board as 'political', Felicity Ashbee was 'bitterly disappointed' that it did not reach the wide public it deserved.

In 1939 Ashbee volunteered for the Women's Auxiliary Air Force to fight fascism and had ambitions to fly in combat, but it was the Royal Air Force and not the Red Air Force and she was consigned to women's work as a clerk, special duties, before becoming an Officer in Intelligence and Administration.

In the WAAF she painted murals for dining halls and in 1943 she designed a fine poster for Russian Relief. Her posters give a tantalising glimpse of a talent that could easily have made Felicity Ashbee one of the most outstanding political poster artists of her generation.

'The "Military" Practice of the Rebels' is a scene of twentieth century phenomenon, a modern crucifixion. The dead child, unidentified, lies tagged and numbered, a victim of fascism. Aerial bombardment may have begun during the First World War, but it was during the rebel onslaught on the Spanish Republic that the techniques of terror, the mass bombing of civilians and the machine-gunning of refugees, was perfected by the airforces of Germany and Italy – Luftwaffe training for Warsaw, Rotterdam, London and Coventry. The poster was produced by the Ministry of Propaganda, drawn by an unknown artist. It is a powerful indictment of the fascist enemy; it is also a call to resist and defend.

The posters produced for the Republican cause, and there were hundreds of designs, displayed a common purpose, a sense of urgency, the need to mobilise to defeat the aggressor, to expose the barbaric nature of the enemy, to fuse the popular spirit of resistance into a unified force strong enough to smash fascism.

Amid the destruction of war, amid the agony and the outrage, the graphic art of Spanish poster artists flourished, giving visual form to the concept of the Popular Front and the peaceful aims of the Spanish Republic. The artists, members of the Spanish Artists' Union, often worked under difficulty, during air raids, under shellfire, by candlelight in bomb-damaged studios. Printers too shared the problems and shortages created by war yet still contrived to produce work that bears favourable comparison with posters produced in peacetime.

The posters were produced by a wide range of government bodies from all the regions of Spain, from the Council for the Defence of Madrid to the Government of Catalonia. All the organisations that made up and supported the Popular Front

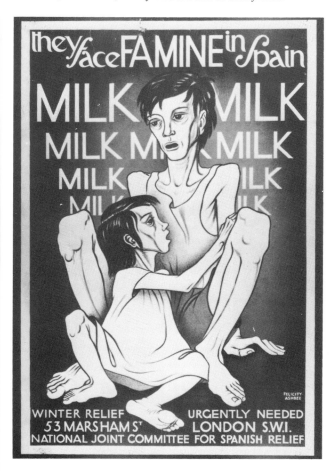

contributed to the pictorial exhortations against fascism and for the welfare of the people. The political parties, Communist, Syndicalist, Socialist, Left Republican, Anarchist; the trade unions, Asturias miners, agricultural workers; the friends of Republican Spain, International Brigades, International Red Aid, Spanish Medical Aid; state organisations, the National League of War Disabled, Office of Press and Propaganda, these and more issued posters to inform and inspire. They were displayed everywhere, in offices, homes, in windows, on hoardings, walls and telegraph poles, a people's gallery of popular art illustrating the will of the government and the indomitable and heroic spirit of the people.

The poster 'Help Wounded Human Beings' was produced in England for the Spanish Medical Aid Committee by the renowned poster artist of the thirties, McKnight Kauffer. The Spanish Medical Aid Committee had been formed by doctors, medical students and nurses on Saturday, 8 August 1936 at a meeting convened in London at less than twenty-four hours' notice. Within two days the work of preparing a unit to go to the front was under way. Two weeks later the unit, consisting of a team of four doctors, five administrative and quartermaster staff, six nurses and five dressers and orderlies, was on its way to

Spain. During the first month they treated over 800 patients and were themselves constantly under fire on their journeys to the front.

Whilst the committee was based behind the loyalist lines and primarily existed to assist the democratic forces, they treated the wounded of both sides with medical impartiality in the cause of humanity. Although supported by the National Council of Labour in Britain and the International Federation of Trade Unions in Europe, the committee was made up of people with differing political opinions, with the Rt. Hon. Christopher Addison, MD, FRCS, as President and Dr Somerville Hastings as Vice Chairman. The volunteers came from all parts of Britain and from many trades and occupations – doctors, clerks, students and one taxi driver were among those who made up the first unit.

McKnight Kauffer was one of a large number of the Artists' International Association who put their talents at the disposal of the Republican cause. A distinguished American designer, he came to Britain in 1913 and made an immediate impact with his firm grasp of geometrical decoration. Of the countless posters he designed (including a stunning angular design for the *Daily Herald*), none were produced for a worthier cause. His use of the El Greco face beneath the word 'Help' speaks for humanity. The

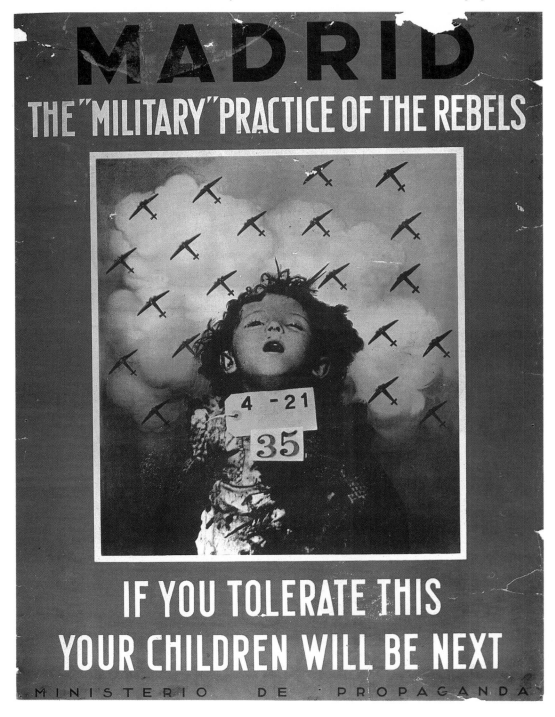

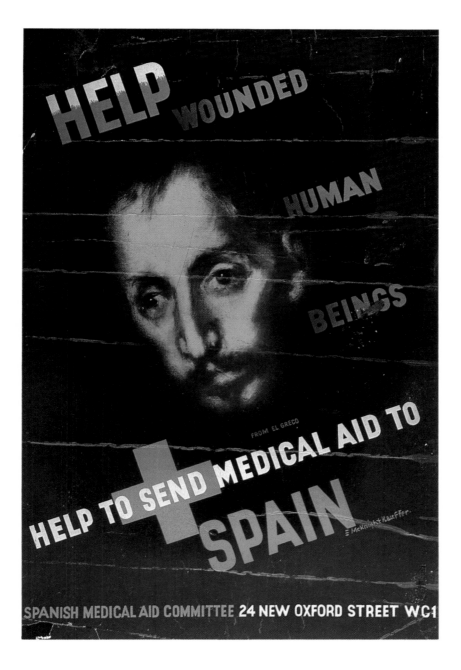

HELP WOUNDED HUMAN BEINGS

FROM EL GRECO

HELP TO SEND MEDICAL AID TO SPAIN

E. McKnight Kauffer.

SPANISH MEDICAL AID COMMITTEE 24 NEW OXFORD STREET WC1

posters of the Spanish conflict are an anti-fascist record, a painted page of history to be viewed with passion and never forgotten.

Three posters linking four historic trade union struggles from 1971 to 1973: the Upper Clyde Shipbuilders' work-in, the 1972 miners' strike and the Briant Colour work-in, where the poster in support of the five dockers imprisoned under the Conservative government's Industrial Relations Act was printed in July 1972.

The decision of the Tory government to liquidate the shipyards that made up the consortium known as Upper Clyde Shipbuilders, with the loss of 6,000 jobs on Clydebank, was announced in the House of Commons on 29 July 1971. The resulting occupation of the yards by the workers began the next day, Willie McInnes, the convenor from Linthouse, saying, 'They will need to get the soldiers from Bogside to get us out of Clydeside.' In a victorious battle that mobilised the support of the labour and trade union movement and won public opinion to the side of the UCS workers, Jimmy Reid, spokesman for the stewards, and Jim Airlie, Chairman of the Shop Stewards' Co-ordinating Committee, became as well known as the government ministers they fought. The poster appealing for unity and funds was produced by the sub-committee responsible

for fund raising, led by Roddy McKenzie. Large donations came from trade unions at home and abroad, but it was the pennies of the old age pensioners and the unemployed that underlined the popular support for the UCS workers in their fight for jobs.

The 1972 miners' strike, the first national miners' strike since 1926, was a fight for higher wages. Faceworkers, the highest paid of Britain's miners, earned a gross wage of about £30 a week, five shifts at £5 a shift, plus £5 bonus. The successful strike, called after the holding of a national ballot of the mineworkers, started on 8 January 1972 and lasted until 28 February. The poster, 'He'll Carry No More', came from the Kent miners, the drawing by pit-top worker, Jimmy Brannen, being based on an idea by Con Connolly, the COSA representative on the Betteshanger colliery liaison committee. The posters were printed by NATSOPA in solidarity with the miners and distributed across the country.

The imprisonment of five dockers, Bernie Steer, Vic Turner, Cornelius Clancy, Edward Merrick and Roy Watkins, for picketing at an East London container depot, brought massive protests from trade unionists throughout Britain. The events that led the dockers to Pentonville began with a demand from dockers that only registered dock workers should handle the loading of containers, at a time when traditional cargo handling was being transferred to depots outside the dock area. Using the provisions of the Tory government's Industrial Relations Act, Midland Cold Storage, the container company at the centre of the dispute, obtained an order from the National Industrial Relations Court forbidding the 'blacking' of their lorries as unlawful industrial action. Ignoring the order, the dockers continued to picket the company and the NIRC responded by ordering their arrest on 22 July 1972. The reaction of Britain's dockers was immediate and decisive. By nightfall, 26,000 had walked out. In a wave of solidarity the picketing switched to Pentonville where workers from other industries joined the dockers in protest. Miners from South Wales joined the picket, as did workers from Upper Clyde Shipbuilders, reciprocating the support given to them by dockers during their own struggle. Throughout the country workers struck, on building sites, newspapers, factories and mines, demanding the release of the imprisoned trade unionists. 'If they're in, we're out' was the slogan echoing across the land as even the Aberdeen trawler crews struck in support. The winning blow came when the TUC voted to call a twenty-four hour general strike of protest. The government unearthed the Official Solicitor and the National Industrial Relations Court found itself able to release the dockers to the jubilant throng of workers outside the prison who cheered and sang as the dockers were carried shoulder high down the Caledonian Road.

While the dockers were in Pentonville, the print workers of Briant Colour Printing Ltd. were occupying the company factory in the Old Kent Road. On 21 June 1972 the 130 workers were given one minute's notice as the company went into voluntary liquidation. The firm was originally established in 1876 and many of the print workers had years of service with the company. Within an hour of the announcement, the workers voted to

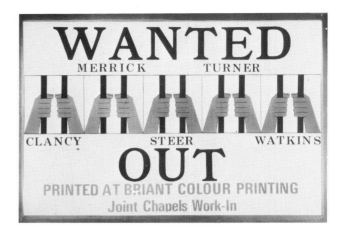

work-in to save their jobs, a decision inspired by the work-in of Upper Clyde Shipbuilders. The work-in brought support from Kent miners, London dockers and UCS workers. The poster produced by the Briant Colour work-in printers and signed by the five imprisoned dockers is a relic that not only marks the two disputes but demonstrates working class solidarity. The work-in involving the members of NATSOPA, SOGAT, NGA, SLADE and the AUEW lasted until 18 May 1973, when beneath the banner of the Briant workers a contract was signed for the purchase of the plant by a new owner, with a guarantee that all the employees would eventually be re-engaged. In the four struggles, of shipyard workers, miners, dockers and printers, there runs the link of solidarity that made for success.

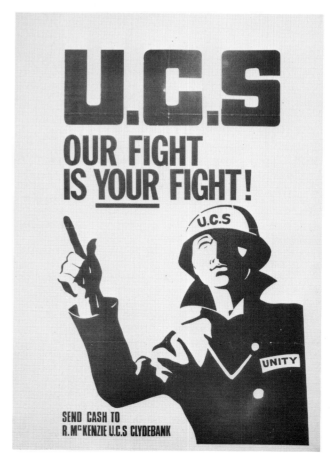

PRINTED EPHEMERA

Preparations for the Social Democratic Federation's fund-raising Christmas bazaar began in the summer of 1900; the target – to raise £1,000, ostensibly to finance the party at the local elections and provide for the expected general election, but also to clear the debt incurred by Central Office. In an appeal for gifts for the bazaar, the secretary of the bazaar committee, Herbert Arthur, reminded readers of *Justice*, 'Life's real heroes and heroines are those who bear their own burdens bravely and give a helping hand to raise the THOUSAND.'

By September the SDF announced the issue of one shilling credit notes, 'excellent examples of lithographic printing', that could be purchased in advance and exchanged for goods on the day of the bazaar, though members were cautioned not to part with them before receiving their money. By the beginning of December an amazing variety of gifts from the branches began to roll into Central Office: five fretwork frames, one violin, bow and case, three pincushions, a smoking cap, two petticoats and from *Clarion* readers a parcel of three framed pictures, two *royal* photographs and various small articles, 'everything of a breakable nature arriving broken due to bad packing'. Madame Alicia Gilson agreed to sing the opening stanzas of 'Internationale' at the opening ceremony of each day of the bazaar and the ubiquitous Walter Crane agreed to design the poster advertising the bazaar.

The tickets were considered an important factor in the success of the venture and were printed in green with an illustration of the Bastille to link revolution with the theme of 'Old Paris'. The committee explained that it had been extremely difficult to obtain an illustration of the Bastille as it had been destroyed and decided to stamp tickets upon entry to the bazaar so that they could be retained as souvenirs.

Although the SDF advertised the bazaar as a national event, it was obvious that few comrades from outside the capital would make the Christmas journey to Charing Cross Road. Those who did were advised to ask for Trafalgar Square, the well-known landmark closest to St Martin's Town Hall. Provincial branches were urged to buy the threepenny handbook, 'a really admirable specimen of artistic printing', containing portraits of SDF candidates for the London School Board elections and an illustration and description of the Bastille. Sheet music of the 'Internationale' was also printed especially for the bazaar, at 3*d.* per copy, full music size, and comrades were recommended to buy it for their Christmas parties.

Still the goods came: two pen wipers, an umbrella stand, a magic lantern, two antimacassars and a bound volume of Hyndman's *India*. Thousands of items were donated and Christmas Eve saw a frenzy of socialist activity as St Martin's Town Hall was recreated inside to a 'realistic representation of the streets of Paris in the seventeenth century, with the Bastille

at one end and the towers of Notre Dame at the other'. The ambitious set surrounded the stalls piled high with the goods for sale, while the centre aisle was decorated with ferns and fruit. Under the gallery at the far end visitors could purchase 'a cheering cup of tea dispensed by fair women's hands'. For those who wanted something stronger, the lower hall was set aside and they could also 'indulge in the fragrant weed'.

On Boxing Day morning the bazaar was opened by James McDonald, secretary of the London Trades Council, who gave a short history of the SDF and was followed by Hyndman, who thought the Christmas festival an appropriate opportunity to point out that the churches were allied with 'all that was infamous and vile'. The following day the opening ceremony was performed by Harry Quelch and W.M. Thompson, the editor of *Reynolds' Newspaper*. Alicia Gilson added the 'Wearing of the Green' to her rendition of the 'Internationale', the band played, people danced and the old Paris Bazaar was a great success, the top-selling line being the mounted photographs of SDF leaders, Hyndman, Bax, Quelch, Pearson and Barwick.

Perhaps because socialists have an aversion to balance sheets, it took until August before the accounts were finalised and the result published in *Justice*. Every penny of expenditure was accounted for, from the 10*s*. 6*d.* for the hire of curtains from Arding and Hobbs to the £1 tip to the hall-keeper. The net profit was £582. 19*s*. 1*d.*, not all that was hoped for, but a solid sum for the war chest.

The designer of the sixpenny admission card remains anonymous and no copy of Walter Crane's poster seems to have survived.

As for the choice of the Bastille for the illustration on the card, W.M. Thompson said, 'The frowning towers of the Bastille were typical of the towers of capitalism, privilege and tyranny and the forces of democracy must unite to overthrow them.' Nobody could doubt the sincerity of those who gave up their precious Christmas holiday in order to raise the money to help their attempt at the overthrow.

It was fitting that the Federated Postmen of Sheffield should have used the postal service to send season's greetings for 1893 to their brothers in other parts of the country and to reiterate their hopes for the success of the national petition. Founded in

1891 on the initiative of postmen from the East Central District Office of the London Post Office, the Federation soon spread to the main offices throughout the United Kingdom and in 1893 had a membership of over 6,000. The union's journal, *The Postman's Gazette*, reporting the first annual conference of the Federation, praised the splendid work of a Mr Bamford in building the Sheffield branch and it is likely that he was responsible for the issue of the Sheffield card.

The national petition was a series of demands on wages, hours, holidays and promotion procedures presented to the Postmaster General on 16 January 1893. The demands were drafted in difficult circumstances, for authorities were hostile to trade unionism in the postal service and victimisation in a tightly organised and disciplined service was easy to inflict and not infrequent. One member who ran a branch of the Federation in in the early years of the union was 'shadowed, persecuted and refused extra duty' and in another branch, the secretary felt 'compelled to withdraw from the secretaryship, owing to the tyrannical manner in which I have been treated'. That the petition was warranted is apparent from the debate that preceded the formulation of the demands. A delegate from Dundee moved that 'the day's work be done within twelve hours of starting', and from Leeds came a motion that condemned the 'system of appointing junior postmen at fourteen shillings a week'.

Attacks were made on the system of promotion by patronage and the demand was made for 'promotion by merit, not favour'. A delegate reported that in this office, not more than two percent of the postmen's staff received promotion as sorting clerks, the appointments being given to the sons of controlling officers. An M.C. Read of the North West District Office moved 'that boy labour being necessary in the department, the messenger service should be the channel for the promotion to appointments instead of a means of recruiting to the army.' Mr Parkes of Dublin, speaking in the course of the discussion of the training of telegraph messengers for the army and the rumour that postmen were to be drilled, said the postmen would have no objection if higher officials were put through the same training.

The final demands of the petition were modest enough, a minimum wage of 20s., with an annual increase of 2s. to a maximum wage of £2, eight hours of work per duty, promotion by merit, payment for Christmas Day and Good Friday and Sunday rate and a total of three weeks' holiday per annum. 20,000 postmen signed the petition, the non-unionists outnumbering the unionists by two to one, who, being ever ready to accept the benefits won for them by trade unionists, were furious when the petition was summarily rejected by the Postmaster General, who said the men 'ought to be satisfied'.

A fighting editorial in the *Postman's Gazette* following the rejection, under the heading 'The thin red line', concluded, 'Comrades, near and far, we appeal to you as men to stand firm! Education and self-discipline follow in the train of organisation, and to organise we must now give our bent. Right is Might, and if we can strengthen our Society to the tune of 20,000, we shall have accomplished a task that will make victory easy of attainment. The "thin red line" have done yeoman service, but you can do more. Hesitate no longer, but throw in your lot for the common good of all, and help to make our Society unique in the history of Trade Unionism.'

Two sisters, Muriel and Susanna Jackson, jointly designed and produced the banner of the Women's Co-operative Guild, unveiled at the Jubilee Congress of the Guild in June 1933. Muriel Jackson was trained as a mural painter and used to working on a large scale, enjoying some success, with her work being exhibited in London, Paris and New York. Her sister Susanna was an embroideress and dressmaker, a talented needlecraft woman holding a diploma in tailor's cutting. Together they made an ideal pair for the creation and making of a new banner for the Guild which traced its history from 1883.

Fortunately and unusually, the full explanation of the design survives.

The figure of Co-operation is seen as a Guildswoman whose emblem is a basket full of Co-operative purchases. There she stands in her simple dress of beautiful colours, carrying her CWS groceries, her *Co-operative News* and a basket of daffodils to brighten her home. Her other arm is around her lively little girl holding a shopping bag, happy and proud to have bought at the store and no doubt thinking of the Luton chocolates she will soon be eating and the

THE NATIONAL BANNER OF
THE WOMEN'S CO-OPERATIVE GUILD.

new pair of CWS shoes she will be wearing tomorrow as she goes to school. Behind the two figures, in the background, is the local Co-operative store with people looking in and admiring the fine display of CWS goods, the red flags flying to show that Co-operation stands for peaceful revolution to establish a more just and humane society. On the left is a man carrying a sack, symbolic of the industry set going by the buyers at the store. Above, across storm clouds, with the light breaking through between them, is a rainbow, the most ancient symbol of hope, recalling the Guild motto, 'Of whole heart cometh hope'. A rainbow is now the symbol of International Co-operation, in which women are vigorously playing their part.

The sisters took great care to select materials that would not fade and that were not too heavy to carry. By using the technique of appliqué, the sisters carefully built up the image by sewing the various coloured materials upon a corn-coloured linen. The problem of how to make the basket was overcome by the use of bias binding interwoven by pieces of brown wool used for rug making. The child's frock was made from the actual material of a CWS dress and the bright gold wedding ring and Women's Co-operative Guild gold brooch were made from a very thin rubbery material, well soaked and manipulated to shape.

Unfurling the banner at the Jubilee Congress, Margaret Llewellyn Davies, who had been Secretary of the Guild from 1889 to 1921, called for 'the control of industry by the people to carry out a peaceful and constructive revolution'. She said of the figure of the Guildswoman depicted on the banner, 'She realises that she is one of a vast host who are helping to uproot the causes of poverty and enmity and creating a civilisation which will lead to a great ennoblement of life. For it is indeed true, as this banner proclaims, that Co-operative buying builds a better world.'

The banner was such a success that the design was reproduced as a coloured postcard, printed by the CWS at Reddish and selling for 2½d. each or 2s. 3d. per dozen.

During the 1860s great advances were made by co-operative societies in the North East of England, the Newcastle-on-Tyne and Sunderland Societies both being formed in 1859 and local societies spreading throughout the shipbuilding, engineering and mining areas during the next decade. Newcastle-on-Tyne was to become one of the main areas of co-operative activity as well as other radical movements during those years, their base being the effective trade union organisation established by the miners of the Durham coalfields.

In 1862 a conference of co-operative societies in Newcastle, chaired by the well-known radical, Joseph Cowen, decided to form a Northern Union of Co-operative Stores for the purposes of wholesale trade. The following year there was a proposal for the foundation of a Newcastle Central Store but the idea foundered for lack of capital. Eventually, the Co-operative Wholesale Society agreed to open a store for the Northern Co-operators and the Newcastle-on-Tyne store was opened at West Blandford Street in 1917 and the bookmark was given to customers to publicise this new venture in co-operation. The importance of the role of women in the co-operative movement is shown by the choice of a woman reader for the illustration in the design at a time when working class women were expected to spend their time in the home, cooking, cleaning and looking after the children.

May Day 1895 started in the early afternoon with a march to Hyde Park and ended at three in the morning with champagne cup and the comrades dancing 'La Carmagnole'. The marchers assembled on the Thames embankment, 4,000 strong, with fifty banners, and made their way to the park, via London's club land, 'ignoring the contemptuous sneers and aristocratic sniffs, the smell of which was at times overpowering'. The array of speakers included Tom Mann, William Morris, H.M. Hyndman, Will Thorne, Eleanor Marx and Pete Curran, who held their audience until a sudden thunderstorm brought the demonstration to an early conclusion.

The revelry at the Holborn Hall, given by the Independent Labour Party, began with a light-hearted concert given by 'stars' of the ILP, followed by a magic lantern show projecting the work of Walter Crane and portraits of labour leaders. The dancing then began and, according to the *Labour Leader*, carried on 'amid a flow of unbroken harmony and merriment'. In a separate room, Frank Smith presented a series of living pictures depicting 'the triumph of Labour', in which Tom Mann appeared in evening dress representing a 'bloated capitalist' while Tom McCarthy played a more familiar role, that of a poor worker. The party occupied both the main hall and the smaller hall, as well as the board room and half a dozen committee rooms, and overflowed onto the stairs and corridors. Robert Blatchford booked half a dozen dances with 'the fair creatures' and although the free-flowing champagne cup was described as innocuous, there seems to have been a good deal of harmless horseplay.

The ticket for the First Socialist Carnival was designed by Walter Crane and printed in black on a thin card. The *Labour Leader* described the design as being in Crane's 'happiest vein' and the cards were later sold at 6d. each as mementoes of the occasion. The price represented an hour's pay for an unskilled worker and it is not recorded how many were sold, though, fortunately, at least one has survived to recall the celebration and provide a further example of the socialist art of Walter Crane.

When Marie Lloyd sent a telegram to the manager of the Tivoli saying, 'I am busy putting a new flounce on my dress so I cannot appear tonight,' it was not a fit of temperament, it was support for a strike. As early as 1885 Charlie Coburn of 'Two lovely black eyes' fame had formed the first performers' trade union, the Music Hall Artistes' Association, in order to combat the Music Halls' Managers' Association. The union failed, but in 1906 Coburn tried again, bringing together twenty-four members from the Grand Order of Water Rats, the International Artistes' Lodge and the Music Hall Artistes' Railway Association to form the Variety Artists' Federation. From the original two dozen, the union grew to 3,799 members when they joined with the National Association of Theatrical Employees and the Amalgamated Musicians' Union in coming out on strike on 22 January 1907.

The music halls were no longer the independent ale houses of Champagne Charlie's day but were commercial 'Palace of Variety' theatres, organised in a series of powerful circuits. It was the refusal of Walter Gibbons, a wealthy theatre owner, to sign a charter of minimum requirements drawn up by the three theatre unions that precipitated the strike. The first evening there were no performances at four London halls and a miserable attempt at the Holborn Empire to put on a performance with a pianist, one drummer and a singer.

The strike soon spread to the halls owned by Gibbons' father-in-law, Adney Payne, theatres closing from Oxford to Walthamstow. The stars appeared on the picket lines and an emergency relief appeal launched to which hundreds subscribed. Stars like Little Tich, Nellie Wallace and Lottie Collins supported the strike while managers deprived of their stars tried to put on shows with third-rate acts of hopeful strikebreakers. They were not a success. Eventually on 9 February the managers, through their London Entertainments' Protection Association, recognised the alliance and went to arbitration. The artistes negotiated with the help of the London Trades Council and, in particular, with the help of Ben Tillett. The printed resolution of the London Society of Compositors in support of the strike was typical of the many expressions of solidarity passed by trade unions. In a profession of highly individual talents, the lesson of co-operation had been learned: unity had achieved fairer and better conditions for all.

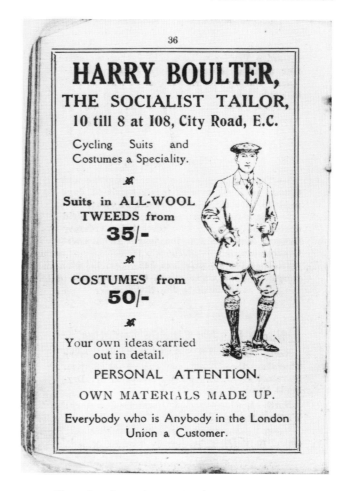

MUSIC HALL WAR. Jan-Feb 1907

COPY of RESOLUTION.

" That this Delegate Meeting of the London Society of Compositors, representing 11,000 members, expresses its sympathy with the Music Hall Employees' Alliance in their endeavour to secure more equitable conditions of employment, and the members pledge themselves not to patronise any place of entertainment which is in dispute with the Alliance."— Carried unanimously.

Similar resolutions have been passed by Trade Union organisations and at public meetings. The Alliance thank their hundreds of thousands of friends who are loyally supporting them, and ask for a continuation of such support, when victory is certain.

Printed by the Co-operative Printing Society Limited, Tudor Street, London, E.C., and Published by J. B. Williams, 9, Great Newport Street, W.C.

Self-employed socialists and small business owners with Labour sympathies had little compunction in trading on their political allegiance in the early days of the socialist movement. Harry Boulter, advertising in the *Clarion* handbook of 1913, proclaimed himself a socialist tailor, trading at 108 City Road from ten in the morning till eight at night. In 1896 the New Age clothing company of Leicester advertised regularly in *Justice*, offering high class tailoring made in a factory without 'sweating' on a forty-eight hour week. An order to New Age would bring a free copy of a book by the 'Bounder', E.F. Fay, a founder of the *Clarion*, and an assurance that your purchase had contributed 'one step towards social salvation'.

Lewis Lyons of Cephas Street in East London offered 'Red Flag' cigarettes, 'handmade by socialists for socialists' at 10 for 2½d. or 100 for 2s. Non-smokers could write to Leeds for penny tablets of 'Red Flag' butterscotch or spend their holidays at Blackpool, sipping tea in the Clarion café.

From the first issue of the *Clarion* on 12 December 1891, a new impetus was given to spreading the message of socialism. Founded by Robert Blatchford and three colleagues from the *Sunday Chronicle*, the first issue sold almost 40,000 and by 1908 had a circulation of over 80,000, making it the largest and most influential socialist newspaper in Britain. Blatchford had the unusual gift of being able to write about socialism in a way that was readily understood by working people and combined his skill with a flair for organisation. The *Clarion* became more than a paper, it became a movement, a fellowship of campaigning socialists who knew the new dawn would break tomorrow.

In 1894 the first Clarion Cycling Club was formed in Birmingham and the idea freewheeled at an astonishing speed. Branches sprung up all over the country but especially in the industrial north where thousands of young people from the mills, mines and factories joined in the adventure to become two-wheeled gospellers for socialism. At weekends they

An appeal for funds and donations in kind for equipping the van met with ready contributions. A comrade offered to send a brand-new harness as soon as the size of the horse was known and in the meantime sent a nosebag, whip, waterproof apron, halter and metal polish. The London Jewish Clarionettes sent 10*s*. 6*d*., a 'Gateshead Soirée' raised 15*s*. 0*d*. and someone who described themselves as sorrow-stricken and destitute sent 1*s*. 0*d*.

Work on the van continued and Julia Dawson was able to report, '. . . the heart of a woman could not wish for a prettier room than the interior of that van. The walls are painted a delicate cream, the ceiling striped with cream and red, the windows are draped with pretty spotted muslin and the comfortable beds form nice wide cushioned seats by day.' The van had its own grate but Dawson reported that they were now the owners of a first class oil cooking stove and looked forward to cooking outside, 'gipsy fashion'. The search for the hire or loan of a suitable horse was not so easy, for the creature had to be stoutly built, of some fifteen or sixteen hands and capable of pulling one and a half tons up a hill. After months of appeals, a horse was offered and after much discussion named by the volunteers as 'Environment'. Julia Dawson wrote, 'Our gee gee is a real beauty, as gentle as a lamb and as strong as a Clarion Women's van horse ought to be.' By May 1896 the contents assembled included cutlery, two dish cloths, two bath towels, seven cups and saucers, one teapot, three tea cloths, six towels, one bundle of *Merrie England* and one packet of *Clarion* leaflets. *Merrie England* was the book by Robert Blatchford compiled from a series of articles he had written for the *Clarion* in the form of letters to an imaginary working man, presenting the case for socialism in plain language. The book was an unparalleled success for a socialist publication, 750,000 copies of the penny edition sold at the first rush. Translated into Welsh, Dutch, German, Swedish, French, Spanish, Hebrew, Danish and

pedalled to the fresh air and beauty of the countryside to hold meetings in the market squares of quiet villages and make Clarion converts. Clarion Clubs, Clarion Scouts, Clarion Cafés, the Clarion Fellowship and Clarion vans, all were inspired by Blatchford's *Clarion* and his persuasive writing.

The Clarion horse-drawn vans brought a new dimension to socialist propaganda in the days before radio and television carried the wider world to the remote rural areas. The vans, mobile homes, enabled supporters to travel for weeks on end carrying the message of socialism to farmworkers and others in the little towns and villages of Britain. Based upon 'The Wanderer', the first purpose-built caravan designed by Dr W. Gordon-Stables in 1885, the vans were homely and equipped with every necessity for an independent life.

The first Clarion van to take to the road in 1896 was not purpose-built but a conversion and it was women volunteers that pioneered the trail. Week by week, the progress in preparing the van was excitedly reported by Julia Dawson in the 'women's letter' column of the *Clarion*. Looking forward to the first journey, she speculated that 'chats by cottage doors and the happy little gatherings on the greens will do more real good than any boisterous meetings,' and she continued, '. . . our van occupants will work steadily and quietly gaining the ears and hearts of the people and will leave behind them some telling pamphlets written in plain simple language which every farm labourer who knows his A.B.C. can understand.' A democratic request to readers for suggested routes brought a large response from those anxious to bring the van and socialism to their own locality. 'The people are so dreadfully respectable in Harrogate, I wish the van would come here and open their eyes.' 'In the village of mid-Sussex the people are intensely ignorant of everything but conservatism. It would be a seed sown in absolutely virgin soil so far as socialism is concerned.'

THE RIGHT TO WORK (the Cry of the Unemployed).

No parish money or loaf,
    No pauper badges for me ;
I'm a son of the soil, with the right to toil,
    Entitled to my fee,
No alms I ask, give me my task,
    Here are the arm—the leg ;"
The strength and sinews of a man,
    To work, and no. to beg.
My honest claim is this,
    To work, and up with the lark ;"
By lawful turn, my living to earn
    Between the light and dark ;
My daily bread, my nightly bed,
    My "baccy" and drop o'beer ;
But all from the hand that holds the land,
    And *none from the Overseer*.—(after) *Tom Hood*.

Norwegian, it sold over 2,000,000 copies and probably made more converts to British socialism than any other political publication.

By June, the van was ready to be brought from Liverpool to Chester by 'Dangle' (A.M. Thompson) of the *Clarion* and Joseph O'Donnell of Liverpool, though not without difficulty. Dangle wrote, '. . . shall never forget the day when the socialist horse stuck on the Cardin Hill and we realised to our dismay that the poor old windless beast was punctured.' Nevertheless, despite the offer of a replacement, the comrades remained loyal to 'Environment' and on 14 June 1896 all was set for the 'land yacht' to set out on its historic journey. Stocked with butter, leaflets, cobs of coal, tins of salmon, harness polish and jam, everything needed for a life of nomadic socialism, the van departed, followed by fifty Clarion cyclists.

The Clarion postcard, illustrated by Cosmo Rowe, was posted on 29 January 1913, by which time Clarion vans were established as a regular part of socialist activity. No longer conversions but built and beautifully decorated by socialists they were named after pioneers, the first being the Caroline Martyn Memorial van. The William Morris van had carved panels designed by Walter Crane and a metal fascia depicting the rising sun of socialism. The vans toured industrial as well as rural areas but life was far from the idyll imagined by Julia Dawson, the reception in some areas being far from friendly. 'Evening meetings disturbed by drunk men', wrote Bruce Glasier in his diary. Stones and muck were thrown, horses refused to climb hills, harnesses rubbed and literature ran out. Despite the hardship, there developed a deep comradeship among vanners and they played a vital role in taking socialism to the people. It is possible that in a barn, somewhere, a Clarion van survives awaiting its place in history.

Drawn by R. Ruttley and printed by the Twentieth Century Press, this postcard was issued during the unemployed struggles of 1906 by the Workers' Committee for the Unemployed. The London Trades Council had established a Central Workers' Committee to carry on agitation on behalf of the unemployed in 1906 and formed twenty local committees. Although the Twentieth Century Press, formed in 1892 for the printing of *Justice*, was the property of the Social Democratic Federation, thousands of pamphlets, booklets and tracts were printed by them for the wider labour movement and it is probable that the card was produced for the London Trades Council during their Right to Work campaign of that time.

The Daily Herald League was launched at a mass meeting at the Memorial Hall, London, on 22 November 1912. The idea was to create 400 or 500 centres throughout Britain, each with at least 150 members who would contribute 3*d*. a week, thus raising £50,000 a year to keep the young independent newspaper in business. If the need for cash was the primary force behind the concept of a nationwide band of supporters, the need to stimulate the spirit of revolt against capitalism was second only by necessity. During a period of intense industrial action the *Daily Herald* voiced that spirit of rebellion in its daily columns of campaigning socialism, with support for strikes and the exposure of government intrigue.

The meeting for the 'christening' of the League was supported by an array of militant orators, George Lansbury opening and immediately followed by Victor Grayson, the first socialist MP, and Tom Mann the pioneer trade unionist and labour leader. Lansbury said what they wanted to do was to 'make the poor hate their poverty' and Grayson joined in the attack, supporting the *Daily Herald*'s exposure of poverty, slums, prostitution and exploitation. He urged the audience, 'Let them go out to work with the *Daily Herald* for a day when no child should be born into the world without the right to live, when no man who was willing to work should go without work and when no woman should pollute her body for bread.' 'Messages from absent friends' were read from a broad spectrum of supporters, including G.K. Chesterton, Conrad Noel, Will Thorne, the

Countess of Warwick, Mrs Despard, Fred Jowett and Josiah Wedgwood. Walter Crane sent more than a message, he sent a design for a button badge for the League. Charles Lapworth, the editor of the *Daily Herald*, said with more prophecy than he knew, 'The *Daily Herald* is out to give expression to all forms of revolt. It is a rank and file paper and if it changes in any respect it ought to die.'

The opportunity for the Herald League to give practical support to revolt came in August 1913 with the great Dublin lock-out of trade unionists that became one of the bloodiest and most ferocious disputes in the history of British trades unionism. The working people of Dublin lived in tenements and poverty. A report the previous year by Sir Charles Cameron revealed that 9,000 families lived six in a room, 6,000 lived seven in a room and the death rate was ten percent higher than in London, including the East End. Of every 1,000 that died, 250 died in the workhouse. Men were working seventy hours for 12*s*. to 17*s*. a week; wages that spelt starvation. Against the destitution, poverty and vicious exploitation stood the trade unions and in the forefront of the struggle was the Irish Transport and General Workers' Union. Determined to smash the Transport Union and all it stood for was the Dublin Employers' Federation, to whom trades unionism was anathema. The employers' attack on the union was precipitated by William Martin Murphy who discovered that men and boys in the dispatch department of his newspapers and in the parcels office of the tramway company were members of the Irish Transport and General Workers' Union. His ultimatum was swift and direct: leave the union or be sacked. The union replied by blacking his newspapers. Following a big and enthusiastic union meeting, James Larkin, P.T. Daly, Thomas Lawlor, William O'Brien and W.P. Partridge were charged with seditious libel and seditious conspiracy and a proclamation was issued by the Dublin police prohibiting as unlawful and seditious any assembly that 'would cause terror and alarm to, and dissension between, His Majesty's subjects.' The proclamation was burned in the streets and the simmering class hatred between workers and employers erupted to molten fury. The employers were assured of the support of the Dublin Metropolitan Police, the Royal Irish Constabulary and if need be, the British army. Political demonstrations were ruthlessly smashed, running battles fought, heads broken and hundreds arrested. One union member, James Nolan, on his way to Liberty Hall, the HQ of the Transport Union, was so savagely beaten by police that he died of his wounds. Sean O'Casey, who was also a member of the union, saw the corpse laid out in its coffin and wrote, 'There he was asprawl under a snowy sheet, looking like a mask on a totem pole, one eye gone, the other askew, the nose cracked at the bridge and bent sideways, the forehead and cheek royal purple, from a distance it looked like a fading iris on a wide patch of snow. The mighty baton!' The funeral was a great demonstration of solidarity and suppressed rage; Keir Hardie came and marched in the funeral procession. O'Casey watched from the pavement in O'Connell Street and penned a moving description, 'Here it comes, the "Dead March in Saul", flooding

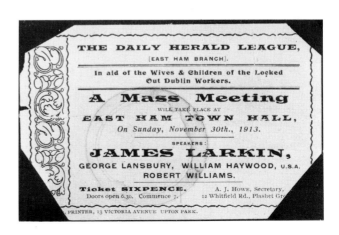

the street, and flowing into the windows of the street's richest buildings, followed by the bannered labour unions, the colours sobered by cordons of crepe, a host of sodden grey following a murdered comrade.'

On Sunday, 31 August thousands came from the slum tenements and dockside hovels to gather in O'Connell Street to hear James Larkin, who was released on bail, speak to them. Disguised as an elderly clergyman Larkin appeared on a balcony of the Imperial Hotel, cast off his disguise and began to speak. While some constables rushed into the hotel to arrest Larkin, hundreds began to baton the crowd, mounted police charged, women screamed, blood flowed in the gutters and in minutes the scene was that of a battlefield and another 'bloody Sunday' was given to history. Hundreds were injured, hospitals filled and the employers from 400 firms agreed not to employ any persons that were members of the Transport and General Workers' Union. They produced a document for the workers to sign reminiscent of the hated 'document' that English employers had tried to foist upon building workers in 1830. The workers refused the humiliation and 20,000 were sacked from their jobs.

In England, the Daily Herald League embarked on a nationwide campaign of meetings of solidarity with the Dublin workers. At a great meeting at the Albert Hall, George Bernard Shaw described the Dublin police as 'mad dogs in uniform' and went on to say that if policemen were to continue on the footing of mad dogs, there could only be one end – all respectable men would have to arm themselves. The atmosphere in the Albert Hall was that of a revivalist crusade, the women stewards all wore red caps and the thousand League supporters cheered as Lansbury said, 'We are out for the fight.' James Larkin was unable to be present as he was under arrest but his sister Delia spoke with quiet passion of the struggle and related a story of a seventy-nine year old man, starving on a pension of 5s. a week, who had sent 6d. to 'help wipe out Murphyism'. James Connolly brilliantly and methodically exposed the philanthropy of Mr Jacobs who had closed his biscuit factory to help crush the unions: Connolly's own niece worked at the factory being paid 6s. for a fifty-six hour week. Beginners were paid 4s. and before the union came into the factory were only paid 2s. 6d. 'You cannot build a free nation on the basis of slavery,' he declared.

Other speakers included Sylvia Pankhurst, who had eluded the police to be present, George Russell, the Irish poet, Mrs Despard, Ben Tillett and Dora Mountefiore. Robert Williams brought the audience to their feet when he said, 'The militants could combine propaganda by deed with public utility by burning down Dublin.'

The Albert Hall rally was followed by Herald League meetings all over the country to win support and give aid to the workers of Dublin, calling on English workers to strike and succeeding in starting strikes in Liverpool, Manchester and Birmingham. The TUC collected and sent £150,000 to the Irish workers and the CWS in a magnificent demonstration of support sent food ships to the hungry families of Dublin.

The ticket for the Daily Herald League meeting in East Ham carries the name of William Haywood, USA, as one of the speakers. This was Big Bill Haywood, leader of the American syndicalist movement, the Industrial Workers of the World, who had arrived in Britain for a speaking tour 'to carry the fiery cross' in support of the Dublin workers. No newspaper had ever given so much practical support to a workers' struggle and the Herald League made an enormous contribution to arousing the labour movement to the plight of the people of Dublin.

What to do with men who simply refused to fight was a problem for the military that arose with the introduction of conscription into Britain in January 1916. More than 6,000 men were refused exemption and handed over to the military, who were totally unprepared for the challenge to military discipline that followed. Refusal to obey orders led to summary punishment and continued refusal led inevitably to court martial. Despite the wishes of some officers to shoot those who refused to fight, the only sanction allowed was imprisonment,

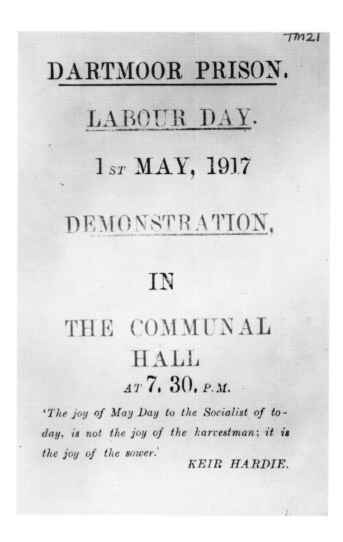

but conscientious objectors were no ordinary prisoners. Among the objectors were more than a thousand socialists, some of them pacifists but the majority political objectors who saw the conflict as a capitalist war in which only capitalists could benefit. The strongest group of political objectors came from the Independent Labour Party who opposed the war and saw conscription as 'the thin edge of the wedge of Czarism'. They were supported by a variety of socialist organisations, the most prominent of them being the British Socialist Party. Together with other radical groups and a number of anarchists they were a revolutionary and disruptive influence, a challenge to authority and a threat to discipline.

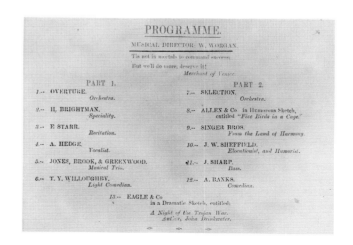

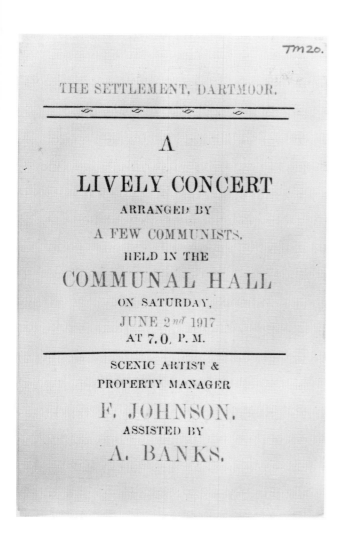

Eventually, responsibility had to be moved from the military to the Home Office under the operation of a scheme devised by William Brace, a Labour MP, and an under-secretary at the Home Office. A tribunal began interviewing men who had been court-martialled and a total of 4,522 were released for work under the Brace Committee scheme. More problems arose, as almost all work might be deemed to have a connection with the war effort and was refused on the slightest pretext.

By February 1917 the lack of suitable employment had become critical and a new work centre was urgently required; the offer came from the Prison Commissioners, Dartmoor. The Brace Committee renamed Dartmoor Prison the Princetown Work Centre and by the autumn of 1917 a total of 1,200 objectors were at work on quarrying and reclaiming land for the Duchy of Cornwall. King George V thought the scheme an 'excellent one both as regards the conscientious objectors and the reclamation work at Dartmoor'.

While the slaughter on the Western front continued, a hostile press, led by the *Daily Mail*, whipped up public opinion against the safe and comparatively free life being led by the conchies and reds. A public meeting was held in Princetown against the 'coddled conscience men', a Devonshire VC being brought to the meeting to stir the jingoism and increase the hatred for the men who would not fight. The Bishop of Exeter, with a Christian charity commensurate with his Church's wholehearted support for the war, recommended that the political objectors should be placed in 'that portion of England that is frequently visited by the enemy aeroplane'. The resolute socialist opponents of the war were unmoved by the exhortations of conservative newspapers and clergymen for their blood and organised their own political and social life within the bounds of the prison settlement. They sang the 'Red Flag', walked out of church when the national anthem was played and produced their own political leaflets. The ILP formed a Dartmoor branch of the party, regarding their sentences as certificates of honour. The printed programmes for the Dartmoor Prison May Day demonstration of 1917 and the 'Lively Concert' arranged by a few communists on 2 June give some indication of the degree of freedom allowed to the inmates of the Centre. The May Day celebration included the singing of 'Onward, Friends of Freedom', 'Sons of Labour', the 'Red Flag' and 'A Song of War', a parody by H. Brightman. A resolution was moved, though its content has not been traced, proposed by C.H. Norman and seconded by W. Watson. The concert seems to have had little direct political comment and consisted of an orchestra, humorous sketches, solo singers and a comedian.

In July there was an attempt to satisfy hostile public opinion by tightening the discipline and appointing Captain Stevenson, the Deputy Governor of Wormwood Scrubs, as the full-time inspector of the Brace Committee's camps and work centres. The result of the enforcement of a list of rules and regulations was that the percentage of men refusing work rose! In February 1918 one of the men died of diabetes and a claim was made that the doctor had been negligent and the prisoners struck work on the day of the funeral. Two of the leaders were sent to prison, further citations for bravery in the face of the enemy.

There is no doubt that many people regarded the socialist conscientious objectors as worthless agitators, traitors and cowards. To others they kept above the concept of the brotherhood of man while a generation of young men were sacrificed on the instructions of two capitalist governments.

Two little collection tickets are evidence of working class solidarity and mementoes of two strikes, the first won, the second lost. It was on 1 January 1913 that 5,000 London taxi drivers, members of the London Cabdrivers' Trade Union, came out on strike against an increase in the charge for petrol from 8*d*. to 1*s*. 1*d*. per gallon, imposed by the cab combines. The decision to strike was taken by ballot and was virtually unanimous, 4,695 voting for the strike and only 177 against. Apart from a handful of blacklegs, the strike was solid and the smaller cab companies soon gave in, reducing the price of their petrol to 8*d*. a gallon. Their cabs went back on the road again, the drivers displaying trade union permits tucked in their caps and contributing 2*s*. a day to the strike fund. The Cabdrivers' Union was well funded and made a weekly strike payment of 7*s*. 6*d*., though not all the drivers drew the pay, about 1,000 declining in order to strengthen the union's fight.

If 7*s*. 6*d*. was scarcely enough to exist on, the plight of some 6,000 auxiliary workers was worse. These were the lamp-men, greasers and washers, poorly paid and unorganised, who found themselves locked-out and penniless in the middle of a bitter English winter. The unions did what they could to help, the Cabdrivers' Union making a gift of food parcels and issuing the 2*d*. collection tickets in aid of the washers. The Church Army gave a hundredweight of coal to each man and provided a small amount of winter relief work at the Church Army shelter. The desperate hardship of the washers was vividly described in a letter to the *Daily Herald*: 'I am a taxi washer's wife, I have six little children to keep and I am expecting to be turned out through not being able to pay the rent. All I have coming in is four shillings a week which my husband receives from the Church Army for working two days a week.'

While the taxi drivers continued their strike and the washers struggled to avoid destitution, the rich cab combines fought back. Offers of a bribe of £5 to each driver returning to work failed and tougher action was taken. Captain Lynch of the British Motor Cab Company led the way by selective sacking of men he claimed were the worst drivers and he was quickly supported by the large cab company, Ward G. du Cros, demanding that the men sacked must return their uniforms and collect their licences. This attempt to divide the strikers failed as all the cabbies returned their uniforms in a show of solidarity. Led by the banners of the Marylebone and Paddington branches of the Cabdrivers' Union, they marched at a signal from a bugle, their uniforms on their shoulders, to the singing of 'We All Go the Same Way Home' and cries of 'Old clo'es, old clo'es' to the company offices.

Support for the strikers came from unions of many industries, including the miners. Dockers attacked a blackleg cab in the East End and Chelsea football club supporters gave generously to a collection taken at the gates of the ground. Faced with an unyielding strike gaining in popular support the cab companies gave in, reducing the cost of petrol back to 8*d*. a gallon, reinstating all the men and agreeing to the union's demand that the few blackleg cabbies should be sacked. The strike cost the union £40,000 in strike pay but the owners lost well over £300,000 in their attempt to push up their profits at the expense of the drivers.

The London Cabdrivers' Trade Union eventually joined the amalgamation of unions that formed the Transport and General Workers' Union but they did not lose their identity, neither did they forget their fellow trade unionists who had helped in their great struggle of 1913. When the miners remained locked out and alone to fight on for six hungry months after the General Strike of 1926, the cabbies remembered how the miners had donated to

their strike fund and organised a regular weekly collection for the Miners' Wives' and Children's Fund. The 6*d*. tickets were issued as receipts for the donations and the collection continued until the miners were finally driven back to work under the lash of hunger. The cabbies, like many trade unionists, were generous in their support of the miners but the donations and collections were as crumbs on the tables of 800,000 men and their families.

Neville Chamberlain wrote of the miners in his diary on 20 June 1926, 'they are not within sight of starvation', but he had never served at a soup kitchen in the coalfields of South Wales, Yorkshire or Durham, never lived on cocoa, bread and marge, never gone hungry so that his children might eat. With winter approaching, the miners were forced back to work for longer hours at lower pay, made to accept the deliberately divisive policy of district agreements and subjected to ruthless victimisation.

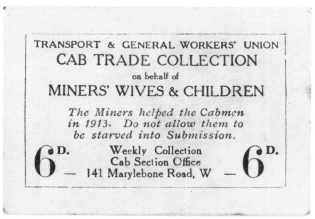

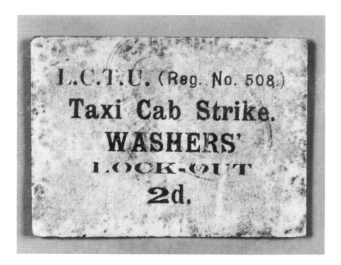

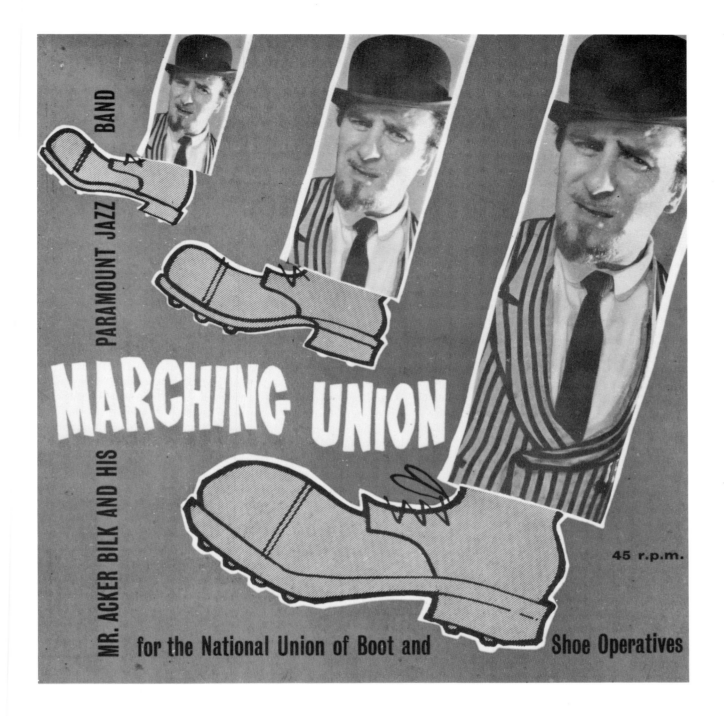

'Marching Union' was a pop record produced in 1961 by the National Union of Boot and Shoe Operatives in a drive to recruit young workers into the union. It was also an adventurous attempt to present the union to young people in a way that would find readier accceptance than the conventional trade union methods of leaflets, speeches and demonstrations. To the tune of 'Marching through Georgia', popular jazz musician Acker Bilk and his Paramount Jazz Band thumped out a recruiting message to a post-war generation that had never seen a hunger march or known unemployment. The union moved into the 'swinging sixties' in a serious and calculated effort to communicate with young workers who had not inherited the same working class commitment to trades unionism as their parents, yet were the future of the union.

The opening verse of the 45 rpm record gave the briefest history of the union ever written:

Back in 1873, twenty-five young men,
organised and organised
and organised again,
Now we're 80,000 strong
a power in the land,
Marching along with the union

Bilk handled the strange words with an easy professionalism,
Leather soles or rubber,
boots and shoes and things,
Make 'em for shop stewards,
presidents and kings
But when it comes to wages
and holidays with pay
We're marching along with the union

and the record received wide coverage from the national press, unaccustomed to receiving gramophone records from trade unions.

Working for London and Peace

Not all NUBSO members were so ready to praise the innovation and at the union's national conference held in Llandudno that year, there was strong criticism of the executive, exemplified by R. Simpson, a shop steward from Nottingham, who said, 'I don't see why we should waste our money on pop records', and was supported by other delegates. Richard Gregson, the union's General Secretary, countered, 'Acker Bilk is better known to young people than the Prime Minister', and defended the decision to make the record, saying, 'Trade unions have for too long neglected public relations, you can't interest youngsters in union affairs by the methods of thirty years ago.' The executive won the argument as the union President moved that 'The Executive Council and General Secretary are to be congratulated on the brochure and the Acker Bilk record.'

The idea and production of the record was the work of Mountain and Molehill, a small advertising agency formed in the late 1950s by Ken Sprague and Ray Bernard to provide a publicity service for the labour movement. The record sleeve was designed by Ken Sprague and the words were written by Solly Kaye, an advertising copy writer and a Stepney Borough communist councillor. 5,000 records were made and distributed free of charge, every probation member of the union under twenty receiving a copy. Despite the apparent success of the venture, the exercise was never repeated and apart from another record made by Mountain and Molehill for the National Union of Tailors and Garment Workers, featuring folk singers Ewan McColl and Peggy Seeger, no other trade union appears to have tried recruitment by record.

1983 was designated as 'Peace Year' by the Labour-controlled Greater London Council and was celebrated by a year of peace-orientated cultural events sponsored by the GLC. To symbolise 'Peace Year', the Council commissioned Peter Kennard, a young socialist artist well known for his work in the medium of photomontage, to design a logo, symbolic of peace, to be used on a varied range of publicity material. The result was the powerful 'breaking of a missile' image, rapidly to become the recognised symbol of opposition to the siting of Cruise missiles in Britain.

Kennard, himself a Londoner, was born in 1949 and at the age of sixteen won a scholarship to the Slade School of Fine Art where he trained as a painter. His involvement in politics began with the student movement in 1968 and Kennard was impelled to reconsider his position as an artist in relation to society. Painting as a means of communication seemed too narrow to him, the production of 'one valuable object for a limited audience'. He turned to making dyeline prints of his work and was soon flyposting giant images, up to twenty feet in length, on empty walls and hoardings of the city, to be viewed by thousands of people.

After finishing his course at Slade, he joined the Workers' Press where he was given freedom of expression in his work as an artist, leaving only when his political views diverged. Kennard freelanced, worked three years as a night-shift telephone operator for the Post Office, and then in 1976 went to the Royal College of Art for a three-year postgraduate course. By 1980 he was active as an artist in the peace movement and using the twentieth century medium of photomontage to give visual expression to his opposition to the nuclear arms race. It was a medium he mastered with technical skill and merged with his artistic talent, it helped to give a new voice to the resurgent peace movement.

Kennard sees his work as a 'resource, an imagebank for the anti-nuclear movement', and has described his work as the 'visual language of opposition'. Through touring exhibitions, video films, television and a massive GLC poster campaign, his images have become familiar to millions, creating a chilling awareness of the doomsday threat and challenging the theory of peace through strength.

His symbol for 'Peace Year' began as a montage of a single hand breaking a missile and was designed for the Labour Party. The graphic logo for the GLC was developed from this image, photographer Ed Barber taking a picture of two hands snapping a tube to provide the basis for the drawing. If it has a resemblance to the older symbol of the War Resisters' International, where the hands broke a rifle, it loses none of its power because of that: it is a symbol of our time.

184

SASHES

In borrowing from the iconography of the craft guilds, the symbolism of freemasonry and the Victorian imagery of the friendly societies, the trade unions also adopted some of the regalia used to give visual identity to office and authority. Initially, during the years of illegality when some unions administered oaths to protect the organisation and identity of their members from police and employers, they sought to embellish their ceremonies with regalia of the kind used by the masonic lodges, Buffaloes, Oddfellows, Druids and other orders. The old Society of Preston Joiners when it came under the influence of the Builders' Union in 1833 provided Kendal Lodge with a subsidy for 'regalah' for the purposes of initiation. In November of that year, the cashbook shows expenditure for union ritual:

By new top hat for Tyler	£1.	4. 6d.
By coct hat for "	£	10. 6d.
By mufstaches for "	£	1. 0d.

The accessories were used to make the ceremony more imposing to the new and apprehensive members, to impress and beguile. The purchase of 'mufstaches' is puzzling and seemingly unnecessary, but the George Tutill catalogue for 1896, under the heading of regalia for the United Ancient Order of Druids, advertises long beards from 5s. 6d. and wigs from 10s. 6d. for a similar ritual. Tutill also supplied 'handsome brass crookheads' for the Loyal Order of Ancient Shepherds and gardeners' aprons for the British Order of Ancient Free Gardners. The Builders were merely aping the older, bourgeois orders in procedure, ceremony, regalia, initiation and oaths.

It is recorded that in 1834 the Nantwich Shoemakers, as part of the Grand National Consolidated Trades Union, were left with about £40 after paying their entrance fee to the National body. Not knowing what better to do with it, they paid Thomas Jones £25 to paint for them a banner emblematical of their craft and 'also purchased a full set of secret regalia, surplices, trimmed aprons etc., and a crown and robe for King Crispin'. When two delegates of the union were arrested by the police at Exeter, they were found to have in their possession 'two wooden axes, two large cutlasses, two masks and two white garments or robes, a large figure of death with dart and hourglass, a Bible and Testament'. In the same year, the Tolpuddle Martyrs were charged with administering an illegal oath and evidence was given against them that they had ordered a painting of a skeleton. To the judges, government ministers and the local squirearchy, their own foolish mummery and paraphernalia of aprons, squares and compasses was respectable enough, but for trade unionists it spelt a conspiratorial plot demanding transportation.

Had fancy taken the government, they might well have prosecuted the Society of Friendly Boilermakers, 'Worthy President, Vice, Officers and Brothers all', formed in the same year, whose opening ceremony and initiation ran to many printed pages and included the secret sign of the Society. 'President: Can you present your right-hand brother with the grip of a Friendly Boiler Maker? Answer: Yes, worthy President, the grip of a Friendly Boiler Maker is thus (here the grip is shown). President: Providing you were in a public house and you saw some person in the same room whom you knew to work at the business, how would you act, to prove whether he was a friendly brother or not? Answer: I would take up my glass and act thus (there the sign of the glass is shown).' Brotherhood was bound stronger by the ritual of mutuality and the promise of solidarity. Secrets and self-discipline gave strength to working people who sought to relieve sickness, unemployment and old age, curtail excessive hours of labour during life and obtain a decent burial upon death and who were regarded as criminals for their humanity.

Cotton spinners and miners, woolcombers and flannel weavers, all subscribed to the mystic rites, doggerel and regalia that were adopted, copied and imitated from the freemasons and friendly societies, with doors opening, tilers waiting, strange knocking and even stranger signs to be given. A closed

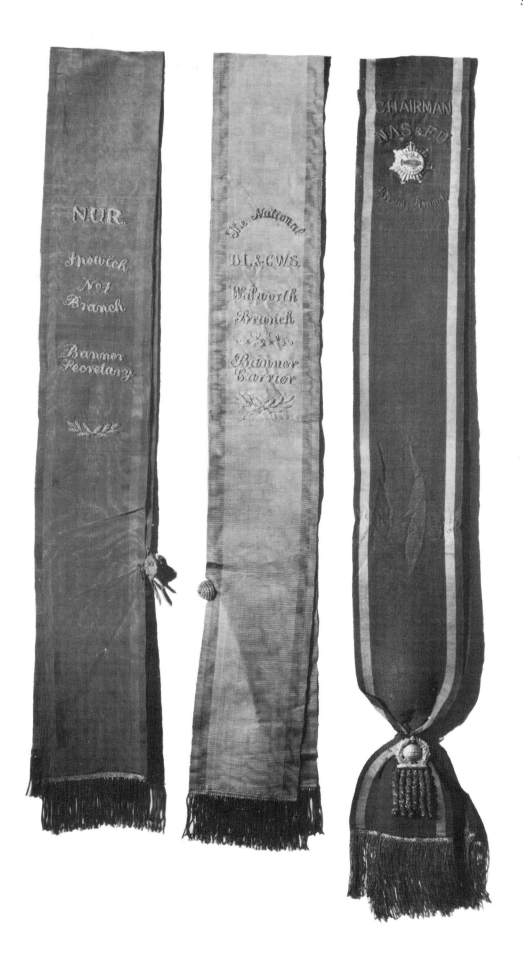

community of visual symbolism that gave assurance to the doubters and bound them in unity and brotherhood. Outwardly, the unions displayed increasing visual evidence of their growing strength as they paraded their imagery in protest and affirmation. 'Operative Dressers and Dyers, six abreast, Grand banner, Unity, Benevolence, Concord, Boiler Makers, six abreast, Success to trade', the banners streamed against the wind to greet Peter McDouall and John Collins, two Chartists, on their release from prison in 1840, silver, gold, green and blue, a dazzling proclamation, no rabble this but the army of labour, craftsmen, workers, men and women, each behind their banner, each behind the union. 1867 – the great Reform League demonstration, with bands, banners and regalia, 'the Plasterers and several Lodges of the Operative Masons wearing their aprons', the procession kept in order by members of the Farriers' Union, mounted on horseback, wearing top hats, scarves and cockades, most of the standard bearers adorned with scarves or cockades. The eight-hours movement demonstration in 1890 saw Tom Mann and George Shipton, Secretary of the London Trades Council, preceded by twenty-five farriers, 'right gallantly mounted on sprightly steeds'; they wore 'blue and white sashes and rode at the head of the procession, smoking cigars'. Rosettes, sashes, wands, aprons, cockades, gloves, hats, all were used to give colour, presence and credibility as the unions paraded to flourish the proud symbols of their skills and their labour. 1882 – the Preston Guild procession, Tin Plate Workers and Gas Fitters, 'two mounted trumpeters clad in ancient costume, the members carried silver mounted staves and were adorned with regalia': the Saddlers and Harness Makers, 'preceding the beautiful banner, steered by four lads in jockey's costume, complete with white unmentionables and pink smocks, being also booted and spurred', the Plumbers and Painters, 'the chief marshall carried a gold baton and his assistants, silver', the Plasterers, 'each man wore an apron bearing the coat of arms of the craft.' The banners emblematic, the regalia as varied as the number of marches and parades, the age of trade union public splendour, each union striving to outshine the other with banners and pageantry.

Ceremonial aprons were mainly worn by masons and other workers allied with the building trades, painters, slaters and bricklayers; however, reference is also to be found to the wearing of aprons in processions by coopers and horseshoemen. In 1857 the Housepainters of Limerick paid 15s. for three aprons for a parade and on 8 November 1876 the Coopers handed over to a new committee thirteen sashes, five aprons and three stands of colour. In 1873 the Limerick Bakers spent £35 on sashes, an enormous sum representing more than half a year's wages for a baker at that time.

It was with the impetus of the new unionism in 1889 that the wearing of sashes gained in popularity and became a necessary part of ceremonial attire for almost every union branch. Photographs from the 1870s until 1926 of trade unionists in demonstrations or posed as the Executive Committee to be recorded for posterity commonly show the officers wearing sashes. Trade union banners carrying widow and orphan scenes invariably depict two union officials at graveside or bedside, bringing condolences and cash, bedecked with the sashes of their office. Chairmen, secretaries and presidents would expect a sash of office as of right, but the practice spread to include stewards and marshals for easy identification on demonstrations and plain sashes for each member of the branch committee. The Ipswich branch of the National Union of Railwaymen had a special sash made for the office of Banner Secretary (giving a clear indication of the importance of the banner to the branch). Elaborate sashes of velvet, heavily embroidered with silver and gold thread, were presented to long-serving officers as a mark of respect by grateful members. The sash presented to S.J. Williams of the number seven branch of the National Union of Vehicle Workers is a typical example, with insignia and inscription surmounted by the 'all-seeing eye'.

The sashes were made of various colours and materials, depending on rank and cost. Tutill, who manufactured sashes of every description for Friendly Societies, Masonic Lodges, Temperance Societies and Sunday Schools as well as trade unions, advertised 'Sashing, any colour, according to office'. For the Independent Order of Oddfellows, Manchester Unity, he supplied them in purple and gold for past and present officers, scarlet and gold for the Grand Master, pink and blue for the Vice Grand Master and blue and white for supporters.

The sashes were mostly made of woven watered silk with better quality being offered in satin or even velvet. Embellishments to the sash in the quality of the fringing, lettering and badge or emblem all added to the cost. In the 1890s a six-inch silk sash, three yards in length, could be bought for 10s. 6d. with an additional charge for silver or gold bullion fringe. For 13s. Tutill advertised a superior brocaded sash with 'designs woven in real silver for members or real gold for officers'. Special metal badges emblematic of the union could be added to the sashes, as in the case of the Bristol Branch of the National Amalgamated Sailors' and Firemens' Union that carried two, one bearing the the union motto 'pull together' and the other depicting the world and the word 'unity'.

A rival to Tutill was the House of Toye, founded by Guillaume Henri Toye, a Huguenot weaver who fled to England to avoid persecution after the revocation of the Edict of Nantes by Louis XIV. He settled in Hope Town (now Bethnal Green) and began weaving silk and velvet and gold and silver lace for the gentry. His sons continued the business until 1793 when Charles, a great-grandson of Guillaume, set up his own factory in Camden Town to produce gold and silver threads, cords, laces and braids for the military. In 1835 William Toye broke away and set up his own firm, Toye and Company, the direct forerunner of the present firm which is still in existence. The business flourished as the Empire grew and braided colonialists ruled with pomp and pageantry. Then, disaster, the rifle became a weapon of deadly accuracy and gold-embroidered officers became easy targets for rebellious natives and rival imperialists. Khaki became the order of the day and Toye was brought close to financial ruin. A man of energy and skill, he turned resourcefully to 'making high quality regalia for friendly societies and masonic lodges. In addition he began making the beautiful embroidered and hand-painted banners for the trade unions together with their ornamental sashes.' The two companies competed for the fast growing market of trade unions, when, in the 1890s, new unions were formed every week and new branches every day. On May Days, hospital days, gala days, funerals and demonstrations of support for or opposition to any cause, the banners sailed forth onto the streets, accompanied by sash-wearing officers, stewards, banner bearers and marshals. The tradition seems to have died away after the General Strike of 1926, when the trade unions were forced to rebuild and consolidate during the years of recession and unemployment. In 1971, during the great TUC demonstration in London to protest against the Conservative government's Industrial Relations Bill, the trade unions brought their old banners to supplement the thousands of placards, posters and modern banners carried on the streets on that February day. Some trade unionists, while rummaging in dusty basements, found sashes tucked away in the banner boxes and perhaps for the last time they were worn 'on the march' in a revival of a past whose regalia has gone, but whose tradition of solidarity and humanity remain to bear witness to the cause of labour, the hope of the world.

SOURCE NOTES

2 Red-Spots *Clarion Handbook*, London, 1912.

6 And Now Win the Peace Report by W.W. Henderson to Campaign Sub-Committee, 24.7.1945, Labour Party Library. Eastwood, G.G., *George Isaacs*, London, 1952.

8 Walter Crane's Cartoon for the *Sun* The Sun, 27.6.1893, 28.6.1893, 1.5.1903. Hyman, Alan, *The Rise and Fall of Horatio Bottomley*, London, 1972.

10 Henry Fry Sculpture Interview with William Lawrence, 3.4.1984. William Lawrence, Leaflet, London, 1983.

32 Society of Women Welders Society of Women Welders, Minute book, TUC Library.

33, 34, 35 Trade Union Badges Smethurst, John B. and Devine, Francis, *Soathar 7, Journal of the Irish Labour History Society*, Dublin, 1981. TUC Library, History file. Loftus, Belinda, *Marching Workers*, Belfast, 1978.

36 Election Button Badges *The Northern Echo*, 11.1.1910. McNair, John, *James Maxton, The Beloved Rebel*, London, 1955. Shinwell, Emanuel, *The Labour Story*, London, 1963.

37 Peace Badges McMichael, Dr Joan K., *The Work of the British Medical Aid Committee for Vietnam*, duplicated 17 pp. *Dick Shepherd*, by his friends, London, 1938. Duff, Peggy, *Left, Left, Left*, London, 1971. National Museum of Labour History, Cabinet, Box 2.

38 War-Time Badges Trachtenberg, Alexander, *History of May Day*, New York, 1929. *Daily Worker*, 2.5.1940. Communist Party Library, Box 86. First of May Demonstration, Official Programme, London 1941. People's Convention, Communist Party Library, Box 27. Joint Committee for Soviet Aid, Communist Party Library, Box 480. Mahon, John, *Harry Pollitt*, London, 1976. Calder, Angus, *The People's War*, London, 1969.

39 Campaign Badges The Great March, TUC, London, 1971.

40 Anniversary and Commemorative Badges Lovell, John, *Stevedores and Dockers*, London, 1969. Cummings, D.G., *History of the United Society of Boilermakers and Iron and Steel Shipbuilders*, Newcastle-on-Tyne, 1905. Anon, *Sixty Years of Trade Unionism*, souvenir of the sixtieth Trades Union Congress, London, 1928. Trades Union Congress, Annual Report, London, 1968. Clegg, H.A., *General Union*, Oxford, 1954. Postgate, R.W., *The Builders' History*, London, 1923. McKillop, Norman, *The Lighted Flame*, London, 1950. Pitt, Malcolm, *The World on our Backs*, London, 1979.

42 Amalgamated Stevedores' Labour Protection League Lovell, John, *Stevedores and Dockers*, London, 1969. Irving, Joseph, *Annals of our Time, 1871-1891*, London, 1892. Tillett, Ben, *Memories and Reflections*, London, 1931. Stafford, Ann, *A Match to Fire the Thames*, London, 1961. London, Jack, *The People of the Abyss*, London, 1903. Smith, H. Llewellyn and Nash, Vaughan, *Story of the Dockers' Strike*, London, 1889.

43 National Union of Agricultural Labourers and Rural Workers Edwards, George, *From Crow-scaring to Westminster*, London, 1922. Groves, Reg, *Sharpen the Sickle*, London, 1959. Interview with Wilfred Page, 2.3.84. Green, F.E., *The Tyranny of the Countryside*, London, 1913. Russell, Rex C., *The Revolt of the Field in Lincolnshire*, Lincoln, 1956. Horn, Pamela, *Joseph Arch*, Kineton, 1971.

44 Poplar Labour League Haw, George, *From Workhouse to Westminster*, London, 1907. Untitled cuttings on Poplar Labour League reports, dated 23.7.1896 to 30.9.1897, Tower Hamlets Library.

45 Social Democratic Federation Lee, H.W. and Archbold, E., *Social Democracy in Britain*, London, 1935. Elton, Godfrey, *England Arise*, London, 1931. *Hyndman, Prophet of Socialism*, London, 1928.

46 Amalgamated Society of Railway Servants Bagwell, Philip S., *The History of the National Union of Railwaymen*, London, 1963. Alcock, G.W., *Fifty years of Railway Trade Unionism*, London, 1922.

46 National Union of Railwaymen, Hither Green Branch Bagwell, Philip S., *The History of the National Union of Railwaymen*, London, 1963. Alcock, G.W., *Fifty years of Railway Trade Unionism*, London, 1922.

47 National Workers' Sports' Association Article by George Elvin, Dorsetshire Labourers' Centenary 1934, Souvenir, London, 1934. Citrine, Walter M., editor, *The Martyrs of Tolpuddle*, London, 1934. Citrine, Walter M., editor, *Centenary Commemoration of the Tolpuddle Martyrs*, Dorchester, 1934. TUC *Dorsetshire Labourers' Centenary, Handbook and Programme*, Dorchester, 1934.

48 Wigan Cotton Operatives Oastler, Richard, *A Letter to Millowners*, Manchester, 1836. Hopwood, Edwin, *A History of the Lancashire Cotton Industry and the Amalgamated Weavers' Association*, Manchester, 1969. Brockway, Fenner, *Socialism over Sixty Years*, London, 1946.

49 Bethnal Green Co-operative Party Shea, Peter, *Times Past*, Reading, 1955. Carbery, Thomas F., *Consumers in Politics*, Manchester, 1969. Rhodes, G.W., *Co-operative-Labour Relations, 1900-1962*, Loughborough, 1962. Letter from Stan Newens, 4.2.1984. Bailey, Jack, *The British Co-operative Movement*, London, 1955. Interview with George Mackley Browne, May 1984.

50 Central Labour College Atkins, John, *Neither Crumbs nor Condescension*, Aberdeen, 1981. Craik, W.W., *Central Labour College*, London, 1964. Millar, J.P.M., *The Labour College Movement*, London, n.d.. Letters from J.P.M. Millar, 7.2.1984, 13.2.1984.

51 National Council of Labour Colleges Atkins, John, *Neither Crumbs nor Condescension*, Aberdeen, 1981. Craik, W.W., *Central Labour College*, London, 1964. Millar, J.P.M., *The Labour College Movement*, London, n.d.. Letters from J.P.M. Millar, 7.2.1984, 13.2.1984.

52 No More War Movement Chamberlain, W.J., *Fighting for Peace*, London, n.d. c.1928. Rae, John, *Conscience and Politics*, Oxford, 1970. *The Autobiography of Bertrand Russell*, vol. ii, London, 1968. Thorne, Will, *My Life's Battles*, London, n.d.. *Daily Mail*, 27.4.1917. Brockway, Fenner, *Inside the Left*, London, 1942.

53 Carshalton Left Book Club Lewis, John, *The Left Book Club*, London, 1970.

54 Tunnel Shelters Haldane, J.B.S., *ARP*, London, 1938. Jackson, Gabriel, *A Concise History of the Spanish Civil War*, London, 1974. Calder, Angus, *The People's War*, London, 1969. Daily Worker, 1.10.1938, 12.1.1939, 19.1.1939, 13.2.1939, 15.2.1939, 15.3.1939.

55 Arms for Spain Jackson, Gabriel, *A Concise History of the Spanish Civil War*, London, 1974. Alexander, Bill, *British Volunteers for Liberty*, London, 1982. Interview with Bill Alexander, 15.7.1984.

55 Young Communist League Klugman, J., *History of the Communist Party of Great Britain, 1919-1924*, vol. i, London, 1968.

56 Royal Group of Docks Interview with Bernie Steer, 21.1.1984. Dash, Jack, *Good Morning Brothers!*, London, 1969. Stewart, Margaret, *Frank Cousins: A Study*, London, 1968. Allen, V.L., *Trade Union Leadership*, London, 1957.

56 Grunwick Strike Committee Dromey, Jack, and Taylor, Graham, *Grunwick: The Workers' Story*, London, 1978. Guerman, Mikhail, *Art of the October Revolution*, English edition, London, 1979. Conversation with Vipin Magdani, 2.12.1983.

58 Peterloo Jug Bruton, E.A., *The Story of Peterloo*, Manchester, 1919. Marlow, Joyce, *The Peterloo Massacre*, London, 1969. Woodward, E.L., *The Age of Reform 1815-1870*, Oxford, 1938. May, John and Jennifer, *Commemorative Pottery*, London, 1972.

58 Reform Jug May, John and Jennifer, *Commemorative Pottery*, London, 1972.

59 Brougham Flask *Jewitt's Ceramic Art of Great Britain, 1800-1900*, revised by Geoffrey A. Godden, London, 1972. May, John and Jennifer, *Commemorative Pottery*, London, 1972.

60 Honley Mechanics' Institute Plate Harrison, J.F.C., *The Early Victorians*, London, 1971. Wallace, Graham, *Life of Francis Place*, London, 1898. Perkin, Harold, *The Origins of Modern Society, 1780-1880*, London, 1969. Langer, L.W., editor, *The Rise of Modern Europe, 1832-1852*, London, 1969. Engels, Frederick, *The Condition of the Working Class in England*, Moscow, 1953.

61 Ramsay MacDonald Plate Weir, Macneill L., *The Tragedy of Ramsay MacDonald*, London, n.d..

61 Tolpuddle Plate Dorset County Museum.

62 Stratford Co-operative Society Jug Co-operative Congress, Stratford 1904, Manchester, 1904. *Co-operative Review*, January, 1979. Brown, W. Henry, *Stratford Co-operative and Industrial Society Limited, 1861-1911*; supplementary chapters by Bate, John M., London, 1911. Co-operative Wholesale Society Annual, Manchester, 1911.

62 Keir Hardie Lamp Hughes, Emrys, *Keir Hardie*, London, 1956. Cole, G.D.H., *James Keir Hardie*, Fabian Pamphlet, London, 1941. Stewart, William, *J. Keir Hardie*, London, 1921.

63 Votes for Women, Figure Letter from Royal Doulton Tableware Ltd., 2.5.1984. Atterbury, Paul and Irvine, Louise, *The Doulton Story*, souvenir booklet for exhibition at the Victoria and Albert Museum, London, 1979.

64 *The Times* Challenger Mug *The Times*, 13.11.1979. Interview with Lou Kenton, June 1984.

64 People's March for Jobs Mug National Organising Committee Minutes, Agenda and Notices, TUC Library, Box 135.591. TUC Annual Report, London, 1983. *Morning Star*, 6.6.1983. *Guardian*, 6.6.1983. Interview with Lou Kenton, June 1984.

66 Ragged School Union Southgate, Walter, *That's the Way it Was*, Oxted, 1982. Bready, J. Wesley, *Lord Shaftesbury and Social-Industrial Progress*, London, 1926. Anon, *Champion of Liberty, Charles Bradlaugh, Centenary Volume*, London, 1933.

67 Labour Crusaders *Labour Leader*, 31.3.1844 to 19.8.1899.

68 Miners' Protection Society Arnot, Robin Page, *The Miners*, London, 1949. George Tutill Trade Catalogue, London, 1896.

69 Democratic League *The Reformers' Year Book*, London, 1902. *Reynolds' Newspaper*, 28.10.1900, 10.4.1901, 28.4.1901.

70 Independent Labour Party *Labour Leader*, 2.4.1914, 16.4.1914. Hughes, Emrys, editor, *Keir Hardie's Speeches and Writings*, Glasgow, n.d.. Johnson, J. and Grentzner, A., *Dictionary of British Artists, 1880-1940*, Suffolk, 1976.

71 Amalgamated Society of Woodworkers Higenbottam, S., *Our Society's History*, Manchester, 1939. *ASW Journal*, February 1929.

72 The Ginger Club Lansbury's Labour Weekly, 28.2.1925, 17.7.1926, 18.12.1926, 22.1.1927, 29.1.1927, 26.2.1927, 5.3.1927, 19.3.1927, 9.7.1927, 16.7.1927.

73 Women's Co-operative Guild Gaffin, Jean and Thomas, David, *Caring and Sharing, the Centenary History of the Co-operative Women's Guild*, Manchester, 1983.

74 Socialist Sunday School Letter from J. Simmons, 14.4.1984. National Museum of Labour History, Socialist Sunday School Cabinet, Box 2.

75 Amalgamated Engineering Union *Amalgamated Engineers' Monthly Journal*, London, 1901. Jefferys, James B., *The Story of the Engineers*, London, 1945. Letter from J.T. van Riemsdijk, Keeper of Mechanical and Civil Engineering, Science Museum, London, 14.5.1984. *Bury Guardian*, 21.10.1899. Leeson, R.A., *United We Stand*, Bath, 1971.

76 50th Anniversary of the Labour Party Labour Party Archives, 50th Anniversary box. Williams, Francis, *Fifty Years' March*, London, 1950. Shinwell, Emanuel, *The Labour Story*, London, 1963. Foot, Michael, *Aneurin Bevan*, vol. ii, London, 1973. Dalton, Hugh, *High Tide and After, Memoirs*, vol. ii, London, 1962.

78 Stone Masons' Friendly Society Leeson, R.A., *United We Stand*, Bath, 1971. Postgate, R.W., *The Builders' History*, London, 1923. Hilton, W.S., *Foes to Tyranny*, London, 1963.

79 Amalgamated Association of Card and Blowing Room Operatives TUC Library, Box File HD.6661 T 4.19. Bullen, Andrew, *The Lancashire Weavers' Union*, Manchester, 1984.

80 Amalgamated Society of General Toolmakers, Engineers and Machinists Jefferys, James B., *The Story of the Engineers*, London, 1945. Society of Amalgamated Toolmakers, 25th Anniversary Souvenir, Birmingham, 1907. Amalgamated Society of General Toolmakers, Engineers and Machinists, 7th Annual Report, Birmingham, 1889. Monthly Record, Birmingham, 1909. Webb, Sidney and Beatrice, *History of Trade Unionism*, London, 1898.

81 The United Society of Boiler Makers and Iron Ship Builders Cummings, D.G., *History of the United Society of Boilermakers and Iron and Steel Shipbuilders*, Newcastle-on-Tyne, 1905. Mortimer, J.E., *History of the Boilermakers' Society*, London, 1973.

82 Amalgamated Society of Painters and Decorators Bromley, John, *The Armorial Bearings of the Guilds of London*, London, 1960. Wood, Leslie W., *A Union to Build*, London, 1979. Fox-Davies, Arthur Charles, *Heraldry Explained*, London, 1906.

84 Printers' Labourers Moran, James, *NATSOPA, Seventy Five Years*, Oxford, 1964. Finch, R.W., *My Lord they are Printers*, London, 1984.

85 Demonstration, Trafalgar Square *The Times*, 15.7.1907. *Justice*, 20.7.1907.

85 H. Quelch Gould, Frederick J., *Hyndman, Prophet of Socialism*, London, 1928. *Justice*, 13.7.1907, 31.8.1907.

86 Salvation Army Sweating Gertrude Tuckwell Collection, TUC Library, Box 207. *Justice*, 12.9.1908, 5.7.1910. Higenbottam, S., *Our Society's History*, Manchester, 1939. Connelly, T.J., *The Woodworkers*, London, 1960. Moran, James, *NATSOPA, Seventy Five Years*, Oxford, 1964.

87 Feed the Children *The Times*, 21.12.1907. *Justice*, 25.1.1908. Brockway, Fenner, *Socialism over Sixty Years*, London, 1946. Bourne, Richard and MacArthur, Brian, *The Struggle for Education*, London, 1970. Sherhard, Robert W., *Child Slaves of Britain*, London, 1905.

88 Churchill-Curran Craig, F.W.S., editor, *British Parliamentary Election Results, 1885-1918*, London, 1974. Wilkinson, Ellen, *The Town that was Murdered*, London, 1939. Thorne, Will, *My Life's Battles*, London, n.d.. Prochaska, Alice, *History of the General Federation of Trade Unions*, London, 1982. *The Jarrow Express*, 12.1.1906.

89 The Railway Crisis Alcock, G.W., *Fifty Years of Railway Trade Unionism*, London, 1922. Bagwell, Philip S., *The Railwaymen*, London, 1963. McKillop, Norman, *The Lighted Flame*, London, 1950.

90 Right to Work Anon, *London Trades Council, 1860-1950*, London, 1950. Anon, *Short History of the London Trades Council*, London, 1935. *Labour Record*, February 1906, March 1906. *Daily News*, 23.1.1906, 29.1.1906, 30.1.1906, 31.1.1906, 9.2.1906, 10.2.1906, 13.2.1906.

91 In Memory of William Morris *Justice*, 2.10.1909. Lindsay, Jack, editor, *Selected Poems of William Morris*, London, 1948. Glasier, J. Bruce, *William Morris, Romantic to Revolutionary*, London, 1955. Cole, G.D.H., editor, *William Morris, Selected Writings*, New York, 1934.

92 Civil Service Socialist Society Clinton, Dr Alan, *Post Office Workers*, London, 1984. *The Postman's Gazette*, 26.6.1910, 22.6.1910, 12.9.1910. *Civil Service Socialist*, April 1908, July 1910, March 1915. *Justice*, 7.5.1910. Swift, H.G., *The History of Postal Agitation*, London, 1929.

93 No Conscription *Labour Leader*, 11.12.1913, 19.12.1913.

94 Burston Edwards, Bertram, *The Burston School Strike*, London, 1974. Brockway, Fenner, *Towards Tomorrow*, St Albans, 1977.

95 Votes for Women Pankhurst, Sylvia, *The Suffragette Movement*, London, 1931. Pankhurst, Emmeline, *Mrs Pankhurst's Own Story*, London, 1914. *Votes for Women*, 8.10.1908, 15.10.1908. *The Times*, 12.10.1908.

96 Sacco and Vanzetti Steele, Henry, editor, *Documents of American History*, vol. ii, New Jersey, 1973. Sharp, Harold S., *Footnotes to American History*, New Jersey, 1977. *Sunday Worker*, 28.8.1928.

97 London Unemployed Workers Hannington, Wal, *Unemployed Struggles*, London, 1936. Hannington, Wal, *A Short History of the Unemployed*, London, 1938. Snowden, Philip, *An Autobiography* , vol. ii, London, 1934. *Daily Herald*, 24.2.1925.

98 John Syme Reynolds, Gerald W. and Judge, Anthony, *The Night the Police went on Strike*, London, 1968. Sellwood, A.V., *Police Strike*, London, 1978.

100, 101 Peckham and Dulwich Branch, SDF Accounts Book of the Peckham and Dulwich Branch of the Social Democratic Federation, Walter Southgate Collection, NMLH.

102, 103 Docks Dispute Letters Original letters and copies from 5 November 1889 to 8 February 1890. Bound vol. i, Dock Strikes, Collection of NMLH. Lovell, John, *Stevedores and Dockers*, London, 1969.

104, 105 Letters of Albert Victor Grayson Groves, Reg, *The Strange Case of Victor Grayson*, London, 1975. Thompson, W., *The Life of Victor Grayson*, London, 1910. Seven original letters and postcards from Victor Grayson to H. Dawson, Collection NMLH.

SOURCE NOTES

106 General Strike Service Records, Southern Railway, 1926 Bagwell, Philip S., *The History of the National Union of Railwaymen*, London, 1963. Symons, Julian, *The General Strike*, London, 1957. *General Strike, May 1926*, Great Western Railway, London, n.d.. *British Gazette*, 10.5.1926. Noel, Gerard, *The Great Lock-out of 1926*, London, 1976.

108 Amalgamated Society of Tin Plate Workers Kidd, Archibald T., *History of the Sheet Metal Workers and Braziers*, London, 1949. Rules of the General Union of Tin-Plate Workers' Trade Society, 1885. Rules of the Operative Tin Plate Workers' Society, Liverpool, 1886. Leeson, R.A., *Travelling Brothers*, London, 1979.

109 The Labour Church *The Labour Prophet*, January 1892, October 1892, March 1893. *The Labour Church Hymn and Tune Book*, Manchester, 1893. Elton, Godfrey, *England Arise*, London, 1931. Silver, Eric, *Victor Feather*, London, 1973.

110 National Union of Corporation Workers, Amalgamated Society of Woodworkers, Amalgamated Engineering Union Craik, William, *Sidney Hill and the National Union of Public Employees*, London, 1968. Higenbottam, S., *Our Society's History*, Manchester, 1939. Jefferys, James B., *The Story of the Engineers*, London, 1945.

111 National Transport Workers' Federation *Dockers' Record*, December 1910, November 1915, July 1916. Mann, Tom, *Tom Mann's Memoirs*, London, 1923. Pelling, Henry, *A History of British Trade Unionism*, London, 1963. Hutt, Allen, *The Post War History of the British Working Class*, London, 1937.

111, 112 London Society of Compositors Musson, A.E., *The Typographical Association*, London, 1954. London Society of Compositors, Annual Report, London, 1938 and 1945. Rowles, George E., *The Line is on, Centenary Souvenir of the LCS 1848-1948*. *The British Printer*, London, 1907. *The London Typographical Journal*, 1915, October 1920, October 1929, October 1955.

113 National Unemployed Workers' Movement Hannington, Wal, *Unemployed Struggles*, London, 1936. *Out of Work*, 19.3.1921.

113 Labour's Bid for Power Ferguson, Lewis B., *The Trade Disputes and Trade Unions Act, 1927*, London, 1927. Renshaw, Patrick, *The General Strike*, London, 1975. Pelling, Henry, *A History of British Trade Unionism*, London, 1963. The Labour Party Annual Report, London, 1929.

114 The Social Democratic Party and Penny Nails Lee, H.W. and Archbold, E., *Social Democracy in Britain*, London, 1935. Crane, Walter, *An Artist's Reminiscences*, London, 1907. Thompson, E.P., *William Morris*, London, 1955.

115 Carnet De Honor Castells, Andreu, *Las Brigades Internacionales de la Guerra de Espana*, Barcelona, 1974. Alexander, Bill, *British Volunteers for Liberty*, London, 1982.

116 Surrey Spain Foodship *Famine Faces a Million in Spain*, pamphlet issued by National Joint Committee for Spanish Relief, London, 1937. *The Surrey Advertiser and County Times*, 4.2.1939, 11.3.1939. *The Surrey Times and Weekly Press*, 10.2.1939, 3.3.1939. *Surrey and Hants. News, Aldershot Gazette and Guildford Times*, 2.2.1939.

118 RACS 'Check Box' Davis, Walter T., *The History of the Royal Arsenal Co-operative Society Ltd.*, London, 1922. Holyoake, George Jacob, *History of Co-operation*, London, 1908. Hall, F. and Watkins, W.P., *Co-operation*, Manchester, 1937. Roffey, R.A., Secretary, RACS, *Dividend Tokens, A Summary*.

119 Independent Labour Party Collecting Box Thompson, Laurence, *The Enthusiasts*, London, 1971. *James Maxton, The Beloved Rebel*, London, 1955. Hughes, Emrys, *Keir Hardie*, London, 1956.

120 Thomas Paine Table Rickman, Thomas Clio, *The Life of Thomas Paine*, London, 1819.

121 Widows' Weeds Loftus, Belinda, *Marching Workers*, Dublin, 1978. Gorman, John, *Banner Bright*, London, 1973. Morley, John, *Death, Heaven and the Victorians*, London, 1971. Lovell, John, *Stevedores and Dockers*, London, 1969.

122 Co-operative Wholesale Society Box Hall, F. and Watkins, W.P., *Co-operation*, Manchester, 1937. Holyoake, George Jacob, *History of Co-operation*, London, 1913.

123 Amalgamated Society of Engineers' Chest Webb, Sidney and Beatrice, *Industrial Democracy*, vol. i, London, 1897. Jefferys, James B., *The Story of the Engineers*, London, 1945. Kiddier, William, *The Old Trade Unions*, London, 1931. Pelling, Henry, *A History of British Trade Unionism*, London 1963. Howell, George, *Trade Unionism, New and Old*, London, 1891.

124 Dockers' Money Bag Tillett, Ben, *Memories and Reflections*, London, 1931. Mann, Tom, *Tom Mann's Memoirs*, London, 1923. Smith, H. Llewellyn and Nash, Vaughan, *The Story of the Dockers' Strike*, London, 1889.

126 Operative Bricklayers' Society Postgate, R.W., *The Builders' History*, London, 1923. Explanation of Certificate of Membership, n.d. *c*.1890. Hilton, W.S., *Foes to Tyranny*, London, 1963. Operative Bricklayers' Society, 22nd Annual Report, 1869-1870, pub. 1871, UCATT Deposit, Modern Records Centre, University of Warwick Library.

127 Railway Worker and Child Deposit Record, NMLH.

128 Walter Crane Crane, Walter, *An Artist's Reminiscences*, London, 1907. Spencer, Isobel, *Walter Crane*, London, 1975. *The Easter Art Annual*, London, 1898.

129, 130, 131, 132 Electrical Trades Union Murals Lansbury, George, *The Miracle of Fleet Street*, London, n.d.. Schaffer, Gordon, *Light and Liberty*, ETU, 1949. Interview with Cliff Rowe, June 1984. Interview with Frank Haxell, July 1984. Morris, Lynda and Radford, Robert, *The Story of the Artists' International Association*, Oxford, 1983.

133, 134 General Strike/*Yours Fraternally* Sprague, Ken, preface to *Yours Fraternally* folio, London, 1968. Interview with Ken Sprague, February 1979.

135 History of the British Working Class, Maureen Scott Interview with Maureen Scott, November 1984. Explanation of the Mural, Collection of the National Museum of Labour History, uncatalogued, dated April 1976.

136 George Lansbury Postgate, Raymond, *George Lansbury*, London, 1951. *Daily Herald*, 12.5.1939. *The City and East London Observer*, 15.7.1939.

136 Henry Mayers Hyndman National Portrait Gallery File, 1947. Gould, Frederick J., *Hyndman, Prophet of Socialism*, London, 1928.

138 Liberty Press *Liberty*, January 1894, February 1894. Thompson, E.P., *William Morris*, London, 1977. Glasier, J. Bruce, *William Morris and the Early Days of the Socialist Movement*, London, 1921.

139 *The Socialist Series* *The Socialist Series*, no. 1, Glasgow, 1918. *The Socialist*, no. 1, Edinburgh, 1903. Bealey, Frank and Pelling, Harry, *Labour and Politics, 1900-1906*, London, 1958. Klugman, James, *History of the Communist Party of Great Britain*, vol. i, London, 1968. McFarlane, L.J., *The British Communist Party, its Origin and Development until 1929*, London, 1966.

140 Young Socialist National Museum of Labour History, Socialist Sunday Schools Collection, Box 2. The *Young Socialist*, October 1901, April 1902, March 1918. Thompson, Laurence, *The Enthusiasts*, London, 1971.

141 Socialism and the Survival of the Fittest *Daily Herald*, 9.2.1929. *Plebs*, London, September, 1959. *Daily Worker*, 9.2.1962. McDonnell, John, editor, *Songs of Struggle and Protest*, Dublin, n.d.. *The Call*, 6.5.1920.

142 The Woman Worker Hamilton, Mary Agnes, *Mary MacArthur*, Newcastle-upon-Tyne, 1925. Goldman, Harold, *Emma Paterson*, London, 1974. Hamilton, Mary Agnes, *Margaret Bondfield*, Edinburgh, 1924.

143 *The Herald* Randall, W., *The Miracle of Fleet Street*, London, 1925. Fienburgh, Wilfred, *25 Momentous Years*, London, 1955. *The Herald*, 26.1.1918. Dutt, R. Palme, 'The Rise and Fall of the Daily Herald', *Labour Monthly*, London, March 1964.

144 *The Workers' Cry* 'Salvationist-Socialist, Frank Smith, MP, Father of Salvation Army Social Work', paper by Norman N. Murdoch, 4th Annual Salvation Army Historical Conference, NYC, 1978. Fairbank, Jenty, *Booths' Boots, the Beginnings of Salvation Army Social Work*. Brockway, Fenner, *Socialism over Sixty Years*, London 1946. McLean, Iain, *Keir Hardie*, London, 1975. Anon, *The General next to God*, London, 1965.

145 *The Labour Woman* Skelton, Christopher, *The Engravings of Eric Gill*, Wellingborough, 1983. Middleton, Lucy, editor, *Women in the Labour Movement*, London, 1977. *The League Leaflet*, February 1913. *The Labour Woman*, May 1913.

146 Plan for Peace Wilkinson, Ellen, *Plan for Peace*, pamphlet, London, 1945. Williams, Francis, *Fifty Years' March*, London, 1950.

148, 149 Portraits, William Morris, Will Thorne, Ben Tillett, Tom Mann, Eleanor Marx Warwick, Frances Evelyn, *William Morris*, London, 1912. Thorne, Will, *My Life's Battles*, London, n.d.. Tillett, Ben, *Memories and Reflections*, London, 1931. Kapp, Yvonne, *Eleanor Marx*, London, 1976. Mann, Tom, *Tom Mann's Memoirs*, London, 1923. Pollitt, Harry, *Tom Mann*, pamphlet, London, n.d.. Peacock, W. Arthur, editor, *Tom Mann, 80th Birthday Souvenir*, London, 1936.

150 Clarion Van Lee, H.W. and Archbold, E., *Social Democracy in Britain*, London, 1935.

152 Sweated Homeworkers Smith, Richard Mudie, editor, *Sweated Industries*, handbook of the *Daily News* Exhibition, London, 1906.

153 Harry Pollitt Pollitt, Harry, *Serving my Time*, London, 1940. Mahon, John, *Harry Pollitt*, London, 1976.

154 *Jolly George* Mahon, John, *Harry Pollitt*, London, 1976. Pollitt, Harry, *Serving my Time*, London, 1940. Bullock, Alan, *The Life and Times of Ernest Bevin*, London, 1960. *The Post War History of the British Working Class*, London, 1937.

155 Hunger Marcher Arrested Hannington, Wal, *Unemployed Struggles, 1919-1936*, London, 1936. McNair, John, *James Maxton*, London, 1955.

156 Herbert Smith Lawson, Jack, *The Man in the Cap*, London, 1941.

157 Christian Socialist, Co-operative Pioneers Binyon, Gilbert Clive, *The Christian Socialist Movement in England*, London, 1931. Hall, F. and Watkins, W.P., *Co-operation*, Manchester, 1937.

158 Not a Penny on the Rent *Daily Worker*, 30.6.53, 27.5.54, 13.6.54, 25.6.54. Personal recollections of the author.

160 Calico Printers Kiddier, William, *The Old Trade Unions*, London, 1931. Webb, Sidney and Beatrice, *History of Trade Unionism*, London, 1898. Ridgway, J., *On Combinations of Trade*, London, 1831. Anon, *The History of the Combination of Journeymen Calico Printers*, pamphlet, Manchester, 1807. Howell, George, *Trade Unionism New and Old*, London, 1891. History of the Brooks Family of Crawshaw Hall, Rossendale Collection, District Central Library, Rawtenstall.

161 Tailors' Strike, 1889 Fishman, William J., *East End Jewish Radicals*, London, 1975. *The East London Advertiser*, 7.9.1889, 21.7.1889, 28.7.1889, 3.10.1899.

162 Social Reconstruction *Cartoons for the Cause*, London, 1896. *Justice*, 1.5.1909. Crane, Walter, *An Artist's Reminiscences*, London, 1907.

163 Khaki Election and Vote Unionist Shinwell, Emanuel, *The Labour Story*, London, 1963. Chester, Lewis, Fay, Stephen and Young, Hugo, *The Zinoviev Letter*, London, 1967. Snowden, Philip, *An Autobiography*, vol. ii, London, 1934. Williams, Francis, *Fifty Years' March*, London, 1950.

164 H. Quelch Rothstein, Andrew, *Marx Memorial Library Bulletin*, London, July-September, 1963. Klugman, James, *History of the Communist Party of Great Britain*, London, 1968. *Justice*, 20.9.1913. Craig, F.W.S., editor, *British Parliamentary Election Results 1885-1918*, London, 1974.

165 Revolution in Russia *Justice*, 27.1.1906. *Labour Leader*, 26.1.1906.

166 'Labour Clears the Way' Labour Party, 11th Annual Conference Report, 1911. Butler, David and Freeman, Jennie, *British Political Facts, 1900-1967*, second edition, London, 1968. Labour Party Library, Labour Party Leaflets, 1906-1910. Cook, Chris, *A Short History of the Liberal Party, 1900-1976*, London, 1976.

167 Equality of Sacrifice Snowden, Philip, *An Autobiography*, London, 1934.

168 Stop War Livingstone, Dame Adelaide, *The Peace Ballot*, London, 1935. *Commercial Art*, vol. xx, January 1936. *Dick Shepherd*, by his friends, London, 1938.

169 Famine in Spain Interview with Felicity Ashbee, 1984. *Famine Faces a Million in Spain*, pamphlet issued by National Joint Committee for Spanish Relief, London, October 1937. Stansky, Peter, *William Morris, C.R. Ashbee and the Arts and Crafts*, London, 1984.

170 'The "Military" Practice of the Rebels' Tisa, John, editor, *The Palette and the Flame*, New York, 1979.

171 'Help Wounded Human Beings' Tisa, John, editor, *The Palette and the Flame*, New York, 1979. *British Medical Aid in Spain*, *News Chronicle*, pamphlet, 1937. Barnicoat, John, *A Concise History of Posters*, London, 1972. Morris, Lynda and Radford, Robert, *The Story of the Artists' International Association*, Oxford, 1983.

172 Upper Clyde Shipbuilders Thompson, Willie and Hart, Finlay, *The UCS Work-in*, London, 1972.

172 'A Miner Carries' Pitt, Malcolm, *The World on our Backs*, London, 1979.

172 'Wanted Out' and Briant *Morning Star*, 15.6.1972 to 27.7.1972. *Morning Star*, 21.6.1972, 28.6.1972, 30.6.1972, 20.10.1972, 12.4.1973.

174 The Federated Postmen of Sheffield Clinton, Alan, *Post Office Workers*, London, 1984. *The Postman's Gazette*, 1.10.1892, 29.10.1892, 18.2.1893.

174 Bazaar and Fancy Fair. *Justice*, 18.8.1900, 1.9.1900, 8.12.1900, 15.12.1900, 22.12.1900, 5.1.1901.

175 Women's Co-op Guild Davies, Margaret Llewellyn and Morris, Lilian, *The National Banner of the Womens' Co-operative Guild*, pamphlet, Manchester, 1933. Speech by Margaret Llewellyn Davies to the 12th Congress of the Women's Co-operative Guild, 19-22 June 1933. British Library of Political and Economic Science, Collection Misc. 268, vol. x.

175 Co-operative Wholesale Society Bookmark Cole, G.D.H., *A Century of Co-operation*, Manchester, 1944.

176 May Day 1895 *Labour Leader*, 11.5.1895.

177 Harry Boulter *The Clarion*, 4.4.1896. *Justice*, all issues, 1910.

177 Music Hall War 'When Elephants were Blacklegs', article by Peter Honri, *The Performer*, January-February, 1907.

178 'The Right to Work' Anon, *London Trades Council, 1860-1950*, London, 1950.

178 The Clarion Van Lyons, A. Neil, *Robert Blatchford*, London, 1910. Thompson, Laurence, *The Enthusiasts*, London, 1971. *The Clarion*, 20.2.1896 to 3.10.1896.

179 The Daily Herald League Randall, W., *The Miracle of Fleet Street*, London, 1925. Anon, *Fifty Years of Liberty Hall*, Dublin, 1959. Boyd, Andrew, *The Rise of the Irish Trade Unions, 1729-1970*, Dublin, 1972. *Daily Herald*, 15.11.1912, 16.11.1912, 23.11.1912, 3.11.1913.

180 Dartmoor Prison Rae, John, *Conscience and Politics*, London, 1970. *Daily Mail*, 24.4.1917, 27.4.1917.

181, 182 Taxi Cab Strike, Cab Collection *Daily Herald*, 1.1.1913 to 20.3.1913.

183 Marching Union *Daily Mail*, 24.5.1961. *Daily Herald*, 10.5.1961, 11.5.1961. *Melody Maker*, 13.5.1961. *Daily Sketch*, 16.5.1961. *The Shoe and Leather Record*, 12.5.1961. *The Evening News*, 16.5.1961.

184 GLC, Working for London and Peace Interview with Peter Kennard, 6.9.1984. *No Nuclear Weapons*, London, 1981. *Sanity*, December-January 1981-2, article by John Berger.

185, 186, 187, 188, 189 Sashes Cummings, D.C., *History of the United Society of Boilermakers and Iron and Steel Ship Builders*, Newcastle-on-Tyne, 1905. Anon, *Memorial of the Preston Guild, 1882*, Preston, 1882. Webb, Sidney and Beatrice, *History of Trade Unionism*, London, 1898. Citrine, Walter M., *The Martyrs of Tolpuddle*, London, 1934. Loftus, Belinda, *Marching Workers*, Dublin, 1978. Webb, Sidney and Beatrice, *Industrial Democracy*, vol. i, London, 1897. Postgate, R.W., *The Builders' History*, London, 1923. George Tutill Trade Catalogue, London, 1896. Draper, Alfred, *The Old Firm*, London, 1974. *The Pictorial News*, 13.10.1890. *Daily Chronicle*, 5.5.1890.

INDEX